Louisville Slugger

BATTING AROUND

A COMPREHENSIVE COLLECTION OF HITTING ACHIEVEMENTS, ANECDOTES, AND ANALYSES

DOUG MYERS AND BRIAN DODD

CB

CONTEMPORARY BOOKS

Library of Congress Cataloging-in-Publication Data

Myers, Doug, 1964– .
    Louisville slugger presents batting around : a comprehensive collection of
hitting achievements, anecdotes, and analyses / Doug Myers and Brian Dodd
        p.   cm.
    Includes bibliographical references (p.) and index.
    ISBN 0-8092-2519-0
    1. Batting (Baseball).   2. Baseball—United States—History.
I. Title: Batting around.   II. Title.
GV869.M94   2000
796.357'26—dc21
                                                            99-86838
                                                            CIP

Photos on pages 4, 6, 54, 59, 91, 194, 319, 320, and 346 courtesy Library of
Congress; photos on pages 26 and 62 courtesy of the University of Louisville;
photos on pages 85, 95, and 243 copyright © AP/Wide World Photos; photos on
pages 172, 182, 261, and 287 courtesy of the National Archives; photos on pages
186 and 261 courtesy of the Cleveland Public Library. All other interior photos
courtesy of Mountain Lion, Inc.

Cover design by Nick Panos
Cover photograph copyright © Corbis/Bettmann-UPI
Interior design by Hespenheide Design

Published by Contemporary Books
A division of NTC/Contemporary Publishing Group, Inc.
4255 West Touhy Avenue, Lincolnwood (Chicago), Illinois 60712-1975 U.S.A.
Copyright © 2000 by Mountain Lion, Inc.
Printed in the United States of America
International Standard Book Number: 0-8092-2519-0
00 01 02 03 04 05 VH 18 17 16 15 14 13 12 11 10 9 8 7 6 5 4 3 2 1

To my wife, Cindy, and other doubles hitters everywhere

DM

To my Dad, David Dodd, who founded the Kanata Baseball Association in 1970 so that my brother and I would know the sights and sounds of the diamond

BD

Contents

Acknowledgments

Thanks to Mark Gola for his contributions to "Walk Softly and Carry a Big Stick" (Chapter 14) and "The Left-Hander's Advantage and Switch-Hitters" (Chapter 20); to Randy Voorhees for his contributions to "Coming Through in a Pinch: The Best Pinch Hitters" (Chapter 6) and "Different Strokes for Different Folks" (Chapter 18); and to John Monteleone for his contributions to "Darwin at the Bat: The Evolution of Baseball" (Chapter 1), "Newton at the Bat" (Chapter 15), and to civilized political discourse.

Thanks, as always, to Cindy, Penny, Maggie, and Sammy; Mom and Dad; The Motel 6 Baseball League; Debbie Crisfield; Sammy Sosa and Mark McGwire; Helen Warren and Frank Juliano; the 1977–78 Yankees; and to every pitcher who ever threw me offspeed stuff on 0–2.

And Mickey Mantle facade-crashing thanks to Mountain Lion for coming up with the idea, and to Contemporary for buying it.

DM

Thanks to my wife, Dana, to my mom and dad, and to all who had a role in making me what I am. The blame is yours.

Thanks to the 1986 Kanata Krusaders, Gurza Custom Brokers, the Hockey Stick men, and everyone else who pretended I had athletic ability.

Special thanks to Nick Shiver, the only person I know who drinks from a bag at breakfast. Cheers!

BD

Introduction

"Hitting a baseball is the most difficult thing there is in sports."
—TED WILLIAMS

"There's no skill involved. Just go up there and swing at the ball."
—JOE DIMAGGIO

A classmate of mine at the Wharton School of Business came up big in April 1992, scoring six tickets to an Orioles-Tigers game at a new stadium called Camden Yards. But when he said he'd take care of transportation for the trip from Philadelphia, I didn't expect to find myself in an Econoline cargo van, sliding around in the back on a thrift-shop couch. Nor did I expect—among the psychotically ambitious that clog the base paths of the world's finest business school—to find myself sharing a breakfast of cheese puffs and malt liquor with a twisted Canadian who could take my best baseball trivia punches without so much as blinking, seeing that Rick Bosetti and raising me John Boccabella.

Seven years later, when casting about for a literate and knowledgeable collaborator on a book about the who, what, when, where, and why of hitting—a companion to the other *Louisville Slugger®* books, the *Ultimate Book of Hitting* and the *Complete Book of Pitching*—my mind went immediately to that nutjob banker from Toronto. He knew his stuff—even if he couldn't spell *offence* or *centrefield*, and even if his mind occasionally wandered to Pat Boutette and the '79 Maple

Leafs—and he was as devout a believer in the church of baseball as you can find in these days of Fehr and bloating.

So we carved up the various topics we wanted to cover and got busy, resisting the urge to put too much of our Wharton training to use. We would not heed the call of the spreadsheet, the need to reduce all complex issues to mind-numbing mathematical formulas that bring everything back to profit and loss. We did some math, but only in moderation, putting our emphasis instead on what the true believers talk about in the back of Econolines: baseball's great moments, engaging personalities, eternal arguments, and whatnot.

This book is a tribute to the lumber barons. Joe DiMaggio is in here not for his great glove, while countless others are in despite their disinterested, disappointing, or downright dangerous defensive play. Kirk Gibson is in here not for his leadership, while more than a few are in despite a single-minded focus on personal stats and a habit of playing small in the fall. But what better way to tell the story of twentieth-century baseball than from the point of view of the man with the club in his hands and bad intentions in his head? From Ty Cobb and Tris Speaker to Babe Ruth and Lou Gehrig, to Jimmie Foxx and Hank Greenberg, to Joe DiMaggio and Mickey Mantle, to Stan Musial and Ted Williams, to Willie Mays and Willie McCovey, to Hank Aaron and Frank Robinson, to Willie Stargell and Mike Schmidt, to Barry Bonds and Mark McGwire—the chain of great hitters is an unbroken one, like a lineup batting around, a side that may never be retired.

This trip around the bases traces the evolution of offense from the deadball days of 3–2 baseball in 1901 to the home run highlight reels of 1999. It will take you to the great, through the memorable, and on to the how and why, before bringing it all back home with a summary of the game's most impressive records and how they came to be. Among other things, you'll read about

- The evolution of offense from the nineteenth to the twenty-first century: Darwin at the bat.
- The 25 greatest hitters of all time: a tribute to those with power and patience, unsettling questions raised about the hallowed 3,000-hit club, and the greatest hitter we never really knew.
- The greatest hitting tandems: the most devastating 1-2 punches from Ruth and Gehrig to Mays and McCovey to McGwire and Canseco to the troubling lack of long-term hitting relationships in these days of big money and small markets.
- The greatest hitting teams: from Murderers' Row to the Big Red Machine to Harvey's Wallbangers, the most productive lineups the game has seen. Take into account when and where the games were played, and some unexpected lineup cards find their way to the top of the deck.

- What might have been: players taken too soon or betrayed by injuries, minor league bashers who never got enough of a chance in the big leagues, and Negro League stars who never got any chance at all. A time at bat for Pete Reiser, Joe Hauser, and Josh Gibson.
- Great regular season and postseason hitting moments: game-winners, series-turners, dramatic flourishes, and tearful farewells.
- Great pinch hitters and pinch hits: where have you gone, Chuck Essegian?
- The left-hander's advantage: why lefties are overly represented at the top of baseball's hit list, why switch-hitters are made and not born, and why it makes sound financial sense to have little Sammy taking his T-ball hacks from the left side of the plate at least half of the time.
- Park effects and expansion: how changes in where the game is played and in how many players are gainfully employed by major league clubs has affected offense. About 300 pitchers in the big leagues today, with 10 of them chucking and ducking in Coors Field 81 times a year? Might as well let Molotov pitch mop-up.
- 1930 and 1968: the year everyone hit and the year no one hit. In only 38 years, the AL's leading batting average fell below the NL's league average. How did it come to this?
- The Game's Most Impressive Records: welcome to Valhalla. Walk softly and pitch around the big sticks.

So, in the words of the noted philosopher Crash Davis, "Bring it, Meat."

THE BEST
AND THE
BRIGHTEST

1

Darwin at the Bat
The Evolution of Baseball

"Hitting is the most important part of the game. It is where the big money is, where much of the status is, and the fan interest."
——TED WILLIAMS

It's often been said that one of the beauties of baseball is that fans from the nineteenth century could witness one of today's games and have no difficulty recognizing it as the same sport played by the Boston Beaneaters, Brooklyn Bridegrooms, Chicago Colts, Cleveland Spiders, and Louisville Colonels in 1897. Truth be told, since the National League was formed in 1876 just about everything except the length of the bases has changed. These changes, along with other external forces such as World War II, expansion, and civil rights, have created several eras in major league baseball—eras characterized by dramatically different tactics and results from both hitters and pitchers.

Fast and Loose: 1876–1900

"Keep your eye clear and hit 'em where they ain't."
——WILLIE KEELER, 1898

In 1876, baseball bore little resemblance to today's game. The pitcher stood 45 feet from home plate, threw underhand, and faced batters who could request high or low pitches. Foul balls weren't strikes, and balls bouncing over fences were home runs—even though some fences were less than 210 feet from home plate! Things

Baseball had quite a different look during its developmental stages in the nineteenth century.

weren't all bad for pitchers; a foul ball caught on one bounce was an out, and it took nine balls to walk a batter.

During the first 25 years of the National League's history, tinkering with the rules was an annual event. Here are some of the highlights.

In 1880, a walk was issued after eight balls rather than nine.

In 1881, the pitcher's mound was moved back from 45 feet to 50 feet.

In 1882, it was ball seven, take your base.

In 1883, a foul ball caught on one bounce was no longer an out.

In 1884, a pitcher was allowed to pitch from as high as his shoulder, rather than underhand. That was the good news for the hurlers; the bad news was six balls now meant a free pass. This went back up to seven in 1886, but came down to five the following year.

In 1887, batters could no longer call for a high or low pitch, but it required two called third strikes to be caught looking.

In 1888, it was back to three strikes and you're out, and the ground rule double was established for balls bouncing over fences less than 210 feet from home plate.

In 1889, they finally arrived at ball four.

In 1892, the ground rule double was pushed back to fences less than 235 feet from home plate.

In 1893, flat-sided bats were outlawed, but the mound was moved back to 60 feet 6 inches from home plate—marked by a new thing called a pitching rubber.

It wasn't until 1895 that a foul tip was a strike, and it wasn't until 1900 that home plate was widened from a 12-inch square to a 17-inch wide, five-sided polygon.

Three things are worth noting at this point:

- Comparing twentieth-century and nineteenth-century statistics can often be a meaningless exercise. The rules that governed play—and the equipment used by the players—led to high-scoring, error-filled contests where the objective was to simply put the ball in play. In 1876, the *average* game featured more than 7 unearned runs (in most seasons since World War II, there has been an average of less than 1 unearned run per game). Few batters struck out, fewer still drew bases on balls, and batters such as Willie "Hit 'Em Where They Ain't" Keeler choked halfway up the bat. Home runs were rare despite the short porches in many ballparks, yet the typical game in 1894 was still an 8–7 affair.
- Most of the rule changes were made to help the hitter. *That* is one thing that has not changed in the twentieth century.
- These rule changes tended to have a dramatic impact initially, but the players quickly adjusted. In 1884, when pitchers were allowed to throw overhand, strikeouts per game shot up from less than 7.5 to nearly 10. Strikeouts per game declined in 1885, and would not reach that level again until 1957. In 1893, when the pitchers were moved back 10 feet, runs went up by 3 per game, and another 1.5 per game the following year—to levels that have never been reached again in major league baseball. Forced to innovate, the defense tightened up and the pitchers got creative. By 1898, runs per game were less than they'd been before the mound was moved five years before—a remarkable accomplishment, aided in large part by trick pitches such as the spitball.

This cycle of the pitchers innovating, and the hitters—or the rulemakers—responding would continue for the next 100 years.

Ty Cobb (middle) talking hitting with teammates

Deadball: 1901–19

"Every great hitter works on the theory that the pitcher is more afraid of him than he is of the pitcher."

—TY COBB

When the National League (NL) began to call strikes on all foul balls in 1901—followed by the American League (AL) in 1903—it ushered in the lowest-scoring era in baseball. It also marked just about the last time the rulemakers would do the pitchers any favors.

Both the AL and NL would bat .254 and play 5–3 games during this period. If the defense had been up to current standards, runs per game would have dropped even further, to all-time lows of 6.5 runs per game. A league batting average of .254 is nothing new; more often than not, league averages have been in the .250s since 1942. It was the lack of punch that held down the scoring. Slugging averages (total bases divided by at-bats) were around .330, an all-time low, during this period. To put some faces next to these numbers, consider that the average hitter in today's game looks a lot like Todd Zeile and J. T. Snow—in the high .260s with around 15 home runs. The average hitter in the deadball era looked a lot like Gary DiSarcina and Mike Bordick—two slick-fielding shortstops who aren't in the big leagues today for their bats. The name of the game on offense was bat control, with hitting for power an untested art. Ty Cobb was the game's greatest hitter during this period. He played cat-and-mouse games with the fielders, bunting for a base hit if they played deep, slapping the ball past them if they played in. Success at the plate was more about brains than brawn.

Swinging for the Fences: 1920–41

"I have only one superstition. I make sure I touch all the bases when I hit a home run."

—BABE RUTH

The deadball era came to an end when Babe Ruth was sold to the Yankees after the 1919 season. Ruth brought to the plate a new style of swinging the bat—rotational. Instead of shifting his weight forward and slapping at the ball to ensure contact, Ruth spun on the ball in a corkscrew-like motion, generating tremendous bat speed. The Babe didn't just shatter home run records; his strikeouts were unprecedented, too.

Ruth would benefit from a livelier, cork-centered ball, hitting an unheard-of 54 home runs in 1920—and 611 more after that. It also helped that home runs were no longer judged fair or foul by where they landed, but rather by where they cleared the fence. Perhaps most significant of all for Ruth and other sluggers was the outlawing of the spitball, which stripped many hurlers of their "out pitch."

When Ray Chapman was killed by a pitched ball on August 16, 1920, more baseballs began to be used during games. No longer were balls brown, difficult to see, with the life beaten out of them by the fifth inning. Just about the only good news for the pitchers came in 1931, when the ground rule double was established for all balls that bounced over the outfield fence.

Despite the fact that defenses continued to improve—unearned runs dropped steadily during the '20s and '30s, and were approaching 1 per game by 1940—offensive production was up by about 2 runs a game. Home runs increased threefold, but batting averages were up, too. The league averages were around .280, by far the highest of any era. The National League as a whole hit .303 in 1930 (see Chapter 17 for a more detailed discussion). Usually when home runs increase, strikeouts do as well, reflecting the big strides and longer, looping swings of most power hitters. In the '20s and '30s, both power *and* contact were in style. Without trick pitches such as spitballs to contend with, strikeouts were down by about 15 percent.

The War Years: 1942–45

Baseball during World War II gives us a glimpse of what replacement baseball might have looked like in 1995. All able-bodied players reported for military duty, including countless Hall of Famers, so the quality of pitching and hitting remained *relatively* the same. Some might expect that the same offensive numbers would result. They didn't. Batting averages fell back into the .250s and slugging averages fell to nineteenth-century levels. Runs declined by 1 per game in 1942. There aren't many people on the planet who can hit a baseball solidly and consistently and occasionally 400 feet—regardless of who happens to be throwing it.

Mays, Aaron, and Two Robinsons: 1946–60

"The pitcher has got only a ball. I've got a bat. So the percentage in weapons is in my favor and I let the fellow with the ball do the fretting."

—HANK AARON

Rule changes were minimal between World War II and expansion in 1961–62. In 1950, the strike zone was lowered from the top of the shoulder to the armpit, and raised from the bottom to the top of the knee. In 1959, minimum dimensions were established for new ballparks (325 down the lines and 400 feet to center). But the most significant change during this period was not a rule, but the breaking in 1947 of the "gentlemen's agreement" that banned blacks from the major leagues. With black stars like Willie Mays, Jackie Robinson, Hank Aaron, and Frank Robinson now allowed to play—and expansion yet to come—baseball's talent pool was arguably at its deepest point in history.

With this influx of talent, offense changed dramatically from 1941 to 1960. Home runs per game increased by about 50 percent, though runs per game actually declined. Batting averages were lodged in the high .250s, and strikeouts per game were up by 2 in the AL and 4 in the NL. The advent of night games, along with more strenuous road trips created by westward franchise movements to Milwaukee, Kansas City, Los Angeles, and San Francisco, proved to be tougher on hitters than pitchers. And, as pitchers had adjusted in the 1890s with the spitball, so they adjusted in the 1950s—with a hard curveball that eventually became known as a slider.

Expanding the Strike Zone: 1961–68

> *"They give you a round bat and they throw you a round ball. And they tell you to hit it square."*
>
> —WILLIE STARGELL

In 1961, the American League expanded to 10 teams, followed by the National League in 1962. Much has been made of the diluting effect of expansion on pitching, with Roger Maris's 61 home runs in 1961 offered as Exhibit A. Some forget that Ruth lost *two* records that year, as Whitey Ford broke his record of consecutive scoreless innings pitched in World Series competition. Pitching was very much alive. Maris notwithstanding, expansion in 1961 and 1962 appears to have had little to no impact on offense. In 1961, runs per game in the AL went up by .3 and home runs per game by .14—hardly seismic events. The league batting average was virtually flat. In 1962, runs per game in the NL actually declined, as did batting average, slugging average, and home runs per game.

Nevertheless, the strike zone was returned to its original dimensions in 1963, helping to usher in a 6-year period of pitching dominance unseen in 50 years. The defense was doing its part, holding unearned runs below 1 per game. By 1968, total runs per game had dropped below 7 for the first time since 1908, while strikeouts had doubled from prewar levels. Home runs also steadily declined. The American League hit .230 in 1968, lowest in history, while Bob Gibson recorded a 1.12 ERA in the National League (see Chapter 17 for a more detailed discussion).

Artificial and Designated: 1969–92

"Taters, that's where the money is."

—REGGIE JACKSON

The period between 1969 and 1992 saw more significant rule changes than any time in the twentieth century. It began in 1969, when, as a reaction to the low-scoring 1968 season, the changes made to the strike zone in 1963 were undone. More significantly, the pitcher's mound was lowered from 15 inches to 10. Both leagues expanded to 12 teams in 1969. If expansion did indeed dilute pitching, then this combination of changes would have been expected to usher in a hitting bonanza reminiscent of 1893 or 1920. The impact lasted exactly two years.

By 1972, runs per game in the AL were back to 1968's low levels, and home run production had eroded even further. New stadiums and those minimum dimensions required by the league had something to do with this, too. Parks with short porches, such as the Polo Grounds and Ebbets Field, had given way to less hitter-friendly places like Shea Stadium, Candlestick Park, and Dodger Stadium—the latter two among the best pitcher's parks in baseball.

Linking diminished offense with diminished attendance, the AL instituted the designated hitter rule for the 1973 season, relieving the pitchers of the burden of all that swinging and missing. *This* changed what the mound and the strike zone could not. The league batting average went up 20 points and runs per game went up 1.6, the greatest jump since 1911 (when they first started tinkering with the baseball). By 1974, strikeouts per game had dropped below 10 for the first time since 1960.

In 1977, the American League expanded to 14 teams, and this seemed to finally dilute pitching in the major leagues. Runs per game and home runs per game jumped in both leagues. With older parks giving way to new multipurpose stadiums, artificial turf was on half of the fields in the National League. Teams such as the St. Louis Cardinals were building their offense around slap hitters with gap power and speed, to take advantage of the fast track.

Forced again to innovate, this time pitchers followed the lead of Cubs reliever Bruce Sutter, who threw a split-fingered fastball. The splitter was thrown like a forkball, only harder. To the hitter it looked like a fastball, but it dropped sharply as it approached the plate. Many batters were unable to lay off, swinging at and missing balls that ended up in the dirt. As other pitchers began to adopt the pitch, strikeouts per game climbed back to mid-'60s levels—and past them in the NL. Fortunately for hitters, not every pitcher followed Sutter's lead. The pitch put greater strain on the arm and was believed to end careers prematurely.

In 1987, the strike zone was reduced again, from the middle of the torso to the top of the knees. The high, hard fastball that few hitters could handle had been taken away from the pitchers. When home runs jumped to nearly 2 per game in the NL, and well past that in the AL, people began to talk of a "juiced ball." Major league baseball has consistently denied doing anything to the ball, but the fact that home runs per game have fluctuated more in recent years than at any other time in history has fueled the speculation of conspiracy theorists. Others point to the increased use of weight training by hitters, which had been taboo among flexibility-conscious baseball players until a soft-hitting backup catcher named Brian Downing turned his career around in the late '70s by bulking up. There is no shortage of theories, including those who link home runs to weather patterns—suggesting that as our climate has become more extreme from year to year, even the flight of baseballs has been affected.

Home Runs for *SportsCenter*: 1993–?

> *"You don't dream about hitting forty-nine (or fifty-eight or seventy) home runs when you're a kid. You just dream about hitting the ball, you don't dream about numbers."*
>
> —MARK MCGWIRE

In 1993, the National League expanded to 14 teams and offensive production again increased—by more than one run per game in the NL and by nearly as much in

Ken Griffey Jr. hit 398 home runs before the age of 30.

the AL. Newer, smaller ballparks, and 81 games a year played in the hitter-friendly, thin air of Denver, contributed to this increase in offense. Others pointed to an unwillingness of pitchers to come inside to back hitters off the plate, allowing batters to dive into pitches and increase their plate coverage—either out of fear of a batter charging the mound with malice aforethought, or bad habits developed in college and high school where aluminum bats can't be "sawed off," or simply due to union solidarity. Some suggested, tongue only halfway in cheek, that hitters were swinging from the heels because they liked looking at themselves on ESPN's *SportsCenter.*

In 1996, the strike zone was lowered from the top of the knee to the bottom of the knee, though this was not so much a change as a formalization of a practice already in place. And 1996 was by no means a pitcher's year, regardless of how big the strike zone was supposed to be. Runs per game in the NL reached their highest level since 1953. Things were even more dramatic in the AL, where runs per game climbed toward 11, to their highest point since 1938. Home runs per game were up to 2.4, highest in history, as the league ERA approached 5.00. Unfortunately, so too were the lengths of games—as pitchers nibbled more, taking hitters deep into counts. The combination of strikeouts and walks is at its highest point in history, and these outcomes of an at-bat take much longer than any other. There's one surefire way to make pitchers throw more strikes, but baseball fans might not be ready for ball three, take your base.

Some fans are complaining about *too much* offense, but the spinning turnstiles when Big Mac, Sammy Sosa, and Junior Griffey come to town is what major league owners choose to hear. Although the number of runners crossing the plate might make a nineteenth-century fan think back to the offensive explosion of 1893–97, nothing much else about the sport is the same. Today, it's a whole new ballgame.

2

Mount Olympus

The 25 Greatest Hitters of All Time

"Baseball is the only field of endeavor where a man can succeed three times out of ten and be considered a good performer."

—TED WILLIAMS

"If I had my career to play over, one thing I'd do differently is swing more. Those 1,200 walks I got, nobody remembers them.

—PEE WEE REESE

The list of big-league hitters extends from Major League home run champ Hank Aaron to Federal League home run champ Dutch Zwilling, with thousands of names in between. With so many to choose from, how to go about selecting the 25 best of all time? Turns out that having so many to choose from is just the beginning of the challenges.

- How do you compare hitters across eras? Ty Cobb and Barry Bonds have a lot in common, but the eras in which they played could not be more different. The same could be said for Harmon Killebrew and Hank Greenberg.
- How do you take into account the quality of a player's teammates? Ernie Banks put up some big numbers for some wretched ballclubs; but as impressive as his RBI and runs scored totals are, they could be topped by lesser hitters on better teams.

- How do you make a fair comparison between the short but brilliant career of Ralph Kiner and the long and consistent career of Willie Stargell?
- How do you reward the player who piles up numbers in underappreciated categories such as doubles and walks, when batting average treats all hits the same and ignores bases on balls completely?
- And how do you do all that without a hideous mathematical formula that is as out of place in a baseball book as artificial turf in Wrigley Field?

Here is a simple method that addresses all of those issues without making your eyes glaze over. It doesn't require any more information than what you can find on the back of a baseball card. And it's built on two basic assumptions that any knowledgeable fan can buy into:

- Honus Wagner's stats might not look like Alex Rodriguez's, but what any two great players *should* have in common is performance well above that of the average players of their day.
- While a hitter may not have control over how many runs he scores or knocks in, he does have control over how many total bases and walks he piles up during the course of a season.

That's it: Total bases and walks compared to the player's average contemporaries on a season-by-season basis. It's simple without being simplistic. There's even a simple name for it: bases. And a simple abbreviation: B.

The comparison to the league's average player is done with *bases* and *base average*. Bases equals total bases plus walks. Base average is a modified version of slugging average—taking total bases and walks, then dividing by at-bats and walks. This works out to the number of bases a hitter reaches for each plate appearance. To see how it works, let's use Honus Wagner and Alex Rodriguez as an example.

When looking at the big three statistics—home runs, RBI, and batting average—there appears to be no comparison between what Wagner did in 1908 and what Rodriguez did in 1996.

	HR	RBI	BA
Wagner 1908	10	109	.354
Rodriguez 1996	36	123	.358

But things change when you look at statistics that capture more of a hitter's offensive contribution: total bases and walks. Things change even more when you take into account what the average hitter looked like in the deadball National League of 1908 compared to the rabbitball American League of 1996. It's time to reconsider Honus.

	At-bats + walks	Bases	Base average
Wagner 1908	622	362	.582
NL 1908	622	221	.355
Rodriguez 1996	660	438	.664
AL 1996	660	329	.499

In 1998, Alex Rodriguez became the first infielder to hit 40 home runs and steal 40 bases in the same season.

PATIENCE AND POWER

To gauge the significance of total bases and walks, consider how different these .320 to .330 lifetime hitters look when evaluated on the dimensions of hitting for power and hitting with patience. The ones with the highest batting averages—Tony Gwynn and Mike Piazza—actually make the most outs. And though even the casual fan knows that Frank Thomas has greater power than Wade Boggs, did you know that Thomas's total bases per hit were *that much* higher than Boggs's? Take both factors into account, and the one with the lowest batting average—the patient and powerful Frank Thomas—is actually the most productive hitter.

	Puts the ball in play	Waits for his pitch
Slap hitter	Tony Gwynn .339* Outs per 600 plate appearances: 366	Wade Boggs .329* Outs per 600 plate appearances: 349
	Total bases per hit: 1.35	Total bases per hit: 1.35
Power hitter	Mike Piazza .333* Outs per 600 plate appearances: 362	Frank Thomas .321* Outs per 600 plate appearances: 333
	Total bases per hit: 1.73	Total bases per hit: 1.82
	*through 1998	

So how much better were Wagner and Rodriguez than their peers in the same number of plate appearances? As good as A-Rod was, Wagner was even better. Rodriguez put up huge numbers in 1996 during one of the best offensive seasons in baseball history. When you consider that the average baseball game in 1908 was a 3–2 pitchers' duel, Wagner's performance was significantly better. In fact, by these criteria it happens to be the greatest season any shortstop has ever had.

	Bases	Base average
Wagner 1908	362	.582
NL 1908	221	.355
Wagner vs. NL	141 additional bases	64% better
Rodriguez 1996	438	.664
AL 1996	329	.499
Rodriguez vs. AL	109 additional bases	33% better

This method doesn't just level the playing field for hitters who toiled during a pitching era, it gives the doubles hitter with a good eye his just due. Compare Hall of Fame third baseman Pie Traynor's best season to one of the "worst" of Cooperstown-snubbed third baseman Ron Santo.

	HR	RBI	BA	
Traynor 1930	9	119	.366	
Santo 1968	26	98	.246	

No comparison, right? Well, yes, actually, but not how it might initially appear. For one thing, 1930 was the most explosive year in baseball history, while 1968 was a year of pitching dominance unmatched in the modern era. For another, Ron Santo led the league in walks in 1968 (for the third consecutive season), doubling Traynor's output (which was actually an uncharacteristically high total for him).

	At-bats + walks	Bases	Base average
Traynor 1930	545	301	.552
NL 1930	545	268	.491
Santo 1968	673	339	.504
NL 1968	673	262	.389

Despite a career-high .366 batting average, Traynor was only 12 percent better at "producing bases" than the *average* National Leaguer of 1930. Despite an uncharacteristically low .246 batting average, Santo was still 30 percent better than his peers, relying on walks and extra-base hits to pile up more than double the number of additional bases of Traynor in a much, much tougher year for hitters.

	Bases	Base average
Traynor 1930	301	.552
NL 1930	268	.491
Traynor vs. NL	33 more bases	12% better
Santo 1968	339	.504
NL 1968	262	.389
Santo vs. NL	77 more bases	30% better

So which is a better indicator—bases or base average? Rather than try to answer that question, we've looked at hitters from both perspectives. Base average relative to the league helps out the deadball players, since it's harder to pile up additional bases when you're running them one or two rather than four at a time. Relative base average also helps out the players who dominated for shorter periods of time. Additional bases favor today's players, whose careers are longer and who play in an era when extra bases are easier to come by.

As you'll see, players didn't get into the top 25 without being very impressive in both relative base average and additional bases. They also didn't get there by simply being consistently good for a long period of time. Many of them were frequently great, with 17 of these 25 gentlemen accounting for 45 of the 50 best individual seasons that any hitter has ever had—including the 29 best!

The top 25 follow, in reverse order. But before reading on, can you name:

- The three players on the list still active in 1999?
- The top National League hitter?
- The top right-handed hitter?
- The only switch-hitter?
- The only retired player on the list who is not in the Hall of Fame?
- The five players who produced a top 50 season without cracking the top 25?

NEW STATISTICS, NEW TARGETS

Even a casual baseball fan knows about a .300 average, 200 hits, and 100 RBI in a season, 500 home runs and 3,000 hits for a career. So what are the comparable levels for base average and bases?

Base Average–Season

The league leader has been at .600 for the vast majority of seasons since the deadball era ended.

A base average of .750 has only been done 24 times by 10 players (with a base average of .800 even more rare than a batting average of .400). One hitter flirted with .900 twice, but it's never been reached.

When looking at relative base average, you'll find that outproducing one's peers by 33 percent is usually enough to lead the league. Only 12 hitters (a total of 29 times) have outproduced their league by two-thirds (67 percent). And only one player has ever outproduced his league by more than 100 percent—essentially being twice as good as the average player of his day.

Base Average–Career

A career base average of .600 is as rare as a lifetime .333 hitter. Only 23 hitters with at least 4,000 plate appearances have maintained this level—with a number of today's sluggers lacking only the necessary service time to join the crowd. (Whether they can stay there remains to be seen; Frank Robinson and Duke Snider are two notable examples of players who spent most of their careers above .600, but retired below.)

Even more rare is the 40-percent club. Only 16 hitters have put up base averages 40 percent higher than their league average for an entire career.

Bases–Season

Compiling 400 bases in a season is usually more than enough to lead the league, while 500 bases is a legendary performance, having only been done 21 times by eight players. One player even topped 600 for a season.

Producing 100 *additional* bases is a very solid season that will put a hitter near the top of the league. Producing 200 additional bases will earn a hitter a prime seat in Valhalla, having been done only 21 times by just seven players.

Bases—Career

Recording 6,000 bases for a career is akin to joining the 3,000-hit club. Only 20 hitters have topped 6,000—with one reaching 8,000. Only 11 of the 23 members of the 3,000-hit club have done it, with the newest 3,000-hit men, Tony Gwynn and Wade Boggs, still a long way from 6,000 bases.

Even more exclusive than the 6,000-bases club is the 1,500-additional-bases club, of which Barry Bonds became the 16th member in 1999.

Example: Jeff Bagwell

To get a handle on what a great hitter's base average, bases, relative production, and additional bases will look like, let's take a look at Jeff Bagwell's seasons through 1999.

		AB	H	2B	3B	HR	BB	B	BA	SA	A	LGE	+/−	Additional
Hou	1991	554	163	26	4	15	75	317	.294	.437	.504	.428	18%	48
Hou	1992	586	160	34	6	18	84	344	.273	.444	.513	.421	22%	62
Hou	1993	535	171	37	4	20	62	338	.320	.516	.566	.449	26%	70
Hou	1994	400	147	32	2	39	65	365	.368	.750	.785	.464	69%	149
Hou	1995	448	130	29	0	21	79	301	.290	.496	.571	.459	24%	59
Hou	1996	568	179	48	2	31	135	459	.315	.570	.653	.460	42%	136
Hou	1997	566	162	40	2	43	127	462	.286	.592	.667	.464	44%	141
Hou	1998	540	164	33	1	34	109	410	.304	.557	.632	.463	37%	110
Hou	1999	562	171	35	0	42	149	481	.304	.591	.677	.485	40%	136
		4759	1447	314	21	263	885	3477	.304	.545	.616	.454	36%	910

AB—at-bats; H—hits; 2B—doubles; 3B—triples; HR—home runs; BB—walks; B—bases (total bases + walks); BA—batting average; SA—slugging average; A—base average (total bases + walks/at bats + walks); LGE—the NL or AL's base average for that season; +/−—the hitter's base average relative to the league's base average (A/LGE); Additional—the number of additional bases a hitter accumulated relative to the league's average hitter in the same number of plate appearances)

Base Average—Jeff Bagwell was in the midst of one of the best seasons in baseball history in 1994 when a broken hand shut him down for the year within days of the players strike. He finished with a base average over .750 (.785), outproducing the National League by more than two-thirds (69 percent), but without enough plate appearances to qualify for the all-time "short list." If he can maintain a career base average of more than .600 (.616) and continue to outproduce the league by more than one-third (36 percent) for another 10 years, he'll be knocking someone out of the all-time top 25.

Bases—Bagwell has topped the 400-bases plateau four times in his career (410, 450, 459, and 462), and was making a run at 500 bases in 1994. In recent years, he has consistently produced more than 100 additional bases (110, 136 twice, and 141) and would almost certainly have produced 200 additional bases in 1994. Though he's probably not going to reach 3,000 hits for his career, he is more than halfway to 6,000 bases (3,477) and 1,500 additional bases (910).

Not bad for a guy with one of the most awkward-looking batting stances the game has ever seen. Think the Red Sox would take him back?

The Top 25

25. Frank Thomas, 1B/RH, 1990–. Chicago White Sox.

Top 50 seasons: None yet

		AB	H	2B	3B	HR	BB	B	BA	SA	A	LGE	+/–	Additional
ChiA	1990	191	63	11	3	7	44	145	.330	.529	.617	.443	39%	41
ChiA	1991	559	178	31	2	32	138	447	.318	.553	.641	.450	43%	133
ChiA	1992	573	185	46	2	24	122	429	.323	.536	.617	.441	40%	123
ChiA	1993	549	174	36	0	41	112	445	.317	.607	.673	.463	46%	139
ChiA	1994	399	141	34	1	38	109	400	.353	.729	.787	.489	61%	152
ChiA	1995	493	152	27	0	40	136	435	.308	.606	.692	.483	43%	131
ChiA	1996	527	184	26	0	40	109	439	.349	.626	.690	.499	38%	121
ChiA	1997	530	184	35	0	35	109	433	.347	.611	.678	.480	41%	126
ChiA	1998	585	155	35	2	29	110	391	.265	.480	.563	.483	16%	55
ChiA	1999	486	148	36	0	15	87	316	.305	.471	.551	.493	12%	34
		4892	1564	317	10	301	1076	3880	.320	.573	.650	.473	37%	1055

At 6′5″ and 260 pounds, Frank Thomas is able to drive balls more than 500 feet while committing the cardinal sin of hitting off his front foot, his back foot off the ground. A former Division-I football player and one of the most intimidating-looking hitters to ever enter the batter's box, he's more than made up for the 90-year dearth of great White Sox hitters all on his own.

"The Big Hurt" moved into the top 25 after only eight seasons; but if his struggles of 1998 and 1999 continue, he may not be able to stay there. He was his league's best hitter in 1991, 1992, and the strike-shortened 1994 season. When that campaign was interrupted two-thirds of the way through by the players union, attention was focused on Matt Williams's and Ken Griffey's lost chances at Roger Maris's home run record. But it was Frank Thomas and Jeff Bagwell who were having the greatest seasons.

In 1994, Thomas was on his way to a 54-homer, 202-hit, 156-walk, 145-RBI, and 152-run season for a division-leading White Sox team. Had the 1994 season been allowed to continue and Thomas maintained his torrid pace, his mark of 218 additional bases would have placed him in the top 10 of all time—shouldering aside no less than Babe Ruth and Ted Williams in the process.

Even if Thomas had slumped down the stretch, he would have easily accumulated the 100 bases he needed to reach 500 for the season. In the process, he would have become only the eighth player to ever do that—joining a list with names like Babe Ruth, Lou Gehrig, Jimmie Foxx, Ted Williams, Hack Wilson,

Rogers Hornsby, and Stan Musial. Had Thomas been able to keep on keeping on, he would have piled up 574 bases for the season.

Only one man would have ever exceeded that total for a season—but more on him later.

24. Ralph Kiner, LF/RH, 1946–55. Pittsburgh Pirates, Chicago Cubs, Cleveland Indians. Hall of Fame: 1975.

Top 50 seasons: 1949 (39th), 1951 (47th)

		AB	H	2B	3B	HR	BB	B	BA	SA	A	LGE	+/−	Additional
Pitt	1946	502	124	17	3	23	74	290	.247	.430	.503	.417	21%	50
Pitt	1947	565	177	23	4	51	98	459	.313	.639	.692	.449	54%	161
Pitt	1948	555	147	19	5	40	112	408	.265	.533	.612	.441	39%	114
Pitt	1949	549	170	19	5	54	117	478	.310	.658	.718	.446	61%	181
Pitt	1950	547	149	21	6	47	122	445	.272	.590	.665	.459	45%	138
Pitt	1951	531	164	31	6	42	137	470	.309	.627	.704	.447	58%	172
Pitt	1952	516	126	17	2	37	110	368	.244	.500	.588	.430	37%	99
Pitt/ChiN	1953	562	157	20	3	35	100	388	.279	.512	.586	.465	26%	80
ChiN	1954	557	159	36	5	22	76	347	.285	.487	.548	.463	18%	54
Clev	1955	321	78	13	0	18	65	210	.243	.452	.544	.445	22%	38
		5205	1451	216	39	369	1011	3863	.279	.548	.621	.447	39%	1086

"Home run hitters drive Cadillacs; singles hitters drive Fords."

—RALPH KINER

Before he was butchering his native tongue as a Mets announcer, Ralph Kiner was dominating the National League the way no other power hitter has. The 6′2″, 195-pounder from New Mexico led the league in home runs in each of his first seven seasons. He couldn't keep up the pace, and when his power stroke slowed he had no other baseball skills to fall back on.

Ralph Kiner had the shortest career of any member of the top 25, but he crammed a lot of production into those 10 years, averaging 37 home runs and 101 walks per season—outproducing his league's average player by 39 percent and 109 bases. He led the National League in home runs seven times and slugging average three times, despite playing in a pitcher's park for a string of bad ballclubs.

Kiner led the National League in bases three times (1947, 1950, and 1951), though his best season was 1949 (39th best of all time), when he took a run at Babe Ruth's single-season home run record. No hitter has ever hit so many home runs with a weaker-hitting lineup around him. Take a look at this lineup card and ask yourself why he ever saw a strike.

1949 Pirates

		HR	RBI	BA
Walker Cooper	C	4	21	.237
Johnny Hopp	1B	5	39	.318
Monty Basgall	2B	2	26	.218
Stan Rojek	SS	0	31	.244
Pete Castiglione	3B	6	43	.268
Ralph Kiner	LF	54	127	.310
Dino Restelli	CF	12	40	.250
Wally Westlake	RF	23	104	.282

23. Willie Stargell, LF/LH, 1962–82. Pittsburgh Pirates. Hall of Fame: 1988.

Top 50 seasons: None

		AB	H	2B	3B	HR	BB	B	BA	SA	A	LGE	+/−	Additional
Pitt	1962	31	9	3	1	0	3	17	.290	.452	.500	.446	12%	2
Pitt	1963	304	74	11	6	11	19	149	.243	.428	.461	.413	12%	16
Pitt	1964	421	115	19	7	21	17	228	.273	.501	.521	.420	24%	44
Pitt	1965	533	145	25	8	27	39	306	.272	.501	.535	.423	26%	64
Pitt	1966	485	153	30	0	33	48	330	.315	.581	.619	.429	44%	101
Pitt	1967	462	125	18	6	20	67	282	.271	.465	.533	.414	29%	63
Pitt	1968	435	103	15	1	24	47	239	.237	.441	.496	.389	28%	52
Pitt	1969	522	160	31	6	29	61	351	.307	.556	.602	.425	42%	103
Pitt	1970	474	125	18	3	31	44	286	.264	.511	.552	.449	23%	53
Pitt	1971	511	151	26	0	48	83	404	.295	.628	.680	.419	62%	155
Pitt	1972	495	145	28	2	33	65	341	.293	.558	.609	.420	45%	106
Pitt	1973	522	156	43	3	44	80	417	.299	.646	.693	.432	61%	157
Pitt	1974	508	153	37	4	25	87	360	.301	.537	.605	.426	42%	106
Pitt	1975	461	136	32	2	22	58	296	.295	.516	.570	.427	33%	74
Pitt	1976	428	110	20	3	20	50	246	.257	.458	.515	.417	24%	47
Pitt	1977	186	51	12	0	13	31	133	.274	.548	.613	.450	36%	35
Pitt	1978	390	115	18	2	28	50	271	.295	.567	.616	.427	44%	83
Pitt	1979	424	119	19	0	32	47	281	.281	.552	.597	.438	36%	75
Pitt	1980	202	53	10	1	11	26	124	.262	.485	.544	.426	28%	27
Pitt	1981	60	17	4	0	0	5	26	.283	.350	.400	.419	-4%	-1
Pitt	1982	73	17	4	0	3	10	40	.233	.411	.482	.425	13%	5
		7927	2232	423	55	475	937	5127	.282	.529	.578	.424	36%	1367

"I never saw anything like it. He doesn't just hit pitchers. He takes away their dignity."

—HALL OF FAME PITCHER DON SUTTON ON WILLIE STARGELL

Some may be surprised to see Willie Stargell on this list—though you'd get no argument from Don Sutton or any other pitcher who ever tried to sneak a low-and-in fastball by him. Stargell played in the shadow of Roberto Clemente in Pittsburgh, and Hank Aaron and Willie Mays in the National League. His home run totals in the 1960s were diminished by spacious Forbes Field. And his only MVP (1979, shared with Keith Hernandez) was the baseball equivalent of a lifetime achievement award, a tribute to his leadership in the clubhouse more than to his production at the plate.

Stargell had two trademarks: pinwheeling his bat while waiting for the pitch, and tape-measure home runs. The landings of some of his moon shots have been marked by specially colored seats in the remote sections of upper decks all over the National League (with the exception of Dodger Stadium, where two of his bombs left the building completely).

These spectacular aspects of his game notwithstanding, Stargell's presence on this list is more of a tribute to his longevity and his consistent production during a pitcher's era. Read on for some eerie parallels to another Willie who is on the list for the same reasons.

22. Joe DiMaggio, CF/RH, 1936–42, 1946–51. New York Yankees. Hall of Fame: 1955.

Top 50 seasons: None

		AB	H	2B	3B	HR	BB	B	BA	SA	A	LGE	+/−	Additional
NYA	1936	637	206	44	15	29	24	391	.323	.576	.592	.479	24%	75
NYA	1937	621	215	35	15	46	64	482	.346	.673	.704	.473	49%	158
NYA	1938	599	194	32	13	32	59	407	.324	.581	.619	.476	30%	94
NYA	1939	462	176	32	6	30	52	362	.381	.671	.704	.466	51%	122
NYA	1940	508	179	28	9	31	61	379	.352	.626	.666	.463	44%	115
NYA	1941	541	193	43	11	30	76	424	.357	.643	.687	.450	53%	147
NYA	1942	610	186	29	13	21	68	372	.305	.498	.549	.417	32%	89
NYA	1946	503	146	20	8	25	59	316	.290	.511	.562	.424	33%	78
NYA	1947	534	168	31	10	20	64	343	.315	.522	.574	.429	34%	86
NYA	1948	594	190	26	11	39	67	422	.320	.598	.638	.450	42%	124
NYA	1949	272	94	14	6	14	55	217	.346	.596	.664	.453	47%	69
NYA	1950	525	185	33	10	32	80	414	.352	.636	.684	.470	46%	130
NYA	1951	415	109	22	4	12	61	236	.263	.422	.496	.445	11%	24
		6821	2241	389	131	361	790	4765	.329	.583	.626	.454	38%	1311

A brief marriage to Marilyn Monroe and a 56-game hitting streak have begun to obscure much of what DiMaggio actually accomplished throughout his career: hitting at least .300 in all but two of his seasons, homering nearly as often as he struck out (361 to 369), leading his team to 10 World Series and 9 championships in 13 seasons, and doing it all with remarkable grace. When asked what made DiMaggio so great, teammate Yogi Berra shrugged and said, "He was perfect." Michael Jordan has often been compared to Babe Ruth, but between the lines it's to DiMaggio that the comparison should be made.

Joe DiMaggio makes the short list of great hitters despite losing three seasons to military service (at the prime ages of 28 through 30), parts of other seasons to injury, and playing in a ballpark with a power alley of 461 feet to left-center. DiMaggio is one of only six hitters among the top 25 to have played "up the middle": catcher, second, short, or center. Take his exquisite fielding at a critical position and the unparalleled success of the team, compare it to the glovework and rings of the other hitters on this list, and you begin to understand why so many who saw him play consider him the greatest to ever take the field.

21. Willie McCovey, 1B/LH, 1959–80. San Francisco Giants, San Diego Padres, Oakland A's. Hall of Fame: 1986.

Top 50 seasons: 1969 (22nd)

		AB	H	2B	3B	HR	BB	B	BA	SA	A	LGE	+/−	Additional
SF	1959	192	68	9	5	13	22	148	.354	.656	.692	.451	53%	51
SF	1960	260	62	15	3	13	45	167	.238	.469	.548	.440	24%	33
SF	1961	328	89	12	3	18	37	198	.271	.491	.542	.457	19%	31
SF	1962	229	67	6	1	20	29	164	.293	.590	.636	.446	43%	49
SF	1963	564	158	19	5	44	50	369	.280	.566	.601	.413	46%	116
SF	1964	364	80	14	1	18	61	211	.220	.412	.496	.420	18%	32
SF	1965	540	149	17	4	39	88	379	.276	.539	.604	.423	43%	113
SF	1966	502	148	26	6	36	76	370	.295	.586	.640	.429	49%	122
SF	1967	456	126	17	4	31	71	315	.276	.535	.598	.414	44%	97
SF	1968	523	153	16	4	36	72	357	.293	.545	.600	.389	54%	126
SF	1969	491	157	26	2	45	121	443	.320	.656	.724	.425	70%	183
SF	1970	495	143	39	2	39	137	440	.289	.612	.696	.449	55%	156
SF	1971	329	91	13	0	18	64	222	.277	.480	.565	.419	35%	57
SF	1972	263	56	8	0	14	38	144	.213	.403	.478	.420	14%	18
SF	1973	383	102	14	3	29	105	314	.266	.546	.643	.432	49%	103
SD	1974	344	87	19	1	22	96	270	.253	.506	.614	.426	44%	82
SD	1975	413	104	17	0	23	57	247	.252	.460	.526	.427	23%	46
SD/Oak	1976	226	46	9	0	7	24	100	.204	.336	.400	.417	-4%	-4
SF	1977	478	134	21	0	28	67	306	.280	.500	.561	.450	25%	61
SF	1978	351	80	19	2	12	36	175	.228	.396	.452	.427	6%	10
SF	1979	353	88	9	0	15	36	178	.249	.402	.458	.438	5%	8
SF	1980	113	23	8	0	1	13	47	.204	.301	.373	.426	-12%	-7
		8197	2211	353	46	521	1345	5564	.270	.515	.583	.428	36%	1483

Wille Mays came to the big leagues and went 0 for 12 until connecting for a home run off Warren Spahn. A few years later, in 1959, Mays's teammate Willie McCovey came to the Show and debuted with a 4 for 4 off Hall of Famer Robin Roberts.

Like his contemporary Willie Stargell, McCovey played Hall of Fame–caliber ball in the shadow of a living legend (Mays). Both Stargell and McCovey played more than 20 years in the big leagues, producing impressive (and strikingly similar) numbers without dominating their leagues. For their careers, they both outperformed the average player in their league by 36 percent, with McCovey's greater patience at the plate allowing him to accumulate more bases than Stargell despite lower batting and slugging averages.

	AB	H	2B	3B	HR	BB	B	BA	SA	A	LGE	+/−	Additional
Stargell	7927	2232	423	55	475	937	5127	.282	.529	.578	.424	36%	1367
McCovey	8197	2211	353	46	521	1345	5564	.270	.515	.583	.428	36%	1483

Coincidentally, they also both had one final fling at the age of 39, Stargell in his 1979 MVP season and McCovey in 1977 with 28 home runs in a triumphant return to the Giants.

		AB	H	2B	3B	HR	BB	B	BA	SA	A	LGE	+/−	Additional
Stargell	1979	424	119	19	0	32	47	281	.281	.552	.597	.438	36%	75
McCovey	1977	478	134	21	0	28	67	306	.280	.500	.561	.450	25%	61

Had he just gotten under that Ralph Terry pitch in 1962 (see Chapter 5), his name might be spoken with more of the reverence it deserves.

20. Tris Speaker, CF/LH, 1907–28. Boston Red Sox, Cleveland Indians, Washington Senators, Philadelphia Athletics. Hall of Fame: 1937

Top 50 seasons: None

		AB	H	2B	3B	HR	BB	B	BA	SA	A	LGE	+/−	Additional
BosA	1907	19	3	0	0	0	1	4	.158	.158	.200	.354	−43%	−3
BosA	1908	118	26	2	3	0	4	38	.220	.288	.311	.349	−11%	−5
BosA	1909	544	168	26	13	7	38	279	.309	.443	.479	.356	35%	72
BosA	1910	538	183	20	14	7	52	304	.340	.468	.515	.366	41%	88
BosA	1911	510	167	34	13	8	59	310	.327	.492	.545	.409	33%	77
BosA	1912	580	222	53	12	10	82	411	.383	.567	.621	.403	54%	144
BosA	1913	520	190	35	22	3	65	343	.365	.535	.586	.393	49%	113
BosA	1914	571	193	46	18	4	77	364	.338	.503	.562	.382	47%	116

		AB	H	2B	3B	HR	BB	B	BA	SA	A	LGE	+/−	Additional
BosA	1915	547	176	25	12	0	81	306	.322	.411	.487	.390	25%	61
Clev	1916	546	211	41	8	2	82	356	.386	.502	.567	.385	47%	114
Clev	1917	523	184	42	11	2	67	321	.352	.486	.544	.379	44%	97
Clev	1918	471	150	33	11	0	64	269	.318	.435	.503	.382	32%	65
Clev	1919	494	146	38	12	2	73	287	.296	.433	.506	.412	23%	53
Clev	1920	552	214	50	11	8	97	407	.388	.562	.627	.438	43%	123
Clev	1921	506	183	52	14	3	68	340	.362	.538	.592	.458	29%	77
Clev	1922	426	161	48	8	11	77	335	.378	.606	.666	.448	49%	110
Clev	1923	574	218	59	11	17	93	443	.380	.610	.664	.442	50%	148
Clev	1924	486	167	36	9	9	72	320	.344	.510	.573	.451	27%	68
Clev	1925	429	167	35	5	12	70	318	.389	.578	.637	.462	38%	87
Clev	1926	540	164	52	8	7	94	347	.304	.469	.547	.448	22%	63
Was	1927	523	171	43	6	2	55	287	.327	.444	.497	.451	10%	26
PhiA	1928	191	51	22	2	3	10	96	.267	.450	.478	.447	7%	6
		10208	3515	792	223	117	1381	6485	.344	.500	.560	.412	36%	1702

The appreciation of Tris Speaker's greatness has diminished with the passage of time and the rise of the home run as an offensive measuring stick. Against some fairly stiff competition, however, Speaker was the most productive hitter in his league four times: 1912, 1914, 1916, and 1918. In addition to being a great defensive center fielder who helped three teams to World Series victories, he is one of only five players to reach 3,500 hits, owns the fourth-highest career batting average among twentieth-century players, and is one of only two deadball hitters on this list of the greatest ever. Despite only 117 home runs—the fewest among the top 25—his .500 lifetime slugging average is one of the 50 highest in baseball history.

There was no lack of respect for Speaker 60 years ago. He was great enough to go into the Hall of Fame in the second wave, after only Cobb, Wagner, Ruth, Mathewson, and Johnson.

Tris Speaker holds the perfect Louisville Slugger bat for his style of hitting. The thick handle and short length provide excellent bat control for line-drive hitters.

19. Harmon Killebrew, 1B/RH, 1954–75. Washington Senators, Minnesota Twins, Kansas City Royals. Hall of Fame: 1984.

Top 50 seasons: None

		AB	H	2B	3B	HR	BB	B	BA	SA	A	LGE	+/−	Additional
Wash	1954	13	4	1	0	0	2	7	.308	.385	.467	.435	7%	0
Wash	1955	80	16	1	0	4	9	38	.200	.363	.427	.445	-4%	-2
Wash	1956	99	22	2	0	5	10	49	.222	.394	.450	.459	-2%	-1
Wash	1957	31	9	2	0	2	2	19	.290	.548	.576	.440	31%	4
Wash	1958	31	6	0	0	0	0	6	.194	.194	.194	.438	-56%	-8
Wash	1959	546	132	20	2	42	90	372	.242	.516	.585	.440	33%	92
Wash	1960	442	122	19	1	31	71	307	.276	.534	.598	.447	34%	78
Minn	1961	541	156	20	7	46	107	435	.288	.606	.671	.454	48%	141
Minn	1962	552	134	21	1	48	106	407	.243	.545	.619	.450	37%	111
Minn	1963	515	133	18	0	45	72	358	.258	.555	.610	.432	41%	104
Minn	1964	577	156	11	1	49	93	409	.270	.548	.610	.435	40%	117
Minn	1965	401	108	16	1	25	72	273	.269	.501	.577	.425	36%	72
Minn	1966	569	160	27	1	39	103	409	.281	.538	.609	.422	44%	126
Minn	1967	547	147	24	1	44	131	436	.269	.558	.643	.406	58%	161
Minn	1968	295	62	7	2	17	70	194	.210	.420	.532	.394	35%	50
Minn	1969	555	153	20	2	49	145	469	.276	.584	.670	.430	56%	168
Minn	1970	527	143	20	1	41	128	416	.271	.546	.635	.437	45%	130
Minn	1971	500	127	19	1	28	114	346	.254	.464	.564	.422	34%	87
Minn	1972	433	100	13	2	26	94	289	.231	.450	.548	.399	37%	79
Minn	1973	248	60	9	1	5	41	127	.242	.347	.439	.437	0%	1
Minn	1974	333	74	7	0	13	45	165	.222	.360	.437	.424	3%	5
KC	1975	312	62	13	0	14	54	171	.199	.375	.467	.437	7%	11
		8147	2086	290	24	573	1559	5702	.256	.509	.587	.430	36%	1526

"I didn't have evil intentions, but I guess I did have power."

—HARMON KILLEBREW

At 5′11″ and 215 pounds, Harmon Killebrew was a strong, compact country boy from Idaho who played his first big league game at 17. It took him 6 years to finally win a starting job, and then he settled in for the next 14 years. He made his way with the Senators to Minnesota when they became the Twins in 1961 and bounced around the playing field too—from third base to the outfield to first base, back to third, and finally to designated hitter before he finally hung up the spikes.

Killebrew's lifetime batting average of .256 is the lowest in the top 25. This did not keep him from being one of the most productive hitters of the pitcher-dominated 1960s, leading the American League in bases in 1959, 1962, 1964, and 1969. In fact, Killebrew is the only hitter to lead the league in bases despite a batting average below .250, doing it in 1959 and 1962.

Harmon Killebrew may be the finest example of the shortcomings of batting average as an offensive statistic.

18. Dick Allen, 1B/RH, 1963–77. Philadelphia Phillies, St. Louis Cardinals, Los Angeles Dodgers, Chicago White Sox, Oakland A's.

Top 50 seasons: 1972 (36th)

		AB	H	2B	3B	HR	BB	B	BA	SA	A	LGE	+/−	Additional
Phil	1963	24	7	2	1	0	0	11	.292	.458	.458	.413	11%	1
Phil	1964	632	201	38	13	29	67	419	.318	.557	.599	.420	43%	125
Phil	1965	619	187	31	14	20	74	380	.302	.494	.548	.423	30%	87
Phil	1966	524	166	25	10	40	68	399	.317	.632	.674	.429	57%	145
Phil	1967	463	142	31	10	23	75	337	.307	.566	.626	.414	51%	114
Phil	1968	521	137	17	9	33	74	345	.263	.520	.580	.389	49%	114
Phil	1969	438	126	23	3	32	64	315	.288	.573	.627	.425	48%	102
SL	1970	459	128	17	5	34	71	328	.279	.560	.619	.449	38%	90
LA	1971	549	162	24	1	23	93	350	.295	.468	.545	.419	30%	81
ChiA	1972	506	156	28	5	37	99	404	.308	.603	.668	.399	67%	163
ChiA	1973	250	79	20	3	16	33	186	.316	.612	.657	.437	50%	62
ChiA	1974	462	139	23	1	32	57	317	.301	.563	.611	.424	44%	97
Phil	1975	416	97	21	3	12	58	218	.233	.385	.460	.427	8%	15
Phil	1976	298	80	16	1	15	37	180	.268	.480	.537	.417	29%	40
Oak	1977	171	41	4	0	5	24	84	.240	.351	.431	.456	-6%	-5
		6332	1848	320	79	351	894	4273	.292	.534	.591	.421	40%	1231

"There was never an ounce of phoniness in Dick. What you see is what you get. He was his own man and he still is. I saw him recently, and to this day I still love the guy."

—RICH GOSSAGE ON DICK ALLEN,
HIS TEAMMATE ON THE 1972 WHITE SOX

If he were a football player, Dick Allen would have been an Oakland Raider. He had his own way of doing things both on and off the field—drawing messages in the infield dirt, smoking cigarettes in the dugout (and on the cover of *Sports Illustrated*), dropping a racist teammate with one punch, nearly severing his hand pushing it through his car's headlight, and admittedly drinking before, after, and sometimes *during* games. But when the bell rang, he got it done.

The only non–Hall of Famer in the top 25—and, along with number 17 and 6, one of only two to play for five different teams—Dick "Don't Call Me Richie" Allen swung a 42-ounce bat and could still turn around any fastball he saw. He was such a great fastball hitter that Nolan Ryan couldn't restrain himself from turning one of their confrontations into a true gunfight—the only time Ryan ever told a hitter he would throw him nothing but fastballs. (They proceeded to get into a foul-ball duel that ended in neither a dinger nor a whiff, but merely a long fly, so call it a draw.)

When looking at the surface level of his 1972 statistics, greatness doesn't hop off the page. His performance for the White Sox during a punchless 1972 season has yet to be topped by any American League hitter since, as he nearly carried a truly lousy ballclub past an emerging Oakland A's dynasty into the postseason. He outproduced his league by 67 percent, a truly Ruthian performance. Junior Griffey hit 56 home runs in 1998 and outproduced his counterparts by only 35 percent. In the high-powered American League of 1998, Griffey would have needed to bat .303 with *68* home runs to exceed his peers by the same level that Dick Allen did in 1972.

Unlike the wildly popular Griffey, Allen was reviled by the press as a lazy, malingering underachiever. Imagine an injury-prone and slow-healing Barry Bonds who was prone to walking out on his ballclubs in midseason. But bear in mind that Barry Bonds never had to play in Philadelphia. Fans in the City of Brotherly Love are the acknowledged masters of ill will, but with Allen they raised it to an art form, heaping abuse on one of the greatest hitters they will ever see. Allen played angry for most of his time in Philadelphia, channeling it into wicked line drives and tape-measure home runs that rattled around a decaying Connie Mack Stadium. He spent his final days in Philadelphia doodling in the dirt around first base and begging to be traded (which he eventually was, to the Cardinals, for Curt Flood, who chose to challenge baseball's reserve system rather than play for the Phillies).

In 1970, at 28 and in the prime of his career, coming off a 101-RBI season (in 122 games) for the Cardinals, Allen was traded to the Dodgers for Ted Sizemore and Bob Stinson. Never willing to "bleed Dodger blue," Allen lasted one season in L.A. and was traded to the White Sox for Tommy John.

Controversy, Dick Allen maintained, always seemed to find him. In his 15-year career, injuries, suspensions, and retirements shortened Allen's seasons seven times.

Season	Games played	Time lost due to
1967	122	Hand injury
1969	118	Suspension by team
1970	122	Hamstring tear
1973	72	Broken leg
1974	128	Retirement
1976	85	Shoulder injury
1977	54	Suspension by team, retirement

Had Allen managed to play only 150 games in these seasons, it would have been a lot harder to keep him out of Cooperstown. These interruptions kept him from reaching 400 home runs, 2,000 hits, and a plaque in the big room.

It is hard to reconcile how one can be both an underachiever *and* one of the most productive hitters in the history of the game. A fairer assessment is that Dick Allen may be one of the most underrated hitters the game has seen—his accomplishments obscured by controversy, incomplete seasons, and stats deflated by a pitcher's era.

17. Frank Robinson, RF/RH, 1956–76. Cincinnati Reds, Baltimore Orioles, Los Angeles Dodgers, California Angels, Cleveland Indians. Hall of Fame: 1982.

Top 50 seasons: 1966 (38th)

		AB	H	2B	3B	HR	BB	B	BA	SA	A	LGE	+/−	Additional
Cinc	1956	572	166	27	6	38	64	383	.290	.558	.602	.453	33%	95
Cinc	1957	611	197	29	5	29	44	367	.322	.529	.560	.450	25%	73
Cinc	1958	554	149	25	6	31	62	341	.269	.504	.554	.457	21%	59
Cinc	1959	540	168	31	4	36	69	384	.311	.583	.631	.451	40%	109
Cinc	1960	464	138	33	6	31	82	358	.297	.595	.656	.440	49%	118
Cinc	1961	545	176	32	7	37	71	404	.323	.611	.656	.457	44%	123
Cinc	1962	609	208	51	2	39	76	456	.342	.624	.666	.446	49%	151
Cinc	1963	482	125	19	3	21	81	294	.259	.442	.522	.413	26%	62
Cinc	1964	568	174	38	6	29	79	390	.306	.548	.603	.420	43%	118
Cinc	1965	582	172	33	5	33	70	384	.296	.540	.589	.423	39%	108
Balt	1966	576	182	34	2	49	87	454	.316	.637	.685	.422	62%	174
Balt	1967	479	149	23	7	30	71	347	.311	.576	.631	.406	55%	124
Balt	1968	421	113	27	1	15	73	260	.268	.444	.526	.394	34%	65
Balt	1969	539	166	19	5	32	88	379	.308	.540	.604	.430	41%	109
Balt	1970	471	144	24	1	25	69	314	.306	.520	.581	.437	33%	78
Balt	1971	455	128	16	2	28	72	304	.281	.510	.577	.422	37%	82
LA	1972	342	86	6	1	19	55	206	.251	.442	.519	.420	24%	39
Cali	1973	534	142	29	0	30	82	343	.266	.489	.557	.437	27%	74
Cali/Clev	1974	477	117	27	3	22	85	301	.245	.453	.536	.424	26%	62
Clev	1975	118	28	5	0	9	29	89	.237	.508	.605	.437	39%	25
Clev	1976	67	15	0	0	3	11	35	.224	.358	.449	.416	8%	3
		10006	2943	528	72	586	1420	6793	.294	.537	.595	.433	37%	1850

"They say you can't hit if you're on your back. But I didn't hit on my back. I got up."

—FRANK ROBINSON

Like Dick Allen, Frank Robinson was an independent, strong-willed black man before the country of baseball was ready for that. It's no coincidence that they were both given away at the peaks of their careers by organizations that felt threatened by them.

After the 1965 season, the Cincinnati Reds traded Frank Robinson to the Baltimore Orioles for a pitcher named Milt Pappas. Few players have made their original teams regret a trade as much and as quickly. Robinson responded by not only becoming the American League's best hitter in 1966, but producing one of the 50 greatest seasons of all time. Milt Pappas went 12–11 with an ERA of 4.29. The Reds dropped 10 games in the standings and finished seventh. The Orioles gained 17 games and swept the Dodgers in the World Series, with Robinson homering twice off Don Drysdale, his second providing the only run in a 1–0 Game 4 victory.

Frank Robinson punished the Reds further with his two home runs against them in the 1970 World Series. Baltimore took care of Cincinnati in five games, and Robinson's second shot came in the first inning of the decisive final game—quickly turning an early 3–0 Cincinnati lead into an uneasy one-run edge that didn't last past the second.

For so many years, the Reds saw Frank Robinson be sent sprawling by fastballs at his head only to dust himself off, take his customary stance on top of the plate, and drive the next offering back through the box or over the Crosley Field wall. They should have known he would make them regret shipping him out of town.

16. Hank Greenberg, 1B/RH, 1930, 1933–41, 1945–47. Detroit Tigers, Pittsburgh Pirates. Hall of Fame: 1956.

Top 50 seasons: None

		AB	H	2B	3B	HR	BB	B	BA	SA	A	LGE	+/−	Additional
Detr	1930	1	0	0	0	0	0	0	.000	.000	.000	.470	-100%	-0
Detr	1933	449	135	33	3	12	46	256	.301	.468	.517	.447	16%	35
Detr	1934	593	201	63	7	26	63	419	.339	.600	.639	.457	40%	119
Detr	1935	619	203	46	16	36	87	476	.328	.628	.674	.459	47%	152
Detr	1936	46	16	6	2	1	9	38	.348	.630	.691	.479	44%	12
Detr	1937	594	200	49	14	40	102	499	.337	.668	.717	.473	52%	170
Detr	1938	556	175	23	4	58	119	499	.315	.683	.739	.476	55%	178
Detr	1939	500	156	42	7	33	91	402	.312	.622	.680	.466	46%	126
Detr	1940	573	195	50	8	41	93	477	.340	.670	.716	.463	55%	169
Detr	1941	67	18	5	1	2	16	47	.269	.463	.566	.450	26%	10
Detr	1945	270	84	20	2	13	42	189	.311	.544	.606	.405	49%	63
Detr	1946	523	145	29	5	44	80	396	.277	.604	.657	.424	55%	140
Pitt	1947	402	100	13	2	25	104	296	.249	.478	.585	.449	30%	69
		5193	1628	379	71	331	852	3994	.313	.605	.661	.455	45%	1241

"No one can tell you how to hit home runs. You either have the natural strength and reflexes, or you don't."

—HANK GREENBERG

A tall, powerful first baseman for the Detroit Tigers, Hank Greenberg makes the list despite playing only nine full seasons—because he was head-shoulders-and-chest above the average player during those seasons. He is one of only five players to produce a career slugging average in excess of .600. Greenberg was the AL's most productive hitter in 1935, 1937, and 1940, though his best season (1938) saw him place second to Jimmie Foxx's 50 home runs and .349 batting average. He twice

(1937 and 1938) missed by only one base joining the elite 500-base club (current membership: eight).

In 1935, Greenberg led the Tigers to the World Series, but an injury kept him out of most of the series as Detroit brought home the first championship in its history. He returned from the war halfway through the 1945 season and led them back to the series to face the Cubs again. This time he stayed injury free, the Tigers won in seven, and he blasted a game-winning three-run homer in the fifth inning of Game 2 and a game-tying home run in the eighth inning of Game 6.

15. Mike Schmidt, 3B/RH, 1972–89. Philadelphia Phillies. Hall of Fame: 1995.

Top 50 Seasons: None.

		AB	H	2B	3B	HR	BB	B	BA	SA	A	LGE	+/−	Additional
Phil	1972	34	7	0	0	1	5	15	.206	.294	.385	.420	-8%	-1
Phil	1973	367	72	11	0	18	62	199	.196	.373	.464	.432	7%	14
Phil	1974	568	160	28	7	36	106	416	.282	.546	.617	.426	45%	129
Phil	1975	562	140	34	3	38	101	395	.249	.523	.596	.427	39%	112
Phil	1976	584	153	31	4	38	100	406	.262	.524	.594	.417	43%	121
Phil	1977	544	149	27	11	38	104	416	.274	.574	.642	.450	43%	124
Phil	1978	513	129	27	2	21	91	314	.251	.435	.520	.427	22%	56
Phil	1979	541	137	25	4	45	120	425	.253	.564	.643	.438	47%	136
Phil	1980	548	157	25	8	48	89	431	.286	.624	.677	.426	59%	160
Phil	1981	354	112	19	2	31	73	301	.316	.644	.705	.419	68%	122
Phil	1982	514	144	26	3	35	107	388	.280	.547	.625	.425	47%	124
Phil	1983	534	136	16	4	40	128	408	.255	.524	.616	.432	43%	122
Phil	1984	528	146	23	3	36	92	375	.277	.536	.605	.423	43%	113
Phil	1985	549	152	31	5	33	87	379	.277	.532	.596	.429	39%	106
Phil	1986	552	160	29	1	37	89	391	.290	.547	.610	.436	40%	111
Phil	1987	522	153	28	0	35	83	369	.293	.548	.610	.458	33%	92
Phil	1988	390	97	21	2	12	49	207	.249	.405	.472	.415	14%	25
Phil	1989	148	30	7	0	6	21		.203	.372	.450	.420	7%	5
		8204	2204	401	59	542	1486	5835	.269	.530	.602	.430	40%	1666

Michael Jack Schmidt led the National League in bases a record seven times. Unfortunately, the greatest third baseman in baseball history spent too much of his career in front of fans who focused too much on his strikeouts and his batting average. He also had to share too much of the credit for bringing Philadelphia its only championship with the vastly overrated Pete Rose, and saw his greatest season cut short by the players strike of 1981. Had the '81 season not been interrupted, Schmidt had a good chance at 50 home runs and an even better one at joining the short list of the 50 greatest seasons a hitter has ever had.

You can do that kind of damage when you have the bat speed that allows you to look for offspeed pitches and still hit the hard stuff.

14. Johnny Mize, 1B/LH, 1936–42, 1946–53. St. Louis Cardinals, New York Giants, New York Yankees. Hall of Fame: 1981.

Top 50 seasons: 1940 (46th)

		AB	H	2B	3B	HR	BB	B	BA	SA	A	LGE	+/−	Additional
StLN	1936	414	136	30	8	19	50	289	.329	.577	.623	.432	44%	88
StLN	1937	560	204	40	7	25	56	389	.364	.595	.631	.431	47%	124
StLN	1938	531	179	34	16	27	74	400	.337	.614	.661	.426	55%	142
StLN	1939	564	197	44	14	28	92	445	.349	.626	.678	.437	55%	158
StLN	1940	579	182	31	13	43	82	450	.314	.636	.681	.426	60%	168
StLN	1941	473	150	39	8	16	70	323	.317	.535	.595	.418	42%	96
NYN	1942	541	165	25	7	26	60	342	.305	.521	.569	.401	42%	101
NYN	1946	377	127	18	3	22	62	279	.337	.576	.636	.417	52%	96
NYN	1947	586	177	26	2	51	74	434	.302	.614	.658	.449	46%	138
NYN	1948	560	162	26	4	40	94	410	.289	.564	.627	.441	42%	121
NYN/NYA	1949	411	108	16	0	19	54	235	.263	.440	.505	.446	13%	28
NYA	1950	274	76	12	0	25	29	192	.277	.595	.634	.470	35%	50
NYA	1951	332	86	14	1	10	36	168	.259	.398	.457	.445	3%	4
NYA	1952	137	36	9	0	4	11	68	.263	.416	.459	.428	7%	5
NYA	1953	104	26	3	0	4	12	53	.250	.394	.457	.442	3%	2
		6443	2011	367	83	359	856	4477	.312	.562	.613	.432	42%	1321

Despite 2,000 hits, a .312 lifetime batting average, four home run titles, three RBI crowns, and a batting championship, the original "Big Cat" had to wait 28 years for Cooperstown to call. World War II cost him 2,500 hits, 450 home runs, and an even higher position on this list. One of the most underrated hitters in the game's history, Mize was the NL's most productive hitter in both 1939 and 1940. His 1940 season, during which he outproduced the average National Leaguer by 60 percent, was very quietly one of the greatest in the game's history.

13. Ty Cobb, CF/LH, 1905–28. Detroit Tigers, Philadelphia Athletics. Hall of Fame: 1936.

Top 50 seasons: None

		AB	H	2B	3B	HR	BB	B	BA	SA	A	LGE	+/−	Additional
Detr	1905	150	36	6	0	1	10	55	.240	.300	.344	.361	−5%	−3
Detr	1906	350	112	13	7	1	19	161	.320	.406	.436	.362	20%	27
Detr	1907	605	212	29	15	5	24	310	.350	.473	.493	.354	39%	88

		AB	H	2B	3B	HR	BB	B	BA	SA	A	LGE	+/−	Additional
Detr	1908	581	188	36	20	4	34	310	.324	.475	.504	.349	44%	95
Detr	1909	573	216	33	10	9	48	344	.377	.517	.554	.356	56%	123
Detr	1910	509	196	36	13	8	64	346	.385	.554	.604	.366	65%	136
Detr	1911	591	248	47	24	8	44	411	.420	.621	.647	.409	58%	151
Detr	1912	553	227	30	23	7	43	367	.410	.586	.616	.403	53%	127
Detr	1913	428	167	18	16	4	58	287	.390	.535	.591	.393	50%	96
Detr	1914	345	127	22	11	2	57	234	.368	.513	.582	.382	52%	80
Detr	1915	563	208	31	13	3	118	392	.369	.487	.576	.390	48%	126
Detr	1916	542	201	31	10	5	78	345	.371	.493	.556	.385	44%	106
Detr	1917	588	225	44	23	7	61	397	.383	.571	.612	.379	61%	151
Detr	1918	421	161	19	14	3	41	258	.382	.515	.558	.382	46%	81
Detr	1919	497	191	36	13	1	38	294	.384	.515	.550	.412	33%	74
Detr	1920	428	143	28	8	2	58	251	.334	.451	.516	.438	18%	38
Detr	1921	507	197	37	16	12	56	358	.389	.596	.636	.458	39%	100
Detr	1922	526	211	42	16	4	55	352	.401	.565	.606	.448	35%	92
Detr	1923	556	189	40	7	6	66	327	.340	.469	.526	.442	19%	52
Detr	1924	625	211	38	10	4	85	366	.338	.450	.515	.451	14%	46
Detr	1925	415	157	31	12	12	65	313	.378	.598	.652	.462	41%	91
Detr	1926	233	79	18	5	4	26	145	.339	.511	.560	.448	25%	29
PhiA	1927	490	175	32	7	5	67	303	.357	.482	.544	.451	21%	52
PhiA	1928	353	114	27	4	1	34	186	.323	.431	.481	.447	7%	13
		11429	4191	724	297	118	1249	7112	.367	.513	.561	.405	39%	1973

> *"I had to fight all my life to survive. They were all against me . . . but I beat the bastards and left them in the ditch."*
>
> —TY COBB

A miserable human being but a brilliant ballplayer, "the Georgia Peach" is the greatest hitter of the deadball era. There truly is no modern comparison to Ty Cobb as a ballplayer—he would have to be assembled with Willie Mays's baserunning, Rod Carew's bat-handling, Jackie Robinson's will to win, and then coated with a viciousness and paranoia that makes Albert Belle look like Dale Murphy. His hits record was eclipsed, but it's doubtful that even Albert will ever be suspended for anything more disgraceful than climbing into the stands to stomp a disabled fan for heckling him.

Though Cobb's lifetime batting average is the best of all time at .367 and will never be topped, his slugging average of .513 is "only" 38th on the list behind players such as Jeff Heath, Bob Johnson, Hal Trosky, Ken Williams, and Dick Allen, to name just five. Cobb's greatness emerges when he is judged against the average player of his day. During a low-scoring era, he was his league's most productive hitter six times, in 1907, 1908, 1909, 1911, 1915, and 1917. In 1911, when he hit .420, he became the first player to ever top 400 bases in a season—a mark that stood until the deadball era ended in 1920.

He was sadistic and racist, he was despised by opponents and teammates alike, and he died angry and alone. But the man could hit.

12. Mark McGwire, 1B/RH, 1986–. Oakland Athletics, St. Louis Cardinals.

Top 50 seasons: 1998 (7th), 1999 (50th)

		AB	H	2B	3B	HR	BB	B	BA	SA	A	LGE	+/−	Additional
Oak	1986	53	10	1	0	3	4	24	.189	.377	.421	.461	-9%	-2
Oak	1987	557	161	28	4	49	71	415	.289	.618	.661	.478	38%	115
Oak	1988	550	143	22	1	32	76	339	.260	.478	.542	.443	22%	62
Oak	1989	490	113	17	0	33	83	312	.231	.467	.545	.437	25%	61
Oak	1990	523	123	16	0	39	110	366	.235	.489	.578	.443	30%	85
Oak	1991	483	97	22	0	22	93	278	.201	.383	.483	.450	7%	19
Oak	1992	467	125	22	0	42	90	363	.268	.585	.652	.441	48%	117
Oak	1993	84	28	6	0	9	21	82	.333	.726	.781	.463	69%	33
Oak	1994	135	34	3	0	9	37	101	.252	.474	.587	.489	20%	17
Oak	1995	317	87	13	0	39	88	305	.274	.685	.753	.483	56%	109
Oak	1996	423	132	21	0	52	116	425	.312	.730	.788	.499	58%	156
Oak/SL	1997	540	148	27	0	58	101	450	.274	.646	.702	.472	49%	147
SL	1998	509	152	21	0	70	162	545	.299	.752	.812	.463	76%	235
SL	1999	521	145	21	1	65	133	496	.278	.697	.758	.485	57%	179
		5652	1498	240	6	522	1185	4501	.265	.587	.658	.463	42%	1334

With forearms as big as a mere mortal's thigh, it comes as no surprise when Mark McGwire reaches the Uecker seats. The only cheap home run of his 70 in 1998 was, ironically enough, the low line drive off the Cubs' Steve Trachsel that just cleared the wall for number 62.

Once the big redhead was able to stay healthy and make more consistent contact at the plate, he strung together four of the game's greatest power seasons in 1996, 1997, 1998, and 1999. These came on the heels of three injury- and strike-shortened seasons in which he came to bat only 536 times. But in that full season's worth of at-bats, McGwire managed 57 home runs. This did not go unnoticed by the Maris Watchers.

McGwire's record-shattering 1998 season saw him produce the sixth-highest number of bases in a single year. His base average wasn't bad either—.812 (fifth-highest ever). In a season where his league's average was .463, this meant that Big Mac was 76 percent better than the average player. Even though 1998 was a hitter's season, McGwire was good enough to outproduce his league by a higher level than any other National Leaguer in history.

ONE GREAT SEASON

Forty-five of the 50 greatest seasons were produced by men on the top 25 list. The five hitters whose best seasons put them in the class of these immortals include

- two career years from stout, self-destructive individuals,
- a truly flukish performance in 1961 by someone whose name is not Roger Maris,
- some big numbers from a Colorado Rockie who actually managed to do some hitting on the road, and
- a season in which a Hall of Famer almost singlehandedly carried his team to an improbable world championship.

Here they are, along with their ranking in the top 50 seasons of all time.

48. Hack Wilson, 1930

"Built along the lines of a beer keg and not unfamiliar with its contents" was how one writer described Hack Wilson. The 5'6", 190-pound center fielder with the size 5½ shoes had been plucked from the Giants' system in the annual minor league draft held after the 1925 season. John McGraw had sent Wilson to the minors to learn the strike zone. From 1926 through 1930, Wilson showed McGraw just how much he'd learned. He was the Babe Ruth of the National League during this stretch, leading in home runs four times in five years.

Wilson peaked in 1930. In a league that hit .303, Hack Wilson was the best. Even relative to such high levels of offensive production—and without even taking into account his major league record *190* RBI—Wilson earns a spot on this list thanks to 56 home runs, 105 walks, a .356 batting average, and a .723 slugging average. He piled up 189 additional bases and outproduced the very powerful league average by 56 percent.

Unfortunately for Wilson, the Cubs fell a few games short of the pennant, which caused manager Joe McCarthy to be fired and the neurotic Rogers Hornsby to be named player-manager. Hornsby was notoriously intolerant, forbidding his players from even having soda pop. Wilson probably had little trouble staying off the pop—it was the harder stuff that did him in. Hornsby tried to tame Wilson's wild ways off the field, while humiliating him on the field with frequent "take" signs. Add this to the fact that the National League loosened up the 1930 rabbitball, which caused the league average to fall to .277, and one can begin to understand how Wilson could tumble all the way to 13 home runs in 1931.

Wilson was traded to the Dodgers after the 1931 season, had a brief resurgence in 1932 in cozy Ebbets Field, then struggled through two more alcohol-soaked seasons before lurching to the end of the line. He quietly died a pauper in Babe Ruth's hometown of Baltimore in 1948, only a few months after the Babe's massive public funeral at Yankee Stadium.

43. Norm Cash, 1961

Detroit Tigers first baseman Norm Cash hit 20 fewer home runs than Roger Maris in 1961, but he accumulated more bases in fewer at-bats. As out of character as Maris's 1961 season was, what the 26-year-old Texan did proved to be even more so. Cash led the league at .361 with a league-leading 193 hits and 124 bases on balls. He fell off to

.243 in 1962, and never again hit higher than .283, retiring in 1974 with a career average of .271. He did continue to hit for power—at least 20 home runs in 10 of the next 11 seasons—and draw walks, producing some of the AL's best offense during a pitcher's era of the 1960s.

When all is crunched and done, Norm Cash's relative offensive production is actually more impressive than that of Reggie Jackson, Al Kaline, Carl Yastrzemski, Eddie Murray, and Roberto Clemente, to name just five. Yet he has received a grand total of six votes for the Hall of Fame in all of his years of eligibility and will never receive serious consideration by the Veterans Committee.

40. Kevin Mitchell, 1989

By 1987, Kevin Mitchell was already on his third team in less than one year. The Mets, in an effort to rid their clubhouse of any troublesome individuals (and, as it turned out, any chemistry), had traded him to the Padres for Kevin McReynolds. Mitchell didn't last long in his hometown of San Diego, where he had once been a gang member. They sent him to San Francisco for the immortal Chris Brown. After a decent, 19-homer season in 1988, the Giants moved Mitchell to left field, where he hit a thoroughly unexpected 47 home runs, knocking in 125 runs, batting .291, and drawing 87 walks. He even made a highlight reel with his glove—without it, actually, as he overran a fly ball down the left-field line and reached back to catch it barehanded.

Mitchell went on to hit 35 home runs in a less potent 1990, then from 1991 through 1998 changed teams six times (and countries once, as he had a brief, disastrous stay in Japan, where they don't have as much tolerance for overweight, injured, check-cashing players) without ever even topping 400 at-bats again. Based on what Kevin Mitchell showed he was capable of in 1989, some consider his subsequent injury-plagued efforts to be colossal underachievement. More likely, Kevin Mitchell's 1989 season was the greatest year an average baseball player has ever had.

35. Larry Walker, 1997

The Colorado Rockies should have an asterisk for a mascot. Some ballparks add home runs while stealing doubles, and others add singles while limiting home runs, but Coors Field increases all hits by a game-distorting amount. As a result, mediocre players like Dante Bichette, who couldn't hold down a full-time job in Anaheim or Milwaukee, start putting up big numbers with Colorado and calling up Ted Williams to talk hitting. With castoffs like Bichette, Vinny Castilla, Andres Galarraga, and even Charlie Hayes putting up big numbers in Denver, fans wondered what would happen if an established star ever signed to play for the Rockies.

Larry Walker did just that after the 1994 season, but the anticipated avalanche of statistics didn't follow. He hit a fairly average .306 in 1995, then tumbled to .276 in an injury-plagued 1996 season. Like the rest of his Coors-inflated teammates, Walker's statistics were a blend of average road numbers and pinball-machine home numbers. Except in Walker's case, the road numbers were wretched, suggesting that seeing hanging curveballs for a week at a time was making it very difficult for him to adjust to big-league pitching when he saw it on the road.

Well, Walker figured it out in 1997, answering his critics loudly with an injury-free MVP season that not even the most ardent purist could use Coors Field to explain away.

Walker did just as much damage at home as he did on the road, batting .366 with 49 home runs and 130 RBI, connecting for 208 hits while walking 78 times.

Despite Larry Walker's offensive explosion, the Rockies could do no better than 83 wins and third place in a weak, four-team NL West field. Hack Wilson kept his Cubs in contention until the final week in 1930. Norm Cash led the Tigers to an ultimately futile 101-win campaign in 1961. Kevin Mitchell helped the Giants reach the World Series for the first time in 27 years.

The final player on the list carried his team from ninth place to the seventh game of the World Series.

30. Carl Yastrzemski, 1967

> "... I've never watched a player have one complete year like Yastrzemski had. I don't expect to see it again, either. It was just phenomenal in all phases—running, throwing, fielding, hitting, hitting with power. He was the ultimate team leader...."
>
> —RED SOX MANAGER DICK WILLIAMS
> ON CARL YASTRZEMSKI'S 1967 SEASON

Like Ted Williams in 1946, Carl Yastrzemski's offensive heroics carried the Red Sox to within one game of their first championship since 1918. (Unlike Williams, Yastrzemski won a few games with his glove in 1967, and had a productive World Series.) In a season dominated by pitching, Yastrzemski hit 44 home runs, knocked in 121, and batted .326, leading the league in all three categories, as well as runs and hits, while also walking 91 times. He outproduced his league by 66 percent despite batting in a lineup that offered little in the way of protection after Tony Conigliaro's face was caved in at midseason by a Jack Hamilton fastball. Yastrzemski saved his best baseball for the most pressure-packed final days of a frenetic four-team race that went down to the final game of the season (see Chapter 4). Appropriately, Yaz credited Ted Williams with suggesting a slight change in his batting stance that helped him hit 28 more home runs, knock in 41 more runs, and hit 48 points higher than he had in 1966.

Yastrzemski won the batting title the following season with a .301 mark, the lowest in history. He also drew 119 walks, the first of six 100-plus walk campaigns in the next seven seasons. He hit 40 home runs in both 1969 and 1970, then never again topped 30. After hitting .329 in 1970, he only topped .300 again once—.301 in 1974. His dropoff after the age of 31 was attributed by some to his very unorthodox batting stance: holding his bat straight up in the air with his hands higher than his head required very quick wrists. As he got older and his hands got slower, he tinkered with his stance to compensate with mixed results, and never again dominated the Red Sox lineup.

Carl Yastrzemski, like Williams, played into his 40s—44 to be exact—piling up 3,419 hits and 452 home runs in the process. His 3,308 games played are second only to Pete Rose. When looking at his Hall of Fame plaque, the lasting memory of veteran Red Sox fans is not the 39-year-old Yastrzemski of the 1978 one-game playoff, trying to get around on a Goose Gossage fastball, but the 28-year-old Yastrzemski in the 1967 World Series, valiantly trying to slay the dragon that is the Curse of the Bambino.

11. Mel Ott, RF/LH, 1926–47. New York Giants. Hall of Fame: 1951.

Top 50 Seasons: None.

		AB	H	2B	3B	HR	BB	B	BA	SA	A	LGE	+/−	Additional
NYN	1926	60	23	2	0	0	1	26	.383	.417	.426	.433	-2%	-0
NYN	1927	163	46	7	3	1	13	75	.282	.380	.426	.432	-1%	-1
NYN	1928	435	140	26	4	18	52	280	.322	.524	.575	.447	29%	62
NYN	1929	545	179	37	2	42	113	459	.328	.635	.698	.474	47%	147
NYN	1930	521	182	34	5	25	103	404	.349	.578	.647	.491	32%	98
NYN	1931	497	145	23	8	29	80	351	.292	.545	.608	.433	40%	101
NYN	1932	566	180	30	8	38	100	440	.318	.601	.661	.436	51%	149
NYN	1933	580	164	36	1	23	75	346	.283	.467	.528	.404	31%	82
NYN	1934	582	190	29	10	35	85	429	.326	.591	.643	.437	47%	138
NYN	1935	593	191	33	6	31	82	411	.322	.555	.609	.434	40%	118
NYN	1936	534	175	28	6	33	111	425	.328	.588	.659	.432	52%	146
NYN	1937	545	160	28	2	31	102	387	.294	.523	.598	.431	39%	108
NYN	1938	527	164	23	6	36	118	425	.311	.583	.659	.426	55%	150
NYN	1939	396	122	23	2	27	100	330	.308	.581	.665	.437	52%	113
NYN	1940	536	155	27	3	19	100	345	.289	.457	.542	.426	27%	74
NYN	1941	525	150	29	0	27	100	360	.286	.495	.576	.418	38%	99
NYN	1942	549	162	21	0	30	109	382	.295	.497	.581	.401	45%	118
NYN	1943	380	89	12	2	18	95	254	.234	.418	.535	.404	32%	62
NYN	1944	399	115	16	4	26	90	307	.288	.544	.628	.417	51%	103
NYN	1945	451	139	23	0	21	71	296	.308	.499	.567	.420	35%	77
NYN	1946	68	5	1	0	1	8	17	.074	.132	.224	.417	-46%	-15
NYN	1947	4	0	0	0	0	0	0	.000	.000	.000	.449	-100%	-2
		9456	2876	488	72	511	1708	6749	.304	.533	.605	.432	40%	1927

Mel Ott and the following four National League hitters are the most tightly bunched in the top 25, and to rank one above the other is to some extent misleading. The third member of the 500-homer club, Ott was a consistent hitter who frequently led his league in bases—1934, 1935, 1936, 1938, and 1942—but never laid waste to it the way some of his contemporaries did. He only topped 40 home runs and .330 in a season once, yet ended his career at 511 and .304. A lefty, he strode toward the pitch with a high kick of his front leg echoed years later by Darryl Strawberry and Japanese home run king Sadaharu Oh.

Hitting 324 of his 511 home runs in the Polo Grounds, with its short porch down the line in right, Ott benefited more from his ballpark than any player in the top 25.

10. Hank Aaron, RF/RH, 1954–76. Milwaukee-Atlanta Braves. Hall of Fame: 1982.

Top 50 seasons: 1971 (33rd)

		AB	H	2B	3B	HR	BB	B	BA	SA	A	LGE	+/−	Additional
MilN	1954	468	131	27	6	13	28	237	.280	.447	.478	.463	3%	7
MilN	1955	602	189	37	9	27	49	374	.314	.540	.575	.462	24%	73
MilN	1956	609	200	34	14	26	37	377	.328	.558	.584	.453	29%	84
MilN	1957	615	198	27	6	44	57	426	.322	.600	.634	.450	41%	124
MilN	1958	601	196	34	4	30	59	387	.326	.546	.586	.457	28%	85
MilN	1959	629	223	46	7	39	51	451	.355	.636	.663	.451	47%	144
MilN	1960	590	172	20	11	40	60	394	.292	.566	.606	.440	38%	108
MilN	1961	603	197	39	10	34	56	414	.327	.594	.628	.457	38%	113
MilN	1962	592	191	28	6	45	66	432	.323	.618	.657	.446	47%	139
MilN	1963	631	201	29	4	44	78	448	.319	.586	.632	.413	53%	155
MilN	1964	570	187	30	2	24	62	355	.328	.514	.562	.420	34%	90
MilN	1965	570	181	40	1	32	60	379	.318	.560	.602	.423	42%	112
Atla	1966	603	168	23	1	44	76	401	.279	.539	.591	.429	38%	109
Atla	1967	600	184	37	3	39	63	407	.307	.573	.614	.414	48%	133
Atla	1968	606	174	33	4	29	64	366	.287	.498	.546	.389	41%	106
Atla	1969	547	164	30	3	44	87	419	.300	.607	.661	.425	56%	150
Atla	1970	516	154	26	1	38	74	370	.298	.574	.627	.449	40%	105
Atla	1971	495	162	22	3	47	71	402	.327	.669	.710	.419	69%	165
Atla	1972	449	119	10	0	34	92	323	.265	.514	.597	.420	42%	96
Atla	1973	392	118	12	1	40	68	320	.301	.643	.696	.432	61%	122
Atla	1974	340	91	16	0	20	39	206	.268	.491	.544	.426	28%	44
MilA	1975	465	109	16	2	12	70	235	.234	.355	.439	.437	1%	1
MilA	1976	271	62	8	0	10	35	135	.229	.369	.441	.416	6%	8
		12364	3771	624	98	755	1402	8258	.305	.555	.600	.435	38%	2273

"The only man I idolize more than myself is Henry Aaron."

—MUHAMMAD ALI

Hank Aaron was a consistently excellent performer for many years, eclipsing Babe Ruth's home run record without ever topping 50 home runs in a season. In fact, no other retired player in the top 25 has as great a disparity between his absolute performance (third all-time with 2,273 additional bases) and his relative performance (38 percent better than the average player of his day, good for "only" 23rd on the all-time list).

Aaron led the league in bases four times—1959, 1963, 1966, and 1967—though his finest season was in 1971, when he hit a career-high 47 home runs at the age of 37, outproducing a league of youngsters by 69 percent. By the time he was through swinging the bat, Aaron had piled up more bases than anyone in history, passing Babe Ruth late in the 1974 season after hitting home run number 715 early in the season.

When you consider that Ruth's home run record fell to a man who debuted just seven years after the color barrier was broken, it makes you wonder just how much damage Josh Gibson and his contemporaries might have done had they gotten their chance (see Chapter 13).

9. Barry Bonds, LF/LH, 1986–. Pittsburgh Pirates, San Francisco Giants.

Top 50 seasons: 1992 (32nd), 1993 (28th)

		AB	H	2B	3B	HR	BB	B	BA	SA	A	LGE	+/–	Additional
Pitt	1986	413	92	26	3	16	65	237	.223	.416	.496	.436	14%	28
Pitt	1987	551	144	34	9	25	54	325	.261	.492	.537	.458	17%	48
Pitt	1988	538	152	30	5	24	72	336	.283	.491	.551	.415	33%	83
Pitt	1989	580	144	34	6	19	93	340	.248	.426	.505	.420	20%	57
Pitt	1990	519	156	32	3	33	93	386	.301	.565	.631	.436	45%	119
Pitt	1991	510	149	28	5	25	107	369	.292	.514	.598	.428	40%	105
Pitt	1992	473	147	36	5	34	127	422	.311	.624	.703	.421	67%	170
SF	1993	539	181	38	4	46	126	491	.336	.677	.738	.449	64%	192
SF	1994	391	122	18	1	37	74	327	.312	.647	.703	.464	51%	111
SF	1995	506	149	30	7	33	120	412	.294	.577	.658	.459	43%	125
SF	1996	517	159	27	3	42	151	469	.308	.615	.702	.460	53%	162
SF	1997	532	155	26	5	40	145	456	.291	.585	.674	.464	45%	142
SF	1998	552	167	44	7	37	130	466	.303	.609	.683	.463	48%	150
SF	1999	355	93	20	2	34	73	292	.262	.617	.682	.485	41%	85
		6976	2010	423	65	445	1430	5328	.288	.559	.634	.446	42%	1577

No one can dispute Barry Bonds's numbers. By the time he's through, he might be as high as fifth on this list and the greatest hitter in National League history. He's already ninth, though he doesn't have a .300 lifetime average and only surpassed the 2,000-hit mark in 1999. Bonds has led the league in bases four times, including two of the game's greatest seasons in 1992 and 1993. A rare injury in 1999 kept him from becoming only the fourth player to string together 10 consecutive seasons of 100 additional bases.

However, Bonds also has, by far, the worst postseason performance of any of these great hitters (see Chapter 5 for the October numbers of all 25 of these hitters). Compare "Mr. May's" average regular-season performance to his postseason performance in a comparable number of at-bats (and those numbers don't include yet another shutout in the one-game playoff with the Cubs in 1998, which was technically a regular-season game). Bonds's big-game shortcomings defy the imagination.

Barry Bonds, much like home run king Hank Aaron, uses a short, quick stroke that provides both power and consistency.

	AB	H	2B	3B	HR	BB	B	BA	SA	A
Avg season	80	23	5	1	5	16	61	.290	.556	.631
Postseason	80	16	4	0	1	14	37	.200	.288	.394

His dour personality and crunch-time failings won't keep him out of the Hall of Fame, but they will keep many from appreciating how extraordinary a hitter he's been.

8. Stan Musial, LF/LH, 1941–44, 1946–63. St. Louis Cardinals. Hall of Fame: 1969.

Top 50 seasons: 1948 (21st)

		AB	H	2B	3B	HR	BB	B	BA	SA	A	LGE	+/−	Additional
StLN	1941	47	20	4	0	1	2	29	.426	.574	.592	.418	42%	9
StLN	1942	467	147	32	10	10	62	291	.315	.490	.550	.401	37%	79
StLN	1943	617	220	48	20	13	72	419	.357	.562	.608	.404	51%	141
StLN	1944	568	197	51	14	12	90	402	.347	.549	.611	.417	46%	128

		AB	H	2B	3B	HR	BB	B	BA	SA	A	LGE	+/−	Additional
StLN	1946	624	228	50	20	16	73	439	.365	.587	.630	.417	51%	148
StLN	1947	587	183	30	13	19	80	376	.312	.504	.564	.449	26%	76
StLN	1948	611	230	46	18	39	79	508	.376	.702	.736	.441	67%	204
StLN	1949	612	207	41	13	36	107	489	.338	.624	.680	.446	52%	168
StLN	1950	555	192	41	7	28	87	418	.346	.596	.651	.459	42%	123
StLN	1951	578	205	30	12	32	98	453	.355	.614	.670	.447	50%	151
StLN	1952	578	194	42	6	21	96	407	.336	.538	.604	.430	40%	117
StLN	1953	593	200	53	9	30	105	466	.337	.609	.668	.465	44%	141
StLN	1954	591	195	41	9	35	103	462	.330	.607	.666	.463	44%	140
StLN	1955	562	179	30	5	33	80	398	.319	.566	.620	.462	34%	102
StLN	1956	594	184	33	6	27	75	385	.310	.522	.575	.453	27%	82
StLN	1957	502	176	38	3	29	66	373	.351	.612	.657	.450	46%	118
StLN	1958	472	159	35	2	17	72	321	.337	.528	.590	.457	29%	72
StLN	1959	341	87	13	2	14	60	206	.255	.428	.514	.451	14%	25
StLN	1960	331	91	17	1	17	41	202	.275	.486	.543	.440	23%	38
StLN	1961	372	107	22	4	15	52	234	.288	.489	.552	.457	21%	40
StLN	1962	433	143	18	1	19	64	284	.330	.508	.571	.446	28%	63
StLN	1963	337	86	10	2	12	35	171	.255	.404	.460	.413	11%	17
		10972	3630	725	177	475	1599	7733	.331	.559	.615	.441	39%	2182

> *"The secret of hitting is physical relaxation, mental concentration, and don't hit the fly ball to center."*
>
> —STAN MUSIAL

When Stan Musial took his place in the left-hander's batter's box, his back was toward the pitcher and his eyes were peering out from behind his shoulder. Out of this impossible stance, Musial hit for average and power for a longer stretch than nearly anyone who's ever played the game. From 1943 to 1958, he slugged at least .500 every season—a longevity exceeded by only Babe Ruth. Just for perspective, the man who broke Musial's NL record for most hits—Pete Rose—slugged .500 exactly once. Musial's combination of 3,000 hits, .330 batting average, and 400 home runs is unmatched; none of the members of the 3,000/.330 club have even produced 120 home runs.

A seven-time league leader in bases (1943, 1946, 1948–49, 1952–54), Musial regularly topped 400 bases and a .600 base average, outproducing his league by at least 40 percent and piling up 100 additional bases more than 10 times. His finest season was 1948, when he won the batting title by 43 points and missed the Triple Crown by one home run. In the process, he topped 500 bases and outproduced his league by two-thirds—the last National Leaguer to join both exclusive clubs until Mark McGwire 50 years later.

Amazingly, Musial did all this without any real protection in the lineup for most of his career. (See the "No Protection" sidebar in Chapter 9.)

PITCHING TO STAN THE MAN

"Once Musial timed your fastball, your infielders were in jeopardy."

—HALL OF FAMER WARREN SPAHN

"Walk him and then try to pick him off first base."

—CATCHER JOE GARAGIOLA ON HOW TO PITCH TO STAN MUSIAL

"I've had pretty good success with Stan—by throwing him my best pitch and backing up third."

—DODGERS ACE CARL ERSKINE

"You wait for a strike. Then you knock the crap out of it."

—STAN MUSIAL

7. Willie Mays, CF/RH, 1951–73. New York–San Francisco Giants, New York Mets. Hall of Fame: 1979.

Top 50 Seasons: 1965 (41st)

		AB	H	2B	3B	HR	BB	B	BA	SA	A	LGE	+/−	Additional
NYN	1951	464	127	22	5	20	56	275	.274	.472	.529	.447	18%	43
NYN	1952	127	30	2	4	4	16	68	.236	.409	.476	.430	10%	6
NYN	1954	565	195	33	13	41	66	443	.345	.667	.702	.463	52%	151
NYN	1955	580	185	18	13	51	79	461	.319	.659	.700	.462	52%	157
NYN	1956	578	171	27	8	36	68	390	.296	.557	.604	.453	33%	97
NYN	1957	585	195	26	20	35	76	442	.333	.626	.669	.450	49%	145
SF	1958	600	208	33	11	29	78	428	.347	.583	.631	.457	38%	118
SF	1959	575	180	43	5	34	65	400	.313	.583	.625	.451	38%	111
SF	1960	595	190	29	12	29	61	391	.319	.555	.596	.440	35%	102
SF	1961	572	176	32	3	40	81	415	.308	.584	.636	.457	39%	117
SF	1962	621	189	36	5	49	78	460	.304	.615	.658	.446	48%	148
SF	1963	596	187	32	7	38	66	413	.314	.582	.624	.413	51%	140
SF	1964	578	171	21	9	47	82	433	.296	.607	.656	.420	56%	156
SF	1965	558	177	21	3	52	76	436	.317	.645	.688	.423	62%	168
SF	1966	552	159	29	4	37	70	377	.288	.556	.606	.429	41%	110
SF	1967	486	128	22	2	22	51	271	.263	.453	.505	.414	22%	49
SF	1968	498	144	20	5	23	67	310	.289	.488	.549	.389	41%	90
SF	1969	403	114	17	3	13	49	225	.283	.437	.498	.425	17%	33

		AB	H	2B	3B	HR	BB	B	BA	SA	A	LGE	+/−	Additional
SF	1970	478	139	15	2	28	79	321	.291	.506	.576	.449	28%	71
SF	1971	417	113	24	5	18	112	313	.271	.482	.592	.419	41%	91
SF/NYN	1972	244	61	11	1	8	60	158	.250	.402	.520	.420	24%	30
NYN	1973	209	44	10	0	6	27	99	.211	.344	.419	.432	−3%	−3
		10881	3283	523	140	660	1463	7529	.302	.557	.610	.437	39%	2130

Willie Mays could have stayed in the big leagues for 15 years on his glove, his wheels, and his competitiveness alone. Because he also happened to be one of the game's most dangerous hitters, many consider him to be the greatest player ever. Though he is Barry Bonds's godfather, it's Ken Griffey Jr. who most reminds the veterans of Willie Mays.

Mays was his league's greatest hitter six times. His finest hour came in 1965, when he hit 52 home runs and batted .317 in a pitcher's year, outproducing the National League by 62 percent. When comparing Mays's career averages for 500 at-bats to Henry Aaron's in an identical number of plate appearances, the similarities are astounding. Mays comes up higher on the all-time list because his slightly better patience at the plate enabled him to generate a mere *four* additional bases every season, which is enough to rank Mays 17th all-time in relative performance, compared to Aaron at 23rd.

	AB	H	2B	3B	HR	BB	B	BA	SA	A	LGE	+/−	Additional
Willie Mays	500	151	24	6	30	67	344	.302	.557	.610	.437	39%	98
Hank Aaron	509	155	26	4	31	58	340	.305	.555	.600	.435	38%	94

Tightly bunched indeed.

6. Rogers Hornsby, 2B/RH, 1915–37. St. Louis Cardinals, New York Giants, Boston Braves, Chicago Cubs, St. Louis Browns. Hall of Fame: 1942.

Top 50 seasons: 1924 (20th), 1922 (19th), 1925 (16th)

		AB	H	2B	3B	HR	BB	B	BA	SA	A	LGE	+/−	Additional
StLN	1915	57	14	2	0	0	2	18	.246	.281	.305	.380	−20%	−4
StLN	1916	495	155	17	15	6	40	260	.313	.444	.486	.374	30%	60
StLN	1917	523	171	24	17	8	45	298	.327	.484	.525	.374	40%	85
StLN	1918	416	117	19	11	5	40	213	.281	.416	.467	.375	25%	42

		AB	H	2B	3B	HR	BB	B	BA	SA	A	LGE	+/-	Additional
StLN	1919	512	163	15	9	8	48	268	.318	.430	.479	.380	26%	55
StLN	1920	589	218	44	20	9	60	389	.370	.559	.599	.400	50%	129
StLN	1921	592	235	44	18	21	60	438	.397	.639	.672	.436	54%	154
StLN	1922	623	250	46	14	42	65	515	.401	.722	.749	.448	67%	207
StLN	1923	424	163	32	10	17	55	321	.384	.627	.670	.440	52%	110
StLN	1924	536	227	43	14	25	89	462	.424	.696	.739	.435	70%	190
StLN	1925	504	203	41	10	39	83	464	.403	.756	.790	.458	73%	195
StLN	1926	527	167	34	5	11	61	305	.317	.463	.519	.433	20%	50
NYN	1927	568	205	32	9	26	86	419	.361	.586	.641	.432	48%	137
BosN	1928	486	188	42	7	21	107	414	.387	.632	.698	.447	56%	149
ChiN	1929	602	229	47	8	39	87	496	.380	.679	.720	.474	52%	169
ChiN	1930	104	32	5	1	2	12	57	.308	.433	.491	.491	0%	0
ChiN	1931	357	118	37	1	16	56	261	.331	.574	.632	.433	46%	82
ChiN	1932	58	13	2	0	1	10	28	.224	.310	.412	.436	-6%	-2
StLN/StLA	1933	92	30	7	0	3	14	60	.326	.500	.566	.404	40%	17
StLA	1934	23	7	2	0	1	7	19	.304	.522	.633	.437	45%	6
StLA	1935	24	5	3	0	0	3	11	.208	.333	.407	.434	-6%	-1
StLA	1936	5	2	0	0	0	1	3	.400	.400	.500	.432	16%	0
StLA	1937	56	18	3	0	1	7	31	.321	.429	.492	.431	14%	4
		8173	2930	541	169	301	1038	5750	.358	.577	.624	.424	47%	1836

"Guys who can field you can shake out of any old tree. Give me a guy who can hit."

—ROGERS HORNSBY

The only middle infielder in the top 25, Rogers Hornsby is also one of the most traveled in the group. He played for five teams—including four in four seasons from 1926 through 1929. By most accounts an arrogant, compulsive, and insufferable individual, Hornsby was traded from the Cardinals after player-managing his team to a World Series title in 1926, and received not a penny from his former teammates when the Cubs reached the World Series in 1932 though he'd player-managed the team for half the season.

Hornsby also happens to be the greatest hitter in the history of the National League. He was his league's best hitter seven times, reaching that level for a record three different teams—a mark among active hitters that, appropriately enough, Albert Belle may someday match. He won six consecutive slugging average titles, won the Triple Crown *twice*, and finished his career with the second-highest batting average in baseball history. In 1922, he didn't just lead the league in home runs, RBI, and batting average, but hits (250!), runs, doubles, on-base average, and slugging average, as well.

Unconvinced? His .756 slugging average—a record that has stood longer than Ruth's 60 and Maris's 61 *combined*—remains the highest in the NL even after McGwire's assault in 1998.

5. Mickey Mantle, CF/SH, 1951–68. New York Yankees. Hall of Fame: 1974.

Top 50 seasons: 1961 (29th), 1956 (27th), 1957 (24th)

		AB	H	2B	3B	HR	BB	B	BA	SA	A	LGE	+/−	Additional
NYA	1951	341	91	11	5	13	43	194	.267	.443	.505	.445	14%	23
NYA	1952	549	171	37	7	23	75	366	.311	.530	.587	.428	37%	99
NYA	1953	461	136	24	3	21	79	308	.295	.497	.570	.442	29%	69
NYA	1954	543	163	17	12	27	102	387	.300	.525	.600	.435	38%	106
NYA	1955	517	158	25	11	37	113	429	.306	.611	.681	.445	53%	149
NYA	1956	533	188	22	5	52	112	488	.353	.705	.757	.459	65%	192
NYA	1957	474	173	28	6	34	146	461	.365	.665	.744	.440	69%	188
NYA	1958	519	158	21	1	42	129	436	.304	.592	.673	.438	54%	152
NYA	1959	541	154	23	4	31	94	372	.285	.514	.586	.440	33%	92
NYA	1960	527	145	17	6	40	111	405	.275	.558	.635	.447	42%	120
NYA	1961	514	163	16	6	54	126	479	.317	.687	.748	.454	65%	189
NYA	1962	377	121	15	1	30	122	350	.321	.605	.701	.450	56%	125
NYA	1963	172	54	8	0	15	40	147	.314	.622	.693	.432	61%	55
NYA	1964	465	141	25	2	35	99	374	.303	.591	.663	.435	52%	128
NYA	1965	361	92	12	1	19	73	236	.255	.452	.544	.425	28%	52
NYA	1966	333	96	12	1	23	57	236	.288	.538	.605	.422	44%	72
NYA	1967	440	108	17	0	22	107	298	.245	.434	.545	.406	34%	76
NYA	1968	435	103	14	1	18	106	279	.237	.398	.516	.394	31%	66
		8102	2415	344	72	536	1734	6245	.298	.557	.635	.436	46%	1954

"No man in the history of baseball had as much power as Mickey Mantle. No man. You're not talking about ordinary power . . . when you're talking about Mickey Mantle it's an altogether different level. Separates the men from the boys."

—BILLY MARTIN

"He was the best one-legged player I ever saw play the game."

—CASEY STENGEL

You would be hard-pressed to find a hitter who strung together eight better seasons than Mickey Mantle did from 1954 to 1961, at the top of his league every year until his body gave out. His performances in 1956, 1957, and 1961 are great enough to merit inclusion in the top 50 seasons ever produced. Like Barry Bonds, his great batting eye puts him in the top 10 with a sub-.300 batting average for his career. Despite battling ever more severe injuries for the final seven years of his career, Mantle still managed to outproduce his league by 46 percent for his career—the sixth best mark of all time. He was the game's greatest player during the game's greatest decade—the 1950s—after the color barrier was broken and before expansion diluted competition.

It is one thing to imagine what might have been had Pete Reiser not run into so many walls, Tony Conigliaro not been beaned, and Bo Jackson not wrecked his hip in a football game. Maybe they, too, could have been like Mick for at least one season. But when you consider what might have been had Mantle not torn up his leg *twice* and drank like a man who didn't expect to live past 1971—well, who would Mickey have been like, given how great he was hung over and on one leg? Maybe like no one else who ever played the game.

4. Jimmie Foxx, 1B/RH, 1925–42, 1944–45. Philadelphia Athletics, Boston Red Sox, Chicago Cubs, Philadelphia Phillies. Hall of Fame: 1951.

Top 50 seasons: 1938 (42nd), 1933 (23rd), 1932 (11th)

		AB	H	2B	3B	HR	BB	B	BA	SA	A	LGE	+/−	Additional
PhiA	1925	9	6	1	0	0	0	7	.667	.778	.778	.462	68%	3
PhiA	1926	32	10	2	1	0	1	15	.313	.438	.455	.448	1%	0
PhiA	1927	130	42	6	5	3	14	81	.323	.515	.563	.451	25%	16
PhiA	1928	400	131	29	10	13	60	279	.328	.548	.607	.447	36%	73
PhiA	1929	517	183	23	9	33	103	426	.354	.625	.687	.460	49%	141
PhiA	1930	562	188	33	13	37	93	451	.335	.637	.689	.470	46%	143
PhiA	1931	515	150	32	10	30	73	365	.291	.567	.621	.449	38%	101
PhiA	1932	585	213	33	9	58	116	554	.364	.749	.790	.460	72%	232
PhiA	1933	573	204	37	9	48	96	499	.356	.703	.746	.447	67%	200
PhiA	1934	539	180	28	6	44	111	463	.334	.653	.712	.457	56%	166
PhiA	1935	535	185	33	7	36	114	454	.346	.636	.700	.459	52%	156
BosA	1936	585	198	32	8	41	105	474	.338	.631	.687	.479	43%	144
BosA	1937	569	162	24	6	36	99	405	.285	.538	.606	.473	28%	89
BosA	1938	565	197	33	9	50	119	517	.349	.704	.756	.476	59%	192
BosA	1939	467	168	31	10	35	89	413	.360	.694	.743	.466	59%	154
BosA	1940	515	153	30	4	36	101	400	.297	.581	.649	.463	40%	115
BosA	1941	487	146	27	8	19	93	339	.300	.505	.584	.450	30%	78
BosA/ChiN	1942	305	69	12	0	8	40	145	.226	.344	.420	.401	5%	7
ChiN	1944	20	1	1	0	0	2	4	.050	.100	.182	.417	−56%	−5
PhiN	1945	224	60	11	1	7	23	117	.268	.420	.474	.420	13%	13
		8134	2646	458	125	534	1452	6408	.325	.609	.668	.458	46%	2017

" . . . I don't know which stories in particular you've heard, but I'd say you wouldn't go far wrong if you believed them all."

—HALL OF FAMER TED LYONS ON JIMMIE FOXX

They didn't call Jimmie Foxx "the Beast" for nothing. Yankee ace Lefty Gomez said that he had muscles in his hair. Others said that he wasn't scouted, he was trapped.

Foxx and the remaining three players on this list produced 14 of the 15 greatest seasons of all time. He is one of only seven players to top 2,000 additional bases for his career. He is one of only four players with a career base average greater than .666. He is one of only three players to top 200 additional bases in consecutive seasons, and only one man ever piled up more bases in a two-year span than Foxx did in 1932 and 1933. A victim of Connie Mack's Depression-era purge of the Philadelphia Athletics, Foxx is one of only a handful of players to lead the league in bases for two different teams and, along with Mark McGwire, is the only man to hit 50 home runs for two different teams.

Due to the stiff hitting competition in the 1930s—namely, the three greatest first basemen in the league's history—Foxx only led the AL in bases three times, and had to put up legendary numbers to do it. He came within one base in 1933 of becoming only the third player to reach 500 bases in a season three times.

The gap between Foxx and Hornsby, Mays, and Aaron is by no means a wide one. But because he dominated his league by so much for so long, Foxx is a worthy choice for the greatest right-handed hitter in the game's history.

3. Lou Gehrig, 1B/LH, 1923–39. New York Yankees. Hall of Fame: 1939.

Top 50 seasons: 1936 (44th), 1931 (37th), 1930 (31st), 1934 (25th), 1927 (5th)

		AB	H	2B	3B	HR	BB	B	BA	SA	A	LGE	+/−	Additional
NYA	1923	26	11	4	1	1	2	22	.423	.769	.786	.442	78%	10
NYA	1924	12	6	1	0	0	1	8	.500	.583	.615	.451	37%	2
NYA	1925	437	129	23	10	20	46	278	.295	.531	.576	.462	25%	55
NYA	1926	572	179	47	20	16	105	419	.313	.549	.619	.448	38%	116
NYA	1927	584	218	52	18	47	109	556	.373	.765	.802	.451	78%	243
NYA	1928	562	210	47	13	27	95	459	.374	.648	.699	.447	56%	165
NYA	1929	553	166	33	9	35	122	444	.300	.582	.658	.460	43%	134
NYA	1930	581	220	42	17	41	101	520	.379	.721	.762	.470	62%	199
NYA	1931	619	211	31	15	46	117	527	.341	.662	.716	.449	60%	197
NYA	1932	596	208	42	9	34	108	478	.349	.621	.679	.460	48%	154
NYA	1933	593	198	41	12	32	92	451	.334	.605	.658	.447	47%	145
NYA	1934	579	210	40	6	49	109	518	.363	.706	.753	.457	65%	203
NYA	1935	535	176	26	10	30	132	444	.329	.583	.666	.459	45%	138
NYA	1936	579	205	37	7	49	130	533	.354	.696	.752	.479	57%	194
NYA	1937	569	200	37	9	37	127	493	.351	.643	.708	.473	50%	164
NYA	1938	576	170	32	6	29	107	408	.295	.523	.597	.476	26%	83
NYA	1939	28	4	0	0	0	5	9	.143	.143	.273	.466	−42%	−6
		8001	2721	535	162	493	1508	6567	.340	.632	.691	.460	50%	2195

"Gehrig never learned that a ballplayer couldn't be good every day."

—CATCHER HANK GOWDY

Overshadowed by a teammate named Babe Ruth and a consecutive-games streak that lasted for more than a half-century, Lou Gehrig was very quietly one of the game's most devastating hitters. He outproduced his league by 50 percent for his career, though he played during the game's greatest hitting era. He topped 100 additional bases for a record *12* consecutive seasons. He led the league in bases six times, topping the lofty 500 mark *five* times in the process. Gehrig's greatest season was 1927, when he matched Babe Ruth home run for home run until the ill health of his mother sent him into a September tailspin. In the end, he still managed to produce more bases than Ruth and his 60 home runs.

Gehrig's illness kept him from reaching 3,000 hits and 500 home runs, but you'll find him third on the career slugging average list at .632. How high is .632? It's .340 with 38 doubles, 12 triples, and 35 home runs in an *average* year. For perspective, 6 of the 15 members of the 500-homer club never even slugged .632 in a *season*.

Gehrig walked away in 1939 after the debilitating illness that now bears his name had reduced him to a .143 hitter who was mobbed by teammates for fielding a routine ground ball. On the 4th of July, Lou Gehrig Day at Yankee Stadium, knowing that he didn't have long to live, Gehrig told the packed house: "Today, I consider myself the luckiest man on the face of the earth." He went into the Hall of Fame in a special election that year, and died two years later.

When you consider that the Yankees put Lou Gehrig on the field with both Babe Ruth and Joe DiMaggio at their best, it's a wonder any other teams ever got to play in October.

2. Ted Williams, LF/LH, 1939–60. Boston Red Sox. Hall of Fame: 1966.

Top 50 seasons: 1954 (45th), 1949 (34th), 1947 (18th), 1957 (14th), 1942 (13th), 1946 (10th), 1941 (9th)

		AB	H	2B	3B	HR	BB	B	BA	SA	A	LGE	+/−	Additional
BosA	1939	565	185	44	11	31	107	451	.327	.609	.671	.466	44%	138
BosA	1940	561	193	43	14	23	96	429	.344	.594	.653	.463	41%	125
BosA	1941	456	185	33	3	37	145	480	.406	.735	.799	.450	78%	210
BosA	1942	522	186	34	5	36	145	483	.356	.648	.724	.417	74%	205
BosA	1946	514	176	37	8	38	156	499	.342	.667	.745	.424	76%	215
BosA	1947	528	181	40	9	32	162	497	.343	.634	.720	.429	68%	201
BosA	1948	509	188	44	3	25	126	439	.369	.615	.691	.450	54%	153
BosA	1949	566	194	39	3	43	162	530	.343	.650	.728	.453	61%	200

		AB	H	2B	3B	HR	BB	B	BA	SA	A	LGE	+/−	Additional
BosA	1950	334	106	24	1	28	82	298	.317	.647	.716	.470	52%	103
BosA	1951	531	169	28	4	30	144	439	.318	.556	.650	.445	46%	139
BosA	1952	10	4	0	1	1	2	11	.400	.900	.917	.428	114%	6
BosA	1953	91	37	6	0	13	19	101	.407	.901	.918	.442	108%	52
BosA	1954	386	133	23	1	29	136	381	.345	.635	.730	.435	68%	154
BosA	1955	320	114	21	3	28	91	316	.356	.703	.769	.445	73%	133
BosA	1956	400	138	28	2	24	102	344	.345	.605	.685	.459	49%	114
BosA	1957	420	163	28	1	38	119	426	.388	.731	.790	.440	79%	189
BosA	1958	411	135	23	2	26	98	338	.328	.584	.664	.438	52%	115
BosA	1959	272	69	15	0	10	52	166	.254	.419	.512	.440	16%	23
BosA	1960	310	98	15	0	29	75	275	.316	.645	.714	.447	60%	103
		7706	2654	525	71	521	2019	6903	.344	.634	.710	.445	59%	2576

"They said he had no weakness, won't swing at a bad ball, has the best eyes in the business, and can kill you with one swing; he won't swing at anything bad, but don't give him anything good."

—PITCHER BOBBY SHANTZ, ON THE SCOUTING
REPORT HE WAS GIVEN ON TED WILLIAMS

"All I want out of life is that when I walk down the street folks will say, 'There goes the greatest hitter who ever lived.'"

—TED WILLIAMS, 1939

Legend has it that when the 20-year-old Ted Williams joined the Red Sox, a teammate told him, "Wait till you see Jimmie Foxx hit." Williams replied, "Wait till Foxx sees me hit."

The game's first scientific hitter, Ted Williams debuted with the greatest season any rookie has ever had, knocking in 145 runs to lead the league. He kept hitting until age 42, hitting his 29th home run of the 1960 season in his final at-bat in Fenway Park, then rode off into the sunset. He has seven seasons in the top 50, including five in the top 20. He led the league in bases for six consecutive seasons, and the only things that kept that streak from being 15 were two wars, Hank Greenberg, and a broken elbow suffered in the 1950 All-Star Game.

The accomplishments go on and on:

- Last man to hit .400, batting .406 in 1941.
- Only batted below .316 once, in 1959, at the age of 41.
- Six batting titles, including consecutive crowns at the ages of 39 (.388) and 40.
- His .731 slugging average (at the age of 39) wasn't topped until Mark McGwire did it in 1998.

WAR, PEACE, AND TEDDY BALLGAME

The Second World War and perhaps the Korean War (following so soon and therefore involving many of the same people) had the most profound effect on the lives and careers of major league players. Great hitters like Joe DiMaggio (three seasons), Hank Greenberg (three seasons), and Johnny Mize (three seasons) all lost significant portions of their major league careers to military service. No player, however, gave up more of his major league career than Ted Williams, who missed the equivalent of five seasons while serving in World War II and the Korean War.

Following the 1942 season, the 24-year-old Williams joined the Marines, becoming a fighter pilot. In both of the previous two seasons he had led the league in batting, runs scored, walks, on-base percentage, and slugging percentage. In 1941 he batted .406, a level that has not been matched by any player since, while in 1942 he won the first of his two Triple Crowns. In 1946, Williams returned to baseball and demonstrated, at 28, that his skills were undiminished. He hit .342, leading the American League in runs scored, walks, on-base percentage, and slugging percentage while hitting a then career high of 38 home runs.

In 1952, the Korean War put Williams's career on hold once more. Early in the 1952 season he got in 10 at-bats, and late in the 1953 season 91 more. In between, he was flying combat missions in Korea, making life difficult for international communism. In his next full season, 1954, Williams once more proved, at age 35, that he was still among the best in the game. He batted .345 with 29 homers while playing in only 117 games, but nevertheless managed to lead the American League in walks and on-base percentage.

Assume there was no interruption to Williams's career and that he had only hit as well as he did after each interruption during each interruption. Certainly this is conservative since it is likely that he would have had some monster seasons between the ages of 24 and 28. The following table illustrates what might have been (with the speculative seasons in italics).

	GP	BA	AB	R	H	2B	3B	HR	RBI	BB
1939–42	586	.356	2104	54	749	154	33	127	515	493
1943–45	*450*	*.342*	*1542*	*426*	*528*	*111*	*24*	*114*	*369*	*468*
1946–51	835	.340	2982	732	1014	212	28	196	746	832
1952–53	*234*	*.345*	*772*	*186*	*266*	*46*	*2*	*58*	*178*	*272*
1954–60	828	.337	2519	506	850	153	9	184	541	673
	2933	.343	9919	2391	3407	676	96	679	2349	2738

The addition of the five seasons that Williams lost to military service would make him the all-time leader in runs scored (over Ty Cobb with 2,245), RBI (over Hank Aaron with 2,297), and walks (over Babe Ruth with 2,056). It would also allow him to join the 3,000-hit club and move him into third place on the all-time home run list behind only Hank Aaron and Babe Ruth. It is even possible (given that he hit 29 homers in his last season) that he might have stuck around a few years longer to take a run at Ruth's mark of 714 home runs.

- Reached base more frequently than any hitter in the league in 12 of his 13 full seasons.
- Thanks to more than 2,000 walks (second all-time), Williams reached base more frequently than any hitter in history, including Babe Ruth.

Ted Williams never wanted to be anything other than the greatest hitter the game has ever seen—and he damn near pulled it off.

1. Babe Ruth, RF/LH, 1914–35. Boston Red Sox, New York Yankees, Boston Braves. Hall of Fame: 1936.

Top 50 seasons: 1932 (49th), 1919 (26th), 1930 (17th), 1931 (15th), 1928 (12th), 1924 (8th), 1926 (6th), 1927 (4th), 1923 (3rd), 1921 (2nd), 1920 (1st)

		AB	H	2B	3B	HR	BB	B	BA	SA	A	LGE	+/−	Additional
BosA	1914	10	2	1	0	0	0	3	.200	.300	.300	.382	-22%	-1
BosA	1915	92	29	10	1	4	9	62	.315	.576	.614	.390	57%	23
BosA	1916	136	37	5	3	3	10	67	.272	.419	.459	.385	19%	11
BosA	1917	123	40	6	3	2	12	70	.325	.472	.519	.379	37%	19
BosA	1918	317	95	26	11	11	57	233	.300	.555	.623	.382	63%	90
BosA	1919	432	139	34	12	29	101	385	.322	.657	.722	.412	75%	165
NYA	1920	458	172	36	9	54	148	536	.376	.847	.884	.438	102%	271
NYA	1921	540	204	44	16	59	144	601	.378	.846	.879	.458	92%	288
NYA	1922	406	128	24	8	35	84	357	.315	.672	.729	.448	63%	138
NYA	1923	522	205	45	13	41	170	569	.393	.764	.822	.442	86%	263
NYA	1924	529	200	39	7	46	142	533	.378	.739	.794	.451	76%	231
NYA	1925	359	104	12	2	25	59	254	.290	.543	.608	.462	31%	61
NYA	1926	495	184	30	5	47	144	509	.372	.737	.797	.448	78%	223
NYA	1927	540	192	29	8	60	138	555	.356	.772	.819	.451	81%	249
NYA	1928	536	173	29	8	54	135	515	.323	.709	.768	.447	72%	215
NYA	1929	499	172	26	6	46	72	420	.345	.697	.736	.460	60%	157
NYA	1930	518	186	28	9	49	136	515	.359	.732	.787	.470	68%	208
NYA	1931	534	199	31	3	46	128	502	.373	.700	.758	.449	69%	205
NYA	1932	457	156	13	5	41	130	432	.341	.661	.736	.460	60%	162
NYA	1933	459	138	21	3	34	114	381	.301	.582	.665	.447	49%	125
NYA	1934	365	105	17	4	22	103	299	.288	.537	.639	.457	40%	85
BosN	1935	72	13	0	0	6	20	51	.181	.431	.554	.434	28%	11
		8399	2873	506	136	714	2056	7849	.342	.690	.751	.445	69%	3197

"Ruth had become simply impossible, and the Boston club could no longer put up with his eccentricities. I think the Yankees are taking a gamble."

—BOSTON RED SOX OWNER HARRY FRAZEE, AFTER SELLING BABE RUTH TO THE YANKEES IN 1920

Babe Ruth crosses home plate after hitting one of his 714 career homers.

"Ruth made a grave mistake when he gave up pitching. Working once a week, he might have lasted a long time and become a great star."

—TRIS SPEAKER, 1921

"To understand him, you had to understand this: He wasn't human."

—TEAMMATE JOE DUGAN

". . . I stopped talking about the Babe for the simple reason that I realized that those who had never seen him didn't believe me."

—TOMMY HOLMES

"I coulda hit a .400 lifetime average easy. But I woulda had to hit them singles. The people were payin' to see me hit them home runs."

—BABE RUTH

He was so good they had to invent the Hall of Fame for him.

And the All-Star Game and Yankee Stadium, too.

Babe Ruth hit 714 home runs, though he wasn't a regular in the starting lineup until he was 24—earning his keep as one of the game's best pitchers. Then the Red Sox finally got clever in 1918 and began to find some playing time for him in their outfield. In 1918, Ruth led the league in home runs while playing in less than 100 games. Then, from 1919 to 1932—with the exception of an illness-plagued 1925 season—Ruth slugged at least .720 every season. Only Rogers Hornsby and Lou Gehrig could come close to keeping pace with him. His mark of 60 home runs fell in 1961—the same season that his record for consecutive scoreless innings pitched in World Series play also was broken. His record of 714 career home runs was eclipsed in 1974. But Ruth owns several other records that neither Roger Maris nor Hank Aaron nor Mark McGwire nor Sammy Sosa ever even caught a glimpse of on the horizon:

- Career slugging average of .690, 56 points higher than Ted Williams.
- Career base average of .751, 41 points higher than Williams.
- Outproduced his league by 69 percent for his career, 10 percent higher than Williams.

- 3,197 additional bases for his career, more than 600 ahead of Williams.
- Base average of .884 in 1920, first of four .800-plus campaigns—the .800 level only reached by two other players (Lou Gehrig in 1927 and Mark McGwire in 1998).
- 601 bases in 1921, first of three 550-plus seasons—the 550 level only reached by two other players (Lou Gehrig in 1927 and Jimmie Foxx in 1932).
- Outproduced his league by more than 100 percent in 1920, first of four 80-percent–plus efforts—the 80-percent level never reached by any other player.
- 288 additional bases in 1921, second of three 260-plus seasons—the 250 level never reached by any other player.
- Outhomered every *team* in the American League twice, in 1920 and 1927.

In 1998, Mark McGwire became the first hitter in 52 years to crack the list of all-time top 10 seasons. But as great as McGwire was in '98, he would have had to hit 84 home runs and hit .326 to reach Ruth's base, additional base, and base average bests. As for outproducing his league by 102 percent, that would have required 91 home runs, a .340 batting average, 629 bases, and a .935 base average.

Babe Ruth didn't just change the way the game was played, he reinvented it. Imagine a 7-foot point guard averaging a triple double every game for a decade and you might begin to get the picture.

HEY, WHY ISN'T PETE ROSE ON THIS LIST?

The two most hallowed lifetime achievements are home runs and hits. At the end of the 1999 season, 22 modern major leaguers had 3,000 hits and 21 had 450 home runs (and six men had both). Five of the 22 (23%) with 3,000 hits made the list of top 25 hitters, while 14 of the 21 (67%) with 450 home runs made it. Are home runs worth that much more than singles? Or is there something about the 3,000-hit club that is deceiving? Compare the 3,000 club with the 450 club and make your own call:

3,000 Hits	Bases	Add'l. Bases	Base Avg.	+/– vs. League	Rings	450 HRS	Bases	Add'l. Bases	Base Avg.	+/– vs. League	Rings
Rose	7318	676	.469	10%	3	Aaron*	8258	2273	.600	38%	1
Cobb	7112	1973	.561	39%	0	Ruth	7849	3197	.751	69%	4
Aaron*	8258	2273	.600	38%	1	Mays*	7529	2130	.610	39%	1
Musial*	7733	2182	.615	39%	3	Robinson	6793	1850	.595	37%	2
Speaker	6485	1702	.560	36%	4	Killebrew	5702	1526	.587	36%	0
Yastrzemski*	7384	1402	.534	23%	0	Jackson	6209	1291	.552	26%	5
Wagner	5831	1408	.511	32%	1	Schmidt	5911	1666	.602	40%	1
Molitor	5948	461	.499	8%	1	Mantle	6245	1954	.635	46%	7

3,000 Hits	Bases	Add'l. Bases	Base Avg.	+/− vs. League	Rings	450 HRS	Bases	Add'l. Bases	Base Avg.	+/− vs. League	Rings
Collins	5766	1073	.503	23%	4	Foxx	6408	2017	.668	46%	2
Mays*	7529	2130	.610	39%	1	McGwire	4501	1334	.658	42%	1
Murray*	6730	998	.531	17%	1	McCovey	5564	1483	.583	36%	0
Lajoie	4989	1088	.494	28%	0	Williams	6903	2576	.710	59%	0
Brett	6140	1026	.536	20%	1	Banks	5469	1009	.537	23%	0
Waner	5562	968	.527	21%	0	Mathews	5793	1376	.580	31%	1
Yount	5696	337	.476	6%	0	Ott	6749	1927	.605	40%	1
Winfield*	6437	990	.527	18%	1	Murray*	6730	998	.531	17%	1
Carew	5016	535	.485	12%	0	Gehrig	6567	2195	.691	50%	6
Brock	4999	285	.451	6%	2	Musial*	7733	2182	.615	39%	3
Kaline	6129	1185	.538	24%	1	Stargell	5127	1367	.578	36%	2
Clemente	5113	746	.507	17%	1	Winfield*	6437	990	.527	18%	1
Gwynn	4927	582	.501	13%	0	Yastrzemski*	7384	1402	.534	23%	0
Boggs	5476	588	.517	12%	1						
AVERAGE	5938	1070	.502	21%	23	AVERAGE	6176	1670	.580	36%	39

*members of both exclusive clubs

On average, the 450-homer club actually accumulated more bases than the 3,000-hit club, while outproducing their league by nearly twice as much. In one season, Babe Ruth had more additional bases than Tony Gwynn, Lou Brock, Rod Carew, Robin Yount, and Paul Molitor managed in their entire careers.

While only two members of the 450-homer club outproduced their league by less than 20 percent for their careers (Dave Winfield and Eddie Murray), 10 members of the 3,000-hit club were below 20 percent. Molitor, Yount, and Brock were below 10 percent. Pete Rose finished his career only 10 percent better than the average player in his league, which is less than Al Oliver, Vada Pinson, and Jose Cruz, and equivalent to Graig Nettles. Three players who outproduced their league by more than 10 percent for their careers while accumulating more additional bases than Rose: Dave Parker, Enos Slaughter, and Ken Singleton.

Want further evidence that home run hitters with shorter, more dominating careers are worth more than singles hitters who hang on? The 22 members of the 3,000-hit club have combined to win 23 championships. The 21 members of the 450-homer club have combined to win 39. Of the 23 championships won by the 3,000-hit club, 7 were won by members of the 450-homer club and 9 were won by deadball superstars. That leaves 7 titles from the 10 post–WWII singles hitters with 3,000 hits. There have been 11 post–WWII 450-plus home run hitters without 3,000 hits. They've combined not for 7 titles, but for 19.

The case can be made that 3,000 hits is the most overrated offensive accomplishment in baseball.

3

From Murderers' Row to Harvey's Wallbangers

The Greatest Hitting Teams

Baseball is the most individual of team sports. By its nature it highlights individual performance. Whether hitting, fielding, pitching, or running the bases, a player is center stage and succeeds or fails based upon his own skills or weaknesses. Tony Gwynn must hit Nolan Ryan's fastball on his own. Ken Griffey Jr. must catch Bernie Williams's sinking line drive on his own. Randy Johnson must retire Mark McGwire on his own. Each test of skill is a measurable event with honor or blame clearly apportioned. As a result, a plethora of statistics exist to dissect a player's performance and determine his contribution in each aspect of the game. This bounty of numbers perhaps explains baseball fans' obsession with individual performance.

However, baseball players compete in a team context. No one player can carry a team to a pennant. Too many great hitters—Ernie Banks, Luke Appling, and George Sisler, to name a few—have toiled through long and distinguished careers without ever playing in the postseason. Teams win pennants. Teams endure pennant races, outlasting their rivals. Teams struggle through a season with different players coming to the fore in different games. It is over the course of the season that the importance of the team becomes evident. Our fondest memories and allegiance are reserved for our favorite teams. Brooklyn was brokenhearted not because it lost Duke Snider and Gil Hodges, but because it lost the Dodgers.

Some of the greatest hitting teams of the twentieth century are presented here, beginning with an underappreciated bunch from the early 1900s that benefited from a "corporate merger," moving on through three different Yankees dynasties covering 24 seasons between 1927 and 1961, a string of Brooklyn Dodgers teams that had the misfortune of having to face many of those Yankees teams in October, then on to the Big Red Machine and Harvey's Wallbangers and a strange, under-achieving bunch from the late 1980s known more for its pitching and personal problems, and ending with the greatest hitting team of the wild 1990s.

1901–03 Pittsburgh Pirates

The first great hitting team of the twentieth century was the Pittsburgh Pirates, who won three straight National League pennants between 1901 and 1903. The Pirates benefited from Barney Dreyfus's merger of the Louisville Colonels with the Pirates after the 1899 season, which allowed the guts of the Louisville lineup, including Fred Clarke, Tommy Leach, and Honus Wagner, to be added to Pittsburgh's for the 1900 season. The Pirates reached their pinnacle in 1902 when they won the National League pennant by a stunning 27½ games. The team led the National League in runs, hits, doubles, triples, home runs, batting average, on-base percentage, and slugging percentage during 1902, generating 5.7 runs per game, or 42 percent more than the National League average of 3.98 runs per game. In a league that batted .259 and slugged at a .319 clip, the Pirates' mix of high team batting average (.286) and team power (.375 slugging percentage) was head and shoulders above their competitors.

Here are the offensive numbers for the heart of the Pirates' lineup in 1902:

	GP	BA	R	H	HR	RBI	BB	OBP	SA	SB
Kitty Bransfield, 1B	102	.305	49	126	0	69	17	.336	.395	23
Tommy Leach, 3B	135	.280	97	143	6	85	45	.341	.426	25
Fred Clarke, LF	114	.316	103	145	2	53	51	.401	.449	29
Ginger Beaumont, CF	130	.357	100	193	0	67	39	.404	.418	33
Honus Wagner, RF	136	.330	105	176	3	91	43	.394	.463	42

The top of the Pirates' batting order included the league leader for almost every individual offensive category and was extremely deep, providing the Pirates with an offensive punch no team in the National League could match. Additionally, the Pirates carried a long bench for the time with Lefty Davis, Jimmy Burke, Jack O'Connor, and Chief Zimmer providing offensive contributions. Underlining the Pirates' offensive ascendancy, Honus Wagner, Fred Clarke, Ginger Beaumont, and Tommy Leach finished 1-2-3-4 in runs scored, a feat that has never been repeated. The Pirates' supremacy over the National League during 1902 is partially attributed to the establishment of the American League as an "outlaw" major league in 1901. The American League raided National League clubs between 1900 and 1902, taking such established stars as Cy Young and Jimmy Collins. The Philadelphia Phillies, one of the Pirates' primary rivals, were particularly hurt, losing Napoleon Lajoie, Elmer Flick, and Ed Delahanty to the new loop. Dreyfus, on the other hand, was able to keep his Pirates teams intact, and they ran roughshod over their weakened competition.

1910–14 Philadelphia Athletics

Connie Mack's Philadelphia Athletics of the early 1910s featured the "$100,000 infield" and won four American League pennants and three World Series titles between 1910 and 1914. The Athletics' batting order was relatively stable during this five-year period and peaked in 1913 and 1914, outscoring their nearest rival by 163 runs in 1913 and by 134 runs in 1914. These were huge margins in a league with an average of 3.5 to 4.0 runs per game, allowing the Athletics to waltz to pennants despite their mediocre pitching.

The Athletics probably had their best season in 1913, when they led the American League in runs, hits, doubles, home runs, walks, batting average, on-base percentage, and slugging percentage. The Athletics scored 794 runs, or 5.2 runs per game, in 1913 to easily outdistance the

The first player to put his autograph on a Louisville Slugger bat, Honus Wagner amassed 3,418 hits during his career.

American League average of 3.9. Notably, the Athletics dominated the American League's offensive statistics while playing in Shibe Park, the second-worst hitter's park in the American League during 1913.

	GP	BA	R	H	HR	RBI	BB	OBP	SA	SB
Stuffy McInnis, 1B	148	.324	79	176	4	90	45	.382	.416	16
Eddie Collins, 2B	148	.345	125	184	3	73	85	.441	.453	54
Frank Baker, 3B	149	.337	116	190	12	117	63	.413	.493	34
Jack Barry, SS	134	.275	62	125	3	85	44	.349	.365	15
Rube Oldring, LF	136	.283	101	152	5	71	34	.328	.394	40
Eddie Murphy, RF	137	.295	105	150	1	30	70	.391	.356	21

The Athletics' infield featured two Hall of Famers: second baseman Eddie Collins was the team's offensive spark plug, while third baseman Frank Baker provided the punch. Collins, with his high batting average, good strike zone judgment, and excellent speed, batted first, second, or third for the Athletics and led the American League in runs scored from 1912 to 1914. "Home Run" Baker, who carried a 52-ounce fence post to the plate, was the top power hitter of his day, leading

BEST HITTING TEAM OF THE NINETEENTH CENTURY

Just prior to the opening of the 1893 season, the National League eliminated the pitcher's box and added the pitcher's rubber five feet behind what had been the back line of the pitcher's box, thereby establishing the modern pitching distance of 60 feet 6 inches. In the half-decade that followed, the hitters dominated baseball as pitchers adjusted to the new distance. The year 1894 was the pinnacle of the hitters' domination when the National League batted .309, the highest league batting average in major league history.

In 1894, the Philadelphia Phillies, en route to a fourth-place finish, batted an astounding .349 as a team to set the all-time team record. The Phillies' high-octane offense was anchored by Hall of Famers Billy Hamilton, Ed Delahanty, and Sam Thompson, who comprised one of the greatest hitting outfields of all time.

	GP	BA	R	H	HR	RBI	BB	OBP	SA	SB
Billy Hamilton, CF	131	.404	192	220	4	87	126	.523	.528	98
Ed Delahanty, LF	114	.407	147	199	4	131	60	.478	.585	21
Sam Thompson, RF	99	.407	108	178	13	141	40	.458	.686	24

Billy Hamilton, a diminutive 5'6" and one of the greatest leadoff hitters in baseball history, set the table for the Phillies. The 1894 season was the best of Hamilton's stellar career as he set the all-time major league record for runs scored in a single season and led the league in runs, walks, on-base percentage, and stolen bases. Both of the Phillies' slugging outfielders, Big Ed Delahanty and Big Sam Thompson, were in the primes of their careers and were coming off big seasons in 1893, when Delahanty had led the National League in home runs, RBI, and slugging percentage and Thompson had led the circuit in hits and doubles. While neither Delahanty nor Thompson led the league in any categories during 1894, they were the best 1-2 slugging combination in the majors. Thompson would have certainly led the league in RBI if he had not missed a significant portion of the season to injuries. As it was, he fell 4 RBI short, but his RBI per game of 1.4 is the highest in the history of major league baseball.

The Phillies' amazing outfield was supported by Lave Cross and Tuck Turner. Cross, playing third base, chipped in with a .386 batting average, 123 runs, and 125 RBI. He would play for over 20 seasons and become one of the first players recognized as a great pinch hitter, but would not really approach his 1894 numbers again until a decade later, playing for Connie Mack's Philadelphia Athletics in the early days of the American League. Turner was the classic flash in the pan, batting .416, scoring 91 runs, and driving in 82 in part-time play in the outfield. Despite his excellent season, Turner would never establish himself as an everyday player and was out of baseball by 1898. The Phillies also received excellent production from the catcher's spot, which was split among three players: Mike Grady (44 games), Dick Buckley (42 games), and Jack Clements (45 games), who collectively hit .336 with 102 RBI.

With a league batting average of .309, it is not surprising that other teams recorded remarkable offensive numbers during 1894. The pennant-winning Baltimore Orioles batted .343 during the season, while the third-place Boston Beaneaters, led by Triple-Crown winner Hugh Duffy, checked in with a .331 mark. In fact, both the Orioles and the Beaneaters outscored the Phillies over the course of the season; however, both teams played in much better hitter's parks than the Columbia Street Grounds, the Phillies' home park. The Phillies' inability to contend during 1894 was primarily attributable to their pitching staff, whose team ERA of 5.63 was third-worst in the league, and seemed to have more trouble adjusting to the new pitching distance than other teams' pitching staffs.

the American League in RBI in both 1912 and 1913, winning by margins of 36 and 24, respectively. He led the American League in home runs in every year between 1911 and 1914 and earned his nickname for his exploits in the 1911 World Series, hitting long balls off Christy Mathewson and Rube Marquard.

At first base, Stuffy McInnis, who was originally a middle infielder, was a consistent contact line-drive hitter in the Keith Hernandez or Mark Grace mold, finishing in the top five in RBI from 1912 to 1914. In essence, the Athletics' offense was predicated on Eddie Collins, Eddie Murphy, and Rube Oldring getting on base and Frank Baker, Stuffy McInnis, and Jack Barry driving them home, a system that worked to perfection in 1913. The bottom part of the Athletics' batting order was below average; however, they had a strong bench with Amos Strunk, Wally Schang, and Danny Murphy available. The 1913 Philadelphia Athletics were a young team with an average age of 25 and looked ready to dominate the American League for many years to come, but it was not to be. With the birth of the Federal League in 1914, Connie Mack decided not to compete with the rebel league for players and sold his team away. After winning one more pennant in 1914, the Athletics, without Eddie Collins, Jack Barry, Frank Baker, and Eddie Murphy, fell to last place in 1915.

1927–33 New York Yankees

With the rule changes of 1919 and 1920 and the advent of Babe Ruth, major league batting averages and power statistics rose to new levels, and many individual stars such as Rogers Hornsby and George Sisler recorded Herculean numbers. In this hitter's era, the New York Yankees came to dominate. With the arrival of Lou Gehrig in 1925 and Tony Lazzeri in 1926, Murderers' Row was born. For a seven-season period from 1927 to 1933, the New York Yankees of Babe Ruth and Lou Gehrig were arguably the seven greatest hitting teams of all time, recording team offensive numbers that so exceeded league performance that their relative excellence has never been matched. The combination of two players with the hitting abilities of Ruth and Gehrig on a single team is unparalleled in baseball history and at the heart of the enduring greatness of Murderers' Row. Imagine teaming up Joe

DiMaggio and Ted Williams in the 1940s, or Willie Mays and Mickey Mantle in the 1950s, and you still would not have a combination of the magnitude of Ruth and Gehrig. The cast surrounding Ruth and Gehrig would change over the seven-year run of Murderers' Row, but Ruth and Gehrig were the constants propelling the Yankees' offense with nary an off-season between them.

The top hitting team from the first half of the Yankees' seven-year run was the storied 1927 squad, which cruised to the American League pennant with 110 wins and swept the Pittsburgh Pirates in the World Series. The 1927 New York Yankees led the American League in runs, hits, triples, home runs, walks, batting average, on-base percentage, and slugging percentage, scoring 975 runs, or 6.3 runs per game, which dwarfed the 1927 major league average of 4.9 runs per game by 28 percent. Their team slugging percentage of .489 remains the highest in major league history.

	GP	BA	R	H	HR	RBI	BB	OBP	SA	SB
Lou Gehrig, 1B	155	.373	149	218	47	175	109	.474	.765	10
Tony Lazzeri, 2B	153	.309	92	176	18	102	69	.383	.482	22
Bob Meusel, LF	135	.337	75	174	8	103	45	.393	.510	24
Earle Combs, CF	152	.356	137	231	6	64	62	.414	.511	15
Babe Ruth, RF	151	.356	158	192	60	164	138	.487	.772	7

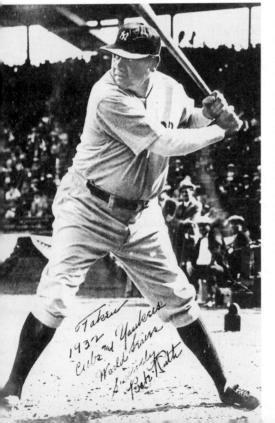

During 1927, both Ruth and Gehrig had career years, posting stupendous offensive numbers. Ruth one-bettered his single-season home run mark of 59 while posting his usual otherworldly on-base and slugging percentages. Gehrig, who won the League Award (a forerunner of the MVP), arrived as a superstar in 1927, recording career highs in hits, extra-base hits, doubles, home runs, and slugging percentage. In fact, Gehrig led Ruth in home runs on August 1 with 38 roundtrippers to Ruth's 35 but suffered a power outage over the remainder of the season, managing only 9 home runs during August and September. In the meantime, Ruth caught fire, hammering 25—including 17 in September. The

By combining explosive hip movement and a thunderous swing, Babe Ruth revolutionized baseball.

two Yankees legends combined for 214 extra-base hits, including 107 home runs and 339 RBI, and provided their team with matchless production in the 3 and 4 slots in the batting order.

The 1927 Yankees were not deep, as the bottom half of the order and bench hit at or below the American League batting average of .285 with no power. The strength of the top of the batting order, however, more than compensated. Ruth and Gehrig were ably supported by the best leadoff hitter in baseball and two superior line-drive power hitters who filled out the top five spots in the batting order. Earle Combs's contribution to the Yankees' success is often overlooked, but he was a productive leadoff man who hit for a high average with reasonable extra-base power. During 1927, Combs reached base safely almost 300 times, setting the table for the meat of the order. Tony Lazzeri, who batted second for the Yankees, was a phenom from the Pacific Coast League, where he had hit 60 home runs in 1925 for the Salt Lake City Bees. In the majors, Lazzeri was a consistent 100-RBI man with good extra-base power over his 13-year career. Bob Meusel, the Yankees' fifth-spot hitter, was a star in his own right and had led the AL in both homers and RBI in 1925, the year of Ruth's bellyache. Over the course of his career, Meusel was a consistent .300 hitter with good power and a lifetime .500 slugging percentage.

The top hitting team of the second half of the Yankees' Ruth-Gehrig era was the 1931 team, which was deeper than the 1927 squad and probably the greatest hitting team of all time. The 1931 Yankees scored 1,067 runs, or 6.88 runs per game— the highest totals in major league history, easily exceeding the American League average of 5.18 runs per game by 32.8 percent. While it is true that the early 1930s was a high-scoring era, it is also true that Yankee Stadium was among the most difficult parks to hit in during 1931, reducing runs scored by about 6 percent. Despite these gaudy and peerless offensive statistics, it is interesting to note that the 1931 Yankees were also-rans, finishing 13½ games behind Connie Mack's Philadelphia Athletics. While the Athletics could not match the Yankees' hitting, they had sufficient power from Hall of Famers Mickey Cochrane, Jimmie Foxx, and Al Simmons that their substantial edges in pitching and fielding were more than enough to outdistance the Bronx Bombers.

	GP	BA	R	H	HR	RBI	BB	OBP	SA	SB
Bill Dickey, C	130	.327	65	156	6	78	39	.378	.442	2
Lou Gehrig, 1B	155	.341	163	211	46	184	117	.446	.662	17
Lyn Lary, SS	155	.280	100	171	10	107	88	.376	.416	13
Joe Sewell, 3B	130	.302	102	146	6	64	61	.390	.388	1
Ben Chapman, LF	149	.315	120	189	17	122	75	.396	.483	61
Earle Combs, CF	138	.318	120	179	5	58	68	.394	.446	11
Babe Ruth, RF	145	.373	149	199	46	163	128	.495	.700	5

In 1931, Lou Gehrig had the kind of season that defines greatness. He set the all-time American League RBI record of 184 while rapping out over 200 hits, walking over 100 times, and scoring 163 runs. Ruth chipped in with what was his last Ruthian season, posting a .700-plus slugging percentage while scoring and driving home more than 1 run per game. Together Gehrig and Ruth lashed out 172 extra-base hits, including 92 home runs and 347 RBI.

The 1931 Yankees' supporting cast was comprised of players who could get on base. Lyn Lary, "Camera Eye" Joe Sewell (who struck out less than 10 times in nine consecutive seasons), Ben Chapman, and Earle Combs were solid contact or line-drive hitters who could take a pitch. With Gehrig and Ruth in the lineup, all four reached the century mark in runs scored. While both Sewell and Combs were veterans who were reaching the latter stages of extremely consistent careers, both Lary and Chapman were youngsters playing over their heads and contributing more than might have been expected. Bill Dickey was the emerging star on the 1931 Yankees and was establishing himself as one of the top hitting catchers in the major leagues. Later in his career, he would learn to pull the ball and become more of a home run hitter, but in 1931 he was a line-drive hitter.

With the decline of Babe Ruth, the mantle of the best hitting team in baseball briefly passed to the Detroit Tigers, who went to back-to-back World Series in 1934 and 1935. The Tigers of the mid-'30s featured the G-Men—Hall of Famers Hank Greenberg, Charlie Gehringer, and Goose Goslin, who were ably abetted by player-manager Mickey Cochrane. The torch, however, quickly returned to the Yankees in 1936 with the arrival of Joe DiMaggio and the beginning of another dynasty.

1936–39 New York Yankees

Between 1936 and 1939, Joe McCarthy's New York Yankees mixed league-leading pitching and slugging to stroll to four straight American League pennants and World Series championships. The Yankees of the late 1930s were a truly dominant team and never faced a sustained pennant race or a seventh game during their four-year run at the top. The 1936 squad was the best hitting team, scoring 1,065 runs or 6.9 runs per game, the second-highest totals in major league history, which comfortably exceeded the American League runs per game average of 5.7 by 21 percent. The 1936 Yankees dominated their opponents with power, slamming 182 home runs, or 1.2 home runs per game, in a league that averaged half that. The 1936 Yankees' team slugging percentage of .483 is the third-highest in major league history. While the mid-1930s was a high-scoring period, and 1936 in particular was the second–highest-scoring season in major league history, the relative production of the '36 Yankees still places them squarely among the most efficient offensive teams of all time.

	GP	BA	R	H	HR	RBI	BB	OBP	SA	SB
Bill Dickey, c	112	.362	99	153	22	107	46	.428	.617	0
Lou Gehrig, 1b	155	.354	167	205	49	152	130	.478	.696	3
Tony Lazzeri, 2b	150	.287	82	154	14	109	97	.397	.441	8
Frank Crosetti, ss	151	.288	137	182	15	78	90	.387	.437	18
Red Rolfe, 3b	135	.319	116	181	10	70	68	.392	.493	3
Joe DiMaggio, lf	138	.323	132	206	29	125	24	.352	.576	4
George Selkirk, rf	137	.308	93	152	18	107	94	.420	.511	3

The core of the 1936 Yankees was Gehrig, DiMaggio, and Dickey. Gehrig, still untouched by the disease that would claim his life, was a perennial MVP candidate. In 1936, he posted Triple-Crown–type numbers while leading the league in five offensive categories. Joe DiMaggio, who joined the Yankees in 1936 after distinguishing himself in the Pacific Coast League with the San Francisco Seals, was the antidote to the loss of Babe Ruth, immediately establishing himself as one of the top outfielders in the game. Bill Dickey became a power hitter in 1936 when he began to pull the ball in Yankee Stadium, hitting over 20 home runs for the first time in his career—including 18 at Yankee Stadium. The 1936 Yankees' supporting cast of Tony Lazzeri, Frank Crosetti, Red Rolfe, and George Selkirk showed good batting averages, decent slugging percentages, and high on-base percentages, the necessary prerequisites for a successful serial offense. Lazzeri was at the end of his tether as a top-flight player and would not be a contributor over the remaining years of the Yankees' run, while Crosetti, Rolfe, and Selkirk would be strong contributors into the early 1940s. Unlike the Yankees' teams of the Ruth-Gehrig era, the 1936 Yankees had some effective bats coming off the bench, including Jake Powell (.306), Myril Hoag (.301), and pitcher Red Ruffing (.291 and 5 home runs).

An Interlude

With the onset of World War II, major leaguers began to enter military service in large numbers. In 1942, 71 players missed the season as a result of military service. By 1945, 384 players were saving the world from tyranny. With so many of major league baseball's better players serving their country, teams were forced to scramble to fill out their lineups. Youngsters like 15-year-old Joe Nuxhall and over-the-hill veterans like Paul Waner and Jimmie Foxx were forced onto the field to keep the game alive. To make matters worse, the baseballs used during the war years were of inferior quality as critical materials were diverted to the war effort. As such, runs and home runs plummeted, and a low-scoring game more akin to the deadball era became prevalent.

With the end of World War II, many desperately missed major leaguers came back, and the baseball world returned to normal. In the 1950s, as America's economy boomed, major league baseball entered an era of great hitting teams, with the Cleveland Indians, New York Yankees, Brooklyn Dodgers, and Milwaukee Braves assembling intimidating lineups.

1952–54 Cleveland Indians

The Cleveland Indians of the early 1950s are best remembered for their starting rotation of Bob Feller, Bob Lemon, Mike Garcia, and Early Wynn. What is generally forgotten is that the Indians of the time were also an extremely strong hitting team. They played in cavernous Municipal Stadium, which, due to its expansive foul territory, was a strong pitcher's park. Taking that into account, the Indians' offensive statistics, while not as superficially impressive as some other teams', improve under scrutiny. Their best hitting season, however, came not during their 111-win campaign of 1954 but their close second of 1952:

	GP	BA	R	H	HR	RBI	BB	OBP	SA	SB
Luke Easter, 1B	127	.263	63	115	31	97	44	.337	.513	1
Bobby Avila, 2B	150	.300	102	179	7	45	67	.371	.415	12
Al Rosen, 3B	148	.302	101	171	28	105	75	.387	.524	8
Dale Mitchell, LF	134	.323	61	165	5	58	52	.387	.415	6
Larry Doby, CF	140	.276	104	143	32	104	90	.383	.541	5

The key players in the Cleveland offense were Luke Easter, Al Rosen, and Larry Doby. Interestingly, all three were power hitters who for different reasons had relatively short careers, but reached the peak of their abilities at the same time. Easter was a Negro League star who found his way to the major leagues in 1949 at the age of 34. He would have three strong years in the major leagues, hitting 86 home runs and driving in 307 runs between 1950 and 1952, but was gone by 1954. Al Rosen's ascent to the major leagues was delayed by World War II and playing behind third baseman Ken Keltner; he would play only seven seasons when his major league career was ended at 32 due to injuries. Between 1950 and 1954, Rosen won two home run titles, two RBI titles, and came within one hit of winning the Triple Crown in 1953. Larry Doby was the first African-American to play in the American League, joining the Indians during the 1947 season. Doby was a multitalented player who hit for average with power and excellent strike zone judgment. He was a perennial American League All-Star between 1949 and 1955, winning home run titles in 1953 and 1955. But he entered a rapid decline phase in 1957 and was out of baseball by 1959 after only 10 full-time seasons. The other key offensive contributors on the Indians were the table-setter, Bobby Avila, who had his career year during the 111-

win campaign of 1954, batting .341 to lead the league, and Dale Mitchell, who later in his career while playing for the Brooklyn Dodgers would take the most famous called third strike in baseball history.

1949–60 New York Yankees

The New York Yankees, led by the "Old Professor," Casey Stengel, dominated the 1950s, winning eight American League pennants and six World Series championships. The Yankees were at their peak as a hitting team in the first half of the decade with Yogi Berra and Mickey Mantle leading the way; however, under Stengel they were very much a team, not dependent on a few star players. Through the liberal use of platooning and role players, Stengel employed his whole roster to gain situational advantages and wear down opposing teams. This was a new kind of baseball, recalling the use of platooning by John McGraw and George Stallings during Stengel's playing days. The 1953 Yankees were probably the best hitting team during Stengel's years and led the American League in runs scored, batting average, on-base percentage, and slugging percentage. After Berra and Mantle, who hit just below .300 with power, Yankees starters like Gene Woodling, Hank Bauer, Joe Collins, Billy Martin, or Gil McDougald contributed between 10 and 15 home runs with 50 to 80 RBI in 350 to 450 at-bats. This, in combination with the Yankees' extremely strong bench that included Irv Noren, Johnny Mize, Don Bollweg, Bill Renna, and Andy Carey, gave the Yankees an extremely flexible and fearsome hitting lineup.

	GP	BA	R	H	HR	RBI	BB	OBP	SA	SB
Yogi Berra, c	137	.296	80	149	27	108	50	.363	.523	0
Joe Collins, 1B	127	.269	72	104	17	44	59	.365	.439	2
Billy Martin, 2B	149	.257	72	151	15	75	43	.314	.395	6
Gil McDougald, 3B	141	.285	82	154	10	83	60	.361	.415	3
Gene Woodling, LF	125	.306	64	121	10	58	82	.429	.468	2
Mickey Mantle, CF	127	.295	105	136	21	92	79	.398	.497	8
Hank Bauer, RF	133	.304	77	133	10	57	59	.394	.446	2

1949–56 Brooklyn Dodgers

The fruit of Branch Rickey's labor during the 1940s were the Brooklyn Dodgers teams of the 1950s. The Dodgers' slugging lineup that would lead the National League in home runs in every year between 1949 and 1955 was substantially in place by 1949 and remained intact at the top of the National League until 1956. During that period the Dodgers would dominate the National League, winning five pennants and one World Series championship despite mediocre or poor pitching. There is something wistful and tragic about the Boys of Summer and their struggles in the shadow of the wrecking ball, but they were a truly great hitting team and the most identifiable symbol of a city whose day had come and gone. The Dodgers' best season was 1953, when they won the National League pennant by 13 games with a franchise-best 105–49 record. The Dodgers had a perfectly balanced attack that year, leading the National League in batting (.285), home runs (208), and stolen bases (90) en route to scoring 955 runs, or 6.2 runs per game, which exceeded the National League average of 4.75 runs per game by 30 percent.

	GP	BA	R	H	HR	RBI	BB	OBP	SA	SB
Roy Campanella, C	144	.312	103	162	41	142	67	.395	.611	4
Gil Hodges, 1B	141	.302	101	157	31	122	75	.393	.550	1
Jim Gilliam, 2B	151	.278	125	168	6	63	100	.383	.415	21
Pee Wee Reese, SS	135	.271	108	142	13	61	82	.374	.420	22
Carl Furillo, LF	132	.344	82	165	21	92	34	.393	.580	1
Duke Snider, CF	153	.329	132	198	42	126	82	.419	.627	16
Jackie Robinson, RF	136	.329	109	159	12	95	74	.425	.502	17

The depth of the 1953 Brooklyn Dodgers' lineup was astounding. Jim Gilliam, the National League Rookie of the Year in 1953, and Pee Wee Reese were solid contributors at the top of the order with high on-base percentages and good speed. Jackie Robinson showcased his broad-based abilities in 1953, hitting for average with line-drive power and excellent strike zone judgment, making him equally valuable to the Dodgers at the top of the order or in an RBI spot. More than any other player, Robinson symbolized the Dodgers' rise to the top of the National League. By integrating first and more quickly than their competitors, the Dodgers presaged the major leagues of the future. Robinson, by his success, figuratively made room for Roy Campanella, Don Newcombe, and Jim Gilliam to follow. Ironically, Robinson literally made room for Gilliam in 1953 by moving from second base to the outfield so that Gilliam could become an everyday player. The middle of the Dodgers' batting order provided awesome power and production. Roy Campanella, a three-time MVP, was a squat, powerful slugger whose offensive contributions varied widely depending upon his health. Nineteen fifty-three was an "on" year for Campy as he won the National League MVP award while setting then major league standards for home runs and RBI by a catcher. An athletic slugging center fielder, Duke Snider led the major leagues in home runs and RBI during the 1950s and was the Dodgers' answer to Mickey Mantle and Willie Mays. The rapid decline phase of Snider's career due to a bad back has dimmed the public perception of his abilities, but in the mid-'50s he was as good a hitter as anyone could be, slamming 40 home runs in five straight seasons between 1953 and 1957. Gil Hodges, the Dodgers' first baseman, was a consistently outstanding hitter in his own right. Although overshadowed by Campanella and Snider, he drove in more than 100 runs in seven straight seasons between 1949 and 1955 and hit more than 20 home runs in 11 consecutive seasons between 1948 and 1959. The forgotten man in the 1953 Dodgers' lineup was National League batting champion Carl Furillo. Furillo was an aggressive line-drive hitter in the Bill Buckner mold who neither walked nor struck out.

1956–61 Milwaukee Braves

The Milwaukee Braves, who won back-to-back National League pennants in 1957 and 1958, were the top hitting team in the National League between 1956 and 1961. The 1957 Braves led the National League in runs scored, home runs, and slugging percentage despite playing their home games in Milwaukee County Stadium, a ballpark that would reduce runs scored by 3 percent and home runs by 12 percent over its history. The Braves were led by all-time greats Henry Aaron and Eddie Mathews, who combined for 227 runs, 146 extra-base hits (including 76 home runs), and 226 RBI during 1957, with Aaron taking home the National League MVP award. In addition to Aaron's and Mathews's heroics, the Braves received substantial contributions from various platoon or shared positions. At catcher, Del Crandell, Carl Sawatski, and Del Rice combined for 30 home runs and 83 RBI while Frank Torre and Joe Adcock combined for 17 home runs and 78 RBI at first base. In the outfield, the Braves used a smorgasbord of players due to injuries, with Wes Covington (21 home runs in 89 games) and Hurricane Bob Hazle (.403 batting average in 41 games) standing out.

	GP	BA	R	H	HR	RBI	BB	OBP	SA	SB
Del Crandell, c	118	.253	45	97	15	46	30	.309	.410	1
Frank Torre, 1B	129	.272	46	99	5	40	29	.341	.393	0
Joe Adcock, 1B	65	.287	31	60	12	38	20	.352	.541	0
Red Schoendienst, 2B	93	.310	56	122*	6	32	23	.345	.434	2
Eddie Mathews, 3B	148	.292	109	167	32	94	90	.388	.540	5
Wes Covington, LF	96	.284	51	93	21	65	29	.345	.537	4
Hank Aaron, RF	151	.322	118	198	44	132	57	.379	.600	1

* Joined Braves during season from Giants. Led NL in hits with 200.

1961 New York Yankees

With the advent of the 1960s, expansion came to major league baseball and home runs climbed. The 1961 Yankees, led by the "M&M Boys," slammed 240 roundtrippers to set an all-time single season team home run mark. Roger Maris and Mickey

Mantle combined for 115 home runs, with Maris breaking Ruth's record by slamming 61. Four other Yankees—Moose Skowron, Yogi Berra, Elston Howard, and Johnny Blanchard—topped the 20-homer mark to give the Yankees broad-based power. Nineteen sixty-one was a high-scoring season, with the American League averaging 4.5 runs per game. The 1961 Yankees are considered by some to be the greatest hitting team in history, but they only outscored the American League average by 12 percent and did not even lead the American League in scoring. That honor went to the Detroit Tigers, who received a couple of career years of their own from Norm Cash and Rocky Colavito.

	GP	BA	R	H	HR	RBI	BB	OBP	SA	SB
Elston Howard, C	129	.348	64	155	21	77	28	.390	.549	0
Bill Skowron, 1B	150	.267	76	150	28	89	35	.320	.472	0
Tony Kubek, SS	153	.276	84	170	8	46	27	.307	.395	1
Yogi Berra, LF	119	.271	62	107	22	61	35	.333	.466	2
Mickey Mantle, CF	153	.317	132	163	54	128	126	.452	.687	12
Roger Maris, RF	161	.269	132	159	61	142	94	.376	.620	0
Johnny Blanchard, UT	93	.305	38	74	21	54	27	.383	.613	1

1969–71 Baltimore Orioles

After the 1962 season, the size of the strike zone was increased and batting averages and home runs plummeted, reaching a nadir in 1968. With hits hard to come by, the power game became the only workable strategy, and several teams topped the 200-homer mark, including the 1963 and 1964 Minnesota Twins and the 1966 Atlanta Braves. The strike zone was returned to its previous size after the 1968 season, and although batting averages did not return to previous levels, they did improve. The Baltimore Orioles stepped into the void as the top hitting team in baseball between 1969 and 1971, winning three straight American League pennants and a World Series championship. The Orioles of the late 1960s and early 1970s were known for their pitching and defense but were also a potent hitting team, building offense around walks and home runs (or, as Earl Weaver said, "a hit, a walk, and a three-run home run"). The 1971 team was the best hitting squad, leading the American League in runs, batting average, and on-base percentage. The 1971 Orioles scored 742 runs, or 4.7 runs per game—it sounds low, but that exceeded the American League average of 3.9 runs per game by 21 percent. The main men for the Birds were Boog Powell, Brooks Robinson, and Frank Robinson, who each hit over 20 home runs and drove in more than 90 runs in what was an extremely low-scoring season. The spark at the top of the order was provided by Don Buford and Merv Rettunmund, who were numbers 4 and 2, respectively, in on-base percentage in the American League and combined for 180 runs.

	GP	BA	R	H	HR	RBI	BB	OBP	SA	SB
Boog Powell, 1B	128	.256	59	107	22	92	82	.383	.459	1
Davey Johnson, 2B	142	.282	67	144	18	72	51	.353	.443	3
Brooks Robinson, 3B	156	.272	67	160	20	92	63	.345	.413	0
Don Buford, LF	122	.290	99	130	19	54	89	.415	.477	15
Merv Rettunmund, RF	141	.318	81	156	11	75	87	.424	.448	15
Frank Robinson, UT	133	.287	82	128	28	99	72	.390	.516	3

WORST HITTING TEAM OF THE NINETEENTH CENTURY

The worst hitting team of the nineteenth century was the American Association's 1886 Baltimore Orioles, who posted an execrable .204 team batting average and nosed out the National League's 1888 Washington Nationals, who stung the ball at a .208 clip. The Orioles were one of the weaker franchises in the American Association and had played the doormat in the 1882, 1883, and 1885 seasons. As may be expected of a team hitting as poorly as the Orioles did in 1886, their lineup was a revolving door, with only four players appearing in over 100 games.

	GP	BA	R	H	HR	RBI	BB	OBP	SA	SB
Joe Sommers, LF	139	.209	79	117	1	52	24	.245	.261	31
Jack Manning, RF	137	.223	78	124	1	45	50	.291	.286	24
Milt Scott, 1B	137	.190	48	92	2	52	22	.239	.242	11
Mike Muldoon, 2B	101	.199	57	76	0	23	34	.269	.276	12

Of Baltimore's four regulars, three would not play in the majors again after the 1886 season, with only Joe Sommers struggling on through five more seasons of mediocre play. Jack Manning was the team's most consistent player and may be the only player in baseball history to be cut loose after leading his team in batting, hits, doubles, bases on balls, on-base percentage, and slugging percentage. Manager Billy Barnie would try numerous players at other positions over the course of the season, but none would hit with the consistency of his "big four."

The Orioles finished in last place during 1886 with a 48–83 record, but their pitching was quite respectable, with Matt Kilroy carrying the load. Kilroy, who started 68 games that year, posted a 29–34 record with a 3.37 ERA and set an all-time major league record, racking up 513 strikeouts. In 1887, the Orioles would make wholesale changes to their starting lineup, vaulting to third place in the American Association and beginning the climb that would see them become one of the dominant teams of the National League.

1975–76 Cincinnati Reds

The Cincinnati Reds team of the mid-1970s was the offensive juggernaut of the decade. Never a deep hitting team, the Reds won back-to-back World Series championships in 1975 and 1976 by assembling perhaps the best top of the order in the history of baseball. The Reds reached their peak in 1976 when they led the National League in runs, hits, doubles, triples, home runs, batting average, walks, on-base percentage, and slugging percentage en route to a 102–60 record. The 1976 Reds scored 857 runs, or 5.3 runs per game, in a low-scoring season and dwarfed the 1976 National League average of 4.0 runs per game by 33 percent. When taking into account the time and place in which they played, this is the greatest offensive team after the New York Yankees' squads of Babe Ruth and Lou Gehrig.

	GP	BA	R	H	HR	RBI	BB	OBP	SA	SB
Johnny Bench, c	135	.234	62	109	16	74	81	.350	.394	13
Tony Perez, 1B	139	.260	77	137	19	91	50	.330	.452	10
Joe Morgan, 2B	141	.320	113	151	27	111	114	.453	.576	60
Pete Rose, 3B	162	.323	130	215	10	63	86	.406	.450	9
George Foster, LF	144	.306	86	172	29	121	52	.369	.530	17
Ken Griffey Sr., RF	148	.336	111	189	6	74	62	.403	.450	34

The table-setters for the 1976 Reds were Pete Rose and Ken Griffey Sr. Rose, baseball's all-time hits leader and one of the game's most intense competitors, led off. Griffey, with his speed and spray-hitting style, was the quintessential artificial turf player and well suited to the National League's multipurpose mausoleums. "Little Joe" Morgan, who won back-to-back MVP awards in 1975 and 1976, was the straw that stirred the drink for the Reds. Only 5′7″, Morgan was an intense competitor who brought a unique combination of speed (60 stolen bases), power (27 home runs), and strike zone judgment (114 walks) to the game. Morgan put pressure on the pitcher and fielders whenever he came to the plate. The Reds' RBI men were Tony Perez, George Foster, and Johnny Bench. Tony Perez, the Reds' cleanup hitter, was a consistent RBI man in the Joe Carter mold with a well-deserved reputation as a clutch hitter. He drove in 90 or more runs in 11 consecutive seasons between 1967 and 1977. With his black bat and glowering manner, George Foster was an intimidating pres-

No hitter in baseball history worked harder at his craft than Pete Rose.

ence at the plate. He reached the pinnacle of his career between 1976 and 1978 when he hit 121 home runs and drove in 390 runs, leading the National League in home runs twice and RBI three times and winning the MVP award in 1977. Johnny Bench, a two-time MVP who drove in over 100 runs on six occasions in his career, had a disappointing season in 1976 but still provided decent run production. The remainder of the Reds' everyday lineup, Dave Concepcion and Cesar Geronimo, played regularly due to their defensive prowess—however, both had good years offensively in 1976, with Concepcion batting .281 and Geronimo .307. The Reds' bench was weak, providing little offensive support on the rare occasions that manager Sparky Anderson allowed them between the white lines.

1980–83 Milwaukee Brewers

As the 1970s came to an end, another great hitting team returned to Milwaukee, as the Brewers assembled a team of free-swinging sluggers that hearkened back to the Braves' teams of the late 1950s. Ultimately known as "Harvey's Wallbangers" after one of their managers, Harvey Kuenn, the Brewers' teams between 1980 and 1983 lived by the long ball, hitting over 200 home runs in both 1980 and 1982 despite playing in a pitcher's park. In 1980, the Brewers hit only 90 of their 203 home runs at Milwaukee County Stadium, while in 1982 they hit only 89 of 216 home runs at home. Harvey's Wallbangers got their name in 1982, posting a 95–67 record and winning the American League pennant. The 1982 Brewers lost the World Series championship to Whitey Herzog's run-and-gun St. Louis Cardinals in one of baseball's starkest philosophical confrontations.

	GP	BA	R	H	HR	RBI	BB	OBP	SA	SB
Ted Simmons, C	137	.269	73	145	23	97	32	.312	.451	0
Cecil Cooper, 1B	155	.313	104	205	32	121	32	.345	.528	2
Robin Yount, SS	156	.331	129	210	29	114	54	.384	.578	14
Paul Molitor, 3B	160	.302	136	201	19	71	69	.368	.450	41
Ben Ogilvie, LF	159	.244	92	147	34	102	70	.327	.453	3
Gorman Thomas, CF	158	.245	96	139	39	112	84	.349	.506	3

The top of the 1982 Brewers' lineup featured two Hall of Famers, Paul Molitor and Robin Yount. Molitor, number 8 on the all-time hit list with 3,319 career hits, was a complete hitter, combining a high batting average and line-drive power with speed and baserunning savvy. Molitor's 1982 season was typical of his career, and in fact matches up almost identically with his career batting average (.306), on-base percentage (.372), and slugging percentage (.448). Yount, the American League MVP in 1982 and 1989, was the captain and team leader. A career 3,000-hit man, Yount hit for average with boatloads of extra-base hits. Although he was a good RBI man and clutch hitter, Yount's primary role in the Brewers offense was to score runs, which he did successfully, scoring over 100 runs in every full major league season between 1980 and 1984. Cecil Cooper was a high-average slugger who put the ball in play. Cooper combined a Rod Carew approach to plate coverage with a Hank Aaron approach to inside pitches. The muscle men for the 1982 Brewers were Gorman Thomas and Ben Ogilvie. Thomas, a two-time American League home run champion, was a star pupil from the Dave Kingman "swing hard you might just hit something" school of hitting, but exhibited a little better strike zone judgment than the Master. Ogilvie, a tall, thin left-handed batter, was another hard swinger who briefly flourished as a top-flight power threat between 1980 and 1982, winning the American League home run title in 1980. Almost lost in the 1982 Brewers' wealth was Ted Simmons, one of the top hitting catchers in major league history. Simmons's contribution in 1982 was typical of his career, in which he hit over 20 home runs on six occasions and drove in over 90 runs eight times. The 1982 Brewers also received a strong contribution from a platoon arrangement at designated hitter, with Don Money and Roy Howell combining for 20 home runs and 93 RBI.

1985–88 New York Mets

The 1980s was a pitcher's decade. With the exception of 1987, when an extraordinary heat wave in the eastern and central U.S. increased home runs, major league runs per game average hovered around the 4.3 mark, with the National League average being significantly lower. Between 1985 and 1988, the New York Mets were the league's best hitting team, winning the National League East crown in 1986 and 1988 and finishing second to Whitey Herzog's speedy St. Louis Cardinals in 1985 and 1987. Playing in a pitcher's era in a pitcher's park, the Mets' hitting statistics look very ordinary. When they are adjusted for the effect of playing in Shea Stadium half the time and normalized for the league average, the lie is exposed. The 1985 to 1988 Mets were an excellent hitting team who, despite the reputation of their pitching staff (which included such greats as Dwight Gooden and David Cone), won many more games because of their hitting than as a result of pitching. The Mets had their best hitting season in 1988 when they led the National League in runs scored with 703, or 4.3 runs per game, which outdistanced the National League average by 13 percent.

	GP	BA	R	H	HR	RBI	BB	OBP	SA	SB
Mookie Wilson, OF	112	.296	61	112	8	41	27	.346	.431	15
Lenny Dykstra, CF	126	.270	57	116	8	35	30	.323	.385	30
Kevin McReynolds, LF	147	.288	82	159	27	99	38	.338	.496	21
Darryl Strawberry, RF	153	.269	101	146	39	101	85	.371	.545	29
Howard Johnson, 3B	148	.230	85	114	24	68	86	.348	.422	23

The 1988 Mets were a mix of old and young players, and manager Davey Johnson was forced to use his whole roster. Gary Carter and Keith Hernandez, the aging superstars who had played significant roles in the 1986 World Series championship, were both at the end of the line. Carter, in his last full-time season, caught 119 games but batted only .242 with 11 home runs, while Hernandez could manage only 93 games at first base and a .276 batting average. The players who propelled the 1988 Mets' offense were Howard Johnson, Kevin McReynolds, and Darryl Strawberry. Notwithstanding his low batting average, Hojo was a strong offensive player with home run power, good strike zone judgment, and speed. He was one of the top offensive players in the National League between 1987 and 1991—so good that Whitey Herzog regularly had his bat checked for cork. Kevin McReynolds, whose career eventually collapsed almost as quickly as Hojo's, was not as multi-talented but was a consistent 25-homer, 80- to 90-RBI man between 1986 and 1990 and a key performer during the Mets' run. Darryl Strawberry was the Mets' bona fide superstar. Touted as a savior upon his signing as a teenager, he provided the Mets with awesome power and production. In its context, his 1988 season was all-world—and although he came in second in the MVP voting, he would have been a deserving winner.

Keith Hernandez and the New York Mets perfectly meshed youth and experience to win the World Series in 1986.

EIGHTY-SIXED METS

The 1986 Mets were not the beginning of the dynasty many expected them to be. The unraveling of the franchise began in Game 4 of the 1988 NLCS, when Mike Scioscia's home run in the ninth inning off Dwight Gooden tied up what should have been a Mets victory and a 3–1 lead in games. The Mets eventually lost the series in seven. Looking back, with only one championship to show for their efforts, it is hard to overstate how disappointing the Mets of the late '80s really were. In many ways, in fact, it was unprecedented.

One must approach a season resigned to the fact that the best team will lose one-third of its games and the worst team will win one-third of its games. It's in that middle one-third that the success or failure of the season plays out. If so, the '86 Mets were as successful as a team can get. They ran the table in that middle third, racking up 108 wins and a .666 winning percentage. In the modern era, only 19 teams have ever won two-thirds of their games: the '98 Yankees, the '95 Indians, '86 Mets, '75 Reds, '69–70 Orioles, '61 Yankees, '54 Indians, '54 Yankees, '53 Dodgers, '46 Red Sox, '42–44 Cardinals, '39 Yankees, '32 Yankees, '31 Athletics, '29 Athletics, and '27 Yankees.

Unlike all but the '54 Indians, '46 Red Sox, and '31 Athletics, the Mets did not return to the World Series within four years. The Red Sox had to wait 31 years, the Athletics and Indians 41 years. Forty-one? The Mets better hope that's not a tradition.

The 1954 Indians won 111 games, the modern record, but were an old team that overachieved. The 1946 Red Sox were even older than the 1954 Indians, lost their first of four Game 7 tragedies, then went on to lose to the Indians in a one-game playoff in 1948, lose the pennant to the Yankees on the last game of the season in 1949, and finish 4 games out in 1950 despite a .302 team batting average. The 1931 Athletics went to their third World Series in a row, and featured five Hall of Famers, young or in their prime—all eventually sold off along with the rest of the pitching staff and starting lineup for half a million bucks, a depression-induced fire sale that sent the team into a four-decade tailspin.

The 1986 Mets can't blame old age for their difficulties. Among this select group of 19 teams that won two-thirds of its games, the Mets were by far the youngest. In fact, their pitching staff (with an average age of 26)—led by Dwight Gooden (21), Sid Fernandez (23), Rick Aguilera (24), Ron Darling (25), and Roger McDowell (25)—was among the youngest ever to win a World Series. Only five other teams have won it all with a staff as young (the '81 Dodgers, '69 Mets, '63 Dodgers, '55 Dodgers, and '42 Cardinals), and you have to go back to the 1918 Red Sox and a 23-year-old lefty named Babe Ruth to find a younger championship staff.

The 1986 Mets also can't blame Bostonian bad luck in the years after their 108-win season. More like New York overconfidence. They lost the division in 1987 to a Cardinals team that didn't have a 12-game winner and whose only .300 hitter was Ozzie Smith. They lost in the playoffs in 1988 to Orel Hershiser and a Dodgers team that hit .210 and featured Mickey Hatcher, Alfredo Griffin, Jeff Hamilton, and John Shelby prominently in their offense.

By most accounts, the '86 Mets can blame much of their underachievement on hard living—and not just from Darryl Strawberry and Doc Gooden. Many insiders have suggested that as much as half of the team was partying out of bounds. Whether this was the reason the Mets were broken up so quickly, only GM Frank Cashen knows for sure. But only the '86 Mets and '31 Athletics had none of their eight starting position players remaining five years later. By 1991, the Mets were in fifth place and only Doc, Sid, and former bench player Howard Johnson were left from the championship team.

The suits did their part to wreck this team by making a series of astonishingly bad personnel decisions. Fearing that Kevin Mitchell would be a "bad influence" on Darryl and Doc, they traded him for "foundation player" Kevin McReynolds. McReynolds was a good ballplayer, but he also happened to be a country boy who couldn't abide NYC. Hustling second baseman Wally Backman was forced out after the 1988 season to make room for an immature phenom named Gregg Jefferies, who popped up and pouted frequently, and had his game bats sawed in half by his teammates. Despite a crying need for punch in their lineup, the Mets' big move in midseason 1989 was to acquire Frank Viola in a deal that cost them Rick Aguilera and Kevin Tapani. That same year, unable to decide between Lenny Dykstra and Mookie Wilson in center field, the Mets dumped both of them—Mookie to the Blue Jays for Jeff Musselman, and Jefferies's two biggest tormentors, Dykstra and McDowell, to the Phillies for Juan Samuel.

As bad as the Samuel deal was, the Mets only made it worse by playing him out of position in center field for a few months, then dealing him to the Dodgers after the season for Mike Marshall, one of the biggest dogs to ever play the game. Marshall lasted 53 games before they then dumped him on the Red Sox for a bag of used baseballs.

Gary Carter and Keith Hernandez were allowed to leave and decay elsewhere, but there was no one left to fill their leadership roles, and Dave Magadan and Mackey Sasser—a catcher who had a mental block about throwing the ball back to the pitcher— were the best they could come up with to fill their positions. They let Darryl Strawberry go free agent after the '90 season, and spent the money they saved on Vince Coleman— whose time in New York was highlighted by throwing a firecracker at a child, hitting Dwight Gooden while swinging a golf club in the locker room, and complaining that the Shea Stadium infield was keeping him out of the Hall of Fame. To round things out, they got nothing for Bob Ojeda and Sid Fernandez, and, because they waited so long for Ron Darling to reestablish himself, next to nothing for him.

By 1991, half of their starting lineup was playing out of position. After clearing out the guts of the ballclub—Backman, Dykstra, McDowell, and Mitchell—to make room for McReynolds and Jefferies, both were given up on and dealt to Kansas City for Bret Saberhagen before the 1992 season. By 1993, the Mets would be the worst team in baseball—and if not for the emergence of Randy Myers, the evolution of Howard Johnson, and the grand larceny of Ed Hearn for David Cone, it would have been an even swifter and steeper fall.

Though these personnel moves were a slow-motion train wreck—bad enough to turn a 100-win team to a 100-loss team in five years—it can't be overlooked that many of the players on the '86 team have proven to be among the most self-destructive in baseball.

Dykstra, Darryl, Doc, Mitchell, and Ojeda have had dark clouds following them for the past 13 years. No problem. There's a lot of blame to go around for the eighty-sixed Mets: to many of the players for wasting their gifts, and to a front office that panicked, dismantling one of the greatest teams in baseball history almost as quickly as they built it. There have been almost as many fingers pointing at one another in Flushing as there were in the '86 Red Sox clubhouse after Game 6.

But don't be surprised if it turns out that the biggest dark cloud to emerge from all this waste is the one that will hang over this franchise for, say, the next 41 years. 41. Tom Seaver's number. Nice touch.

Mets in '27. You heard it here first.

1990s

Beginning in 1993, not so coincidentally the year that the Colorado Rockies entered the National League, an upsurge in offense began that has carried through the remainder of the decade, putting the 1990s on an equal footing with the late 1920s and early 1930s as one of the greatest hitter's eras in major league history. This upsurge has been based on the home run, which has increased to historically high levels of frequency. While overall hitting has increased and individual players have excelled during the 1990s, the major leagues have not seen one clearly dominant hitting team. The 1993 Philadelphia Phillies with Lenny Dykstra, John Kruk, and Darren Daulton, who combined power with patience to win the National League pennant, are notable. The strike-shortened 1994 season saw both the Houston Astros and New York Yankees post fabulous offensive numbers. The Astros were almost a one-man show propelled by Jeff Bagwell's awesome .750 slugging percentage, while the Yankees fielded an enormously deep lineup with Don Mattingly, Wade Boggs, Paul O'Neill, Bernie Williams, Mike Stanley, Danny Tartabull, and Jim Leyritz either getting on base or hitting home runs.

The top hitting team of the 1990s has been the Seattle Mariners, who in 1998 became the first team to hit 200 or more home runs in three consecutive seasons. In 1997, the Mariners had probably their best season, striking a major league single-season record 264 home runs while posting the decade's best production even after taking into account their hitter's park.

	GP	BA	R	H	HR	RBI	BB	OBP	SA	SB
Paul Sorrento, 1B	146	.269	68	123	31	80	51	.346	.514	0
Joey Cora, 2B	149	.300	105	172	11	54	53	.364	.441	6
Alex Rodriguez, SS	141	.300	100	176	23	84	41	.351	.496	29
Ken Griffey Jr., CF	157	.304	125	185	56	147	76	.389	.646	15
Jay Buhner, RF	157	.243	104	131	40	109	119	.384	.506	0
Edgar Martinez, DH	155	.330	104	179	28	108	119	.460	.554	2

The top dog in the 1997 Mariners' offense was center fielder Ken Griffey Jr., who led the American League in runs, home runs, RBI, and slugging percentage en route to winning the MVP award. Griffey, who was significantly ahead of Henry Aaron's career home run pace at the end of the 1999 season, is the full offensive package, hitting for average, hitting for power, and running well.

The key supporting players in the 1997 Mariners' lineup were Edgar Martinez, Jay Buhner, Alex Rodriguez, and Paul Sorrento. Martinez, who usually batted in front of Griffey, was an extraordinary offensive player in 1997, batting over .300 with excellent strike zone judgment and good power. These numbers are completely consistent with his performance since converting to a full-time designated hitter in 1995 and mark him as one of the top offensive players in the game.

Jay Buhner, a "grip it and rip it" slugger, hit over 20 home runs in every season between 1991 and 1997 and had one of his strongest seasons in 1997. Buhner received an extraordinary number of walks (in the context of his career numbers) during 1997, suggesting that other teams were pitching around him to get to the bottom of the order.

Lenny Dykstra was the main spark plug for the 1993 Philadelphia Phillies, leading the National League in hits (194), walks (129), and runs scored (143).

Alex Rodriguez and Paul Sorrento made similar contributions to the 1997 Mariners; however, Rodriguez made his contribution while struggling through a sophomore jinx while Sorrento made his by having the best season of his career. Rodriguez, a can't-miss phenom, made a big splash in 1996, his first full season, winning the American League batting title while batting .358 with 36 home runs and 123 RBI. With a Griffey-like skill set, Rodriguez's 1997 season, while splendid, was below expectations. Sorrento, who had been used primarily as a platoon player during his years with Minnesota and Cleveland, was given a chance to play full-time by the Mariners and responded positively.

Whether the major leagues will ever again see dominant hitting teams like the New York Yankees of the Ruth-Gehrig era or the Brooklyn Dodgers of the early 1950s remains to be seen. Unprecedented player movement due to free agency and the dispersion of talent among 30 major league teams argue against it. Perhaps an improving competitive balance is at work, with teams drafting players from all parts of the world and pushing the quality of play higher and higher. On the other hand, the "have and have-not" phenomenon of the big-market and small-market teams argues that a competitive imbalance could develop whereby some big-market club might be able to assemble a truly formidable hitting team. As with most open questions involving baseball, the best course of action is to stay tuned.

200-HOMER CLUB

Number of Teams by Decade with 200 Home Runs

1900–09: 0	1940–49: 1	1980–89: 9
1910–19: 0	1950–59: 3	1990–99: 33
1920–29: 0	1960–69: 6	
1930–39: 0	1970–79: 3	

The 200-homer club tells the story of the rise of slugging as the predominant offensive strategy. Prior to the rule changes of 1919 and 1920, teams were constrained by the quality of game baseballs and the preferred style of hitting. The 1913 Philadelphia Phillies, led by Gavvy Cravath and Fred Luderus playing in the friendly confines of the Baker Bowl, set the deadball-era record for home runs at a paltry 73.

The high league batting averages of the 1920s and 1930s allowed serial offenses to flourish and biased player selection toward contact hitters who put the ball in play. By the mid-'20s, most teams would include sluggers but were unlikely to go more than two deep in players who could consistently hit the long ball. So while the Yankees had Ruth and Gehrig and the Athletics had Foxx and Simmons, the remainder of their respective lineups, while including many fine hitters, did not contain a legitimate home run threat.

1927 Yankees	HR	% of Team	1930 Athletics	HR	% of Team
Babe Ruth	60	38.0	Jimmie Foxx	37	29.6
Lou Gehrig	47	29.8	Al Simmons	36	28.8
Other starters	44	27.8	Other starters	41	32.8
Bench	7	4.4	Bench	11	8.8
	158	100.0		125	100.0

The major leagues of the 1920s and 1930s were not ready for low-average sluggers, and as such teams did not have the depth necessary to hit 200 home runs. Only the teams' top hitters would swing for the downs, while the remainder of the lineup was comprised of contact hitters. This prejudice may help to explain why the slow-footed Joe Hauser, after belting 16 home runs in 300 at-bats during 1928, was basically waived out of the majors even though there was little doubt that he could contribute at the plate. The 1938 Yankees were the first team to show significant power depth with five players contributing over 20 home runs—Lou Gehrig (29), Joe Gordon (25), Tommy Heinrich (22), Joe DiMaggio (32), and Bill Dickey (27).

Home runs increased steadily through the 1930s and 1940s with a five-year hiatus for World War II, when home runs declined due to loss of talent and to lower-quality base-balls. With the return of the major leaguers from military service, home runs began to increase while, perhaps more important, batting averages began to plummet. League batting averages that had stood in the .280s and .290s during the 1920s reached the .260s by the end of the 1940s. With batting averages falling, serial offenses became more and more difficult to sustain and the major leagues began to draft hard-swinging power hitters.

The 1947 New York Giants, led by Johnny Mize, Willard Marshall, Walker Cooper, and Bobby Thomson, were the first team to break the 200-homer barrier, swatting 221 roundtrippers. This total was primarily attributable to the Giants' home park—the peculiarly shaped Polo Grounds—and a cluster of career years among the Giants' key sluggers. During its history, the Polo Grounds increased home runs by approximately 70 percent over a neutral park, and in most seasons the Giants hit substantially more home runs at the Polo Grounds than they did on the road. The 1947 season was true to form, with the Giants ripping 131 (59 percent) of their 221 home runs at the Polo Grounds. What was different in 1947, however, was that three players in the middle of the Giants' batting order experienced career years in the same season. The Big Cat, Johnny Mize, hit a career-high 51 home runs, while both Willard Marshall and Walker Cooper had completely out-of-context seasons, hitting 36 and 35 home runs, respectively. In his 10-year career, Marshall would never hit more than 17 home runs in any other season, while Cooper would never manage more than 20 during his 16-year career. "The Flying Scot," Bobby Thomson, who would hit 25 or more home runs on five occasions during his Giants career, had one of his better seasons, chipping in with 29 home runs. In 1948, the Giants would manage "only" 164 roundtrippers as its big four fell back to earth, managing only 86 home runs compared to the 151 they hit in 1947.

Home runs continued to increase through the 1950s as the mighty Brooklyn Dodgers' teams featuring Duke Snider, Roy Campanella, and Gil Hodges exceeded 200 dingers in both 1953 and 1955, while the 1956 Cincinnati Reds led by Frank Robinson, Ted Kluszewski, and Wally Post matched the 1947 Giants' mark of 221 roundtrippers.

The slugging ethos reached a peak in the American League expansion season of 1961 when the two circuits slammed 2,730 home runs, an increase of 602 home runs (28.3 percent) over the 1960 season. The major league home run per game average reached a record 0.95 in 1961, a number that would not be matched until 1987. This increase in home runs is partially attributable to expansion, but was also assisted by the addition of two strong hitter's parks to the American League, Wrigley Field in Los Angeles and Metropolitan Stadium in Minneapolis. Wrigley Field in Los Angeles, which was the site of 248 home runs during the 1961 season, is particularly notable because of its extremely short power alleys in both left-center and right-center. The 1961 New York Yankees took advantage of these factors to slam 240 home runs, setting a team single-season home run record. The 1961 Bombers were powered by the greatest 1-2 home run combination in major league history, Roger Maris and Mickey Mantle, who combined for 115 home runs; and by substantial power depth with four other players exceeding 20 home runs, including Moose Skowron (28), Yogi Berra (22), Elston Howard (21), and Johnny Blanchard (21).

With the rule changes of 1962 and 1963, the pitchers came to dominate through the 1960s and 1970s, and home runs declined. The primary offensive strategy through this period, especially in the American League, continued to be slugging, and teams playing in strong hitter's parks, such as the Minnesota Twins, the Atlanta Braves, or the Boston Red Sox, reached the 200-homer plateau on occasion. The most notable team to hit 200 roundtrippers during this period was the 1973 Atlanta Braves, the first team to have three players with 40 or more home runs—including Davey Johnson with 43, Darrell Evans with 41, and Hank Aaron with 40.

The first 200-homer club of the 1980s was the Milwaukee Brewers, who became known as Harvey's Wallbangers after their manager, Harvey Kuenn. The Brewers of the early 1980s were enormously deep, with five genuine home run threats—including Gorman Thomas, Ben Ogilvie, Cecil Cooper, Robin Yount, and Ted Simmons, ably supported by line-drive hitter Paul Molitor and supersub Don Money. This depth allowed the Brewers to hit more than 200 home runs on two occasions, 1980 and 1982, when they stroked 203 and 216, respectively. Harvey's Wallbangers are notable as the first team to hit over 200 home runs while playing in a poor home run park. In 1980, the Brewers hit 113 (56 percent) of their home runs on the road, while in 1982 they hit 127 (59 percent) on the road.

Home runs per game spiked upward between 1985 and 1987, reaching an unprecedented level of 1.06 in 1987. This accelerated upward movement is attributed to an informal lowering and widening of the strike zone that created a period of adjustment in which the hitters dominated. The 1987 season was the denouement of this home run explosion, with five teams surpassing the 200-homer mark. In 1988, home runs per game plummeted to 1984 levels, and an equilibrium between the pitchers and hitters was reestablished.

Since the strike season of 1994, home runs have risen to 1987 levels and have remained there ever since with home runs per game exceeding 1.00 in every year. The reasons for this prolonged increase in home runs are many, including expansion in 1993 and 1998, strong trends in stadium architecture favoring home run hitters, improved strength and conditioning of players, the use of smaller and lighter bats to generate increased bat speed, and the adjustment of hitters to become low-ball hitters and drive low pitches with authority. Under these conditions, the 200-homer club has become commonplace, with 33 teams exceeding 200 home runs since 1994.

With so many teams hitting 200-plus home runs, the all-time single-season team record for home runs has been in real jeopardy in every season since 1994. During 1996, three teams passed the 1961 Yankees, with the Baltimore Orioles setting the pace. Baltimore was led by Brady Anderson, who had one of the most extreme career seasons in major league history, slamming 50 home runs. The Orioles fielded an extremely deep lineup that featured six other players with 20 or more home runs: Rafael Palmeiro, Bobby Bonilla, Chris Hoiles, Cal Ripken, Roberto Alomar, and B. J. Surhoff. The Seattle Mariners, who slammed 245 homers, and the Oakland Athletics, with 243 roundtrippers, were close runners-up to Baltimore in the 1996 season, which featured eight clubs with over 200 home runs. The 1996 Baltimore Orioles all-time single-season home run record was short-lived, as the Seattle Mariners, led by Ken Griffey Jr. and Jay Buhner, surpassed it with 264 home runs in 1997.

Needless to say, the all-time team home run record will remain in permanent jeopardy for the foreseeable future while the *SportsCenter* hit-it-and-watch-it-go era of baseball continues.

4

Greatest Hitting Moments— Regular Season

When you consider that more than 150,000 regular-season major league games have been played during the twentieth century, it becomes extraordinarily difficult to narrow the list of great hitting moments to a manageable number. How to define the greatest? The unexpected home run, or the legend-affirming one? The accumulation of previously unreached statistics, or the determination of a season-long pennant race? The Hollywood ending, or a farewell less scripted and more wrenching?

With the greatest weight given to drama, significance, and grace under pressure, what follows are not the greatest hitting records, but greatest *moments*—a few days' work at most, or at times just one swing of the bat.

This list begins with the end of the line for the game's two greatest hitters, touches on some moments that transformed superstars into legends, passes through the season-turning or record-breaking games that defined the careers of some of baseball's biggest names, and ends with the most dramatic and climactic home runs ever hit.

Farewells

September 26, 1960

"Gods do not answer letters."

—JOHN UPDIKE ON TED WILLIAMS

It was the last game at Fenway Park for **Ted Williams** after 19 seasons with the Red Sox. The weather was foul—dark, cold, and wet—appropriate, given the tempestuous nature of Williams's time in Boston. It had been a strained relationship between "the Kid" and the press, which he held in contempt and blamed for turning the fans against him. For many of the writers who covered the team, Williams was fair game—everything from his love for his mother and his country was considered "in play." When they weren't pressing those buttons, they were downplaying his remarkable achievements; offering backhanded compliments about his exploits in the All-Star Game while deriding his late-season performance under pressure; berating him for not tipping his cap to the fans; accusing him of being a one-dimensional and selfish player who would rather go 4 for 4 and lose, who once spit at the press box after a home run, and who once threw up his hands in disgust when receiving a bases-loaded walk to win a game. Not all of that was untrue, but in retrospect it appeared that Williams's greatest weakness as a player may have been his penchant for reading everything written about him.

In the clubhouse before the game, Williams was his typical irascible self. On the field, his number was retired and he said a few words—which included a few jabs at the "knights of the keyboard" in the press box and a "thank you" to the fans, though only 10,454 showed up. Coming off a good year for most 42-year-olds, but well below Williams's standards, he had returned in 1960 to hit a 500-foot home run in his first at-bat of the season to enter the 500-homer club and to hit a home run off Don Lee, the son of a man he'd taken deep in 1940. Though no one else knew it then, he had already told his manager that he wouldn't be accompanying the team to their final three games in Yankee Stadium, having come close to throwing in his cards several times already that season. The 1960 Red Sox were one of the worst teams he'd ever played for—second to last, going through three managers, and now 30 games off the pace. His protection in the order in his final game: cleanup-hitting catcher Jim Pagliaroni.

The Orioles were throwing young left-hander Steve Barber at the Red Sox. In the first, he walked Williams on four pitches to a chorus of boos, but he wasn't around for the next at-bat. Against Jack Fisher in the third, Williams drove one to deep center, but it stayed in the park. Then in the fifth, he hit one 400 feet toward the bullpen in right field, where Al Pilarcik caught it up against the wall. The balls weren't carrying in the gloomy conditions, and Williams went back to the dugout muttering to himself.

The lights were on by the time Williams came to bat in the eighth inning. The few fans on hand rose to their feet to offer one last ovation. Fisher missed with his first pitch, then Williams swung and missed at a high fastball. Fisher challenged him with another fastball, and Williams deposited it in the bullpen in right-center. No dropping the bat and watching. No high-fives from his opponents. No curtain call. Not even the tip of a cap or a smile. Around the bases, head down, and back into the dugout, ignoring the pleas of the fans, teammates, and even the first-base umpire to come back out to acknowledge the cheers.

Manager Pinky Higgins tricked Williams into giving the fans one last look at a hitter the likes of which they would never see again. He sent Williams to left field in the ninth just so that Carroll Hardy could be sent out moments later to replace him. On his way back in, the legend stood at the top of the dugout steps, held still for a moment, then disappeared, his cap still on his head.

"All I want out of life is that when I walk down the street folks will say, 'There goes the greatest hitter that ever lived.'"

May 25, 1935

"All I can tell 'em is pick a good one and sock it. I get back to the dugout and they ask me what it was I hit and I tell 'em I don't know except it looked good."

—BABE RUTH

Back in the 1920s and 1930s, when a great player came to the end of a long career with a ballclub, he was often named manager—frequently while the player was still in his prime. Somewhere along the line, **Babe Ruth** had gotten it in his head that the Yankees would be doing the same for him—even though Yankees management had shown a liking for tough, no-nonsense individuals who could keep hellions like the Babe in line. The front office was committed to a fellow named Joe McCarthy, who had managed the Yanks to one world championship and three second-place finishes in his first four years with the club. He would go on to manage 24 seasons in the big leagues without ever having a losing record.

The 1934 season would turn out to be Ruth's final one in New York. The Yankees played .610 ball, but finished 7 games off the 101-win pace of a great Detroit Tigers team with as many Hall of Famers in their starting lineup (four) as New York had. A younger Ruth would have made the difference. At 39, he hit 22 home runs, five fewer than Zeke Bonura; and his .288 average was the lowest of his career since his pitching days in 1916, while 30 of his fellow American Leaguers all topped .300. He still managed a flair for the dramatic, his 700th home run on July 13 propelling the Yankees to first place for a brief stay.

At season's end, rather than deal with the distractions he created, the Yankees released him. (Can you imagine the Chicago Bulls ever releasing Michael Jordan, even if he were three years past his prime and angling to take over as coach, general manager, and team president?) Ruth returned to Boston, but this time with the fourth-place Boston Braves. Eager to prove the Yankees wrong, Ruth took the great Carl Hubbell out of the yard in his first National League at-bat. But by June he was hitting .181 and walking away from the game for good.

May 25 wasn't to be his last game, but perhaps it should have been. The Braves came into Forbes Field to play the Pittsburgh Pirates. Forbes Field was a triples park, more than 400 feet to right-center, 435 feet to center, and even deeper around toward left. The grandstand roof in right field was 86 feet high, and had yet to be cleared by any hitter since the park had opened 26 years before. Ruth had only hit two more home runs since his dramatic Opening Day shot off Hubbell, and it looked like any day might be his last and that 711 might be the number that all other power hitters would have to shoot for.

That day, for the major league record 72nd time in his career, Babe Ruth hit two home runs in a game. For good measure, he hit three. The Babe hit that one—number 714—*over* the right-field roof and out of the stadium. The Pirates' pitcher who served it up, Guy Bush, described what it was like to face the man who only three years before had been "calling his shot" in the World Series, as the Yankees dismantled Bush's Cubs: "I never saw a ball hit so hard. He was fat and old, but he still had that great swing."

> *Rising to the glorious heights of his heyday, Babe Ruth, the sultan of swat, crashed out three home runs against the Pittsburgh Pirates today but they were not enough and the Boston Braves took an 11-to-7 defeat before a crowd of 10,000 at Forbes Field.*
>
> *The stands rocked with cheers for the mighty Babe as he enjoyed a field day at the expense of Pitchers Red Lucas and Guy Bush, getting a single besides the three circuit blows in four times at bat and driving in altogether six runs.*
>
> *Ruth left the game amid an ovation at the end of the Braves' half of the seventh inning and after his third home run—a prodigious clout that carried clear over the right field grandstand, bounded into the street and rolled into Schenley Park. Baseball men said it was the longest drive ever made at Forbes Field.*
>
> —ASSOCIATED PRESS

September 30, 1972

"The press was driving him crazy about the 3,000th hit, but to him it was no big deal, because he knew he was going to get it, if not this year, then next year."

—DOCK ELLIS

No one in Pittsburgh knew it would be the final regular-season hit they would ever see their spectacular right fielder **Roberto Clemente** produce. Toward the end of another pennant-winning season in 1972, after 18 years as a Pirate, which featured four batting titles and at least one hit in all 14 World Series games he played, the 38-year-old Clemente was still a .300 hitter. At the start of the season, Clemente needed 118 hits to reach 3,000—and on September 29, in the season's final days, he stood at 2,999.

Tom Seaver was on the mound for the Mets, and 24,000 fans were on hand in Three Rivers Stadium in Pittsburgh to see the game's first Latino superstar became the 11th member of the 3,000-hit club. Clemente hit a high bouncer up the middle that bounded off the glove of second baseman Ken Boswell. The official scorer's ruling took a long time to reach the electronic scoreboard. An H flashed briefly, sending the crowd into hysterics. Toilet paper streamers rained down on the outfield. First baseman Ed Kranepool handed Clemente the ball. Only then did the original ruling finally reach the scoreboard—E4.

Clemente was actually relieved: "I'm glad they didn't call it a hit. I want to get it without any taint." He returned to the lineup the following night against Mets pitcher Jon Matlack. Matlack was cruising through the first three innings, but Clemente reached him for a double off the wall in center field in the fourth inning that triggered a five-run rally.

Days later, Clemente was three outs away from his third trip to the World Series when the Reds rallied for two runs to beat the Pirates 4–3 in Game 5 of the NLCS, the final run scoring on a wild pitch. Two and a half months later, Clemente was on a plane loaded with supplies on a mercy mission to aid earthquake victims in Nicaragua. The plane crashed shortly after takeoff from San Juan, and his body was never recovered. The customary five-year waiting period was waived, and Roberto Clemente and his 3,000 hits went into the Hall of Fame in 1973.

Returns

August 4, 1963

When watching a **Mickey Mantle** highlight reel, it's easy to tell whether a home run has been hit near the beginning or the end of his career. The last 100-odd long balls of his career were hit on upper-body strength alone, the clip revealing a man who still found it easy to put bat on ball but grimaced every time he placed any weight on his legs.

Hall of Famer Nellie Fox once said, "On two legs, Mickey Mantle would have been the greatest ballplayer who ever lived." His leg problems began with a football injury, then became progressively worse from the time he stepped in a drainpipe in the outfield in the second game of the 1951 World Series. He'd been playing in pain through most of his career, even before he tore up his left leg on a rainy June 5 night in 1963. Brooks Robinson hit a drive over his head in Baltimore's Memorial Stadium, and as Mantle went back to the wall to try to run it down, he caught his left foot in the chain-link fence—a gruesome scene. The game's best player, leader of the game's best team, member of the 1951, 1952, 1953, 1956, 1958, 1961, and 1962 champs and 1955, 1957, and 1960 pennant winners, only 31 and just two years removed from a 54-homer season, was carried off the field, torn ligaments in his knee and a broken bone in his foot. Doctors told him he was out for the season, and Mantle himself thought about retiring.

A month later, Mantle was already traveling with the team again. Thanks to the great pitching of Whitey Ford and the contributions of youngsters Jim Bouton, Al Downing, Joe Pepitone, and Tom Tresh, the Yankees were on their way to their fourth consecutive pennant. They didn't mathemically clinch the pennant on August 4 in the second game of a doubleheader in Yankee Stadium against the Baltimore Orioles, but they might as well have. The young Orioles were up 10–9 in the bottom of the seventh and were on their way to a sweep that would inch them closer to the first-place Yankees. Manager Ralph Houk sent Mantle up to pinch hit with the game on the line, though his star hadn't seen live pitching in two months.

Greeted with one of the loudest ovations he'd ever received, Mantle acknowledged getting goose bumps for the first time in his life. "I prayed I wouldn't look bad," he said later. "I said to myself, 'Just meet the ball. Don't strike out, whatever you do.'" On his first swing against left-hander George Brunet, Mantle put one in the seats in left field to tie the game. The Yankees went on to win in 10 innings. "I hit a lot of balls harder," Mantle commented, "but I can't say any of them gave me more satisfaction than that one."

> "At 7:31 last night Mickey Mantle returned to action at Yankee Stadium, swung his bat in anger for the first time in 61 games, and received two of the loudest cheers that have reverberated through the cool, green arches of the House That Ruth Built in a long time."
>
> —NEW YORK TIMES

Mantle would play only 65 games in 1963, hitting 15 home runs and batting .314. He limped through the World Series, a sweep at the hands of the Dodgers. In Game

4, Mantle brought the Yankees even with the Dodgers for the only time in the series when he homered off Sandy Koufax in the seventh inning to tie the game at 1–1. It was only his second hit of the series, the other a bunt single in Game 3. It was only the third hit of the game for New York, which had managed only a single and a lost-in-the-sun double. But the Dodgers responded with an unearned run in the bottom of the inning to take the series with a 2–1 win.

May 14, 1972

The Giants left New York in 1957. **Willie Mays** returned home 15 years later when the Mets traded for the 41-year-old outfielder. In truth, it was a publicity stunt by management, one that generated the desired sellout crowds but was not expected to do much for New York's pennant hopes. Someone forgot to tell Willie that he was just an artifact on display.

Only three years removed from their miracle of 1969, the 1972 Mets were still built around great young pitching. Tom Seaver was only 27 and on his way to another 20-win season. Jerry Koosman struggled, but 22-year-old left-hander Jon Matlack picked up the slack. The offense, however, was moribund, and would end up hitting a league-low .225, atrocious even by early-'70s standards. New York would end the season 13½ games behind the Pirates; but when Mays made his first appearance with the Mets on a Sunday, May 14 afternoon in Shea, they were still in the hunt.

Mays was playing first base and batting leadoff against Sam McDowell and the San Francisco Giants. He walked to lead off the game, then scored on a Rusty Staub grand slam. The Mets blew their 4–0 lead in the fifth as the Giants scored four runs off Ray Sadecki to tie the game. But in the bottom of the inning, Mays sent the 35,000 Shea fans into hysterics with a home run into the Giants' bullpen. It put the Mets up 5–4, and they held on to win the game.

Four days later, Mays got his next start—and perhaps even forgot his age—as he saw his name on the lineup card in center field. He sparked a first-inning rally against the Expos by scoring all the way from first on an extra-base hit. Three days later against the Phillies, down 3–0 to Steve Carlton, Mays got the Mets going with a double in the sixth inning, scoring on a Tommie Agee home run. In the eighth, Mays provided the game winner with a two-run home run of his own. Carlton won 27 games in 1972; Willie Mays singlehandedly kept him from making it 28.

Mays even got to return to the World Series in 1973, after an unexpected division title and an even more unexpected NLCS defeat of the Big Red Machine. The final hit of Mays's career was a two-out, pinch-hit single in the 12th inning of Game 2 of the 1973 World Series off Rollie Fingers, scoring Bud Harrelson with the tie-breaking run and opening the floodgates for a four-run inning.

Last of a Kind

September 28, 1941

"If I couldn't hit .400 all the way I didn't deserve it."

—TED WILLIAMS

Appropriately enough, **Ted Williams** and Babe Ruth are the only players to make this list twice. Williams made it with the exclamation point he placed on one of the few hitting marks that has gone without serious challenge even in this new golden era of hitting.

In only his third season in the big leagues, 22-year-old Ted Williams was hitting .405 at the All-Star break. The Kid actually "slumped" during the second half of the season, dropping all the way to .400 with two games to be played. He was technically at .39955, but his average was rounded up to .400—the first .400 performance in the big leagues since Bill Terry in 1930, and the first in the AL since Harry Heilmann in 1923.

It was suggested to Williams that he sit out the last two games in Philadelphia, but he wanted no part of that. He enjoyed hitting too much, and was too confident to believe that any pitcher could hold him to only 3 hits in 8 at-bats. He played the first game and went 4 for 5 with a home run and 3 singles in a 12–11 victory. Not content with .404, he played the second game, too. Fred Caligiuri held the Sox to 6 hits, but Williams got 2 of them as he went 2 for 3 with a double and a single in a 7–1 loss. He finished the season at .406, 5 RBI from his first Triple Crown (he would win two before he was through). No one has even come close to that level of excellence since.

Going Deep

The next four are season-long accomplishments, followed by a career-long accomplishment that is one of the greatest hitting moments in the game's history.

September 30, 1927

"Sixty, count 'em, 60. Let's see some other SOB match that."

—BABE RUTH

Babe Ruth came into the 1927 season with three failed efforts in four World Series in the Bronx, a suspension-shortened 1922 season, and an illness-shortened 1925 season (it was reported as a bellyache brought on by a gargantuan consumption of hot dogs and soda pop, though it was most likely something far less wholesome).

And his 1926 season had come to an end when he was thrown out stealing for the final out of the seventh game of the World Series (with the Yanks down by one run and Lou Gehrig on deck). A sensation in 1920 and 1921, many believed that at 32, Ruth's best days were behind him.

The Babe did little to dispel that in the early-going. On April 15, 1927, he took Howard Ehmke of the Philadelphia Athletics out of the yard in the first inning. It was his first of only 4 that month. But by the end of May he had 16, and he ended August with 43. Like a truck with brake trouble barreling down a hill, he proceeded to hit 17 during the month of September.

On September 29, Ruth tied his own home run record of 59, set in 1921, with a grand slam off Paul Hopkins of the Washington Senators in the fifth inning. He closed it out the following day in his final at-bat of the season with number 60 in the eighth inning against lefty Tom Zachary of the Senators.

Murderers' Row went on to the 1927 World Series and became the only team to win a championship during batting practice. Before Game 1, the Pirates—no slouches, with three Hall of Famers in their starting lineup and a team batting average of .305—were awed by the performance that Ruth and Gehrig put on. The Pirates had hit only 54 home

Babe Ruth delivering his farewell speech on June 13, 1948, during the celebration for the 25th anniversary of the opening of Yankee Stadium. He died on August 16, 1948.

runs all season, 6 fewer than Ruth and only 7 more than Gehrig. Pittsburgh went down in four and wouldn't return to postseason play for 33 years.

The Yankees went on to sweep the Cardinals in 1928 and the Cubs in 1932. After dropping three of four World Series, Ruth won his final 12 Fall Classic games in a row, going 21 for 46 (.457) with 7 home runs and 17 RBI.

October 1, 1961

> *"It would have been a helluva lot more fun if I had never hit those 61 home runs."*
>
> —ROGER MARIS

Just as Mark McGwire had Sammy Sosa with him as he went after history, so did Roger Maris have a companion. Unfortunately for Maris it was his teammate, Mickey

Mantle, who kept him company. So not only was Maris threatening to break a record that no one wanted to see fall, but in Mantle he was competing with the man the fans—and even his own team's front office—would much rather have seen do it.

Maris later described his 1961 performance as freakish. He'd come out of nowhere to win the AL MVP in 1960 after the Yankees acquired him from the Kansas City A's, leading the league in RBI with 112, hitting 39 home runs, and playing a terrific, strong-armed right field.

In the early part of the '61 season, it did not appear that he would be able to repeat his '60 performance. Coming into play on May 3, 1961, the Yankees had played 16 games and Roger Maris had one home run. His first had come a week before, off Paul Foytack of the Tigers. Maris didn't catch up to the Babe's pace until he hit numbers 19 and 20 off Eli Grba and Johnny James of the Los Angeles Angels in the second game of a doubleheader on June 11. Ironically, Ruth had also hit a pair of home runs on the 11th, both off Garland Buckeye of the Cleveland Indians.

With his 22nd on June 14 against Gary Bell of the Indians, Maris moved ahead of Ruth and stayed there. Mantle, however, was a different story, and the M&M Boys jockeyed for position throughout July and August. On July 25, eight days after commissioner Ford Frick declared that Ruth's record would stand unless broken in 154 games, Maris hit four home runs in a doubleheader against the White Sox (including one off fellow Yankee legend Don Larsen). Maris finished the month at 40, one ahead of Mantle. By September 1, Maris had 51 and Mantle 48. Nagging injuries would cause Mantle to fall farther off the pace throughout the month, as he hit only 6 more.

Maris stayed ahead of Ruth on the home run calendar until the unbearable late-season pressure left him stuck on 60 on September 30, clumps of hair falling out of his head. As Phil Rizzuto shouted happily in the broadcast booth, Maris broke the drought in the fourth inning of New York's final regular-season game with number 61 off Tracy Stallard—a line drive into the right-field seats in Yankee Stadium that had fans climbing all over one another for the ball. It was the only run in a 1–0 Yankees victory, an ironic end to a hitter's season.

Maris went on to hit a game-deciding home run in the 1961 World Series. The Babe hit two of his own in the 1927 Fall Classic, suggesting that 62 should have been the magic number all along. Things might have been a lot easier for Roger Maris had that been the case.

September 13, 1998

With each passing year, the trade of **Sammy Sosa** from the White Sox to the Cubs for George Bell makes its way closer and closer to the top of the list of worst deals ever made. Yet before the 1998 season, the Cubs' patience with Sammy Sosa was wearing thin. He'd had a necklace made to commemorate his 30-homer/30-steal seasons—a piece of jewelry that teammate Mark Grace described as being the size of a manhole cover. Management had confronted him about his selfish play in 1997, running despite having the steal sign blocked on a personal quest for yet another 30/30 season. Ex-Cubs have even blasted the fans for encouraging this type of behavior, for tolerating losing so long as they had a Sammy Sosa home run to cheer. The right offer before the season might have pried him away from the Cubs.

Like Roger Maris, Sammy Sosa got off to a relatively slow start in 1998. Going into play on May 22, the Cubs had played 46 games and Sosa had 8 home runs, putting him on pace for 28 for the season. Little did anyone suspect that Sosa's first-inning solo shot off Greg Maddux on May 22 would trigger an unprecedented avalanche of dingers that would carry him to 66 for the season.

Along the way, he would homer in 18 different ballparks (a new record) and hit 12 home runs against the Brewers alone (one short of the record set when teams faced each other many more times in a season). In June alone he slugged .860 and hit 20 home runs, obliterating the mark for home runs for that month (15, shared by Babe Ruth, Bob Johnson, Roger Maris, and Pedro Guerrero), home runs in any month (18, by Rudy York), and home runs in any 30-day period (21, from May 25 to June 23, which eclipsed the previous mark of 20 set by Ralph Kiner in 1947 and Roger Maris in 1961).

He raced to catch up with the faster-starting Mark McGwire, finally tying him at 47 on August 16 off Sean Bergman of the Astros, then passing him on August 19 with number 48 off Kent Bottenfield in the fifth inning of a game against the Cardinals. McGwire responded with home runs in the 8th and 10th to reclaim the lead and win the game.

It took Sosa five days longer than McGwire to reach 62, but he did so in more dramatic style than even McGwire could muster. In the finale of a wild three-game series with the Milwaukee Brewers in Wrigley Field, the largest crowd of the year was on hand to watch the Cubs try to extend their wild-card lead over the Mets to two games. Sosa propelled the Cubs to an 8–3 lead on the strength of number 61, a fifth-inning, two-run, 480-foot bomb that started out in Bronswell Patrick's hand and ended up on Waveland Avenue. But the Brewers rallied, scoring runs in the sixth and seventh, four in the eighth, and another run in the ninth to go up 10–8. Then, with one out in the ninth, Sosa launched number 62, another 480-foot bomb onto Waveland Avenue off Eric Plunk to bring the Cubs within one run.

The game was held up for six minutes as the fans called Sosa out for three curtain calls. When play finally resumed, the Cubs rallied for another run, then won it in the bottom of the 10th on a Mark Grace home run.

And on that day, at least, there was much joy in Mudville.

September 8, 1998

For **Mark McGwire**, it had always been a question of staying healthy. Like Jose Canseco, Kevin Mitchell, and other muscle-bound hitters of the '80s and '90s, McGwire fell victim to frequent and strange injuries, as if the power of his swings were taking as big a toll on his joints as they were on the ball. He looked finished at 31. Then, late in his career, Big Mac finally found the right recipe.

As if trying to make up for lost time, McGwire started fast in 1998 and never slowed down—never going more than nine games without a home run. Like 1961, it was an expansion season, and fans were expecting someone to take a serious run at Roger Maris's record. After McGwire hit four home runs in his first four games, the Maris Watch went on—and stayed on for six solid months.

McGwire cooled off in the season's second week, then lit up the scoreboards again with three home runs on April 14 against the Arizona Diamondbacks. On May 19, he hit three more against the Phillies, sending one to the warning track in left-center in his final at-bat of the night. All in all, he had 11 multiple-homer days in 1998.

When he tied and broke Hack Wilson's National League record on September 1 with home runs off Livan Hernandez and Donn Pall in Florida, it was no longer a question of if but when. And how many. On Labor Day, he took the Cubs' Mike Morgan deep in St. Louis in the first inning for number 61, earning high-fives from the Chicago infielders, who took a step back from their wild-card race to give McGwire the nod. The following night, on national television and in front of Roger Maris's family, he broke the mark against Steve Trachsel in the fourth inning with his shortest home run of the season—a low line drive that landed beneath the left-field stands, short-circuiting the possibility of any bloody battles for the souvenir ball. A groundskeeper came up with it and gave it to him free of charge.

As the Cubs staggered toward the wild-card finish line, the possibility remained that Sammy Sosa could sneak past McGwire in the final 100 yards. Big Mac went a week before hitting number 63 against Jason Christiansen of the Pirates. He hit two more in Milwaukee and

Mark McGwire watches home run number 70 leave the yard in his final at-bat of the 1998 season.

was robbed by an umpire's decision of a third. On September 24, also in Milwaukee, Sosa pulled even with him with a prodigious blast off Rod Henderson. On the 25th, Sosa hit number 66 off Jose Lima in the fourth inning in Houston, but minutes later McGwire homered off Shayne Bennett of the Expos in St. Louis.

With a spot in the playoffs on the line, Sosa played for the team, frequently shortening his stroke, lining singles through the infield to try to spark rallies. McGwire got to let it all hang out on the final two days of the Cardinals' season, and he homered four times off four different pitchers to put the title away on the last weekend of the season—including a three-run shot off Carl Pavano in his last at-bat of the season for a nice round 70.

Seventy, count 'em, 70. Let's see some other SOB match that!

April 8, 1974

> *"I looked for the same pitch my whole career. A breaking ball. I never worried about the fastball. They couldn't throw it past me. None of 'em."*
>
> —HANK AARON

Hank Aaron never hit 60 home runs in a season. In fact, he never even hit 50. But on April 8, 1974, he hit the most famous and dramatic second home run of any season before or since.

How does it come to this for a man who only had four home run titles all to his own (1957, 1963, 1966, and 1967)? A fairly simple formula. You arrive in the big leagues at age 20, blossom into a star at 21, hit at least 20 home runs for 20 consecutive seasons, and finish stronger than any hitter ever has before or since. Along the way, you manage two batting titles, a 30/30 season, play a very underrated right field, win a World Series in 1957 while hitting .393 with 3 home runs and 7 RBI, nearly win a second in 1958, and just miss a third consecutive trip in 1959.

For year-in, year-out consistency, Henry Aaron has no equal. During his time, however, he was overshadowed by the more spectacular Willie Mays and Mickey Mantle—two superstars who burst onto the scene in New York in 1951, three years earlier than Aaron did in the not-quite-media-capital of Milwaukee, Wisconsin. Leg injuries effectively ended Mantle's days as a feared slugger by the time he turned 33. At 34, Mays was still dominating the National League, hitting 52 home runs and batting .317 in a pitcher's year, but it would prove to be his peak. In 1969, he hit only 13 home runs, his final one the 600th of his career.

By 35, Hank Aaron was just getting started. The Braves had moved to Atlanta in 1966 and were now playing 1,000 feet above sea level at the Launching Pad. Aaron turned 35 before the start of the 1969 season, then celebrated all year long. He hit 44 home runs and batted .300, leading the Braves to the postseason for the first time in 11 years. His batting eye was never better: a career-high 87 walks and a career-low 47 strikeouts. Remarkable for any hitter, extraordinary for a man in his 16th major league season.

In 1971, at the age of 37, he hit a career-high 47 home runs while batting .327. Aaron passed Willie Mays in 1972 for second on the all-time home run list on his way to 34 for the season. Mays, meanwhile, was finishing out his career as an inspirational part-time player for the Mets.

After "falling off" from 47 to 34 home runs in 1972, some expected that the 39-year-old Aaron and his 673 home runs might not have enough left in the tank to reach 714. Thanks to the finishing kick of an Olympic long-distance runner, Aaron nearly reached the Babe in that season alone. He reached 713 by hitting 40 on the season while batting .300 for the 14th time in his career.

Hank Aaron endured a long, hate-mail-filled off-season. Consider the pressure Roger Maris felt in 1961, then multiply it by 10, as a black man playing in the South went after the last hallowed mark of Babe Ruth. The press, which had paid relatively little attention to him throughout his career, suddenly besieged him. As the season approached, the Braves added foolishly to the pressure by floating their desire to use Aaron only in home games. The league offices quashed that notion quickly.

Confused by all the controversy his remarkable performance had generated ("All I want is to be treated as a human being. What am I supposed to do—stop trying to hit home runs?"), Aaron found the challenge of facing major league pitching a welcome relief. Never one to build the drama, he responded to all that swirled around him by hitting number 714 on April 4 off Jack Billingham in his first at-bat of the season. On his first swing, no less. Four days later, back home in Atlanta and in front of a national television audience, Aaron hit the record breaker in the fourth inning off Al Downing and the Dodgers, a drive into the Braves' bullpen in left-center.

The 40-year-old Aaron finished the season with 20 home runs, then was dealt to the Brewers to finish his career in Milwaukee as a designated hitter. At his Hall of Fame induction ceremonies, Aaron succinctly explained, "I never want them to forget Babe Ruth. I just want them to remember Aaron."

That task can be considered complete.

Carrying the Club

With the exception of perhaps Hank Aaron, even the most consistent of stars have that One Great Season that stands out from all the others—when everything comes together, and both injuries and prolonged slumps are avoided . . . when the broken-bat bloops fall between the outfield and the infield, and very few line drives die in a fielder's glove . . . when there always seem to be men on base to knock in and good pitches to hit . . . when the ball seems to be the size of a cantaloupe. Sometimes these players are so good that they can make good teams great, carrying their teammates on their shoulders and into the postseason.

And during those seasons, you can usually find that player's One Great Day—his signature game, the moment he peaked as a ballplayer. Here are four of the finest examples of a hitter taking over a game, and defining a season in the process.

June 23, 1984

> *"There's a drive, way back, it might be out of here, it is! He did it again! He did it again! Oh, the game is tied! Unbelievable! How about that! Listen to this crowd! Everybody has gone bananas! Holy cow! What would the odds be if I told you that twice Sandberg would hit home runs off Bruce Sutter? Come on, you guys, he can't do it all himself."*
>
> —HARRY CARAY

By 1984 the Cubs had not been to a World Series in 39 years, when a collection of aging veterans and 4FS avoiding the draft led a weakened National League in 1945, then fell to the Tigers in seven games. In 1969, they spent more days in first place than any other second-place team in history, collapsing down the stretch to the 1969 Miracle Mets. From 1946 to 1983, they finished higher than third only twice.

Dallas Green, the man who in 1980 managed the Phillies to the only championship in their history, had taken over as general manager of the hapless Cubs. The brash Green made himself many enemies almost immediately, ridiculing Cubs tradition as a tradition of losing, releasing Ferguson Jenkins, and swinging a number of deals that sent out fan favorites for former Philadelphia Phillies in an attempt to inject a winning attitude into a defeatist locker room.

The Cubs responded to Green's leadership by finishing fifth in 1982 and 1983, 19 games off the pace each time. Green's handpicked manager, Lee Elia, launched a profanity-filled tirade at the Wrigley Field fans as they booed his players and doused them with stale beer, and was let go before the end of the 1983 season. In the middle of this mess, a young infielder named **Ryne Sandberg** quietly moved over from third to play a solid second base. He was a throw-in in an initially unpopular trade that sent the flashy Ivan DeJesus to Philadelphia for an aging Larry Bowa.

A good player in 1983, the 24-year-old Sandberg was establishing himself as a star in 1984. Americans found out just how good Sandberg was during a nationally televised Game of the Week broadcast in June. The Cubs were surprising everyone by hanging around near the top of the NL East, and had just made a big trading-deadline move by acquiring Rick Sutcliffe from the Cleveland Indians. Sutcliffe solidified their injury-riddled staff, and Chicago was making another move toward the Mets at the top of the division.

The Cardinals went up 7–1 in Wrigley Field thanks to the hitting of Willie McGee, who hit for the cycle on the day. As hot as he was, he couldn't keep pace with Sandberg, who came into the game with 7 hits in his last 10 at-bats. By the time Sandberg batted in the ninth inning, he had 10 hits in his last 14 at-bats with 4 RBI on the day, but the Cardinals still led 9–8. On the mound was former Cubs closer Bruce Sutter, whose split-fingered fastball made him one of the game's toughest pitchers to hit with any authority. Sandberg responded with a game-tying solo home run. The Cardinals went back on top 11–9 in the top of the 10th, only to see Sandberg hit *another* game-tying home run, this one a two-run shot off Sutter in the bottom of the inning. The Cubs went on to win 12–11 in 11.

With Sandberg having 12 hits in his last 16 at-bats, including two game-saving shots off the best closer in the league, Cardinals manager Whitey Herzog was forced to revise his assessment that Sandberg was one of the best players in the league: "Now I think he's one of the greatest players I've ever seen."

Sandberg went on to win league MVP honors by hitting .314 with 200 hits, 114 runs scored, and 74 extra-base hits in the difficult second spot in the order, all while playing a flawless second base. He continued his hot hitting in the playoffs against the Padres, but the baseball gods had a cruel fifth and final game loss in store for the Cubs in San Diego. It's too bad, because, like in 1945, the Tigers were waiting for them in the World Series.

October 3, 1982

"So much for momentum and inertia."

—EARL WEAVER, MANAGER OF THE 1982 BALTIMORE ORIOLES

It was the last game of the 1982 season. The Milwaukee Brewers—born in 1969 as the hapless Seattle Pilots, doormats of the American League for the first eight years of their existence, frustrated also-rans of the AL East for the past three seasons—were in the process of blowing the pennant. They'd come to Baltimore needing to win just one of four to clinch the pennant, but had dropped three straight—8–3, 7–1, and 11–2—to fall into a first-place tie with the Orioles. Orioles ace and future Hall of Famer Jim Palmer—36 years old, but still one of the AL's best with a 15–4 record and one of the lowest ERAs in the league—stood between them and their first postseason appearance. Milwaukee was countering with another future Hall of Famer—37-year-old Don Sutton, a late-season acquisition.

The Orioles also had the momentum (33–10 down the stretch), the home crowd, several veterans accustomed to the pressures of win-or-go-home baseball, and fiery manager Earl Weaver in his last season at the helm. The Brewers had Harvey Kuenn, a rookie manager who took over after a 23–24 start. And they also had dry mouths, tight throats, and visions in their heads of other famous collapses like the '51 Dodgers, '64 Phillies, and '78 Red Sox.

Milwaukee's players and fans knew they may never get a better shot than this. The Orioles had a solid nucleus, built around 26-year-old Eddie Murray and a 21-year-old shortstop named Cal Ripken, who looked like he might have a future in this game. The Brewers were enjoying career years by thirty-somethings like Cecil Cooper, Gorman Thomas, Ben Ogilvie, and Ted Simmons. Their pitchers were old and thin, propped up by 35-year-old Rollie Fingers and a thoroughly unexpected 18 wins out of the suave Pete Vukovich.

Harvey's Wallbangers were at the top of the league with 214 home runs and 881 runs scored, and 26-year-old shortstop **Robin Yount** was the best of the bunch. Yount had been Milwaukee's shortstop since 1974, coming to the big leagues at the age of 18. He struggled through his first six seasons, even threatening to give up the game and take up golf. Finally fulfilling his potential in 1980, he took it a step further in 1982 with levels of runs, hits, triples, home runs, RBI, batting average, and slugging average that would turn out to be career highs.

Yount took all of the pressure off his teammates immediately with home run number 28 off Jim Palmer in the first inning—an opposite-field drive that broke an 0-for-9 skid. He pulled one into the left-field stands in the third to make it 3–0. With the game still tight at 4–1 in the top of the eighth, Yount led off with a triple and eventually scored. Milwaukee finally loosened up and pushed across five in the ninth, pummeling the Orioles 10–2 to take the pennant. The team would go on to rally from a 2–0 deficit against the Angels to take the series in five, then pushed the Cardinals to seven games in the World Series. Yount led all batters with 12 hits, hitting .414 with 6 RBI in the series.

Later, during an Orioles-Brewers rain delay in Milwaukee, Baltimore catcher Rick Dempsey would pay Yount the ultimate tribute. Donning Yount's number 19 uniform—adding a healthy quantity of Ruthian padding around the stomach—Dempsey pantomimed Yount's two home runs off Palmer to the wild applause of the Milwaukee faithful.

September 30–October 1, 1967

"I was never so sure of myself in my life."

—CARL YASTRZEMSKI

The 1967 AL pennant race was one of the most exciting in baseball history, and **Carl Yastrzemski** just about won it singlehandedly for the Red Sox.

With the Yankees' dynasty having fallen into ruin, there was a power vacuum at the top of the American League. It appeared that the Baltimore Orioles would be the new kings when, fortified by the addition of Frank Robinson in 1966, they had swept the reigning champion Dodgers in the World Series. But injuries had decimated their corps of young pitchers, and they fell below .500 and into the second division. Harmon Killebrew's Minnesota Twins—who had taken the Dodgers to seven games in the 1965 World Series before falling to Sandy Koufax 2–0—were in the thick of it. So was a Detroit Tigers team that would dominate the league the following season. A surprising contender was the Chicago White Sox, led by the best pitching staff and the most aggressive baserunners in the league. And then there were the Boston Red Sox, a ninth-place, 95-loss squad the previous season, which—like the Mets of 1969—everyone expected to fall out of contention but never did. A 100–1 shot at the beginning of the season, Boston jockeyed for position at the top of the standings with Minnesota, Detroit, and Chicago for three solid months.

Boston's pitching was pretty much a one-man show, with Jim Lonborg leading the league in wins and strikeouts, the only member of the Boston staff with more than 12 victories. On offense, Boston became a one-man show when 22-year-old slugging right fielder and fan favorite Tony Conigliaro—the man with more home runs as a teenager than anyone but Mel Ott—was struck in the eye by a Jack Hamilton fastball. It was as bloody and gruesome a scene as you'll ever see on a baseball field; it ruined what could have been a 500-homer career for Conigliaro, and it left Carl Yastrzemski to carry the load for the final two months of the season.

While Boston chased the pennant, Yastrzemski chased the Triple Crown. In his final 19 games, he batted .444 with 26 RBI, tying Killebrew in home runs, pulling away from him in RBI, and leaving Hall of Famers Frank Robinson and Al Kaline in the dust in the batting average race. But Yastrzemski wasn't thinking about the Triple Crown as the season drew to a tumultuous close. The White Sox, having dropped a doubleheader to the lowly Kansas City Athletics despite sending their two best pitchers to the mound, had fallen out of the race. But, having dropped two straight to Cleveland, things didn't look much better for the Red Sox as they entered the final weekend of the season. A game behind in the loss column, Boston did not control its own fate.

End of play, September 29:
Minnesota 91–69
Boston 90–70
Detroit 89–69

Minnesota was coming to Boston to play two, while the Tigers were playing back-to-back doubleheaders in Detroit with the surprising California Angels, who had lurked on the fringes of the pennant race all season. While the Tigers split their first two with the Angels, the Red Sox took on the Twins in Fenway Park. With the score tied 1–1 in the fifth, Yastrzemski knocked in the go-ahead run with a single off Jim Perry on a 3–2 pitch. Two innings later, he put the game away with a two-out home run off left-hander Jim Merritt, his 44th of the season.

End of play, September 30:

Minnesota 91–70

Boston 91–70

Detroit 90–70

A playoff looked like a very real possibility as the Tigers took control of the first game of their doubleheader against the Angels. Boston's ace, Jim Lonborg, was taking on Minnesota's ace, Dean Chance, a 20-game winner and former Cy Young Award winner. The Twins took a 2–0 lead, as the Sox stranded Yastrzemski after an infield single in the first and a double off the wall in right-center in the third. The Red Sox finally got some men on base for Yaz, loading the bases in the fifth. He responded with a line-drive single to center to tie the game. Boston scored three more to go ahead 5–2. Minnesota threatened in the eighth. With two men on, Bob Allison hit a line drive into the left-field corner, but Yastrzemski put an end to that with an unbelievable throw that nailed Allison at second base.

The Tigers dropped their final game to the Angels, and the Red Sox were in the World Series. Only then could Yastrzemski take satisfaction in the fact that he'd won the Triple Crown and had gotten 10 hits in his final 13 pressure-packed at-bats. His hot hitting continued into the World Series, where he hit .400 with 3 home runs, including 5 hits in his final 10 at-bats as the Red Sox made a valiant effort to overcome a 3–1 deficit to the Cardinals, ultimately falling in seven.

In the three games the Red Sox won, the one-man wrecking crew was 7 for 11 with 3 home runs and 5 RBI. In the four games they lost, he was 3–14 with no runs scored or knocked in.

June 28–30, 1949

"Those three days in Boston were the most satisfying of my life."

—JOE DIMAGGIO

By 1948, **Joe DiMaggio** was already assured of baseball immortality. He had been to seven World Series, won six, earned three MVPs, established a 56-game hitting streak that has never been seriously challenged, and been named to the All-Star team every year, starting in all but one. If ever a player had earned the right to take it easy, DiMaggio had. Instead, the 33-year-old Yankee center fielder, hampered by the excruciating pain of a bone spur in his heel, pushed himself to the final weekend of a season that ended with the Red Sox and Indians tied for first and New York 2 games off the pace. Playing through pain that he described as feeling like an ice pick driving through his heel, DiMaggio led the league with 39 home runs and 155 RBI while hitting .320 as he tried to singlehandedly carry the Yankees to a defense of their 1947 title.

The spur was removed in November, but it grew back by spring training and kept him out of the lineup well into June of 1949. The pain only got worse, and it was feared that the career of the game's greatest player was over. Even DiMaggio feared it might be the end of the line—until the day he stepped out of bed and felt no pain. His timing couldn't have been better. The Red Sox were white-hot, winning 10 of 11 and moving past the Yankees into first place.

On June 28, the Yankees began a three-game series with the Red Sox in Fenway Park. Rather than get back in the swing of things against lesser competition, DiMaggio chose this game for his comeback, accelerating his schedule by two weeks. He made the call at noon, getting himself fitted with a spikeless orthopedic shoe and arriving in Boston at 5:00. Other than an exhibition game against the Giants earlier that month, DiMaggio hadn't faced major league pitching for nine months. Nevertheless, he singled in his first at-bat, then followed that in the third with a two-out, two-run homer, propelling the Yankees to a 5–4 victory. The following day the Yankees were down 7–1 when DiMaggio sparked a comeback with a three-run homer. Later he would break the tie with a game-deciding two-run blast in an eventual 9–7 victory. He iced the final game with his fourth home run of the series, a two-out, three-run shot off the light tower in the seventh inning against Boston ace Mel Parnell.

"This was the greatest series of my career," DiMaggio said later. "I've had some fair days in the World Series. I've had thrills in All-Star games, and in pennant competition. But those three straight days in Boston, two weeks ahead of my schedule, gave me the kick of kicks."

The Red Sox never knew what hit them. DiMaggio had risen from the dead to go 5 for 11 with 4 home runs and 10 RBI. He did it again in the final two games of the season, when the surging Red Sox came into Yankee Stadium with a one-game lead. DiMaggio shook off a fever and viral pneumonia to get 2 hits in a 5–4 Game 1 victory. The Yankees wrapped it up 5–3 in the final game. In a half-season, he ended up with 14 home runs, 67 RBI, and a .346 batting average.

Ted Williams took the league MVP honors, but DiMaggio went to the World Series, where the Yankees took the Dodgers in five. Struggling through the first four games with only an infield single in 14 at-bats, DiMaggio homered in the final game of the series, putting the Yankees up 6–1 in an eventual 10–6 victory.

Pennant-Winning Home Runs

October 1, 1950

In 1915, the Phillies went to their first World Series, carried there by one of the game's first sluggers—Gavvy Cravath—and 31-game winner Grover Cleveland Alexander. Before the 1918 season, cash-strapped Phillies owner Bill Baker sent

Alexander to the Cubs in a financially motivated and horribly one-sided deal. The Phillies finished sixth in 1918 and never higher than third until 1949, ending up dead last 16 times in 32 seasons.

Now, with their first pennant in 35 years in sight, the Phillies were falling apart. Only 12 days before, they had been 7½ games ahead of the Boston Braves and 9 games ahead of the Brooklyn Dodgers. They lost 8 of their last 10, including consecutive doubleheader sweeps at the hands of the New York Giants. They lost the second-to-last game of the season to the Dodgers in Brooklyn, leaving them with a one-game lead with one to play.

A pair of 19-game winners would be hooking up in the final game of the season: 24-year-old Don Newcombe and 23-year-old Robin Roberts, who had failed in four previous tries to win his 20th. The game was scoreless through five, until the Phillies pushed across **Dick Sisler** to go up 1–0. Shortstop Pee Wee Reese promptly tied it in the bottom of the sixth with a bizarre home run that wedged itself on the ledge at the base of the Ebbets Field screen in right. One could only conclude that the baseball gods were on the Dodgers' side this time.

In the bottom of the ninth, center fielder Richie Ashburn fielded a Duke Snider single and threw out Cal Abrams at the plate for the first out of the inning. Robin Roberts intentionally walked Jackie Robinson to load the bases, then worked his way out of the jam by popping up Carl Furillo and Gil Hodges, who had combined for 50 home runs and 229 RBI during the season.

This set the stage for the dramatic 10th inning. Manager Eddie Sawyer let Robin Roberts hit leading off the 10th, and the pitcher responded with a single off Newcombe. Eddie Waitkus followed with a single, but Ashburn's sacrifice bunt failed, leaving runners at first and second with one out. The Phillies' number-three hitter, the line-drive-hitting son of Hall of Famer George Sisler, Dick Sisler, came to bat. He played only 799 big-league games, finishing his career with 55 home runs and a .276 average, but Philadelphia fans will remember him as the one who hit the three-run extra-inning home run on the final day of the season to put the Phillies ahead to stay, sending them into their second of only five World Series appearances.

September 28, 1938

"When I got to second base I couldn't see third for the players and fans there. I don't think I walked a step to the plate—I was carried in."

—GABBY HARTNETT

In the 1930s, the lovable, losing Cubbies were a force to be reckoned with. Their failure to build a farm system had yet to catch up with them, as it would from the 1940s on. They benefited from a core of dependable veterans and, believe it or not, solid pitching. In the process, the Cubs were consistent contenders, winning three pennants in the past nine seasons while falling short in 1930 despite a record-setting display of hitting fireworks. In 1938, Chicago was only three years removed from one of the most extraordinary stretch runs in baseball history: 21 consecutive victories in September 1935, which carried them to the pennant.

In late September 1938, they were at it again. A full house was on hand in Wrigley Field because the Cubs had won 8 in a row, 18 of 21, and now trailed the first-place Pirates—whose organization had already been equipping Forbes Field to handle the crush of reporters expected for the World Series—by a half-game. The Cubs would be taking on the Pirates in the second of a three-game series, having already won the first game as sore-armed Dizzy Dean pitched the last great game of his short but brilliant career.

It was a tight game that went to the eighth inning tied at 3–3. The Pirates scored twiced to go up 5–3, but the Cubs rallied to tie the score in the bottom of the inning, with the lead run cut down at the plate by right fielder Paul Waner. It was now 5:30 on an overcast day, and this seesaw battle, filled with pitching changes, was in danger of being called on account of darkness. The umpires agreed to play one more inning—not an insignificant decision, given that the rules of the day did not call for suspended games to be resumed. A tie game would be replayed in its entirety as part of a doubleheader the next day, with the better-rested Pirates' pitchers benefiting greatly.

In the ninth, the game did not appear to be heading for any resolution. The Pirates went out meekly in the top of the inning, while Mace Brown quickly recorded two outs in the bottom of the ninth. To the plate came 37-year-old catcher-manager **Gabby Hartnett**. One of the game's greatest catchers, and certainly one of the most underrated Hall of Famers, Hartnett was nearing the end of the line as a productive hitter. Age had limited him to a half-season of work and brought his batting average below .300 for the first time in four years. A powerful hitter in his prime, Hartnett didn't even have 10 home runs to show for his efforts in 1938.

Hartnett swung twice and fell behind 0–2 to Brown. Instead of wasting a pitch, Brown left a curveball out over the plate. Here's how Hartnett described it later: "Mace Brown wound up and let fly; I swung with everything I had and then I got that feeling I was talking about—the kind of feeling you get when the blood rushes out of your head and you get dizzy. A lot of people have told me they didn't know the ball was in the bleachers. Well, I did—maybe I was the only one in the park who did. I knew it the minute I hit it."

Mace Brown knew it, too, walking toward the dugout as soon as Hartnett hit the ball. The "homer in the gloamin'" lifted the Cubs to the top of the league for the first time since June 8, and broke the collective backs of the Pirates. Chicago went on to win its fourth pennant in 10 years, but fell to a far superior Yankees team in the World Series.

October 2, 1978

"As I rounded second and third and was trotting toward home, Fenway was dead silent. You could hear a pin drop, except for the few Yankee fans. You could hear them clapping."

—BUCKY DENT, ON HIS 1978 PLAYOFF HOME RUN

In Boston, they add an unprintable middle name to **Bucky Dent**.

The Yankees acquired Dent early in the 1977 season as owner George Steinbrenner, desiring an All-Star at every position, grew weary of Fred "Chicken" Stanley and Jim Mason. Oscar Gamble went to the White Sox for Dent and hit 31 home runs despite playing half his games in a pitcher's park, teaming with "Pitch at Risk to" Richie Zisk, Ralph "Roadrunner" Garr, and the immortal Eric Soderholm to help Chicago make an improbable run at the AL West title. Dent hit .247, a nine-point improvement over Stanley.

Dent missed part of 1978 with a leg injury and spent most of the season in the .240s again. He was by far the weakest link in a Yankees lineup loaded with dangerous clutch hitters like Chris Chambliss, Willie Randolph, Graig Nettles, Reggie Jackson, Mickey Rivers, Lou Piniella, and Thurman Munson. When the prettyboy shortstop came to bat in Yankee Stadium, grown men muttered while the teenage girls squealed.

The 1978 Yankees had fallen 14½ games behind the Boston Red Sox in early August before making perhaps the greatest late-season charge of all time. On September 7, having won 12 of 14, the Yankees came to Fenway Park only 4 games behind Boston. They call what happened the "Boston Massacre," as New York left town in a first-place tie, having outscored the Red Sox 42–9. But, as they did in 1949, the Red Sox did not go quietly. Down 3½ games, Boston beat New York in the final game of a three-game series in Yankee Stadium and slowly began to crawl back into contention. They tied the Yankees on the final game of the season, thanks to the shutout pitching of Rick Waits of the Cleveland Indians.

The one-game playoff took place in Fenway Park, where 16-game winner Mike Torrez faced off against the league's best pitcher, 24–3 Ron Guidry and his nine shutouts. Carl Yastrzemski put the Red Sox in front with a line-drive home run just inside the the right-field foul pole, and Mike Torrez carried a 2–0 lead into the seventh inning. With two men on, Red Sox manager Don Zimmer let Torrez face the weak-hitting Bucky Dent. He had only 16 extra-base hits and 37 RBI all season, so Boston fans were counting the number-nine hitter as an easy out before Mickey Rivers and the top of the lineup came around again.

The Sox and their fans had to be feeling even more confident when Dent fouled a ball straight down onto his foot and crumpled in a heap in the batter's box. As Dent tried to walk off the pain, few noticed Mickey Rivers handing Dent a new bat, telling him that he'd spotted a crack in the one the shortstop had been using. Back in the box but down 0–2, Dent responded by lifting a long fly ball that settled into the screen mere inches above the Green Monster in left field to put the Yankees ahead 3–2.

New York went ahead 5–2, the fifth run coming on a majestic Reggie Jackson home run into the seats in center field. The Yankees brought in relief ace Rich Gossage in the bottom of the seventh, and he kept things interesting. Boston closed to 5–4, and put the winning runs on in the bottom of the ninth before Gossage got Carl Yastrzemski to pop up to Graig Nettles at third base to end the game.

The Dodgers' faces bore the same looks of stunned disbelief when Bucky Dent went on to lead the Yankees to their second consecutive championship, hitting .417 and knocking in 7 runs, 3 in the Game 6 finale in L.A.

Don Zimmer later acknowledged having nightmares about Bucky Dent's fly-ball home run throughout the 1978 off-season. It could only make matters worse when, years later, Mickey Rivers admitted that Dent's bat didn't have a crack in it after all. He was just looking for an excuse to hand the light-hitting shortstop a corked bat!

September 30, 1951
October 3, 1951

"The Giants is dead."

—DODGERS MANAGER CHARLIE DRESSEN, AUGUST 1951

In 1951, New York was the center of the baseball universe. Even the most casual baseball fan knows what **Bobby Thomson** did on the third of October, but few can tell you what **Jackie Robinson** did three days before to force the famous playoff in the first place.

The Brooklyn Dodgers had met, and fallen to, their crosstown rivals in the Bronx in the 1947 and 1949 World Series. They narrowly missed meeting them again in 1950, losing to the Phillies on the last day of the season. Jackie Robinson had broken the color line in 1947, taking the inaugural Rookie of the Year award, then establishing himself as the National League's best player in 1949 when he led the league in both stolen bases and batting average. Roy Campanella, Duke Snider, Carl Furillo, and Gil Hodges joined with Robinson to power the game's highest-scoring offense.

The New York Giants, a perennial contender during the 1930s, had bottomed out in 1946 with a last-place finish. They climbed back into the first division in 1947 as the team hit a then record 221 home runs. In 1948, the Dodgers dumped their volatile manager, Leo Durocher, and he did the unthinkable by heading to Coogan's Bluff in Upper Manhattan to replace Mel Ott as leader of the hated New York Giants.

Durocher led the Giants back into the pennant race in 1950, but they ended the season 5 games off the pace. In 1951, the Giants added a 20-year-old center fielder named Willie Mays to their lineup, but they'd dug themselves an early hole by dropping 11 of their first 12. They found themselves 13½ games behind Brooklyn as late as August 12. Motivated in part by the trash talk seeping through the thin clubhouse walls after a Dodgers victory over the Giants, New York went on an unbelievable run. In their final 47 games, the Giants went 39–8, including their final seven in a row.

The Dodgers found themselves in a dead heat with the Giants on the final day of the season. They sent 36-year-old Preacher Roe and his 22–3 record to the mound, but he fell behind the Phillies 6–1 after only three innings. With the Giants beating the Braves in Boston, it appeared that it might be time to shovel the dirt on Brooklyn's pennant hopes.

Jackie Robinson wasn't packing it in yet. He tripled to key a three-run rally in the fifth that cut Philadelphia's lead to one. The Phillies responded with two in the bottom of the fifth, and the bad news only got worse for Brooklyn when the final score of the Giants-Braves game flashed up on the scoreboard. The Dodgers didn't quit, scoring three more in the eighth to tie the game.

Dodgers ace Don Newcombe came in to relieve in the eighth after shutting out the Phillies the day before. But not just Brooklyn was playing for keeps—the Phillies, playing only for pride, countered with their own ace, sending in Robin Roberts, who had also pitched the day before. Newcombe held the Phillies down through the 12th, when Philadelphia loaded the bases with two outs. Eddie Waitkus lined what looked like a certain game-winning single up the middle, only to see Jackie Robinson dive to his right and backhand the ball for the final out, holding onto it despite landing heavily on his elbow and stomach. Robinson lay in pain for a few moments, but was sufficiently recovered to hit the eventual game-winning home run off Robin Roberts in the top of the 14th.

Unlike the American League, the rules of the National League in 1951 called for a three-game playoff to determine who would play the New York Yankees in the World Series. The first game was played in Ebbets Field, where the red-hot Giants ran their winning streak to eight games with a 3–1 win. Bobby Thomson delivered what proved to be the game-winning blow, a two-out, two-run home run off losing pitcher Ralph Branca.

The series shifted to the Polo Grounds in Manhattan, where the Giants had two tries to wrap it up at home. Resting his aces, Larry Jansen and Sal Maglie, Leo Durocher called on Sheldon Jones, who had a losing record on the season. Burt Shotton, his pitching staff exhausted, called on rookie Clem Labine, who had started only a handful of games all season. Labine baffled the Giants, shutting them out on 6 hits, while the Dodgers unloaded for 13 hits and 10 runs off three Giants pitchers.

October 3 was a matchup of 20-game winners, Don Newcombe for Brooklyn and Sal "the Barber" Maglie for the Giants. Maglie didn't have his control early, walking Pee Wee Reese and Duke Snider with one out in the first. Jackie Robinson singled in Reese to give the Dodgers the early lead. Newcombe held the Giants scoreless until the seventh, when Monte Irvin doubled and Bobby Thomson drove him in.

The game didn't stay knotted up for very long. Maglie tired in the eighth, yielding one-out singles to Reese and Snider, then allowing Reese to score on a wild pitch. Robinson was intentionally walked to set up a double play, but Andy Pafko and Billy Cox each singled in a run to put Brooklyn up 4–1. After Newcombe retired the Giants in order in the eighth, the Dodgers were three outs away from redeeming themselves for allowing the pennant to slip out of their hands.

Baseball, as the cliché goes, is a game of inches. That was never more true than the bottom of the ninth inning in the Polo Grounds. Alvin Dark led off the ninth for the Giants with a "ground ball with eyes" that snuck between Robinson and Gil Hodges for a single. Now with a man on first, Hodges decided to hold the runner on, even though a left-handed hitter, Don Mueller, was at the plate. Mueller promptly sent a base hit through the gap where Hodges would have been, and the Giants had runners on first and third, the tying run at the plate, and no one out.

Former Negro League star Monte Irvin, who knocked in 121 runs during the season while hitting .312, stood in against Newcombe. The residents of Brooklyn heaved a collective sigh of relief when he fouled out to Gil Hodges. The Dodgers were a double-play grounder away from the World Series. First baseman Whitey Lockman, a line-drive-hitting lefty, didn't cooperate. He went the other way with a double to left field that scored Dark and sent Mueller to third. Mueller broke his ankle sliding into the base, and while he was being attended to, Dodgers manager Charlie Dressen called for a new pitcher.

These were the days before relief aces, and well before the days of statistical analysis of batter–pitcher matchups. Dressen called on starter Ralph Branca, who'd been taken deep by Bobby Thomson in the first game of the playoff, to face Thomson with the season on the line. On an 0–1 pitch, Thomson drove a fastball into the left-field seats for a 5–4 Giants victory.

In pictures of Thomson rounding the bases while his teammates go wild and the Dodgers hang their heads, you can see Jackie Robinson, competitive to the end, watching Thomson to be certain that he touched every base.

5

Greatest Hitting Moments—Postseason

Though the number of postseason tilts translates to fewer than half of 1 percent of all games played, the pressure and importance of these contests can turn a bloop single into the stuff of legend. As you play back these games in your head, the list of great moments becomes a longer and richer one than what you find when limiting yourself to the regular season alone. From game-winning home runs to series-turning base hits—with some of baseball's greatest outs thrown in along the way—each of these moments helped to determine an entire season's worth of blood, toil, sweat, and tears.

There are the base hits that ended a World Series or turned the tide of a series in the process of being lost; the series-long heroics of Mr. Octobers from the distant and not-so-distant past, and the acts of redemption by players down but not out. Along the way, we look at the postseason performances of the game's 25 greatest hitters (including the only one who never got a chance to play in a postseason game of any kind, and the one whose frequent, nationally televised October failures may make him wish there were two).

The list of the greatest hitting moments in postseason play is a long one, and it begins with the play unique to baseball—the game-winning home run, the sudden, sometimes totally unexpected ending, completed with a slow trot rather than a furious dash.

Game Winners and Series Winners

In the history of postseason play, only 25 games have ended on a home run—more than half in the last 20 years alone.

1949 World Series Game 1:
New York Yankees vs. Brooklyn Dodgers

It wasn't until 1949 that a World Series game ended with a home run trot and a mob of teammates at the plate. "Old Reliable," **Tommy Henrich**, playing first base for the Yankees, led off the bottom of the ninth inning with a solo home run into the right-field stands at Yankee Stadium to beat the Dodgers 1–0 in the 1949 opener. Don Newcombe had been magnificent for Brooklyn, yielding only four hits and no walks while striking out 11 before Henrich's blast. Allie Reynolds took the victory with a two-hit shutout. The Yankees went on to take the Dodgers in five.

1954 World Series Game 2:
New York Giants vs. Cleveland Indians

In 1954, pinch hitter **Dusty Rhodes** of the New York Giants lined a 10th-inning home run into the short porch in right field at the Polo Grounds to take Game 1 from the Indians and Bob Lemon, 5–2. Like Kirk Gibson's home run in 1988, Rhodes's shot set the tone for the series and established the underdog Giants as a very real threat to the 111-win Indians. The Giants went on to sweep the series, with Rhodes having a direct hand in three of the victories (see Chapter 6 for more on Rhodes's exploits).

1957 World Series Game 4:
Milwaukee Braves vs. New York Yankees

One of the least famous but most pivotal game-winning home runs in World Series history took place in the 1957 World Series. The Yankees were the defending champs. They had a 2–1 lead in the series and were in the process of stealing Game 4 from the Braves in Milwaukee. Down 4–1 in the top of the ninth with two outs and no one on, the Yankees rallied against Braves ace Warren Spahn. Yogi Berra and Gil McDougald singled, then Elston Howard hit a 3–2 pitch into the left-field stands to tie the game. The Yankees planted their feet on the Braves' throats in the top of the 10th with another two-out rally. Tony Kubek beat out an infield single, and Hank Bauer followed with a triple off the left-field fence to put New York up 5–4. Spahn didn't unravel with Mickey Mantle at the plate, stopping the bleeding with an inning-ending fly ball to right field.

Nippy Jones batted for Spahn to lead off the 10th. Like Cleon Jones 12 years later, Nippy used shoe polish to prove that he'd been hit with a pitched ball. Casey Stengel called on Bob Grim, who had 12 wins and a league-leading 19 saves for the Yankees during the regular season. A bunt by Red Schoendienst moved pinch runner Felix Mantilla to second. Shortstop Johnny Logan doubled into the left-field corner to tie the game. Slugging third baseman **Eddie Mathews**, who'd been held to 1 for 11 by Yankees pitching, sent the fans home happy with a two-run homer to win the game and even the Series at 2–2. Milwaukee would go on to take the Series in seven on the strength of Lew Burdette shutouts in both Game 5 and Game 7.

1964 World Series Game 3:
New York Yankees vs. St. Louis Cardinals

One of Mickey Mantle's finest World Series performances happened to be his last, and he played through it essentially on one leg. After having dropped the 1964 opener to the Cardinals in St. Louis, New York beat Bob Gibson in Game 2 and returned to Yankee Stadium for a Game 3 pitchers' duel between Curt Simmons and Jim Bouton. The game went to the bottom of the ninth inning tied at 1–1. Cardinals manager Johnny Keane pinch hit for Simmons in the top of the ninth with a man on second and one out. But two well-hit balls settled into the gloves of Maris in center and Mantle in right. The game went into the bottom of the ninth with knuckleball relief ace Barney Schultz facing Mantle. The Yankees' right fielder unloaded on Schultz's first pitch and deposited it deep in the right-field stands. It was World Series home run number 16, sending Mantle trotting past Babe Ruth for first on the all-time list. He would go on to hit number 17 in Game 6 in St. Louis, off the screen on top of the right-field roof at Sportsman's Park. It followed a Roger Maris blast and put the Yankees up 3–1 in a game they would win 8–3 to force Game 7. Down 6–0 to Bob Gibson in the top of the sixth of Game 7, Mantle took Gibson the other way for a three-run blast that cut the Cardinals' lead in half and put a scare into the St. Louis crowd. But as was the case in 1960, Mantle's exploits ultimately went for naught as the Yankees fell in seven games.

Then, from the 1970s on, as home runs began to come more frequently, so did game winners—frequently from very unlikely sources. For every Johnny Bench or Mark McGwire round-trip ticket, you were more likely to find a Bert Campaneris, John Lowenstein, Alan Ashby, George Vukovich, Ozzie Smith, Tony Peña, or Jim Leyritz along for the ride.

1973 NLCS Game 1: Cincinnati Reds vs. New York Mets

The "Ya Gotta Believe" Mets and their meager 83 wins were going up against the Big Red Machine. New York's Tom Seaver nursed a 1–0 lead through seven, but gave up a Pete Rose home run to tie it in the eighth and a **Johnny Bench** home run to win it. (Nothing new for Bench. In the bottom of the ninth of the final game of the NLCS the year before, Bench hit a game-tying home run off Dave Giusti as the Reds rallied for two to beat the Pirates.) The Mets would go on to take the series over the Reds 3–2, though suffering through more late-game home run heroics from Tony Perez and Pete Rose in Game 4.

1973 ALCS Game 3: Oakland A's vs. Baltimore Orioles

The same day that Pete Rose was homering in the top of the twelfth in New York (after hitting only five all season), Oakland shortstop **Bert Campaneris** was going yard against Mike Cuellar to beat the Orioles. Campaneris, who had homered only four times all season, went deep in the bottom of the 11th to beat Baltimore 2–1 and to put the A's up 2–1 in the series. Oakland would go on to take it in five.

1979 ALCS Game 1:
Baltimore Orioles vs. California Angels

Platoon player extraordinaire **John Lowenstein** hit a three-run homer off John Montague in the bottom of the 10th to propel the Orioles past the Angels 6–3. The Orioles beat the Angels in four, then went on to face the Pirates in the World Series.

1981 NL West Division Playoff Game 1:
Houston Astros vs. Los Angeles Dodgers

Catcher **Alan Ashby** had hit only four home runs during the regular season, but he beat the Dodgers and Dave Stewart with a three-run shot that gave Nolan Ryan a two-hit, 3–1 victory. The Astros won 1–0 in 11 the following day, then scored only two runs in dropping the next three games in Los Angeles.

1981 NL East Division Playoff Game 4:
Philadelphia Phillies vs. Montreal Expos

Four days after Ashby's game winner, the Phillies forced a fifth game against the Montreal Expos when pinch hitter **George Vukovich**—with only *one* home run in 26 at-bats—homered off Jeff Reardon in the bottom of the 10th. Reardon had retired eight batters in a row. But the defending champion Phillies fell to Steve Rogers the following day, and the Expos moved on to face the Dodgers, losing in five to a dramatic Rick Monday home run.

1984 NLCS Game 4: San Diego Padres vs. Chicago Cubs

The Padres pushed the Cubs to a decisive fifth game when **Steve Garvey** took Lee Smith deep in the bottom of the ninth for a two-run homer that gave San Diego a 7–5 win. The Padres went on to beat Cubs ace Rick Sutcliffe the following day on a ground ball that the ghost of John McGraw escorted through the legs of first baseman Leon "Bull" Durham.

1985 NLCS Game 5: St. Louis Cardinals vs. Los Angeles Dodgers

Shortly after a graphic flashed on the TV screen about **Ozzie Smith** having *never* hit a left-handed home run, Smith unloaded on a Tom Niedenfuer pitch to give St. Louis a 3–2 win and a 3–2 lead in the series. The Cardinals ended the series in Game 6 in L.A. on the strength of another dramatic home run you'll be reading about later.

1986 NLCS Game 3: New York Mets vs. Houston Astros

After this game, **Lenny Dykstra** told reporters that the last time he'd won a game with a home run was while playing Strat-o-Matic baseball with his brother. Dykstra's two-run homer in the bottom of the ninth off Dave Smith gave New York a 6–5 victory and a 2–1 edge on the Astros. Dykstra had only 8 home runs all season, though this blast is often credited with his subsequent interest in bulking up and going deep.

1988 World Series Game 3: Oakland A's vs. Los Angeles Dodgers

The '88 series is known for one extremely famous game winner in Game 1. Few remember that the only win the heavily favored A's managed against the Dodgers came on a Mark McGwire home run in the bottom of the ninth against Jay Howell. This is the only time that two games in the same World Series have ended on home runs. It was also the only hit McGwire would manage all series. The 2–1 win revived Oakland's hopes, which were promptly dashed by a hard-fought 4–3 loss in Game 4 and a complete-game four-hitter by Orel Hershiser in Game 5.

> *"I was numb after I hit. That was when we started the bash, in '88, so I remember bashing everybody. And I remember a lot of guys were sore the next day because I was doing it so hard. . . . "*
>
> —MARK MCGWIRE ON HIS GAME-WINNING HOME RUN IN GAME 3, 1988 WORLD SERIES

1995 AL Divisional Series Game 1:
Cleveland Indians vs. Boston Red Sox

The Indians rolled through the abbreviated 1995 season with 100 wins in 144 games, finishing 30 games ahead of their nearest competitor. They did it on hitting, with a powerful lineup that featured Albert Belle, Manny Ramirez, Jim Thome, and Eddie Murray. But it was backup catcher **Tony Peña**—a contributor of only 5 of the team's 207 home runs—who ended this marathon, 5–4, in the 13th inning. Peña's shot came two innings after a Tim Naehring home run for Boston was matched by Albert Belle in the bottom of the inning. Belle's blast prompted a corked-bat claim by the Red Sox, to which Albert replied with a finger pointed to his bicep. No one bothered to check Peña's bat.

1995 AL Wild-Card Series Game 2:
New York Yankees vs. Seattle Mariners

The Yankees returned to the postseason in 1995 after a 14-year absence, just in time to give Don Mattingly his first meaningful October baseball before calling it quits. Mattingly responded by hitting .417 with 6 RBI, but it was backup catcher **Jim Leyritz** who stole the show in Game 2 with his only hit of the series. It looked like Junior Griffey's home run in the top of the 12th at Yankee Stadium off John Wetteland was going to decide the game, but New York clawed back with a run in the bottom of the 12th and the game went three more innings. Mariano Rivera and Tim Belcher traded zeroes until the Yankees put two men on in the bottom of the 15th, and Jim Leyritz went the other way with a drive through the early morning mist and into the right-field stands. Little did anyone know at the time that this would just be the first of many dramatic postseason home runs for the journeyman Leyritz.

1996 ALCS Game 1: New York Yankees vs. Baltimore Orioles

In a bizarre game at Yankee Stadium, New York tied the Orioles at 4–4 in the bottom of the eighth inning on a **Derek Jeter** fly ball to right that a 12-year-old fan reached out and took away from right fielder Tony Tarasco. The Orioles screamed bloody murder, but the home run stood—with the little brat treated like royalty the following day. The game remained tied until the 11th, when Bernie Williams untied it with a mammoth blow into the left-field stands against Randy Myers.

1999 ALCS Game 1: New York Yankees vs. Boston Red Sox

Three years later, Bernie Williams did it all over again in a nearly identical situation, though this time from the left side of the plate.

Bernie wasn't the only one repeating history that night. From 1919 to 1999, the Red Sox had managed only four pennants and no titles, falling short of a championship all four times in seven games and falling short of a pennant three times on the last day of the season. Going into play that evening, the Yankees had won 35 pennants and 24 titles over the same stretch—and had twice been the team to deny the Red Sox a pennant on the last day of the season.

In the 1999 best-of-five wild-card series, the Red Sox had fallen behind the Cleveland Indians 0–2 and appeared on their way to yet another postseason sweep. In the 19 postseason games Boston had played dating back to the infamous Bill Buckner game in 1986, the Red Sox had lost 18. Boston's last title: 1918. Still don't believe in The Curse?

But the Red Sox had proceeded to reel off three straight victories over the Indians to set up the first postseason showdown with the Yankees in the storied history of their heated rivalry. Red Sox fans could not be blamed for anticipating more strange doings and unpleasant outcomes. They got both.

Down 3–0 almost immediately in Game 1, the Yankees managed to crawl back to a tie by the seventh inning. A controversial call in the top of the 10th inning robbed Boston of a scoring opportunity. In the bottom of the inning, the Red Sox brought in late-season acquisition Rod Beck to face switch-hitting center fielder Bernie Williams. Beck tried to work Williams inside. He got away with the first pitch; the second one ended up behind the center-field wall. Williams became the first man to end two postseason games with home runs—both in extra innings, no less.

The Yankees went on to take the series in five and eventually bring home pennant 36 and title 25.

1999 NL Wild-Card Series Game 4: New York Mets vs. Arizona Diamondbacks

Across town only four days earlier, the New York Mets had also won a playoff game in 10 innings, 4–3, on a home run to dead center. Had someone told you in advance that the blow would come off of the bat of the Mets' catcher, you would have reasonably concluded that Mike Piazza was finally finishing a season with some gas left in the tank. But Piazza was out of the lineup and on the bench watching a journeyman backup take the hacks.

After blowing a 2–1 lead in the top of the eighth inning, the Mets rallied in the bottom of the inning to tie the score. The game remained knotted up until one out in the bottom of the 10th when the immortal Todd Pratt, who had hit only 3 home runs all season and 16 in his career, took hard-throwing Matt Mantei over the center-field wall to end the series. He became only the fourth man to end a postseason series with a home run—and so to the list of Mazeroski, Chambliss, and Carter is added Pratt.

1999 NLCS Game 5: New York Mets vs. Atlanta Braves

Going into 1999, no one had ever hit a game-winning grand slam to end a post-season game. After **Robin Ventura** did it in the 15th inning of a Game 5 marathon, *still* no one had done it.

Say what?

First, some background from a remarkable game. Having staved off a sweep in Game 4, the Mets scratched and clawed to stay alive in Game 5, using *nine* pitchers along the way. Braves manager Bobby Cox used a mere six as the game stayed locked up at 2–2 from the fourth inning until the 15th. Atlanta broke the tie in the top of the 15th, with the big blow a clutch Chipper Jones double off Octavio Dotel amidst a steady rain and a torrent of verbal abuse from the Shea Stadium faithful.

Three outs and *six* days away from a series date with the Yankees, two of Atlanta's four aces—lefty Tom Glavine and righty Kevin Millwood—warmed up in the bullpen, expecting to get the call from Cox to close out the Mets. Instead, Kevin McGlinchy, just one year removed from Class-A ball, went back out to pitch the 15th. Glavine and Millwood watched, hands on hips, as Shawon Dunston fouled off pitch after pitch after pitch before grounding a single up the middle. They continued to watch as Cox left McGlinchy in to walk pinch hitter Matt Franco. Edgardo Alfonzo bunted them both into scoring position, and McGlinchy intentionally walked John Olerud. McGlinchy then unintentionally walked the immortal Todd Pratt to tie the game.

Atlanta all but waved a white flag when the right-handed McGlinchy remained in to face the left-handed Robin Ventura with the bases loaded. With nowhere to put him and behind in the count, McGlinchy had to challenge Ventura in the strike zone, and the slumping third baseman drove the ball over the drawn-in outfield and over the right-field wall.

With the winning run already across the plate, Ventura's teammates mobbed him between first and second and would not allow him to finish his home-run trot. So, by the official scoring rules, the Mets won the game 4–3 on the longest game-winning single in the game's history.

Two days later, the Braves and Mets hooked up in another wild, extra-inning ball game, with Atlanta coming out on top and setting up a showdown for decade supremacy with the New York Yankees.

1999 World Series Game 3: New York Yankees vs. Atlanta Braves

The Atlanta Braves had laid premature claim to "Team of the '90s" status after beating the Cleveland Indians in the 1995 World Series, their fourth postseason appearance of the decade and first championship. They appeared to be well on their way to cementing their claim in 1996 when they brought a 2–0 series lead home with them from Yankee Stadium—only to watch New York win three straight in Atlanta and the finale in New York.

By 1999, the Braves had been in more postseason series than any team in the 90s—or any decade, for that matter—only to find more ways to lose them than any other team. Until 1999, however, they had never been swept. Down 0–2 in the '99 World Series and heading to Yankee Stadium, Atlanta's best chance for averting such an ignominious close to their decade would come in Game 3.

Bobby Cox called on a flu-ridden Tom Glavine to start, hoping for seven innings. When he got them—and a 5–3 lead—he sent Glavine out for the bottom of the eighth. The Yankees had been digging themselves out of a 5–1 hole since the fifth when Chad Curtis homered, and they completed the climb in the eighth when Joe Girardi led off with a single and Chuck Knoblauch hit a fly ball to right field that was turned into a two-run home run by Yankee Stadium's short porch.

A threat from either side of the plate, Bernie Williams is one of the most complete players in the game today.

This blow knocked Glavine out of the game and led to extra innings for Atlanta yet again. Fearing a pinch-hit appearance by Darryl Strawberry in the 10th, Cox brought in lefty Mike Remlinger to face the right-handed Chad Curtis. Curtis had been part of a revolving door in left field all season, one of the few weak links in the Yankees' lineup, but he drove Remlinger's first pitch for an extra-inning game winner. New York went on to complete the sweep in Game 4, making it twelve straight victories in World Series games, tying their own record set back in 1927, 1928, and 1932.

Of the half-dozen most famous game winners, one set the tone for the entire series, two forced a Game 7, and three were actually series winners.

1976 ALCS Game 5: New York Yankees vs. Kansas City Royals

"Running around the bases, I remember touching first and second, and then somebody tripped me between second and short. I got up and people were trying to steal my helmet, so I took off my helmet and put it under my arm like a football. Third base was ridiculous. There were people all over the

place, and the base had to have been stolen by then. I just went around them and went close to the other team's dugout, then I just took a beeline to our dugout because home plate was also full of people. There was a guy in front of our dugout, and I just walked right over him. I gave him a little shoulder block to get into that dugout."

—CHRIS CHAMBLISS ON HIS 1976 ALCS GAME 5 HOME RUN TROT

It had been 12 long years since the Yankees had played a meaningful game in October. Behind the shrewd trading of GM Gabe Paul, New York assembled a team of clutch, if not particularly flashy, players. Typical of the pre-Reggie, pre-Winfield, pre-Rickey Yankees was first baseman and cleanup hitter **Chris Chambliss**. Son of a Navy chaplain, Chambliss quietly went about his business for 16 years in the big leagues, knocking in runs (though never 100), hitting some home runs (though never more than 20), and putting up a decent batting average (topping out at .304). He quietly endured—or simply ignored—George Steinbrenner's public musings about acquiring Rod Carew to fill out his own personal All-Star team.

Chambliss's finest moments came in the 1976 ALCS against the Kansas City Royals. In Game 3—the first postseason game in Yankee Stadium since Tim McCarver ripped New York's hearts out with a 10th-inning three-run homer in Game 5 in 1964—Chambliss hit a home run to power a Yankees comeback from a 3–0 first-inning deficit. By the eighth inning of Game 5, Chambliss was 10 for 20 on the series, and the Yankees were a handful of outs away from taking on the Reds in the series. But the Yankees' 6–3 lead disappeared in a flash as George Brett crushed a three-run homer off Grant Jackson in the eighth inning to tie the game.

The Royals rallied in the top of the ninth against Dick Tidrow, but a controversial call on a force play ended the inning and kept Brett from coming to the plate with ducks on the pond. The Royals were still hot about the call when Chambliss came to bat against Mark Littell in the ninth. He hit Littell's first pitch deep toward right-center; paused briefly at the plate, standing on his tiptoes to watch its flight; then thrust his arms over his head as the ball disappeared over the wall. As he ran the bases, he was accompanied by a mob of fans who came streaming onto the field. He knocked several of them out of his way as he headed in the general direction of third, flattened one with a body block on his way toward home, then ran for his life into the dugout. Later, he would return to the field with an armed police escort to touch third and home.

In the 1976 World Series, the Reds held the Yankees to a .222 batting average and eight runs in a four-game sweep. Chambliss (.313), Lou Piniella (.333), and Thurman Munson (.529) were the only ones who remembered to bring their bats along. They wouldn't be swinging them in vain in 1977 and 1978, as they brought the championship back to the Bronx for the first time since 1962.

1975 World Series Game 6: Boston Red Sox vs. Cincinnati Reds

"I was in left field, and I caught the ball off the foul pole. It's sitting some-where in my garage at home."

—GEORGE FOSTER, ON CARLTON FISK'S GAME 6 HOME RUN

They call it the greatest game ever played—not just baseball game, but any game.

The Red Sox hadn't won a World Series since 1918—when Babe Ruth was a star pitcher, Boston had won four titles in seven years, Yankee Stadium didn't exist, and New York never won. Now, 57 years later, the Red Sox were in only their third World Series since selling Babe Ruth to the Yankees, after dropping the 1946 and 1967 Series in seven games. They were up against the Big Red Machine, which, like the Braves of the '90s, had been regulars in the postseason who always seemed to come up short—a loss in the 1970 and 1972 series, and an upset at the hands of the 83–79 Mets in the 1973 NLCS.

Boston trailed 3–2 after seeing Cincinnati win Game 2 in their final at-bat and steal Game 3 on a very controversial call in the bottom of the 10th. Now the series was back in Fenway Park, and the Red Sox needed a win to force yet another Game 7. Boston went up 3–0 on Gary Nolan in the first when rookie phenom Fred Lynn hit a three-run homer. It looked like the Sox would put the game away in the third when they loaded the bases, but Cincinnati brought in Jack Billingham and he struck out Rico Petrocelli to end the threat. Red Sox ageless pitching ace Luis Tiant worked in and out of trouble and kept the Reds baffled until the fifth with his whirling dervish pitching motion and variety of arm angles. Ken Griffey Sr. hit a two-run triple to center, and all of New England held its breath as Lynn crashed into the wall and fell to the ground in a daze. He shook it off, but Johnny Bench delivered a clutch two-out game-tying single.

The Reds threatened in the seventh, but it looked as if Tiant would wriggle out of this one as well. After Griffey and Joe Morgan singled to open the inning, Bench pushed Carl Yastrzemski to the base of the Green Monster in left, and Tony Perez flied to right. This time it was George Foster who delivered the big two-out hit, a two-run double off the center-field wall. Defensive specialist Cesar Geronimo chased Tiant in the top of the eighth with a home run to make it 6–3.

Boston rallied in the bottom of the eighth as Fred Lynn singled off the leg of pitcher Pedro Borbon. Borbon then walked Petrocelli and was replaced by rookie closer Rawly Eastwick, who led the NL with 22 saves. Eastwick struck out Dwight Evans and got Rick Burleson to line out to Foster in left. Former Red Bernie Carbo, chafing at the bit to get more playing time in the Series, came on to pinch hit and hit a 3–2 bomb into the center-field bleachers to tie the game—his second pinch-hit home run of the series.

The Red Sox nearly won it in regulation in the bottom of the ninth when Denny Doyle walked to lead off the inning and Yastrzemski singled him to third. Sparky Anderson called on his other young relief ace, Will McEnaney, to try to put out this fire. He walked **Carlton Fisk** intentionally to load the bases and set up the force at home, but it brought Boston's best hitter, Fred Lynn, to the plate. McEnaney couldn't coax a ground ball out of Lynn. Instead, Lynn hit a fly ball down the left-field line. George Foster, known more for his hitting than his fielding, set up his throw perfectly and fired a strike to home plate to nail Denny Doyle. Petrocelli left his fifth and sixth men on base for the game when he grounded out to send the game to extra innings.

The heroics continued in the top of the 11th when Dwight Evans robbed Joe Morgan of a two-run homer with a miraculous grab in right field, then threw to second base to double-up Griffey and end the inning. Rick Wise worked out of trouble in the top of the 12th, stranding two more Reds—the 10th and 11th of the game. But Boston had shown no indication of being able to solve Cincinnati's eighth pitcher, Pat Darcy, going down 1-2-3 in the 10th and 11th and getting only one ball out of the infield. But Carlton Fisk ended the four-hour marathon by drilling Darcy's first pitch in the 12th inning off the left-field foul pole. Television cameras caught Fisk hopping down the first-base line, waving his arms to will the ball to stay fair, then leaping about four feet into the air when the ball ricocheted off the pole to end the game.

The game ended early in the morning of October 22, and the two teams got together later that day to decide things. Unfortunately for Boston, their dramatic victory was not followed with an anticlimactic blowout. The Reds didn't fold up as many teams do when coming so close and falling short. Boston moved ahead 3–0, but couldn't hold off the clutch hitting of Tony Perez, Pete Rose, and Joe Morgan. The Reds won the game 4–3 on a two-out single to center by Joe Morgan in the top of the ninth, their third victory in their final at-bat in the series. Game 7 ended with Carlton Fisk on deck watching Carl Yastrzemski fly to center.

GREATEST OUTS IN THE WORLD SERIES

What would a hitting book be without some outs? In addition to Fisk's and Carbo's dramatic home runs, two of the most famous outs (actually four, given that both catches resulted in double plays) also took place in Game 6 in 1975: Dwight Evans's great grab to rob Joe Morgan, and George Foster's throw to nail Denny Doyle. Here are some others:

Game 3, 1969: New York Mets vs. Baltimore Orioles

When the 1969 World Series switched settings from Baltimore to New York, the ability of the Mets to complete their miracle was still very much in doubt. The Orioles had seen the Mets' best—Seaver and Koosman—and had roughed up Seaver in Game 1 and had fallen just short in Game 2. In Game 3, with 16–4 Jim Palmer going up against 13–12 Gary Gentry, it looked like Baltimore would take command of the series. Though the Mets jumped ahead 3–0 on a home run by Tommie Agee and a two-run double by Gentry of all people, the Orioles looked ready to make some noise in the fourth. After going hitless through three innings, Frank Robinson and Boog Powell put together some singles. After Brooks Robinson struck out, catcher Elrod Hendricks sent a drive to deep left-center. Center fielder **Tommie Agee** sprinted back and made a brilliant backhanded catch at the base of the wall, the ball half in and half out of the webbing of his glove.

Down 4–0, the Orioles rallied again in the seventh. Gentry walked the bases loaded with two outs, and manager Gil Hodges called on a very young, very talented, and very wild pitcher named Nolan Ryan. He got ahead on Paul Blair quickly, then challenged him with another fastball on 0–2. Blair drilled it to right-center, but Agee ran this one down, too, diving headlong on the warning track to come up with it. Later, in the ninth, Blair would bat once more against Ryan with the bases loaded and two outs, falling behind 0–2—but this time the kid froze him with a curveball. (If the Mets are patient with this guy Ryan, they just might have something here.)

Game 6, 1947: Brooklyn Dodgers vs. New York Yankees
The Yankees and the Dodgers were meeting in the World Series for only the second of 11 times in 1947. Brooklyn was down 3–2 in games and needing a win at Yankee Stadium to force Game 6. They led 8–5 in the sixth when the great Joe DiMaggio, who had already hit two home runs in the series, came to bat with two on and two out. DiMaggio hit a drive to Death Valley in left where a little-known and little-used reserve named **Al Gionfriddo**—just into the game as a defensive replacement, who had played in only 37 games all season and would never play in another—raced all the way back to the 415-foot sign to haul it in. It was so great, so timely, and so unlikely a catch that the stoic DiMaggio was moved to actually kick the dirt between first and second in disgust. The Dodgers held on to win 8–6, but the Yankees won Game 7, 5–2.

Game 7, 1955: Brooklyn Dodgers vs. New York Yankees
An even more critical out was recorded by the Dodgers against the Yankees in the 1955 finale. At this point, the Yankees had beaten the Dodgers in 1941, 1947, 1949, 1952, and 1953. Brooklyn had a chance to wrap things up in Game 6, but the Yankees bombed Karl Spooner for five runs in the first, and Whitey Ford did the rest. In Game 7, Johnny Podres was working in and out of trouble as he protected a 2–0 lead. In the bottom of the sixth, Podres walked Billy Martin leading off. Gil McDougald beat out a bunt to put runners on first and second. Yogi Berra came up and sliced a line drive into the left-field corner that another defensive replacement just into the game—**Sandy Amoros**—ran down along the line. Amoros turned a potential game-tying extra-base hit into a double play when he threw to first to double up McDougald. Podres held on for the 2–0 win that gave Brooklyn its only victory over the Bronx Bombers.

Game 4, 1941: New York Yankees vs. Brooklyn Dodgers
In 1941, with two outs in the ninth inning, the Yankees made an out that helped them win the game.

It was the first time the Dodgers and the Yankees would meet in the World Series, and Brooklyn's Hugh Casey had a 4–3 lead on the Yankees and was one strike away from evening the series at 2–2. The Dodgers had not yet made their reputation for post-season near-misses, having only been in two other Fall Classics, back in 1916 and 1920 and losing both. This reputation was born when Casey loaded up a spitter that neither the hitter, **Tommy Henrich**, nor the catcher, Mickey Owen, could handle. Henrich reached first base on the strikeout, and the meat of the order followed. Joe DiMaggio singled. The underrated left fielder Charlie Keller doubled off the right-field wall at Ebbets Field to put New York on top 5–4. Bill Dickey walked, and second baseman Joe Gordon followed with a two-run double over the left fielder's head. Devastated, the Dodgers went down 1-2-3 in the ninth without getting the ball out of the infield, then managed only four hits and one run in the finale the next day.

Game 1, 1954: New York Giants vs. Cleveland Indians

When the topic of great catches comes up, the one **Willie Mays** made in the Polo Grounds in the 1954 World Series goes to the top of the list. Two things get lost in the description of Mays's over-the-shoulder catch on the dead run about 460 feet from the plate: the game situation and the throw he made after the catch. It was the eighth inning of Game 1 of the series between the Giants and the heavily favored Indians, who had set a record with 111 wins during the regular season. The game was tied 2–2, there were no outs, and Cleveland had put its first two men on base, knocking Giants veteran Sal Maglie out of the game. Vic Wertz, who would go on to hit .500 in the Series for a team that hit .190, unloaded on a Don Liddle pitch and sent it to the deepest part of the large, oval stadium. Mays ran it down, then wheeled and fired to second to hold Al Rosen at first and keep Larry Doby from advancing farther than third. Liddle worked out of the inning and the game went into extra innings, setting up Dusty Rhodes's game winner in the 10th.

Game 2, 1978: Los Angeles Dodgers vs. New York Yankees

Not all famous outs in World Series play have been attributable to great defensive play. Two of the most famous were strikeouts of renowned clutch hitters with the game on the line. In 1978, the Dodgers returned to the postseason to face a Yankees team that had beaten them the year before on the strength of three Reggie Jackson home runs in the final game. After unloading on Ed Figueroa in Game 1, L.A. held a 4–3 lead in the ninth inning of Game 2, anxious to put away the defending champs. With two men on and two men out, the only one standing in the way was Reggie Jackson. Tommy Lasorda had put the game in the hands of 21-year-old rookie **Bob Welch**. With the count 3–2, Welch challenged Jackson with fastballs, and Reggie fouled off four of them, nearly screwing himself into the ground with each swing. Determined to further cement his reputation as Mr. October, Jackson was irate when Welch finally blew a fastball by him to end the game.

The Yankees got their measure of revenge by taking the next four, beating Welch in extra innings in a pivotal Game 4, while Reggie got some personal satisfaction by taking Welch very deep in the seventh inning of Game 6 to put the finishing touches on a Series-clinching 7–2 win.

Game 7, 1926: St. Louis Cardinals vs. New York Yankees

"I looked into his eyes and saw that they were bloodshot, but they weren't foggy. I gave him the ball and told him to get Lazzeri."

—ROGERS HORNSBY, ON CALLING FOR GROVER ALEXANDER IN
GAME 7 OF THE 1926 WORLD SERIES

For most of their existence, the St. Louis Cardinals had been the doormats of the National League. With the arrival of Rogers Hornsby, that began to change. The second baseman and manager led the Cardinals to their first World Series in 1926, where they had to face the New York Yankees. The Yankees had been the doormats of the American League until the Red Sox sold them Babe Ruth; but even with the Babe, their results had been mixed. The Giants had beaten them in 1921 and swept them while humiliating Ruth in 1922. The Yankees had earned their first and only championship in 1923 in the first year of a new ballpark called Yankee Stadium.

These teams met in 1926, with the Yankees taking a Series 3–2 lead on a clutch extra-inning sacrifice fly by Tony Lazzeri. The Series shifted back to New York, giving the Yankees two games at home to try to wrap things up. The Cardinals jumped all over them in Game 6, winning 10–2 with **Grover Cleveland Alexander** earning his second complete-game victory of the Series. Alexander was a 300-game winner nearing the end of his career. An alcoholic, epileptic, and a victim of shell shock as a result of his tour of duty in World War I, Alexander had been cut loose by the Cubs earlier in the season after showing up at the park drunk one too many times. He was only 9–7 for St. Louis during the regular season, though his ERA was still the lowest on the staff.

Hornsby had to call on Alexander again in Game 7 the following day. The Cardinals were clinging to a 3–2 lead in the bottom of the seventh, and the Yankees had solved starter Jesse Haines. The bases were loaded with Hall of Famers, two men were out, and another Hall of Famer, Tony Lazzeri, was at the plate. Hornsby brought in Alexander, uncertain whether the veteran would even be sober enough to pitch. He wasn't drunk, but he was badly hung over, and Hornsby was putting the season in his hands. It looked like it was going to be a move that would cost him the Series when Lazzeri drove a 1–1 pitch down the left-field line, but it hooked foul at the last minute. Alexander pulled the string on his next pitch and had Lazzeri way out in front of it, striking him out to end the threat. He retired five in a row without a ball leaving the infield, then pitched gingerly to Babe Ruth with two out in the bottom of the ninth. Ruth walked on a 3–2 pitch, then was thrown out trying to steal second to end the game.

Rejuvenated, Alexander returned in 1927 to win 21 games at the age of 40. He won another 16 in 1928, helping the Cardinals reach another World Series. No heroics this time, however, as the Yankees ran up 11 runs on him in five innings in two appearances. Tony Lazzeri still couldn't figure him out, though, managing only a double on a fly ball lost in the sun.

Game 7, 1962: New York Yankees vs. San Francisco Giants
This is to World Series outs what Bill Mazeroski's home run is to hits.

In 1962, the Giants and Dodgers, out on the West Coast now, once again finished in a tie for first place. And just like 1951, the Giants rallied for four runs in the ninth inning of the final game of the playoff to take the pennant—though no home runs this time, just a lot of walks and defensive lapses by the Dodgers.

The dramatic tension of the World Series was dampened a bit by a long stretch of rain that held up Game 6 in San Francisco for three days. Billy Pierce held up to the delay better than Whitey Ford, pitching a complete-game three-hitter to force a Game 7. The final game was a nail-biter, with **Ralph Terry**—who had been victimized by Bill Mazeroski two years before—and Jack Sanford taking turns setting the side down in order. Through four, Sanford had allowed only one hit—but a pair of singles, a walk to the pitcher, and a double-play grounder put the Yankees up 1–0. Terry, meanwhile, continued to mow down the Giants. He had a perfect game for five and two-thirds, until Sanford broke it up with a single, and then started to weaken in the seventh. Willie Mays hit a line drive into the left-field corner that Tom Tresh ran down. Willie McCovey followed with a triple over Mickey Mantle's head in center, but Terry bore down and got the very dangerous Orlando Cepeda on strikes.

Billy O'Dell bailed the Giants out of a bases-loaded, no-outs jam in the eighth when he coaxed ground balls out of Roger Maris and Elston Howard that were turned into a force play and a double play. In the bottom of the ninth, Matty Alou batted for O'Dell and beat out a bunt. Terry, trying to close a three-hit shutout, struck out both Felipe Alou and Chuck Hiller. Willie Mays lined a double into right field, but Roger Maris kept Alou at third base with a great throw. Now manager Ralph Houk faced a very difficult decision. How much did Terry, a 23-game winner during the regular season and virtually unhittable in the Series, have left? Left-hander Willie McCovey, who had hit 20 home runs in a half-season of play, had struggled during the Series, but two of his hits—a home run in Game 2 and a triple today—had come off the right-hander Terry. On deck was right-handed Orlando Cepeda, who had hit 35 home runs, knocked in 114 runs, and batted .306 during the regular season. He was only 3 for 19 in the Series, however, and had struck out twice and popped up against Terry on the day. Bill Stafford and Bud Daley were warming in the bullpen, but neither was a closer by today's standards—or even those of 1962.

Walk McCovey and let Terry pitch to the slumping Cepeda? Pull him and bring in a lefty to face McCovey? Houk let Terry decide—pitch to McCovey rather than load the bases and have no margin for error against Cepeda—and gave Terry the chance to exorcise the ghost of Bill Mazeroski. McCovey came close to ending it all on the first pitch, but his drive down the right-field line curved foul. On the next pitch, McCovey lined a bullet that would score Alou easily and set up a showdown between the brilliant baserunning of Willie Mays and the strong arm of Roger Maris—except that second baseman **Bobby Richardson** was standing in the perfect spot to catch the line drive without even having to move.

1991 World Series Game 6: Minnesota Twins vs. Atlanta Braves

"He threw me a change-up, and he hung it, and I hit it. I didn't know if it was out when I hit. I didn't know if it was high enough. I thought it was

gonna hit off the Plexiglass. But it just kept going, and it went out about eight or nine rows up. . . . It was unbelievable. Because I've come up in my career lots of times and got the base hit or whatever to win . . . but in order to win a game with a home run, I had never done that. So I guess I picked a hell of a time to do it."

—KIRBY PUCKETT, ON HIS GAME-WINNING HOME RUN IN GAME 6
OF THE 1991 WORLD SERIES

Carlton Fisk's home run in the 1975 World Series was just the final in a string of hero-ics by several players over the course of the evening. In 1991's version of Game 6, **Kirby Puckett** did it all himself.

Fans of the underdog didn't know who to pull for in the '91 Series. Both teams had gone from last in 1990 to first in 1991. While the Twins were only four years removed from a title in 1987, the Braves had been wandering the desert for more than 30 years. Two appearances in the NLCS were washouts. They were swept in '69 by the Mets as their pitchers were pummeled for 27 runs in three games, and they batted .169 with five runs and one extra-base hit in a three-game sweep at the hands of the Cardinals in 1982.

This Braves team had proven to be far more resilient than those two. They didn't know they weren't good enough. They beat the defending NL East champion Pirates in seven games. Down 3–2 and playing the final two games in Pittsburgh after ex-Brave Zane Smith shut them out 1–0 in Game 5, the Braves responded with back-to-back shutouts. Twenty-one-year-old Steve Avery combined with Alejandro Peña for his second 1–0 shutout of the series, then John Smoltz combined with his hypnotist to throw a complete-game 4–0 shutout to send Atlanta to the World Series.

What made Kirby Puckett such a tough out was that he murdered pitches both in and out of the strike zone.

Minnesota solved the Braves' pitching in the first two games in the Metrodome, beating Charlie Liebrandt 5–2 and Tom Glavine 3–2 behind 36-year-old Jack Morris and Kevin Tapani. They pushed the Braves to the brink in Game 3, rallying from a 4–1 deficit on home runs by Kirby Puckett and Chili Davis to force extra innings in Game 3. Mark Lemke won the game for Atlanta in the 12th with a two-out single off Rick Aguilera. The Braves also won Game 4 in their final at-bat, the key blow a triple by the light-hitting Lemke.

The Braves took control of the series with a 14–5, 17-hit blowout in Game 5. Minnesota didn't cave in, however. They scored twice in the first off Steve Avery in Game 6, then kept their lead thanks to a home-run-robbing catch by Kirby Puckett in the third. Terry Pendleton tied the game with a home run in the fifth, but Puckett knocked in the go-ahead run in the bottom of the inning. Scott Erickson couldn't hold the lead for the Twins and was chased in the seventh. The game went to extra innings, and starter Charlie Liebrandt was forced to come out of the bullpen for the Braves in the 11th. Puckett greeted him with a line-drive home run that sent a remarkable series to its seventh game.

Unlike Fisk in 1975, Puckett's heroics were followed with a championship. Jack Morris took on John Smoltz, who grew up near Detroit watching the then Tiger ace. They matched each other pitch for pitch for eight innings, then Smoltz was relieved by Mike Stanton in a scoreless game. The Braves had come closer to scoring. David Justice barely missed the foul pole on a mammoth drive to right field. Lonnie Smith—who had been dumb-lucky enough to be playing for his fourth world championship for four different teams—pulled one of the costliest baserunning blunders in baseball history, failing to score on a Terry Pendleton double to deep left in the seventh. The veteran Smith had been decoyed by a pair of green middle infielders, Greg Gagne and Chuck Knoblauch, into thinking Pendleton's bomb was actually a ground ball.

Jack Morris talked manager Tom Kelly into sending him out for the 10th, and he continued to keep the Braves at bay. Braves manager Bobby Cox, meanwhile, pushed the wrong buttons and watched his bullpen falter in the bottom of the inning. The Twins won 1–0. Unfortunately for Atlanta's fans, this combination of managerial miscalculations and bullpen miscues would continue in October for the rest of the decade.

1988 World Series Game 1: Los Angeles Dodgers vs. Oakland A's

"The man who is the spearhead of the Dodger offense throughout the year, who saved them in the League Championship, will not see any action tonight, for sure."

—ANNOUNCER VIN SCULLY

"I don't believe what I just saw."

—ANNOUNCER JACK BUCK

Easily the most memorable home run of the past 20 years, many who have seen it countless times still don't believe it actually happened. It was hard enough to believe that the 1988 Dodgers were even in the World Series at all.

Their best hitter, MVP **Kirk Gibson**, was hampered by legs so bad that he could barely stand up to swing a bat, and it was assumed that he would miss the entire series. Without him, L.A.'s lineup was arguably the worst to ever reach the postseason, and easily the worst to ever win the whole thing. First base was a revolving door all year, with Tommy Lasorda settling on a platoon of Franklin Stubbs and Mickey Hatcher. They combined to hit 8 home runs and bat .230. Shortstop Alfredo Griffin was below the Mendoza Line at .199. There may be no more obscure fact in all human knowledge than Jeff Hamilton being the third baseman on the '88 championship team. Mike Marshall played right field in his last productive season before whining his way out of baseball, leading the team in RBI with 82. T-Bone Shelby played center, Mike Scioscia caught, and Steve Sax played second. The Mets have never been the same since failing to get past such a mediocre crew.

The Oakland A's, meanwhile, had won 104 games during the regular season, then swept through the Red Sox in four games in the ALCS. They had 24-year-old Mark McGwire, 23-year-old 40/40 man Jose Canseco, and other Bash Brothers Dave Henderson, Don Baylor, and Dave Parker. They had Dave Stewart and Bob Welch on the mound, with Dennis Eckersley's flawless control and 45 saves in the bullpen behind them. It was reasonable to question whether the Dodgers even belonged in the same league with them, much less the same field.

A second-inning grand slam by Jose Canseco off the center-field camera put the A's up 4–2 on Tim Belcher. Canseco would not manage another hit all Series. The Dodgers closed to within 4–3 in the sixth, but Dave Stewart held them off until the ninth, when he handed the ball to Eckersley to close it out. NBC announcer Bob Costas had made his way down to field level to prepare for postgame interviews, and he was close enough to hear the grunts coming from the Dodger runway as Kirk Gibson tried to swing a bat. It was hard to believe that the man would even try to walk, much less try to hit Dennis Eckersley's pitches, but with a man on and two out, Gibson limped out of the Dodgers' dugout to bat for Alejandro Peña.

Through the years, the Dodgers have had hitters who could put up some decent numbers and look pretty doing it. But like the Braves of the '90s, their lineup rarely featured the gruff, dour, chair-throwing cuss who took losing personally. Kirk Gibson was as unlikely a candidate for the Ivory-fresh Dodger whites of Steve Garvey, Steve Sax, and Bill Russell as Thurman Munson or Pepper Martin would have been. But three days' growth and a fearsome glare all wrapped up in Dodger blue was just one of many surreal aspects to the scene that ensued.

With one man on, two outs in the books, and two strikes on Gibson, Eck tried to paint the low outside corner with a back-door slider. The pitch caught a little bit too much of the plate and sped up Gibson's bat enough that he could drive it to deep right-center on arm strength alone. As the camera panned toward the right-field pavilion in Dodger Stadium, you could see the brake lights come on as Dodgers fans on the way out of the park and listening to Jack Buck's call on the radio brought their cars to a screeching halt, not knowing whether to scream with glee or curse their own foolishness.

It was Gibson's only at-bat in the series. If ever a series was won in Game 1, the 1988 World Series was. Orel Hershiser continued the pitching mastery that saw him go the month of September without giving up an earned run, shutting out the A's on three hits. With another complete-game gem in Game 5 to wrap things up for the Dodgers, it would be difficult to deny Hershiser the Series MVP. But if ever a man deserved it for one at-bat, it was Gibson in '88.

The ultimate base hit has never happened: the home run with two outs in the bottom of the ninth inning of the seventh game that turns defeat into victory. These next two guys came the closest.

1993 World Series Game 6: Toronto Blue Jays vs. Philadelphia Phillies

"When he hit it, I couldn't breathe. I knew it was out. When you're down by a run and you're about to get three, you're going to be a world champion. I was pretty good in arithmetic."

—NICK LEYVA, BLUE JAYS THIRD-BASE COACH

"They haven't made up the word yet to describe what the feeling is."

—JOE CARTER

After blowing a 14–9 lead in one inning in Game 4, the Philadelphia Phillies proved resilient against the defending champion Toronto Blue Jays. A Curt Schilling shutout in Game 5 sent the series back to Toronto for the final two games. Down 5–1 in the seventh inning of Game 6, Philadelphia rallied against veterans Dave Stewart and Danny Cox. The big blow was a three-run homer by Lenny Dykstra. The erratic Philadelphia pen kept the Phillies in the game after starter Terry Mulholland failed, but manager Jim Fregosi pulled Roger Mason in the eighth after two and one-third innings of one-hit ball. Things got hairy after a pair of walks, but veteran Larry Andersen retired the side with the 6–5 lead intact. The second-guessers were actually first-guessers that night, as Fregosi brought in closer Mitch Williams—fresh off blowing Game 4 and enduring death threats from citizens of the City of Brotherly Love—to try to get the final three outs. Wild Thing only got one. He walked Rickey Henderson on four pitches, ran the count full on Devon White before getting him to fly out, and gave up a single to Paul Molitor. Sitting on Wild Thing's slider, **Joe Carter** put an end to the series and to the misery of Phillies fans everywhere when he lined a three-run, game-set-and-match home run to left to bring the championship back to Toronto.

1960 World Series Game 7:
Pittsburgh Pirates vs. New York Yankees

It wasn't the prettiest World Series ever played. It wasn't even all that dramatic, as four of the games were lopsided affairs. But the showdown between the Yankees and Pirates in 1960, 33 years after Pittsburgh was humiliated by New York in the Bucs' last Series appearance, was certainly wonderful and strange.

The Bronx Bombers had outscored the Pirates 23–10 in 1927 while batting .279 and slugging .397. The '60 Yankees made that look pretty tame, setting records for runs (55), hits (91), extra-base hits (27), and batting average (.338) that still stand. They scored more than twice the runs that the Pirates did (27), with an average game's output of 8 runs and 13 hits. If it weren't bad enough that Mickey Mantle was hitting .400 with 3 home runs, Moose Skowron was hitting .375 and Elston Howard .462. And they weren't even the most productive hitters. Second baseman Bobby Richardson, who had hit .252 on the season with 26 RBI, hit .367 and knocked in 12 runs, including a record 6 in one game. That's right—Babe Ruth went deep three times in one Series game twice, Reggie Jackson did it once, but neither of them could match the output of the seventh hitter in the lineup, Bobby Richardson, in Game 3.

All that, and the Pirates still found a way to win three games. They lost games 16–3, 10–0, and 10–0, but scratched out 6–4, 3–2, and 5–2 victories. It looked like they were on their way to another low-scoring win when they took a 4–1 lead into the top of the sixth at Forbes Field. Then things got wild. A run-scoring single by Mickey Mantle and a three-run shot by Yogi Berra down the line in right put the Yankees up 5–4. A two-out, none-on walk to Berra in the eighth was followed by three straight hits, including a Clete Boyer double that extended the Yankees' lead to 7–4. The Pirates shocked the Yankees in the bottom of the inning by exploding for five runs, their biggest inning of the series. A double-play grounder to Tony Kubek took a bad hop and hit him in the throat, knocking him out of the game. A scratch single by Dick Groat followed, then a two-out infield single by Roberto Clemente set up a three-run homer by reserve catcher Hal Smith, just into the game as a defensive replacement in the top of the inning.

Down 9–7 and with three outs to live, the Yankees went down swinging. Three straight singles plated a run, and a brilliant baserunning move by Mickey Mantle tied the game: With one out, Mantle on first, and Gil McDougald on third, Yogi Berra hit a hard grounder down the first-base line. Rocky Nelson fielded the ball, stepped on first, and fired to second to try to complete the double play. But Mantle, thinking on his toes, knew that the force had been removed as soon as Nelson touched first. As the throw went down to second, Mantle dove back to first and McDougald raced home to tie the game.

Unfortunately for Mantle and the Yankees, the tie was short-lived. Ralph Terry came on to pitch for the Yankees and gave up the only Game 7 game-winning home run in Series history to second baseman **Bill Mazeroski**.

In addition to Bill Mazeroski in 1960, Chris Chambliss in 1976, and Joe Carter in 1993, 10 other series have ended on hits. These 10 stayed in the ballpark. Four of them came in extra innings in the final game of the series.

1924 World Series Game 7: Washington Senators vs. New York Giants

"Dreams came true in the twelfth—Washington's dream and Walter Johnson's—and when the red September sun dropped down behind the dome of the Capitol the Senators were the baseball champions of the world. Washington waited 25 years for a World Series, but when it came it was the greatest one in history, and the king of pitchers waited eighteen years for the sweetest victory of his career."

—BILL CORUM

Earl McNeely got the Senators' second run-scoring, bad-hop, crucially timed single of the game over third baseman Fred Lindstrom's head, this one coming with one out in the 12th off the New York Giants' Jack Bentley. It scored catcher Muddy Ruel, who had doubled after catcher Hank Gowdy tripped over his face mask on Ruel's foul pop. The Senators beat the Giants 4–3 in Game 7 for their first and only championship. They had already ended Game 2 with a base hit, and just missed taking the opener in the same manner as well. The game's greatest pitcher, 36-year-old **Walter Johnson**, having been uncharacteristically hittable and failing to record victories for Washington in Game 1 and Game 5, pitched four shutout innings of relief for the victory—and nearly won the game with a home run in the 10th. Baseball came very close to having its most dramatic home run come off the bat of a pitcher.

1929 World Series Game 5: Philadelphia Athletics vs. Chicago Cubs

Hack Miller's double off Pat Malone scored Al Simmons in the bottom of the ninth, capping a three-run rally that gave Philadelphia a 3–2 victory over the Cubs. The righty-heavy lineup of the Cubs—stymied by Philadelphia's right-handed pitching and stunned by the use of the game's best pitcher, Hall of Famer Lefty Grove, out of the bullpen—had bottomed out after the Cubs blew an 8–0 lead in the seventh inning the game before to lose their grip on a Series they were favored to win.

1935 World Series Game 6: Detroit Tigers vs. Chicago Cubs

Goose Goslin's bloop single off Larry French scored Mickey Cochrane in the bottom of the ninth, giving Detroit a 4–3 victory over the Cubs. Chicago third baseman Stan Hack had led off the top of the ninth with a triple, but the Cubs were unable to bring him in. With their bench depleted by early ejections for umpire-baiting, pitcher Larry French had to bat for himself with one out.

1953 World Series Game 5: New York Yankees vs. Brooklyn Dodgers

"This feller is going to break up the game."

—CASEY STENGEL TO PHIL RIZZUTO, AS BILLY MARTIN
CAME TO THE PLATE IN GAME 5 OF THE 1953 SERIES

Billy Martin's one-out single off Clem Labine in the bottom of the ninth scored Hank Bauer from second as the Yankees beat the Dodgers 4–3. It was the fourth Series loss to the Yankees in seven years, and crestfallen center fielder Duke Snider couldn't even manage a desperation heave to the plate, picking up the ball and sticking it in his pocket instead. It was the 12th hit in 24 at-bats and the eighth RBI for Martin, an unlikely hero in a lineup featuring Mickey Mantle and Yogi Berra.

1976 NLCS Game 3: Cincinnati Reds vs. Philadelphia Phillies

Ken Griffey Sr.'s bases-loaded single off Tom Underwood in the bottom of the ninth capped a three-run rally that also featured home runs by George Foster and Johnny Bench, as the Reds swept the Phillies in the NLCS.

1978 NLCS Game 4: Los Angeles Dodgers vs. Philadelphia Phillies

For the second time in three years, the Phillies' season ended on a base hit. **Bill Russell**'s single off Tug McGraw scored Ron Cey with the winning run in the 10th inning, giving the Dodgers a 4–3 decision and 3-game-to-1 win over Philadelphia in the NLCS. Cey reached base when the game's premier defensive center fielder, Garry Maddox, dropped a line drive.

1991 World Series Game 7: Minnesota Twins vs. Atlanta Braves

Gene Larkin's pinch-hit single in the bottom of the 10th off Alejandro Peña scored Dan Gladden with the only run of Game 7 against the Atlanta Braves. Considered by many to be the most exciting Series ever played, it was the third extra-inning game, the fifth game won in a team's final at-bat, and the fifth game decided by one run.

1992 NLCS Game 7: Atlanta Braves vs. Pittsburgh Pirates

Capitalizing on an error by Gold Glove second baseman Jose Lind, the Braves rallied for three runs in the bottom of the ninth to beat the Pirates 3–2 in Game 7 of the NLCS. The rally was capped by a two-out, two-run single by the last man on the bench, **Francisco Cabrera**, off Stan Belinda. It scored perhaps the slowest man in baseball, ex-Pirate Sid Bream, with the winning run.

1995 AL Wild-Card Series Game 5: Seattle Mariners vs. New York Yankees

To cap a close, high-scoring, five-game wild-card series—the first of its kind in the AL—**Edgar Martinez**, whose grand slam had broken open Game 4 in the bottom of the eighth, hit a two-run double down the left-field line in the bottom of the 11th off the Yankees' Jack McDowell. Ken Griffey Jr., who hit five home runs in the five games, scored the game winner.

1997 World Series Game 7: Florida Marlins vs. Cleveland Indians

The Cleveland Indians were three outs away from their first world championship in 49 years. They were facing the bottom of the Marlins' order in the 9th, but reliever Jose Mesa yielded a timely single to right by Charles Johnson and a game-tying sacrifice fly from the unlikeliest of sources, light-hitting Craig Counsell. **Edgar Renteria**'s single up the middle in the bottom of the 11th off Charles Nagy gave Florida a 3–2 win and a championship in only the fifth year of the team's existence.

Back Breakers, Tide Turners, and Other Memorable Moments

Maybe in ridiculous movies like *The Natural* a player can hit a home run in the *top* of the ninth that ends the game, but in the real thing a lot of the game's biggest home runs don't end anything. Some just result in counterpunches, while a few suck the life right out of the opposition. Jimmie Foxx hit one of the first such home runs in postseason play, but most of these have come in more recent years—and some pitchers who have served them up have never been the same again.

1930 World Series Game 5: Philadelphia Athletics vs. St. Louis Cardinals

The defending champion Athletics were taking on the St. Louis Cardinals in St. Louis with the series tied at 2–2. The game was tied at 0–0 going into the top of the ninth, with George Earnshaw (with relief help from Hall of Famer Lefty Grove) trading doughnuts with 37-year-old veteran spitballer Burleigh Grimes. Grimes yielded only four hits through eight innings, all singles, one of them a bunt, working out of a bases-loaded jam in the eighth to preserve the tie. In the top of the ninth, Grimes walked Mickey Cochrane leading off, but manager Gabby Street stayed with the veteran. Grimes got Al Simmons on a shallow fly ball, then took on **Jimmie Foxx**, who had struck out in his last at-bat and had been held to only one RBI all series. Foxx unloaded, planting a two-run homer deep into the left-field bleachers at Sportsman's Park to put Philadelphia up 2–0. The Cardinals went meekly in the ninth, and the A's breezed to a 6–1 victory in the sixth game, holding St. Louis scoreless until the ninth inning.

1958 World Series Game 6:
New York Yankees vs. Milwaukee Braves

In nearly all instances where a team has rallied from a 3–1 deficit to take the series in seven, you can find a moment—usually in Game 5 or 6—where the team that is one win away comes tantalizingly close to ending it. With their ace on the mound in Game 6 in Milwaukee, Braves fans had to feel confident that they were on the verge of defeating the Yankees for the second consecutive season. When New York ace Whitey Ford was chased in the second inning, Milwaukee—a major league city for only five seasons—was on the verge of euphoria. The bases were loaded in the second, one man out, Ford out and Art Ditmar in, and shortstop Johnny Logan had just hit a fly ball to Elston Howard in left that looked like it would score Andy Pafko easily. But Howard made a perfect throw to Yogi Berra to complete the inning-ending double play, and the Yankees were down only 2–1. After the Yankees scratched out a run in the top of the sixth, the game remained tied at 2–2 until the top of the 10th, when Gil McDougald, who had hit 14 home runs all year, lined his second one of the Series over the wall in left. Another run made it 4–2, and the Yankees survived a shaky 10th to win 4–3—the last out a line drive to McDougald at second with runners on first and third. The following day, the Yankees beat their nemesis of the 1957 Series, Lew Burdette, snapping a 2–2 tie in the top of the eighth, again on the combination of Berra (double) and Howard (single). After Andy Carey singled, **Moose Skowron** broke Milwaukee's back with a three-run homer to left-center to put New York up to stay, 6–2.

1964 World Series Game 5:
St. Louis Cardinals vs. New York Yankees

Down 2–1 in games after a home run by Mickey Mantle in the bottom of the ninth in Game 3, the Cardinals were on the ropes in Game 4. Young, hard-throwing Al

Downing had St. Louis down 3–0 in the sixth, but two singles and a Bobby Richardson error loaded the bases. Unlike the quick hook that Casey Stengel demonstrated in 1958, manager Yogi Berra elected to stay with Downing to face NL MVP **Ken Boyer**. Boyer responded with a grand slam into the left-field stands. The Yankees didn't manage another hit all day and were held scoreless by Bob Gibson for eight innings in Game 5. The Cardinals led 2–0 and were three outs away from sending the Series back to St. Louis, needing only a win to end it. But an error by Dick Groat put Mickey Mantle on first leading off the ninth. Gibson shook it off, striking out Elston Howard then flagging down a smash up the middle by Joe Pepitone and retiring him for the second out. Young left fielder Tom Tresh then proceeded to knot the game up and revive Yankee hopes with a two-out, two-run, game-tying home run to right. The Cardinals recovered from this train wreck more quickly than the Yankees did the day before. In the top of the 10th, Bill White walked, and home run hero Ken Boyer beat out a bunt. After a force play put runners on first and third, Pete Mikkelsen was taken deep by Cardinals catcher **Tim McCarver**. The Yankees went easily in the bottom of the ninth, then beat up on St. Louis pitching in the sixth game—with Joe Pepitone answering Boyer's grand slam with one of his own in the eighth to put New York up 8–1. But the Cardinals and Bob Gibson held off a furious rush by the Yankees in Game 7 to win 7–5, driving the final nail into the coffin of a New York dynasty that never went more than four years without a World Series appearance for more than 40 years.

1981 NLCS Game 5: Los Angeles Dodgers vs. Montreal Expos

The Montreal Expos reached the postseason for the first time in the strike-torn season of 1981, and they came excruciatingly close to making it all the way to the World Series. They held off the defending champion Phillies in five games, with ace Steve Rogers twice beating Steve Carlton while yielding only one run. His remarkable success continued in Game 3 against the Dodgers, as he threw his second consecutive complete game to beat Jerry Reuss 4–1. Teams have ridden runs like this all the way to championships, so it is hard to criticize Jim Fanning for bringing in Steve Rogers on two days' rest to pitch the ninth inning of Game 5 in relief of Ray Burris. The score was tied 1–1, but not for long, as **Rick Monday** drove a ball over the center-field fence in Olympic Stadium to put L.A. up 2–1. With two outs in the ninth, Dodgers rookie phenom Fernando Valenzuela walked two, but the Expos couldn't deliver the timely hit off reliever Bob Welch. Rogers recovered to have his best year as a pro in 1982, but the Expos have never returned to the postseason, their other best chance at a World Series done in by another strike in 1994.

1985 NLCS Game 6: St. Louis Cardinals vs. Los Angeles Dodgers

In 1985, hard-throwing right-hander Tom Niedenfuer looked to establish himself as a dominant force in an L.A. bullpen that had been thrown into disarray by the drug problems, suspensions, and eventual trading of their closer, Steve Howe. Niedenfuer was 26 years old and had recorded 19 saves during the regular season with a 2.71 ERA and nearly 1 strikeout per inning. But in Game 5 in St. Louis with the game and the series tied at 2–2, Niedenfuer was tagged for Ozzie Smith's first-ever left-handed home run to lose the game in the bottom of the ninth. Two days later, Niedenfuer had a chance to redeem himself. On since the seventh inning, he carried a 5–4 lead into the top of the ninth at Dodger Stadium. But when the Cardinals' best hitter, **Jack Clark**, came to the plate with two men on and first base open, L.A. manager Tommy Lasorda must have been tempted to walk the slugger and call on lefty Steve Howe to face young left-hander Andy Van Slyke, who had been held to only one hit in the series. Howe wasn't there, and the lip-readers watching Lasorda on television could see him say, "Pitch to the SOB." Staying true to the righty-righty "book," he let Niedenfuer pitch to Clark, and the slugger drilled a three-run homer to left-center to bury the Dodgers and send Lasorda into a dugout tantrum. Niedenfuer went backward in 1986, was traded in 1987, and was out of baseball in 1990, the promise of his 1985 season never fulfilled.

1986 ALCS Game 5: Boston Red Sox vs. California Angels

Early in Game 5, the Boston fans and press were fitting Dave Henderson for goat horns after a fly ball by the Angels' Bobby Grich deflected off Henderson's glove and over the fence for a home run. The California Angels had a comfortable 5–2 lead in the game and a 3–1 lead in the series, and Henderson seemed destined to be another sad footnote in Boston's star-crossed postseason history. The Angels, on the other hand, were three outs away from their first World Series appearance since their inception in 1961. Mike Witt, who had already beaten Roger Clemens in Game 1, was sailing along when Don Baylor ignited the Red Sox bench with a two-run homer to cut the lead to 5–4. Manager Gene Mauch, who overmanaged the Phillies during their epic 1964 collapse, was accused of the same when he pulled Witt and brought in lefty Gary Lucas to face lefty catcher Rich Gedman. Lucas shot holes in the lefty-lefty theory when he hit Gedman with a pitch. In came Donnie Moore, the Angels' closer who had saved Game 3. He got to two strikes on **Dave Henderson**, who fouled off one third strike before hitting the next one over the wall to put the Red Sox up 6–5.

The Angels had a little fight left in them, tying the game up in the bottom of the ninth, only to fall 7–6 in the 11th on a Dave Henderson sacrifice fly. The series returned to Boston, and California sleepwalked though both games. After taking a 2–0 lead in the first inning of Game 6, the Red Sox scored eight unanswered runs en route to a 10–4 victory. Boston bombed them again in Game 7, 8–1, and the Angels have never been to the postseason since. In a far sadder footnote, Donnie Moore spiraled into a deep depression. He saved only nine more games for the Angels, retiring after the 1988 season, then killing his wife and himself during the summer of 1989.

1988 NLCS Game 4: Los Angeles Dodgers vs. New York Mets

In retrospect, the Mets of the late '80s were one of the most dominant and disappointing teams in baseball history. After a 108-win season in 1986, the Mets struggled past the Astros in the NLCS and got by the cursed Red Sox on smoke, mirrors, wild pitches, and misplayed ground balls. In 1987, Dwight Gooden's drug suspension derailed the team early, and they lost the division by 3 games. They returned to the 100-win plateau in 1988, and the baseball world waited for the formality of the Dodgers' defeat to be completed so that a showdown with the 104-win A's of Jose Canseco and Mark McGwire could ensue. While the A's were sweeping the Red Sox, the Mets were facing Orel Hershiser—who had finished the season with 59 consecutive scoreless innings—twice in three games, and coming away with two late victories in both games. With Orel in the rearview mirror, a 4–2 lead in Dwight Gooden's hands in the ninth inning of Game 4 with the bottom of the order at the plate, and Game 5 in Shea Stadium, the series looked as good as over. That's when catcher **Mike Scioscia**, who had hit three home runs all season for the Dodgers, tied the game with a two-run homer. The game went 12 innings, with Kirk Gibson homering to put L.A. up 5–4, and Orel Hershiser coming on to record the save in the bottom of the inning. The Mets dropped Game 5, won Game 6, and were shut out by Hershiser in Game 7.

Gooden racked up his share of wins after 1988, though he was never the dominant pitcher he last was in 1988. In fact, the entire Mets' franchise has never been the same since. They finished second in 1989 and 1990, let Darryl Strawberry leave via free agency in 1991, fell to fifth in 1991 and 1992 (more than 20 games off the pace), then bottomed out with a 59–103 mark in 1993.

The Dodgers haven't been the same since Hershiser's arm gave out in 1990. They've been to the postseason twice since 1988, getting swept twice. The Mets finally climbed back into wild-card contention in 1998, but blew their chance at a return to postseason thanks to one of those late-season collapses with which the Mets' Mike Piazza had become familiar during his days in L.A.

1992 World Series Game 2: Toronto Blue Jays vs. Atlanta Braves

To some extent, the Braves were just happy to be in the World Series in 1991. It ended a long stretch of truly wretched baseball, and to even contend in 1991 came as a pleasant and complete surprise. In 1992, the city of Atlanta was ready for its first championship of any kind. Riding the emotional wave of a three-run ninth-inning rally in Game 7 of the NLCS, the Braves were three outs away from taking a 2–0 lead over the Blue Jays in the World Series.

But Atlanta, despite the great young arms of Tom Glavine, John Smoltz, and Steve Avery, had a glaring pitching weakness: the bullpen. They had ridden veteran Juan Berenguer through most of 1991, only to have his arm give out in September and have to turn things over to veteran Alejandro Peña. Peña often had nothing on the ball but his fingers, yet still managed to get the job done—until *his* arm gave out. So Atlanta acquired 36-year-old Jeff Reardon during the '92 season, and counted on the aging closer to regain his form after a rough first half in Boston. With three hitless innings in the NLCS, it looked like the gamble was going to pay off.

Then came the ninth inning of Game 2, when Reardon walked Derek Bell before serving up a two-run, series-turning home run to utility player Ed Sprague, who had hit one all season. Bobby Cox went back to Reardon in the ninth inning of a 2–2 Game 3, only to see him yield a game-winning, bases-loaded single to Candy Maldonado. He was buried for the rest of the Series and never pitched for Atlanta again.

1993 NLCS Game 5: Philadelphia Phillies vs. Atlanta Braves

In 1993, the Braves relied on a combination of the erratic Mike Stanton and the soft-throwing Greg McMichael to save 46 games. They weren't able to replicate their regular-season success in the playoffs against the underdog Philadelphia Phillies. The series turned on two extra-inning games, both of which the Braves' bullpen lost. The most critical of these games was Game 5 in Atlanta, when the Braves, in danger of falling behind 3–2 in the series and heading back to Philadelphia for the final two games, rallied for three runs in the bottom of the ninth off Mitch Williams to tie the game at 3–3. Any momentum this might have given the Braves was taken right back by Len Dykstra in the top of the 10th when he homered off Mark Wohlers. The Phillies and Tommy Greene beat the Braves and Greg Maddux two days later and moved on to take on the Toronto Blue Jays.

1996 AL Wild-Card Series Game 4:
Baltimore Orioles vs. Cleveland Indians

Perhaps no other player has ever performed in a more hostile environment than Baltimore's Roberto Alomar in the 1996 postseason. Near the end of the '96 regular season, as the Orioles fought for a wild-card berth, Alomar sparked a national firestorm when he spit in the face of umpire Mark Hirschbeck. The umpires threatened to walk out when the league refused to suspend Alomar for the postseason. Fans screamed that the Orioles should enforce their own suspension on their star second baseman. And when the series moved to Cleveland for Game 3, the boos in Jacobs Field were deafening. It didn't help the mood of Cleveland's fans any that the underdog Orioles were up 2–0 in games and threatening to short-circuit the Indians' attempt to return to the World Series. A dramatic Game 3 victory for Cleveland, which turned on an Albert Belle grand slam in the seventh, was followed by what looked like a hard-fought 3–2 victory in Game 4, with "money" pitcher Orel Hershiser slated to face Scott Erickson in Game 5. Hard-throwing closer Jose Mesa was on to close out the game, as he'd done 39 times during the regular season.

Roberto Alomar, only 3 for 15 on the series, stood in his way. Amid a torrent of verbal abuse, Alomar delivered a game-tying single. Then, in the 12th, Alomar and Mesa hooked up again, and Alomar hit what proved to be the game-winning home run. In a wonderful twist of irony, Alomar went on to sign with Cleveland before the 1999 season. Jose Mesa went on to blow Game 7 of the 1997 World Series against the Marlins, and by 1998 was no longer an effective pitcher.

One of baseball's most consistent performers in the 1990s, Roberto Alomar also possesses a flare for the dramatic.

ALL-TIME OFFENSIVE LEADERS IN LCS AND WORLD SERIES PLAY

At-Bats
1. Yogi Berra 259
2. Reggie Jackson 249
3. Pete Rose 248

Runs
1. Mickey Mantle 42
2. Yogi Berra 41
3. Babe Ruth, Reggie Jackson 37

Hits
1. Pete Rose 80
2. Reggie Jackson 72
3. Yogi Berra 71

Home Runs
1. Mickey Mantle 18
2. Reggie Jackson 16
3. Babe Ruth 15

RBI
1. Reggie Jackson 44
2. Mickey Mantle 40
3. Yogi Berra 39

Batting Average
1. Pepper Martin .418
2. Lou Brock .391
3. Home Run Baker .363

Slugging Average
1. Babe Ruth .744
2. Lou Gehrig .731
3. Hank Aaron .710

1996 World Series Game 4: New York Yankees vs. Atlanta Braves

By 1996, the Braves looked like they'd finally developed a dominant closer. Mark Wohlers seized the role in 1995 and saved four games in a nearly unhittable postseason, including the 1–0 championship clincher over the Indians—combining with Tom Glavine on a one-hitter, pitching a 1-2-3 ninth that left Albert Belle on deck when the Series ended. Wohlers saved 39 games in an overpowering 1996 regular season and had thrown seven and one-third scoreless and dominant postseason innings when Bobby Cox called on him in the eighth inning of Game 4 to protect a 6–3 lead and put the Braves up 3–1. Wohlers gave up two hits, then hung a slider to **Jim Leyritz** to tie the game at 6–6. Down 6–0 at one point, the Yankees rallied for a 7–6, 10-inning victory, the biggest comeback in their illustrious postseason history. (And if you think you've seen the last of journeyman catcher Leyritz, think again.)

From the moment that Leyritz's fly ball sailed over Andruw Jones's head as Jones climbed the left-field fence, the Braves went 15 innings without scoring, and managed only two runs in the final 21 innings of the series. A 2–0 Series lead that they'd seized with 12–1 and 4–0 victories evaporated, and another championship slipped through the bullpen's fingers. As for Wohlers, he began to struggle with his control in 1997 before losing it completely in 1998 and going on the disabled list for being "unable to pitch."

1998 NLCS Game 1: San Diego Padres vs. Atlanta Braves

Like the Dodgers did to the A's in 1988, the Padres essentially won the series over the heavily favored Atlanta Braves in Game 1. Atlanta had seized the momentum by rallying in the bottom of the ninth for a run off the normally untouchable Trevor Hoffman to tie the game at 2–2. The Padres responded in the top of the 10th inning with an opposite-field blast by **Ken Caminiti** off the Braves' latest closer, Kerry Ligtenberg. Just as Leyritz's blow stunned the Braves into submission for 21 innings in 1996, Atlanta scored one run in the next 22 innings after Caminiti's blow, as they fell behind 3–0 in the series. Ironically, it may have been yet another post-season home run by a cocky Jim Leyritz—who had victimized the Astros in the opening round with a game-tying home run in Game 2, a seventh-inning tiebreaker that proved to be the margin of victory in Game 3, and a first-blood home run in the decisive Game 4 off Randy Johnson—that finally woke the Braves up. They rallied to win Game 4 and Game 5 before going down meekly in Atlanta, managing two hits and no runs in Game 6.

Extra-inning and final-game home runs in October are a hard act to follow. But many, many more championships are won on base hits, not home runs, in pivotal, earlier games, and not always in the ninth inning. Consider these huge base hits—some of the biggest hits you never hear much about—three from underrated players who will most likely never make the Hall of Fame, one from a pitcher with a .110 lifetime batting average, and one from a Dane nicknamed "Swede," a player so obscure that only the most staunch of the Red Sox faithful will even recognize the name.

1912 World Series Game 8: Boston Red Sox vs. New York Giants

That's right, Game 8. Game 2 was called on account of darkness in the 11th, with the score tied 6–6—11 innings of wasted work by New York Giants Hall of Famer Christy Mathewson, perhaps the most popular player of his day. The Boston Red Sox moved on to take a 3–1 lead over the Giants when rookie sensation Hugh Bedient outpitched Mathewson 2–1, with Mathewson retiring the final 17 Boston batters in a row after yielding back-to-back triples in the third. The Giants fought back to even the Series at 3–3, keyed in large part by the clutch hitting of Fred Merkle, who was fighting to atone for his legendary baserunning boner that cost the Giants the pennant in 1908, as well as a 3-for-20 performance in his first World Series appearance the year before.

In the final game, Christy Mathewson and Hugh Bedient hooked up again. Bedient had won 20 games as a rookie, but could he be expected to outpitch the immortal Mathewson yet again? Mathewson's Giants had not won a championship since 1905, when he threw three shutouts over the Philadelphia Athletics.

He was nearing the end of the line by 1912, but he showed that he had at least one more great game in his right arm. Mathewson got one run to work with in the third, and he made it hold up until the seventh.

In the seventh, the Red Sox managed a bloop single and a walk to put runners on first and second with one man out. Mathewson retired the number-eight hitter, bringing the pitcher to the plate with the tying run on second and two men out. Boston manager Jake Stahl made the tough call, lifting Bedient for pinch hitter **Olaf Henriksen**. He had come to bat exactly 149 times in his big-league career, though he had managed to slap enough singles to post a .349 lifetime batting average coming into play that day. He went the other way on Mathewson, doubling down the left-field line to tie the game in his only at-bat of the series.

It's a hit that has gotten lost in the madness that followed in the 10th inning. Smokey Joe Wood, who went 34–5 during the regular season, was on in relief of Bedient. He couldn't keep the Giants off the scoreboard, however, as Fred Merkle singled in the go-ahead run in the top of the 10th. But instead of allowing Merkle to redeem himself, the baseball gods found another New York Giant to stand alongside Merkle in infamy.

Clyde Engle, the leadoff hitter for the Red Sox in the bottom of the 10th, hit an easy fly ball to center that Fred Snodgrass dropped. They remember "Snodgrass's muff," but they don't remember the great catch he made to rob the very next batter, Harry Hooper. Mathewson walked Steve Yerkes and had to face the dangerous Tris Speaker with the winning run on base. It looked like Mathewson had Speaker retired on an easy foul pop between first and home, but Merkle froze and the ball fell—though Mathewson later tried to shoulder the blame by insisting that he'd been incorrectly calling for the catcher to take it. Speaker followed with a run-scoring single, and moments later Larry Gardner hit a sacrifice fly to right to end the Series.

And 74 years before Buckner, it was New York that blew the championship and Boston that accepted the gift.

1940 World Series Game 7: Cincinnati Reds vs. Detroit Tigers

The Cincinnati Reds of 1939–40 are the only team to reach consecutive World Series without a single Hall of Famer on its roster. Perhaps the best among their cast of no-names was first baseman Frank McCormick, who led the NL in hits (209) and RBI (128) in 1939 while batting .332, and followed that up with 127 RBI and a league-leading 191 hits and 44 doubles in 1940. The Reds had been swept in 1939 by the Yankees, but it was the Tigers they had to face in 1940.

This series went seven games, the Reds forcing the finale with a 4–0 Bucky Walters shutout in Game 6 in Cincinnati. Bobo Newsom, 21–5 for the Tigers, hooked up with Paul Derringer, 20–12 for the Reds, in the finale. Just as Walters stymied the Tigers in Game 6, Newsom had the Reds' number in Game 7. Working with a gift run, Newsom took a 1–0 lead into the seventh inning, having scattered three harmless singles through the first five and two-thirds innings. But in the bottom of the sixth, rookie Mike McCormick (no relation to Frank) doubled with two outs and right fielder Ival Goodman just missed a home run to center field.

With Newsom suddenly looking human, Frank McCormick opened the bottom of the seventh with a double off the Crosley Field wall in left that woke up his teammates. Left fielder **Jimmy Ripple** followed with a double off the screen in right field, and eventually came around to score what proved to be the game-winning run on a sacrifice fly. Down to their last few outs, the Reds pulled out the victory and earned their first world championship—and their last for the next 35 years.

1967 World Series: St. Louis Cardinals vs. Boston Red Sox

"I never wanted all this notoriety. I was content to be known as a good ballplayer. Maybe hit 25 to 35 home runs a year, drive in 100 runs, and bat somewhere between .290 and .300. And I wanted to help win pennants."

—ROGER MARIS

For the introverted **Roger Maris**, the pressure from his 1961 run at Babe Ruth's record did not disappear after the season. Expectations to repeat the magical season that many didn't want him to have—and to earn his big new salary—caused the Yankee right fielder to press. In 1962, he hit 33 home runs and knocked in 100 runs—an excellent year for most players, and not far off his 1960 MVP performance—but not enough. In 1963, Maris was bothered by a bad back that limited him to 90 games and 23 home runs. With Mantle suffering a career-threatening leg injury, the M&M Boys played only 30 games together. Maris played only two games in the 1963 series, going hitless in five at-bats. Only 29, Maris had a solid albeit unspectacular season in 1964, then struggled again in the postseason, hitting .200 with one RBI on a solo home run. The bottom fell out of the Yankees in 1965, and they finished 25 games off the pace while Maris played only 46 games. In 1966, the unthinkable happened—the Yankees finished last—and Maris batted .233 and thought about retiring. Instead, the St. Louis Cardinals acquired him, then put him in right field and out of the glare of the spotlight.

The 1967 World Series belonged to Bob Gibson of the Cardinals, who won three games; Lou Brock, who stole seven bases; and to Carl Yastrzemski of the Red Sox, who capped off his Triple-Crown season by hitting .400 with 3 home runs in a losing cause. But Cardinals right fielder Roger Maris made more than his share of significant contributions. Batting third, he knocked in both St. Louis runs in a 2–1 Game 1 victory, put St. Louis up 4–1 in a 5–2 Game 3 victory, and pushed Boston to the wall with a two-run double in the first inning of a Game 4 victory that gave St. Louis a 3–1 lead in games. Boston climbed back up, forcing a Game 7, but Maris put the pressure right back on with a third-inning single that put the Cardinals up

2–0 against Red Sox ace Jim Lonborg in a decisive 7–2 victory. For the series, Maris went 10 for 26 with 7 RBI to lead all batters—quietly, just the way he preferred it.

1968 World Series Game 5: Detroit Tigers vs. St. Louis Cardinals

Down 3–1 in games to the St. Louis Cardinals, the Detroit Tigers trailed 3–2 in the bottom of the seventh inning in Game 5. With one out and no one on, Tigers manager Mayo Smith sent his 17-game winner, automatic-out **Mickey Lolich**, to the plate to hit for himself. While fans second-guessed Smith, Lolich managed to bloop a single into right field that knocked starter Nelson Briles out of the game. Joe Hoerner came in for St. Louis, faced four Tigers, and got none of them out. The worst hitter on the team, Lolich sparked a three-run rally that stunned the Cardinals and won the game. In Game 6, 31-game winner Denny McLain held the Cardinals to one run while the Tigers got him 12. In Game 7, Mickey Lolich returned to the mound on two games' rest to take on legendary big-game pitcher Bob Gibson in St. Louis. The Tigers' offense had to make do without Lolich's offense in this one, but he held St. Louis to one run, a two-out ninth inning home run by Mike Shannon, in a 4–1 Tigers victory—Lolich's third win of the series. In the shadow of Denny McLain all season—and not caring for McLain very much even before that—it was Lolich who got to take the final bow.

1978 ALCS Game 3: New York Yankees vs. Kansas City Royals

Only four men have ever hit three home runs in a post-season game: Babe Ruth, Bob Robertson, Reggie Jackson, and **George Brett**. Brett did it in his first three at-bats in Game 3 in Yankee Stadium, victimizing Catfish Hunter with solo shots each time. Having lost the 1976 and 1977 ALCS to the Yankees in the ninth inning, and knotted up 1–1 in this series, Brett was trying to singlehandedly carry the Royals to their first World Series. Each time Brett homered that afternoon, the Yankees responded. Finally, the Royals scored without benefit of a Brett home run, going up 5–4 in the top of the eighth. What followed in the bottom of the eighth was arguably as impressive a home run as Kirk Gibson's 1988 game winner, though it's earned only a fraction of the acclaim.

The only player in history to win a batting title in three different decades, George Brett was a clutch performer in the postseason.

Yankees catcher **Thurman Munson** had been the American League MVP in 1976 as New York returned to the World Series for the first time in 12 years. While the Reds mopped up the Yankees in four straight, Munson went down swinging, batting .529 for the series, while his opposite number, Johnny Bench, hit .533 for the Reds. When Reggie Jackson arrived in New York in 1977, he announced that he was the "straw that stirs the drink." Jackson needed to be the focal point of the team, and was jealous of Munson, the first Yankees' captain since Lou Gehrig. Munson quietly produced his third consecutive .300/100 RBI season and knocked in five runs in the ALCS while Jackson went 2 for 16. But Reggie earned the headlines when Mr. October hit 3 home runs in the sixth and final game of the 1977 World Series.

By 1978, an injured shoulder had robbed Munson of his extra-base power. He still played 154 games, batting .297 and knocking in 71 runs—the final one forgotten between Bucky Dent's legendary home run and a massive blast by Reggie Jackson in the one-game playoff against the Red Sox. Munson hit only 6 home runs all season, and his shoulder forced him to throw submarine style to nail opposing baserunners. Yet in the bottom of the eighth inning of the pivotal third game of the 1978 NLCS, Munson, with a lump in his right shoulder the size of a baseball, hit a Doug Bird pitch over the 430-foot mark in left-center for what proved to be the winning runs in a 6–5 victory. Few could remember a healthy Munson ever hitting a ball that far. Later in the locker room, Jackson, who had homered in the fourth inning, threw his arm around Munson in the glare of the television lights, and tried to explain the tremendous focus required to do what Thurman had done. Munson just looked uncomfortable, and perhaps a bit amused. New York wrapped it up 2–1 the following day.

Later, in a 1978 World Series remembered for the unlikely hitting heroics of Bucky Dent and Brian Doyle in Game 6, and the spectacular fielding of Graig Nettles in Game 3, Munson quietly knocked in 7 runs, including a game-tying, two-strike double in the bottom of the eighth of Game 4 as the Yankees fought back from a 3–0 deficit to win the game in 10 and even the Series at 2–2. The Yankees would wrap it up in Game 6, as Jackson hit a ball out of Dodger Stadium and Munson quietly crouched behind the plate, nursing an aging Catfish Hunter through one last postseason victory. If nothing else, fate allowed him to catch the game's final out, a pop-up behind the plate.

Thurman Munson died on August 2 of the following year when the plane he was piloting crashed while he was practicing landings in Canton. It's no coincidence that this proved to be the first year in the longest gap between championships at Yankee Stadium.

No discussion of great postseason hitting moments would be complete without the dramatic flourishes, the one-man wrecking crews, and the performances that created nicknames that stuck forever.

MR. OCTOBER

So who has the highest batting average of any Yankee in World Series play? Ruth? Gehrig? DiMaggio? Mantle? Try Thurman Munson, who batted .373, good for fifth all time. He is also the only man in the top 10 in batting average in both World Series and LCS play.

The performance of the top 25 in postseason varies greatly, from the absent (Ralph Kiner) to the woeful (Ted Williams, Barry Bonds) to the productive (Jimmie Foxx, Hank Aaron, Hank Greenberg, Frank Robinson, Joe DiMaggio, Willie Stargell) to the mythic (Babe Ruth, Lou Gehrig, Mickey Mantle):

	G	AB	R	H	2B	3B	HR	RBI	BB	BA	SA
Babe Ruth	41	129	37	42	5	2	15	33	33	.326	.744
Ted Williams	7	25	2	5	0	0	0	1	5	.200	.200
Lou Gehrig	34	119	30	43	8	3	10	35	26	.361	.731
Jimmie Foxx	18	64	11	22	3	1	4	11	9	.344	.609
Mickey Mantle	65	230	42	59	6	2	18	40	43	.257	.535
Rogers Hornsby	12	49	6	12	2	1	0	5	3	.245	.327
Willie Mays	25	89	12	22	5	0	1	10	10	.247	.337
Stan Musial	23	86	12	22	7	1	1	8	12	.256	.395
Barry Bonds	23	80	10	16	4	0	1	5	14	.200	.288
Hank Aaron	17	69	11	25	4	1	6	16	5	.362	.710
Mel Ott	16	61	8	18	2	0	4	10	8	.295	.525
Ty Cobb	17	65	7	17	4	1	0	9	3	.262	.354
Mark McGwire	32	114	12	26	2	0	4	13	16	.228	.351
Johnny Mize	18	42	5	12	2	0	3	9	5	.286	.548
Mike Schmidt	36	140	19	33	9	0	4	16	15	.236	.386
Hank Greenberg	23	85	17	27	7	2	5	22	13	.318	.624
Frank Robinson	35	126	25	30	5	1	10	19	20	.238	.532
Dick Allen	3	9	1	2	0	0	0	0	3	.222	.222
Harmon Killebrew	13	40	6	10	1	0	3	6	14	.250	.500
Tris Speaker	20	72	12	22	3	4	0	3	11	.306	.458
Willie McCovey	8	29	4	9	0	1	3	7	5	.310	.690
Joe DiMaggio	51	199	27	54	6	0	8	30	19	.271	.422
Willie Stargell	33	121	18	31	9	0	7	19	16	.256	.504
Ralph Kiner	0	0	0	0	0	0	0	0	0	.000	.000
Frank Thomas	6	17	2	6	0	0	1	3	10	.353	.529

1911 World Series: Philadelphia Athletics vs. New York Giants

There were the Bambino, Reggie, and Pops, to name just three, but first came the only one they called "Home Run."

In 1911, third baseman and cleanup hitter **Frank Baker** of the Philadelphia Athletics led the AL in home runs—with 11. As the Athletics prepared to defend their title against the New York Giants, he was still Frank. All that changed in Game 2 in Philadelphia.

The Giants, who had beaten Philadelphia in the 1905 World Series on the strength of three Christy Mathewson shutouts, were back in the Series for the first time since. Mathewson picked up where he left off in 1905, throwing a six-hitter in Game 1 and actually yielding a run in a 2–1 New York victory. The Giants and Athletics were locked up in another pitchers' duel in Game 2 when Frank Baker broke the tie with a two-run homer off 24-game winner Rube Marquard. The Giants countered with Mathewson in Game 3 on two days' rest, and he responded with another gem. He was two outs away from a 1–0 victory when Baker struck again, hitting a home run to tie the score. Philadelphia would go on to win 3–2 in 11.

Rains halted the series for a week, so Christy Mathewson took the mound for New York again. Staked to a 2–0 lead, it was Frank Baker who started an uprising in the fourth with a leadoff double. Philadelphia scored three times to take the lead, and Baker added another run-scoring double in the following inning to make it 4–2. That's how it ended, and Philadelphia was up 3–1. The Giants managed to hold Baker hitless in Game 5 as they won 4–3 in 10, but Philadelphia exploded for 13 runs in Game 6. With the score tied 1–1, Baker led off a four-run fourth with a single and added yet another double in a seven-run seventh that buried the Giants.

From Game 3 on, he was Home Run. Except in New York, where Giants fans no doubt called him something less flattering.

1979 NLCS Game 1, World Series Game 7:
Pittsburgh Pirates vs. Baltimore Orioles

Though it wouldn't be announced until after the World Series was played, 38-year-old **Willie Stargell** had been voted his only MVP award in 1979, sharing it with batting champion Keith Hernandez. Stargell got the nod not for his offense so much as for his leadership of the '79 "We Are Family" Pirates. "Pops" had struggled through some difficult postseason series during his prime, but he shone from beginning to end in both the NLCS and the World Series.

Stargell homered in the top of the 11th of Game 1 of the NLCS to snap a 2–2 tie and give the Pirates a 5–2 victory over the Cincinnati Reds. He homered again in the final game of a three-game sweep. He homered in Game 1 of the World Series at Baltimore as Pittsburgh mounted a comeback in frigid conditions, just falling short 5–4. And he capped off Game 7 of the series with a two-run homer in the sixth inning that put Pittsburgh ahead 2–1 in an eventual 4–1 victory, as the Pirates became only the fourth team to come back from a 3–1 deficit to win a World Series.

1926 World Series Game 4, 1928 World Series Game 4:
New York Yankees vs. St. Louis Cardinals

Babe Ruth had a lot to prove in 1926, coming off the worst season of his career. Perhaps he was pressing early on in the 1926 series, as he was only 2 for 10 with no

RBI after hitting 47 home runs and batting .372 in the regular season. St. Louis was up 2–1 in games when he exploded for three home runs in Game 4, starting off with a first-inning, first-pitch missile over the right-field roof at Sportsman's Park in St. Louis. The Cardinals tied it up in the bottom of the first, so Ruth promptly hit another one over the roof in the third. They walked him in the fifth in the middle of a four-run inning that put the Yankees up 7–4, but he came to the plate in the sixth and put the game away with a two-run blast well into the center-field bleachers. With New York up 10–4, Ruth came to bat in the eighth with a chance to hit his fourth and was walked on four pitches.

As much as St. Louis tried to pitch around Ruth—he walked 11 times in seven games—he still got some pitches to hit and did some damage with them. He put New York up 1–0 in the bottom of the third of Game 7 with his fourth home run of the Series. St. Louis rallied for three unearned runs in the top of the fourth and held on for a 3–2 win to take the Series, rendering Ruth's hitting heroics futile.

Ruth got to take out his frustrations on the Pirates in a 1927 sweep, but it must have felt sweeter to do it to the Cardinals in 1928. The Yankees swept them, too, with Lou Gehrig the hitting star with 4 home runs, 9 RBI, and 6 hits in 11 at-bats. But as Ruth was known to do, he overshadowed his teammate in Sportsman's Park in the decisive Game 4. He hit a line-drive home run in the fourth and a moon shot in the seventh. Down 6–2 in the eighth with no one on, St. Louis pitched to Ruth rather than around him, as they'd done in 1926. Getting something to hit, Ruth made the most of it, putting his third home run on the roof.

With Lou Gehrig in his prime batting behind Ruth, the Cardinals could no longer afford to pitch around the Babe. He walked only once in the Series while going 10 for 16.

1932 World Series Game 3: New York Yankees vs. Chicago Cubs

"Maybe I had a smug grin on my face after he took the second strike. Babe stepped out of the box again, pointed his finger in my direction and yelled, 'You still need one more, kid.' I guess I should have wasted the next pitch, and I thought Ruth figured I would, too. I decided to try to cross him and came in with it. The ball was gone as soon as Ruth swung. It never occurred to me then that the people in the stands would think he had been pointing to the bleachers."

—CHARLIE ROOT

Once again Lou Gehrig dominated the series—hitting .529 with 3 home runs and 8 RBI—and **Babe Ruth** stole the show.

Ruth's final World Series home run came in Game 3 of this Series against the Chicago Cubs, and it is easily his most memorable. Legend has it that he "called his shot," pointing to the center-field bleachers in Wrigley Field and putting the next pitch right where he pointed—his second home run of the game and 15th of his postseason career. Eyewitness accounts vary, but it seems more likely that Ruth—who was being ridden mercilessly by the Cubs' bench—either pointed to the Chicago dugout to tell them to shut up; pointed to pitcher Guy Bush, who would be the Cubs' sacrificial lamb in Game 4, to let him know that he'd be due for a beating tomorrow; or pointed to pitcher Charlie Root to remind him that an 0–2 count meant he still had one strike left. As Ruth himself privately acknowledged later, "I'm going to point to the center-field bleachers with a barracuda like Root out there? On the next pitch, they'd be picking it out of my ear with a pair of tweezers."

1977 World Series Game 6: New York Yankees vs. Los Angeles Dodgers

> *"When they brought in Hough, I said, 'Man, I got eight or nine homers off Wilbur Wood, Eddie Fisher, and Hoyt Wilhelm (knuckleballers). They can't be bringing this guy in. The first pitch he threw me was like room service. I mean, the ball looked like a beach ball.'"*
>
> —REGGIE JACKSON

Reggie Jackson became "Mr. October" on this night in 1977. He missed the 1972 World Series with a hamstring pull and put together two good, but not spectacular, Series for Oakland in 1973 and 1974. He was 1 for 14 in the 1977 ALCS when Billy Martin benched him for the decisive Game 5 (though he did deliver a critical, run-scoring pinch-hit single in the top of the eighth).

Reggie wanted to be Mr. October and he willed himself to do it, burying the bad memories of a turbulent first season in New York in the process. He couldn't have scripted it any better. After walking in the second inning on four pitches and scoring on a game-tying Chris Chambliss home run, Jackson faced two first-pitch inside fastballs and lined two laser beams into the right-field stands at Yankee Stadium in the fourth and fifth innings off Burt Hooton and Elias Sosa, then unloaded on a first-pitch fastball from Charlie Hough in the eighth, dropping the bat to watch this one—a towering home run to the black seats in dead center. Three home runs on three swings, with a home run in Game 5 on his final swing of that game. Given the packed house, the national television audience, and the championship he brought back to New York, this game is viewed by many as the greatest hitting performance ever seen—the standard for all other hitters to try to match.

Reggie Jackson said if he ever played in New York, they'd name a candy bar after him. The Reggie bar was born during the 1977 off-season, and Mr. October was showered with them in April when his first swing of 1978 produced yet another home run.

6

Coming Through in a Pinch

THE BEST PINCH HITTERS

"There is only one legitimate trick to pinch hitting, and that's knowing the pitcher's best pitch when the count is 3 and 2. All the rest is a crapshoot."

—EARL WEAVER

"It's like chopping down a tree. You don't warm up. You got work to do and you do it."

—DICK ALLEN, ON PINCH HITTING

Pinch hits (season)		Pinch hits (career)		Pinch-hit average (min. 150 AB)	
28	John Vander Wal, 1995	150	Manny Mota	.320	Tommy Davis
25	Jose Morales, 1976	145	Smoky Burgess	.312	Frenchy Bordagaray
24	Dave Philley, 1961	143	Greg Gross	.307	Frankie Baumholtz
24	Vic Davalillo, 1970	123	Jose Morales	.306	Sid Bream
24	Rusty Staub, 1983	116	Jerry Lynch	.303	Red Schoendienst
24	Gerald Perry, 1993	114	Red Lucas	.300	Bob Fothergill
22	Sam Leslie, 1932	113	Steve Braun	.299	Dave Philley
22	Peanuts Lowrey, 1953	108	Terry Crowley	.297	Manny Mota
22	Red Schoendienst, 1962	108	Denny Walling	.296	Ted Easterly
22	Wallace Johnson, 1988	107	Gates Brown	.295	Harvey Hendrick
22	Mark Sweeney, 1997				

The dictionary defines a pinch hitter as "someone who substitutes for another, especially during an emergency." The term can be traced back to 1891, when baseball's rules first allowed for substitution during the game for instances other than emergencies. For more than a century, managers have been calling on pinch hitters to come through in clutch situations—in a pinch.

In today's version of major league baseball, the team roster is often populated by specialists—middle relievers, setup men, closers, defensive replacements, platoon players, and pinch hitters. A pinch-hitting specialist rarely appears in the starting lineup, being saved instead for late-inning duty when the game is on the line. In the last eight years of his career, all-time pinch-hit leader Manny Mota totalled only 279 at-bats, and 252 were as a pinch hitter. His 79 hits during this period drove in 54 runs. That's excellent productivity—more RBI per hit than all-time RBI king Hank Aaron, and exactly what a manager is looking for in a pinch hitting specialist.

In 1995, when he set the major league record for pinch hits in a season with 28, **John Vander Wal** batted .389 as a pinch hitter—a level of performance he'd never been able to approach as a regular. There was something in his makeup that allowed him to thrive in a difficult role. How difficult? Only six players in history have managed a .300 average as a pinch hitter. Fact is, if you can hit better than .250, you're ahead of the game.

Broadcaster Dave Campbell can testify to the difficulty of reaching .250—he went 2–43 (.047) as a pinch hitter. That's two hits better than shortstop Don Kessinger, who had 1,900 hits in the big leagues but went 0–33 in the pinch. One wonders how sympathetic Billy Martin was to his pinch hitters when he was a manager, considering that as a player he went 3–44 (.068) coming off the bench. Pinch hitting can be a thankless task, too. Gomer Hodge led the league in pinch hits (16) as a rookie for the Indians in 1971 and never played again.

Now consider how some of the greatest hitters in history did when asked to come in cold off the bench:

	Career	Pinch hitting
Ty Cobb	.367	.217
Babe Ruth	.342	.194
Hank Aaron	.305	.198

And these guys didn't have to face today's hard-throwing relief specialists. Just as relief specialists are a fairly modern innovation, pinch-hitting specialists like Vander Wal weren't always the rage in the big leagues. As a result, some of the most dramatic hits in baseball history have been stroked by marginal bench players, aging veterans, relative unknowns, and pinch-hitting novices who were able to create history by being in the right place at the right time. Here's a sampling of some of the most noteworthy pinch hitting . . . and walking . . . and bunting . . . moments in baseball history.

In Game 4 of the 1947 World Series, New York Yankees starter Bill Bevens was one out away from a no-hitter, nursing a 2–1 lead with men on first and second. Brooklyn Dodgers pinch hitter **Cookie Lavagetto**—who had managed only one double and four pinch hits all season—ripped a two-base hit off the right-field wall in Ebbets Field, scoring both runners and giving the Dodgers a Series-tying victory. But it would be hero to goat overnight; the very next day he struck out in the pinch with the tying run at second to end Game 5. The Yankees would go on to take the Series in seven games, and neither Bevens nor Lavagetto would ever play in the majors again.

Greg Gross played 17 years in the major leagues, amassing 143 hits coming off the bench. Playing for the Philadelphia Phillies in 1982, Gross led the league with 19 pinch hits in 53 at-bats (.358).

The most unusual pinch hitter in major league history was 3′7″ **Eddie Gaedel**, a midget employed by St. Louis Browns owner Bill Veeck. Gaedel, wearing uniform number ⅛, walked on four pitches in a game against Detroit on August 19, 1951. The next day Gaedel was banned by the American League for being "detrimental to baseball."

The New York Giants' **Dusty Rhodes** delivered key pinch hits in each of the first three games of the 1954 World Series against the Cleveland Indians, each time batting for Hall of Famer Monte Irvin. He hit a home run to win Game 1 in the 10th inning off Hall of Famer Bob Lemon, and a game-tying single in Game 2 against Hall of Famer Early Wynn. The Giants went on to sweep the powerful Indians, a team that had won a record 111 regular-season games. It was Rhodes's only World Series, and he finished a perfect 3 for 3 as a pinch hitter. He had hit .333 as a pinch hitter during the 1954 regular season, but after his World Series performance he would hit .192 in 177 pinch-hitting opportunities over the final three years of his career.

In Game 4 of the 1969 World Series, the Miracle Mets were on the verge of a 1–0 victory that would give them a commanding 3–1 lead in the Series. The Orioles tied the game in the top of the 9th and came close to taking the lead in the top of the 10th. In the bottom of the inning with men on first and second and no one out, Mets starter Tom Seaver was finally lifted for a pinch hitter. Reserve catcher and

.209 hitter **J. C. Martin** was called on to bunt. Pitcher Pete Richert fielded it cleanly, but his throw to first hit Martin on the wrist, the ball deflecting into the outfield while Rod Gaspar scored the winning run all the way from second. Replays would show that Martin was out of the baseline, but the baseball gods had been on the Mets' side all year and weren't ready to move just yet. It was Martin's only appearance in the Series and his last as a Met.

Six years later, another 10th-inning pinch bunt would prove to be a controversial turning point in a World Series. With no one out, a man on first, and the score tied at 5–5 between the Red Sox and Reds in Cincinnati, pinch hitter **Ed Armbrister** would bunt a ball straight into the ground and then collide with catcher Carlton Fisk as Fisk tried to field the ball. Fisk's throw sailed into center field, and runners ended up on second and third. The Red Sox claimed interference, but umpire Larry Barnett didn't see things the same way. Joe Morgan would eventually end the game with a base hit over the drawn-in outfield, and the Reds would take a 2–1 lead in the Series.

Everyone remembers Carlton Fisk's dramatic 12th-inning home run that squared the 1975 World Series three games later. But it was a three-run pinch-hit homer by BoSox reserve outfielder **Bernie Carbo** in the eighth inning that set the stage for Fisk's heroics. Carbo, who used to play for the Reds, had not even appeared in Boston's ALCS victory over Oakland. He had only two pinch hits all of 1975, but this was his second pinch-hit home run of the series. (Reserve outfielder Chuck Essegian of the Los Angeles Dodgers turned the same trick in 1959, tying Game 2 with a pinch-hit home run in the seventh inning, then putting the icing on the cake in the ninth inning of a Game 6 rout that gave L.A. the championship. He'd hit only one home run all season.)

> *"I worked the count to 3–2, and on the next pitch, a fastball, I hit the ball, probably the best swing I've taken in my career. I'm rounding first base and I'm looking at the ball in center field. (Reds center fielder Cesar) Geronimo turns his back. I'm heading for second base, and I see the ball land in the bleachers. Now I round second base and I'm looking at Pete Rose and I'm yelling at him, 'Don't you wish you were this strong?' And Pete is yelling back, 'Isn't this fun?'"*
>
> —BERNIE CARBO ON GAME 6 PINCH-HIT
> HOME RUN IN 1975 WORLD SERIES

Francisco Cabrera was the unlikeliest of candidates to decide Game 7 of the 1992 NLCS between the visiting Pittsburgh Pirates and Cabrera's Atlanta Braves. Nevertheless, the reserve catcher, last man named to the playoff roster, was ready when manager Bobby Cox called on him to pinch hit in a two-out, bases-loaded situation in the bottom of the ninth inning. It was a situation right out of every kid's daydreams, and with two strikes in the count Cabrera slammed a Stan Belinda fastball between short and third for a game-winning two-run single. His 15 minutes of fame proved to be the most famous pinch hit in league championship history, but he would be out of baseball a year later.

In the 10th inning of Game 4 of the 1996 World Series, with the game tied at 6–6 and men on first and third, the Braves elected to intentionally walk Bernie Williams to load the bases and take their chances with rookie **Andy Fox**. Yankees manager Joe Torre went against "the book," sending up lefty Wade Boggs to face lefty Steve Avery. Unaccustomed though he was to coming off the bench, Boggs drew a free pass on a 3–2 pitch, plating the eventual winning run. The Yankees had completed their comeback from a 6–0 deficit to even the Series at two games apiece, and would go on to take the championship in six games. It might not have been the shot heard 'round the world, but it was certainly the walk heard 'round New York.

Here are some pinch-hitting heroics that aren't as well known:

• **Del "Sheriff" Gainer**'s pinch single in the bottom of the 14th inning of Game 2 of the 1916 World Series made a winner out of a Boston Red Sox left-hander named Babe Ruth. Ruth had pitched the entire 14 innings for the BoSox, while Sherry Smith went all the way and took the hard-luck loss for Brooklyn. The Red Sox would take the Series in five games, but this would be Gainer's only appearance and he would retire with only nine pinch hits to his credit.

• On June 17, 1943, Red Sox player-manager **Joe Cronin** called his own number as a pinch hitter twice in a doubleheader against the Philadelphia Athletics, and both times he hit home runs. Cronin went on to hit five pinch-hit home runs in 1943, one shy of the record set by Brooklyn's Johnny Frederick in 1932.

• **Carroll Hardy**, a .225 hitter in 433 major league games, pinch hit for both Ted Williams and Roger Maris. While pinch hitting for Maris, Hardy slammed a game-winning three-run homer. As a stand-in for Williams, he lined into a double play.

• **Ira Thomas** of the Detroit Tigers managed the first pinch hit in World Series history when he connected for a single against the Cubs in the ninth inning of Game 1 of the 1908 Series.

• The first three hits in **Charley Maxwell**'s career were all pinch-hit home runs off Hall of Fame pitchers (Bob Feller, Bob Lemon, Satchel Paige). Maxwell connected for a grand slam off Paige.

• The first of **Lou Gehrig**'s 2,130 consecutive game appearances took place as a pinch hitter for shortstop Pee Wee Warringer. Though he played 14 more years, Gehrig never again appeared in a game as a pinch hitter.

• Pinch hitter **Willard Brown** of the St. Louis Browns became the first African-American to hit a home run in the American League when he connected off Hal Newhouser of Detroit for an inside-the-park homer on August 13, 1947. It was the only pinch hit and only home run of Brown's one-year career.

• On occasion, the traditional pinch-hitting scenario is reversed, with a pitcher batting for a position player. Two of the best hitting pitchers of all time, **Wes Ferrell** and **Red Ruffing**, posted impressive numbers as pinch hitters. Ferrell totaled 31 career pinch hits, including a 9-for-32 record (.281) in 1935. Ruffing totalled 58 career pinch hits, and twice batted at least .400 for a season as a pinch hitter (.444 in 1935 and .400 in 1941). But the most prolific pinch-hitting pitcher of all time was **Red Lucas**, who toiled primarily for the Cincinnati Reds and Pittsburgh Pirates. By the end of his career in 1938, the left-handed–hitting Lucas recorded an amazing 114 pinch hits, a record that stood until catcher **Smoky Burgess** bested it during the 1965 season.

• **Cliff Johnson**, a catcher and designated hitter, holds the record for the most pinch-hit homers with 20. Johnson managed his score of long balls in only 277 at-bats, meaning he hit one pinch homer per every 13.9 at-bats, an average bettered by only two men (Joe Adcock, 12 in 153 for a ratio of 12.8, and Cy Williams, 11 in 142 for a ratio of 12.9). "Heathcliff" went deep for six different teams from 1974 to 1986.

• Eleven players have made their major league debuts as pinch hitters and gone yard. Most recently, **Marlon Anderson** did it for the Philadelphia Phillies in 1998. **Gates Brown** did it for the Tigers in 1963 and went on to hit 15 more pinch-hit home runs, while neither **Bill Roman** nor **Eddie Morgan** would ever hit another home run in the big leagues.

• **Rusty Staub** finished his 17-year career with more than 2,700 hits, exactly 100 of them coming as a pinch hitter. More than half of these came as a pinch-hitting specialist for the Mets in the final three years of his career, 29 of them after the age of 40. He was called on to pinch hit 94 times in 1983, a major league record—at one point coming through with eight consecutive pinch hits. Dave Philley (of the Phillies, of course) had nine consecutive hits as a pinch hitter during 1958 and 1959.

• **Lee Lacy** of the 1978 Dodgers and Del Unser of the 1979 Phillies each homered in three consecutive at-bats as pinch hitters. Among the 14 American Leaguers who've done it in two consecutive at-bats: Ted Williams in 1957 at the age of 38.

Since the 1973 debut of the designated hitter, pinch-hitting appearances in the American League have declined dramatically—as have the opportunities for

Rusty Staub choked up on his bat to ensure contact when pinch hitting.

understudies to momentarily play the starring role. Since most pinch-hit at-bats are for the pitcher, and AL pitchers don't bat, it is unlikely that any future pinch-hitting records—at least for the number of hits in a season or career—will be set by American League batters. But if the National League continues to let the pitchers bat, an American League reserve in World Series play may get the chance to make history in an NL park. Who knows? Maybe if Joe Torre had let utility infielder Andy Fox hit in Game 4, he'd have taken Steve Avery over the wall.

7

Choosing Up Sides

THE GREATEST HITTERS
BY POSITION

They say that baseball is a game of inches, but that could be said of any sport. When the competition is tight, the difference between winning and losing will eventually be determined by the narrowest of margins. It is more accurate to describe baseball as a game of *balance*: the balance required to control one's body to throw a strike, to turn a double play, or to shift one's weight through a powerful swing. Balance is also required in the clubhouse and on the lineup card—the right blend of personalities, pitching styles, and position players to form a winning team.

To be certain that the greatest hitters have been pulled together on these pages, a similar process has been used. The list of top 25 hitters in Chapter 2 is a balanced one in some ways. For example, there are:

- 13 righties, 11 lefties, and 1 switch-hitter
- 13 players who debuted before the color line was broken, 12 who came after
- 15 players with a lifetime batting average above .300, 10 below .300
- 14 players with more than 500 home runs, 11 with fewer
- 12 players who were primarily National Leaguers, 12 who were primarily American Leaguers, and Frank Robinson, who did plenty of damage in both

But there are a number of areas where the list is unbalanced. A wider net is cast in this chapter:

- Greatest by position
- Greatest by region
- Greatest by team and city
- Greatest by decade

In the process, another batch of great hitters is introduced.

Greatest Hitters by Position

On the list of 25, there are 14 outfielders, 9 first basemen, a second baseman, a third baseman, no shortstops, and no catchers. Hard to field a team that way. When it comes to filling out a great-hitting lineup card, the following is what the depth chart looks like. All but one of the outfielders we've met before, and none of the first basemen. Some new faces appear around the rest of the infield and behind the plate. A player needs a minimum of 1,000 games played at the position to be included on these lists. The greatest active hitters by position are in bold.

Left Field

Career

	Bases	Addl bases	Base avg	+/− vs. league
1. Ted Williams	6903	2576	.710	59%
2. Stan Musial	7733	2182	.615	39%
3. Barry Bonds	**5036**	**1492**	**.631**	**42%**
4. Willie Stargell	5127	1367	.578	36%
5. Ralph Kiner	3863	1086	.621	39%

Note that one team, the Pirates, produced numbers 3, 4, and 5.

Season

	Bases	Addl bases	Base avg	+/− vs. league
1. Ted Williams, 1941	480	210	.799	78%
2. Ted Williams, 1946	499	215	.745	76%
3. Ted Williams, 1942	483	205	.724	74%

Center Field

Career

	Bases	Addl bases	Base avg	+/– vs. league
1. Mickey Mantle	6245	1954	.635	46%
2. Willie Mays	7529	2130	.610	39%
3. Ty Cobb	7112	1973	.561	39%
4. Tris Speaker	6485	1702	.560	36%
5. Joe DiMaggio	4765	1311	.626	38%
Ken Griffey Jr.	**4101**	**977**	**.618**	**32%**

Ken Griffey Jr.

Having just passed Hack Wilson, Ken Griffey is seventh on the list of greatest hitting center fielders, poised to move by Duke Snider and enter the top 25 in the year 2000. Rather than either of his back-to-back 56-homer campaigns of 1997 and 1998, his greatest season to date has been 1993, when he outproduced the AL by 45 percent. He was on his way to bigger and better things in 1994 when the strike cut him off at 40 home runs and a career-high .712 slugging average. Since then his production has remained at its lofty levels while the rest of the AL has gotten better. As you can see in the chart above, as great as Griffey is, Mantle, Mays, Cobb, Speaker, and DiMaggio all were even better relative to their leagues.

Season

	Bases	Addl bases	Base avg	+/– vs. league
1. Mickey Mantle, 1957	461	188	.744	69%
2. Mickey Mantle, 1956	488	192	.757	65%
3. Mickey Mantle, 1961	479	189	.748	65%

Right Field

Career

	Bases	Addl bases	Base avg	+/– vs. league
1. Babe Ruth	7849	3197	.751	69%
2. Hank Aaron	8258	2273	.600	38%
3. Mel Ott	6749	1927	.605	40%
4. Frank Robinson	6793	1850	.595	37%
5. Joe Jackson	3098	906	.563	41%
Larry Walker	**3110**	**819**	**.598**	**32%**

During the 1980s, no hitter was more exciting to watch than Darryl Strawberry.

Joe Jackson
(1908–1920—Philadelphia Athletics, Cleveland Indians, Chicago White Sox)

Had Shoeless Joe Jackson not been banned from baseball near the end of the 1920 season for conspiring with gamblers to throw the 1919 World Series, he would have breezed into the Hall of Fame and placed himself high in the top 25. Only nine men outproduced their league by a higher percentage than Jackson over the course of their careers. But Jackson's career lasted only 11 years, as he was tossed out at 31. He never batted below .308 in a full season, and enjoys the distinction of having hit .408 without winning a batting title (1911). His most lasting legacy may be in providing the inspiration for Babe Ruth's swing, which did nothing short of changing forever the way the game was played.

Larry Walker

The greatest hitting Canadian, Walker has a long way to go before he'll crack the right-field hit list. And it's not likely that he'll make it, even if he does repeat his brilliant 1997 season a few more times. In addition to Hall of Famers Sam Crawford, Chuck Klein (who played most of his career in the Baker Bowl, the Coors Field of its day), Harry Heilmann, Reggie Jackson, and Al Kaline, ahead of him is another Baker Bowl creation, Gavvy Cravath, as well as the very underrated Jack Clark and Reggie Smith, two hitters who displayed power and patience at the plate far in excess of some legendary hitters. If you're looking for Roberto Clemente, see the sidebar at the end of Chapter 2.

Season

	Bases	Addl bases	Base avg	+/− vs. league
1. Babe Ruth, 1920	536	271	.884	102%
2. Babe Ruth, 1921	601	288	.879	92%
3. Babe Ruth, 1923	569	263	.822	86%

Third Base

Career

	Bases	Addl bases	Base avg	+/− vs. league
1. Mike Schmidt	5911	1666	.602	40%
2. Eddie Mathews	5793	1376	.580	31%
3. Ron Santo	4887	944	.528	24%
4. George Brett	6140	1026	.536	20%
5. Home Run Baker	3118	578	.483	23%
Chipper Jones	**1989**	**428**	**.594**	**27%**

Eddie Mathews
(1952–1968—Boston/Milwaukee/Atlanta Braves, Houston Astros, Detroit Tigers. Hall of Fame: 1978)

Eddie Mathews was in the top 25 of greatest hitters until Mark McGwire knocked him off the list. The third baseman for the Braves from 1952 through 1966, he played for the Boston, Milwaukee, *and* Atlanta versions of the club. He was Hank Aaron's hitting partner, though his best season came before Aaron even made it to the majors. In 1953, at the age of 21, Mathews hit 47 home runs, knocked in 135, batted

Mike Schmidt smacked 548 career home runs and won three National League MVP awards.

.302, and walked 99 times, achieving career highs in doubles, home runs, RBI, and slugging average. Mathews had a number of great seasons after that—14 in a row with at least 20 home runs—but none as complete as 1953. Despite finishing with 512 home runs, he still had to wait 10 years for induction into the Hall of Fame. His detractors focus on a .271 career batting average, conveniently overlooking the 1,444 walks (18th all time) that helped him reach 20th on the all-time bases list.

Ron Santo
(1960–1974—Chicago Cubs, Chicago White Sox)
Other than the banned Joe Jackson, Ron Santo is one of only two other non–Hall of Famers you will find in the top 5 by position. Why? Because he was a hack in the field? Hardly. The Cubs' third baseman of the '60s and early '70s was a perennial Gold Glover whose range, at his best, was the equal of Brooks Robinson. Robinson was certainly Santo's superior in the field, but not by as much as one would expect—and Robinson couldn't carry Santo's spikes at the plate. Santo falls victim to

- walks being discounted as an offensive contribution,
- batting average being overrated as a measure of offensive contribution,
- his refusal to stick around to pad his stats (he played only 15 years, hanging it up after one bad year with the White Sox), and
- the perception that his home runs were inflated by playing in Wrigley Field.

The latter is true, but how much were the rest of his offensive statistics deflated by playing so many years with lousy ballclubs? The case can be made that Ron Santo's candidacy never even being given serious consideration is the Hall of Fame's greatest disservice.

George Brett (AL)
(1973–1993—Kansas City Royals. Hall of Fame: 1999)
All George Brett ever did was win three batting titles, including one at 23 and one at 37; produce the highest full-season batting average (.390 in 1980) since Ted Williams hit .401 in 1941; top 3,000 hits; outproduce his league by 20 percent; and accumulate more than 1,000 additional bases in his career. You'll get little argument that he is the greatest hitting third baseman in American League history.

Brett was a line-drive hitter more than a home run hitter, but he did have a remarkably quick bat—so quick that it shouldn't come as much of a surprise that his two most famous home runs came off fireballing Goose Gossage. The first was an upper-deck blast in the 1980 ALCS in Yankee Stadium that turned a 2–1 deficit into a 4–2 lead in the decisive Game 3. The second came on July 24, 1983—the so-called pine tar game. Brett had just drilled yet another game-breaking home run at Yankee Stadium off Gossage, only to have Billy Martin convince the home plate umpire to enforce the rule on pine tar not extending beyond a certain point on the bat. Brett went ballistic; teammate Gaylord Perry, true to his outlaw spirit, tried to steal the evidence; and the Yankees thought they'd stolen the game. Instead, one of the rare team protests was actually upheld as league president Lee MacPhail went against his umpires, reinstated the dinger, and ordered the game to be finished. The Royals and 1,200 fans showed up on August 18 for the final few outs. Pitcher Ron Guidry played center field, Don Mattingly played second base, and the Yankees went three up three down in the bottom of the ninth.

Frank "Home Run" Baker
(1908–1922—Philadelphia Athletics, New York Yankees. Hall of Fame: 1955)
You can read about how Home Run Baker acquired his nickname in Chapter 5. Those unfamiliar with his exploits in the 1911 World Series wonder how a man with 96 career dingers could merit such a nickname. Despite the low total, he actually led the AL in home runs for four consecutive deadball seasons, 1911–14. He also led in RBI in 1912 and 1913, but his batting averages of .347 and .337 weren't enough to lead the league and complete the Triple Crown.

Honorable Mention
Had Al Rosen played 68 more games at third base, he would have been fifth on this list. Rosen played only seven full seasons in the big leagues, exploding on the scene at 26 after three brief and unimpressive trials with the Indians, then fading almost as quickly in 1955 after Cleveland's brilliant 111–43 season in 1954. In between, from 1950 to 1954, Rosen was a force. He knocked in 100 runs each season, capped off by a near–Triple-Crown performance in 1953 when he hit 43 home runs, knocked in 145 runs, and batted .336. Rosen was done in by the most innocuous of injuries— a broken finger in 1954—that permanently affected his batting grip.

Chipper Jones
With Chipper Jones taking his game to new levels in his 1999 MVP season—and former Braves castoff Vinny Castilla producing a mediocre one by late-'90s standards—Jones has vaulted to the top of active third basemen. He is poised to pass Home Run Baker some time in 2001 and may end up right next to fellow Brave Eddie Mathews on the all-time list by the time he's through.

Season

	Bases	Addl bases	Base avg	+/– vs. league
1. Mike Schmidt, 1980	431	160	.677	59%
2. Harmon Killebrew, 1969	469	168	.670	56%
3. Dick Allen, 1966	399	145	.674	57%

Both Killebrew and Allen made the switch from third base to first base mid-way through their careers, with brief detours into the outfield as well. They played the majority of their games at third base when they put up the monster numbers shown here.

Shortstop

Like Roberto Clemente's absence from the right fielders, Wade Boggs from the third basemen, and Pete Rose from any of the positions various teams tried to hide him at throughout his career, you may be surprised not to see Robin Yount's name on this list. Again, see the sidebar at the end of Chapter 2 for the reason why.

Career

	Bases	Addl bases	Base avg	+/− vs. league
1. Honus Wagner	5831	1408	.511	32%
2. Ernie Banks	5469	1009	.537	23%
3. Arky Vaughan	3940	729	.521	23%
4. Vern Stephens	3683	577	.512	18%
5. Joe Cronin	4605	648	.533	16%
Barry Larkin	**3617**	**458**	**.513**	**15%**

Honus Wagner (NL)
(1897–1917—Louisville Grays, Pittsburgh Pirates. Hall of Fame: 1936)

"That goddamned Dutchman is the only man in the game I can't scare."

—TY COBB ON HONUS WAGNER

When Frank Thomas shouldered his way onto the top 25 list, this is who he displaced. Not only was Honus Wagner a charter member of the Hall of Fame, he received as many votes for enshrinement as Babe Ruth did. In a feat indicative of the deadball era, which may never be duplicated, Wagner led the league in slugging average six times without ever leading in home runs. He was an eight-time batting champion who was a doubles- and triples-hitting machine, outproducing his league by 32 percent with 1,408 additional bases for his career. No one has held his spot at the top of his position for as long as Wagner has.

Ernie Banks
(1953–1971—Chicago Cubs. Hall of Fame: 1977)
The Chicago Cubs have the dubious distinction of producing all four MVPs who toiled for teams that did not have winning records. Mr. Cub did it back-to-back and deserved a third, despite playing for the worst teams of the lot. When he did

win, he had to outpoll no less than Willie Mays and Hank Aaron, among others. Today, power-hitting shortstops are not viewed as anything all that special. In Banks's day, there were none. Vern Stephens (see below) had been and gone, and was never viewed as anywhere near the complete player that Banks was. In addition to setting the standard for other power-hitting shortstops to try to meet— though none, as you can see by his position on this list, ever have—he also showed how much power can be generated with a small bat and a whiplike swing.

The tall, skinny kid with the quick wrists and the sunny disposition broke the color line for the Chicago Cubs and very quickly became the most popular Cub of them all. Bad knees forced him to first base after 1,125 games at short, but even after only eight full seasons, he'd established marks that have lasted into the 1990s and beyond.

Arky Vaughan
(1932–1943, 1947–1948—Pittsburgh Pirates, Brooklyn Dodgers. Hall of Fame: 1985)

The Hall kept Johnny Mize waiting 28 years. It was just as much an injustice, if not a greater one, to make Vaughan wait for 37. Vaughan had one of the game's best batting eyes, leading the league in walks three times while never striking out more than 38 times in a season. His big year was 1935, when he hit 19 home runs, knocked in 99 runs, and won a batting title at .385. After Honus Wagner's 1908 season, this is the next best for shortstops. His career totals—2,103 hits and a .318 average—were diminished by his retirement at the age of 31 after the 1943 season, in protest of what he felt to be an unfair decision by Leo Durocher regarding another player. Vaughan didn't return to the Dodgers until Durocher was suspended in 1947, hitting .325 in part-time duty.

As if rewarding him for his integrity, the baseball gods sent Vaughan to the World Series for the first time in 1947, and he almost turned the tide for Brooklyn. After the Dodgers had evened the series at two games apiece—rallying from being one out away from a no-hit loss to seize a dramatic victory in the bottom of the ninth in Game 4—Vaughan took the stage at a crucial point in Game 5 to hit a two-out, pinch-hit double that should have tied the game at 2–2. But there had been no pinch runner for the catcher, Bruce Edwards, who had walked to start off the inning, and he failed to score on the hit. The Yankees' Spec Shea wriggled out of the jam and held on to win 2–1, and New York took the Series in seven.

Vern Stephens
(1941–1955—St. Louis Browns, Boston Red Sox, Chicago White Sox, Baltimore Orioles)

You can hang asterisks on this one until it looks like a Christmas tree. Unlike Ron Santo, Stephens's exclusion from Cooperstown is perfectly understandable. In fact, he never even received a single vote—which is fewer than Clint Courtney, Toby Harrah, and Felix Millan, to name just three.

What goes through the mind of a Hall of Fame voter as he casts a vote for the enshrinement of Felix Millan is a topic for another day. Vern Stephens, though no immortal, certainly merited some token consideration at the very least. When you look at how he did compared to Stan Musial in the beginning of their careers—in the same years and in the same park—he does not embarrass himself. In Fenway Park, he went on to knock in 159 runs in 1949, then followed that up with 144 in 1950. But at 31, Ted Williams left for the Korean War, the injuries piled up, and he limped home from there.

Joe Cronin
(1926–1945—Pittsburgh Pirates, Washington
Senators, Boston Red Sox. Hall of Fame: 1956)

The 1927 Pirates certainly played fast and loose with their Hall of Famers. They had Pie Traynor (age 27) at third base, the Waner brothers (21 and 24) and Kiki Cuyler (29) in the outfield, and Joe Cronin (21) backing up Glenn "Buckshot" Wright at third base. By season's end, Cuyler was on the bench with Cronin, buried by his manager midway through the season for not hustling. He didn't appear in the World Series, as Pittsburgh fell to New York in four. In the off-season, he was traded to Chicago in a lopsided deal that benefited the Cubs and brought another short-stop to Pittsburgh. Suddenly expendable, Joe Cronin was let go and picked up by Washington, and the Pirates were also-rans for the next 33 years. Cronin was a potent offensive force for the Senators and the Red Sox, knocking in 100 runs and batting .300 eight times. He led Washington to their final World Series in 1933, hitting .318 in a losing cause.

Barry Larkin

Of all the positions, this is the one that will change the most dramatically in the early years of the next century. Depending on how much Barry Larkin has left in the tank, he could knock Joe Cronin off the list. However, Larkin's time in the top 5 is likely to be short, with Alex Rodriguez, Nomar Garciaparra, and Derek Jeter all having at least a good chance, if not an excellent one, to knock numbers 3, 4, and 5 from this list.

Season

	Bases	Addl bases	Base avg	+/− vs. league
1. Honus Wagner, 1908	362	141	.582	64%
2. Arky Vaughan, 1935	400	141	.671	55%
3. Rico Petrocelli, 1969	413	141	.652	52%

Rico Petrocelli
(1963, 1965–1976—Boston Red Sox)

Americo Petrocelli? It's not a misprint. Petrocelli was an impatient .250 hitter who was turned by Fenway Park into a 210-homer man. Nearly 20 percent of those home runs came in 1969 when he hit 40, batted .297, slugged .589, and drew 98 walks during a pitcher's year. Thoroughly out of character, Petrocelli never came close to matching it before or since. The Sox moved him to third in 1971. He began to fade in 1972 at the age of 29, and eventually gave way to another creature of Fenway, Butch Hobson, who kept the position lukewarm until Wade Boggs came along.

Second Base

Career

	Bases	Addl bases	Base avg	+/− vs. league
1. Rogers Hornsby	5750	1836	.624	47%
2. Napoleon Lajoie	4989	1088	.494	28%
3. Eddie Collins	5766	1073	.503	23%
4. Joe Morgan	5827	1053	.523	22%
5. Charlie Gehringer	5442	821	.542	18%
Craig Biggio	**3575**	**345**	**.498**	**11%**

Napoleon Lajoie
(1896–1916—Philadelphia Phillies, Philadelphia
Athletics, Cleveland Indians. Hall of Fame: 1937)

Lajoie pretty much singlehandedly legitimized a fledgling outfit called the American League when he jumped from the Phillies to the rival Athletics in 1901. He led the AL in runs, hits, doubles, home runs, RBI, batting average (.422!), on-base average, and slugging average. Lajoie was feasting a bit on weaker pitching, but it was no fluke. He actually outproduced his league by even higher levels in 1904. He was the second member of the 3,000-hit club, with 3,244 for his career and a .338 lifetime batting average. He was almost as adored as Ty Cobb was despised, and his fourth batting title nearly came to him gift-wrapped in 1910, back when the Chalmers Motor Company was giving a car away to the winner. The St. Louis Browns played the infield back to allow Lajoie six bunt singles in a doubleheader, and the official scorer threw a gift his way too, allowing him to go 8 for 8. Cobb, meanwhile, sat out his last two games to protect his lead. Chalmers ended up giving each sportsman a car.

Eddie Collins
(1906–1930—Philadelphia Athletics,
Chicago White Sox. Hall of Fame: 1939)

Collins almost made them forget about Lajoie in Philadelphia. He accumulated 3,311 hits, batted .333, walked more than Lajoie—including a league-leading 119 in 1915—but never won a batting title (something to do with Ty Cobb and Tris Speaker). A true slap hitter, more than 2,500 of his hits were singles and he never reached 40 doubles, 20 triples, or even 7 home runs in a season. Even collecting them one base at a time, he still outproduced his league by 23 percent for his career.

Joe Morgan
(1963–1984—Houston Astros, Cincinnati Reds, San Francisco Giants,
Philadelphia Phillies, Oakland A's. Hall of Fame: 1990)

Joe Morgan's strike zone was small and his batting eye spectacular. He drew 100 walks in a season eight times despite being only a moderate power threat. The second baseman for the Big Red Machine, he hit .300 only twice—in 1975 and 1976, seasons for which he was justly rewarded with back-to-back MVPs. In the 1975 World Series, he provided ninth-inning game-winning hits against the Red Sox in Fenway Park in both Game 2 and Game 7. In 1976, the 5′7″, 160-pound second baseman was moved from second to third in the batting order—thanks to the emergence of the original Ken Griffey, and he responded with 27 home runs, 111 RBI, a .320 batting average, and a league-leading .576 slugging average. He is the greatest second baseman of the postwar era.

Charlie Gehringer
(1924–1942—Detroit Tigers. Hall of Fame: 1949)

"He said 'hello' opening day, 'good-bye' closing day, and in between hits .350."

—HALL OF FAME CATCHER MICKEY COCHRANE,
ON TEAMMATE CHARLIE GEHRINGER

Another quiet second baseman, Gehringer was called the "Mechanical Man" for his German precision. Directly underneath Lou Gehrig in the big book, born a month apart, and competing in the same league for the same teams throughout their careers, Charlie Gehringer was, like the Iron Horse, a model of consistency. From 1927 to 1940, his lowest batting average was .298. You could pretty much write him in for 200 hits (he did that seven times), 40 doubles (though one year he hit 60, one of only six men to do it), between 10 and 20 home runs, 100 RBI (he did that eight times), 130 runs (hitting in front of Hank Greenberg certainly helped), and

.330 (his best was a league-leading .371 in 1937 when he was MVP). Throw in about 70 walks (though he topped 100 twice) and fewer than 30 strikeouts and you have, just like Lou Gehrig, an All-Star for the first six years the Game was played (Gehringer started each game while Gehrig started the first five, moving Jimmie Foxx to third base twice). He slumped badly in 1941 and finished up in 1942 only 161 hits shy of 3,000.

Craig Biggio

As terrific a player as both Craig Biggio and Roberto Alomar are, neither of them is any real threat to the individuals on this list. Even the great Ryne Sandberg wasn't able to crack this group.

Season

	Bases	Addl bases	Base avg	+/− vs. league
1. Rogers Hornsby, 1925	464	195	.790	73%
2. Rogers Hornsby, 1922	515	207	.749	67%
3. Rogers Hornsby, 1924	462	190	.739	70%

First Base

Career

	Bases	Addl bases	Base avg	+/− vs. league
1. Lou Gehrig	6567	2195	.691	50%
2. Jimmie Foxx	6408	2017	.668	46%
3. Mark McGwire	4501	1334	.658	42%
4. Johnny Mize	4477	1321	.613	42%
5. Hank Greenberg	3994	1241	.661	45%

Season

	Bases	Addl bases	Base avg	+/− vs. league
1. Lou Gehrig, 1927	556	243	.802	78%
2. Mark McGwire, 1998	545	235	.812	76%
3. Jimmie Foxx, 1932	554	232	.790	72%

Catcher

Career

	Bases	Addl bases	Base avg	+/− vs. league
1. Johnny Bench	4535	890	.530	24%
2. Gabby Hartnett	3847	720	.539	23%
3. Mickey Cochrane	3327	575	.552	21%
4. Yogi Berra	4347	670	.526	18%
5. Roy Campanella	2634	403	.556	23%
Mike Piazza	**2482**	**615**	**.615**	**33%**

Johnny Bench
(1967–1983—Cincinnati Reds. Hall of Fame: 1989)

At no position does offense define greatness less than at catcher. So when a great-fielding catcher like Johnny Bench comes along and hits the way he did early in his career, it gets attention. Just as Ernie Banks created a sensation in the 1950s by hitting 40-plus home runs at shortstop, so did Johnny Bench in the early 1970s. He peaked early, hitting 45 home runs, knocking in 148 runs, and batting a career-best .293 in 1970 at the age of 22. He knocked in 100 runs five more times; but the physical demands of catching took their toll, and by the age of 30 he was a shadow of his former self. Before moving to the infield to register his 2,000th hit in 1983, Bench passed Yogi Berra for most home runs by a catcher.

Gabby Hartnett
(1922–1941—Chicago Cubs, New York Giants. Hall of Fame: 1955)

Another one of those rare underrated Hall of Famers, Hartnett finishes ahead of three more famous catchers on this list. In 1929, no one would have predicted that for the pudgy, red-faced Cubs catcher. He was 28 years old and had been reduced to limited pinch-hitting duty for most of the Cubs' pennant-winning season due to an arm injury suffered while skeet-shooting in the off-season. He'd performed capably for Chicago for six seasons, but very few catchers improve with age at the plate. Hartnett did. He returned in 1930 to join in the season-long National League slugfest with 37 home runs, 122 RBI, and a .339 batting average for one of the most productive offenses in the game's history. He faded a bit from 1931 to 1933 as the league returned to more normal levels of production, then ramped it up again from the ages of 33 to 36. At 34, he won the MVP in 1935, hitting .344 for a Cubs team that won 21 games in a row in September. He took over the role of player-manager in 1938 and capped off another furious September pennant drive by the Cubs with the team's most storied home run (see Chapter 4 for all the details). He played until he was 40, still catching and still hitting .300.

Mickey Cochrane
(1925–1937—Philadelphia Athletics, Detroit Tigers. Hall of Fame: 1947)

Mickey Cochrane was the backbone of two truly great teams, the 1929–31 Athletics and the 1935 Tigers. His teams won three of four World Series, dropping the fourth in seven games. Cochrane hit .300 for 10 of the 13 seasons he played while hitting plenty of doubles and drawing lots of walks. The latter accomplishments, often overlooked, weren't lost on Mickey Mantle's dad. He thought so much of Cochrane that he named his son after him—and, as the center fielder would recount later, he was grateful that his father didn't know that Cochrane's real name was Gordon.

Yogi Berra
(1946–1963, 1965—New York Yankees, New York Mets. Hall of Fame: 1972)

"You can't think and hit at the same time."

——YOGI BERRA

It would be a shame if people were to remember the Yogi-isms and forget the player. He was short and dumpy and didn't look like much of a ballplayer until he got between the lines. Berra went to 14 World Series as a Yankee, knocked in 100 runs five times (and 98 twice), reached double digits in home runs for 17 consecutive seasons, and won three MVP awards in 1951, 1954, and 1955. He didn't draw many walks because he was so adept at bad-ball hitting; and while playing in a free-swinging, hit-and-miss era, he never struck out more than 38 times in a season. He could have won a fourth MVP in 1950 (Phil Rizzuto took the honors that year) when he hit .322 with 28 home runs, 124 RBI, and 12 strikeouts in more than 650 plate appearances.

Roy Campanella
(1948–1957—Brooklyn Dodgers. Hall of Fame: 1969)

Many a barroom brawl was triggered in New York in the 1950s when the subject of Berra versus Campanella came up. Playing in a smaller ballpark (as Yankees fans were quick to point out), Campanella, like Berra, won three MVPs—in 1951, 1953, and 1955. His best season was 1953, when he hit 41 home runs, knocked in 142 runs, and batted .312. He held the record for home runs hit while catching (as Dodgers fans were quick to point out) until Todd Hundley broke it in 1996. Campanella was also not as consistent as Berra (as Yankees fans were quick to point out), slumping to .207 in 1954, recovering to hit .318 in 1955, then slumping again to .219 in 1956. His career was shortened at the front end by the color line and at the back end by a car accident that broke his neck. Ninety-three thousand fans packed the Los Angeles Coliseum to honor the Dodger on Roy Campanella Night in 1959.

Following a horrific season at the plate in 1954, Roy Campanella (left) won the National League MVP award in 1955 and led the Brooklyn Dodgers to their first world championship.

Mike Piazza

Mike Piazza should catch his 1,000th game sometime in the year 2000. Once eligible, he may very well debut at number 1 on this list. The greatest hitting year for a catcher already belongs to Piazza; in 1997, he hit 40 home runs, batted .362, and outproduced the NL by 46 percent. This pushed him past Johnny Bench's 1972 season, when the Reds' catcher hit 40 home runs and batted .270 in a pitcher's year. Even maintaining his current levels of production, Piazza won't be able to crack the top 25. That's how stiff the competition is. And some time about five years after his $100 million contract with the Mets expires, he will be the first catcher to go into Cooperstown *despite* his fielding.

Season

	Bases	Addl bases	Base avg	+/– vs. league
Mike Piazza, 1997	424	134	.678	46%
Johnny Bench, 1972	391	123	.613	46%
Roy Campanella, 1953	384	112	.655	41%

Greatest by Region

The top 25 list is also unbalanced in terms of geography, with 23 of the players concentrated in four regions of the U.S. In fact, three states alone produced 10 of the game's greatest hitters (Georgia, Alabama, and California).

- South: 7 (Mays, Aaron, Ott, Cobb, Mize, McCovey, Thomas)
- Northeast: 6 (Ruth, Gehrig, Foxx, Musial, Greenberg, Allen)
- Southern Plains: 5 (Mantle, Hornsby, Robinson, Speaker, Stargell)
- Southwest: 5 (Williams, Bonds, McGwire, DiMaggio, Kiner)
- Central: 1 (Schmidt)
- Northwest: 1 (Killebrew)
- New England: 0
- North: 0
- Midwest: 0
- Caribbean: 0

Cities such as San Francisco, New York, and even Donora, Pennsylvania (Stan Musial and Ken Griffey Jr.) and Mobile, Alabama (Hank Aaron and Willie McCovey) have produced more great hitters than entire states. Here is a look at the big three by geography. The top active player is listed in bold.

New England*

	Bases	Addl bases	Base avg	+/– vs. league
Napoleon Lajoie, Rhode Island	4989	1088	.494	28%
Jeff Bagwell, Massachusetts	**3477**	**910**	**.616**	**36%**
Gabby Hartnett, Rhode Island	3847	720	.539	23%

*Connecticut, Rhode Island, Maine, Vermont, New Hampshire, Massachusetts, Quebec, Newfoundland, Nova Scotia

Mo Vaughn of Connecticut should pass Gabby Hartnett eventually and take his place alongside Bagwell and Lajoie.

Northeast*

	Bases	Addl bases	Base avg	+/– vs. league
Babe Ruth, Maryland	7849	3197	.751	69%
Lou Gehrig, New York	6567	2195	.691	50%
Jimmie Foxx, Maryland	6408	2017	.668	46%
Ken Griffey Jr., Pennsylvania	**4101**	**977**	**.618**	**32%**

*New York, Pennsylvania, New Jersey, Maryland, District of Columbia

Three of the game's top four of all time, with two from Maryland alone.

South*

	Bases	Addl bases	Base avg	+/– vs. league
Willie Mays, Alabama	7529	2130	.610	39%
Hank Aaron, Alabama	8258	2273	.600	38%
Mel Ott, Louisiana	6749	1927	.605	40%
Frank Thomas, Georgia	**3880**	**1055**	**.650**	**37%**

*South Carolina, Georgia, Florida, Alabama, Mississippi, Louisiana, Arkansas, Virginia, Kentucky, Tennessee, North Carolina

The southern region is comprised of 11 states, but they grow most of their best hitters in Georgia, Alabama, and Louisiana.

Central*

	Bases	Addl bases	Base avg	+/– vs. league
Mike Schmidt, Ohio	5911	1666	.602	40%
Ed Delahanty, Ohio	3214	922	.545	41%
Chuck Klein, Indiana	4123	1005	.582	32%
David Justice, Ohio	**2883**	**586**	**.574**	**26%**

*Ohio, Indiana, Illinois, West Virginia

This is a diverse group, with Ed Delahanty easily the most bizarre. A slugging sensation in the 1890s and early 1900s who was the second man to hit four home runs in a game, he was also a nasty drunk who disappeared on July 2, 1903, in the midst of another .300 season. The AL's reigning batting champ was ejected from a train near Niagara Falls in the middle of the night for being drunk and disorderly. His body was never found, and it was assumed that he fell off the railroad bridge and went over the falls.

As for Chuck Klein, you can read all about him in Chapter 17. His career numbers are impressive, but they say more about the Baker Bowl in Philadelphia than they do about his ability as a hitter.

David Justice has put together a solid career, but he will be most remembered for a moment in postseason play. Having criticized Braves fans for not being vocal enough before Game 6 of the 1995 World Series in Atlanta, Justice put the pressure squarely on himself—then produced the game's only run when he homered off Indians left-handed reliever Jim Poole. Justice found himself playing for those Indians two years later, and Cleveland manager Mike Hargrove began to second-guess himself as he got to see firsthand how well the left-handed Justice handles both righties and lefties.

North*

	Bases	Addl bases	Base avg	+/- vs. league
Al Simmons, Wisconsin	5300	1012	.565	24%
Larry Walker, Canada	**3110**	**819**	**.589**	**32%**
Jack Fournier, Michigan	3104	659	.536	30%
Dave Winfield, Minnesota	6437	990	.527	18%

*Wisconsin, Michigan, Minnesota, North and South Dakota, Alberta, Saskatchewan, and Ontario

Al Simmons, Aloys Szymanski, or "Bucketfoot Al" for his unorthodox habit of stepping away from the pitch, or "in the bucket"—whatever you call him, he was a star for the great Philadelphia Athletics' teams of the late '20s and early '30s. Simmons is one of only six men to get 250 hits in a season. Jack Fournier didn't establish himself as a regular until he turned 30, despite leading the league in slugging at 25. He had his best seasons from ages 32 to 34 at first base for the Brooklyn Dodgers, and managed only 500 at-bats in a season five times. But he is one those hitters who dominated his league for a brief period of time. Right fielder and DH, Dave Winfield, on the other hand, stuck around long enough to reach 3,000 hits despite one of the most fundamentally unsound swings ever to have an extended stay in the big leagues. Notice that Winfield, despite having more than double the at-bats that Fournier had, didn't generate that many more additional bases.

Southern Plains*

	Bases	Addl bases	Base avg	+/− vs. league
Mickey Mantle, Oklahoma	6245	1954	.635	46%
Rogers Hornsby, Texas	5750	1836	.624	47%
Frank Robinson, Texas	6793	1850	.595	37%
Vinny Castilla, Mexico	**2081**	**344**	**.557**	**22%**

* Oklahoma, Texas, Mexico

They used to grow power hitters in the Southern plains—Willie Stargell and Ernie Banks, in addition to the ones on this list. Now they grow power pitchers.

Midwest*

	Bases	Addl bases	Base avg	+/− vs. league
Sam Crawford, Nebraska	5096	1196	.493	31%
Bob Allison, Missouri	3166	647	.543	26%
Hal Trosky, Iowa	3237	624	.567	24%
Wade Boggs, Nebraska	**5476**	**588**	**.517**	**12%**

*Iowa, Kansas, Nebraska, Missouri

Appropriately, the unassuming Midwest has produced three of the game's most underrated hitters. Wahoo Sam Crawford of Wahoo, Nebraska played alongside Ty Cobb in the Detroit outfield, retired 39 hits shy of 3,000, and was the master of the triple during the deadball era, leading the league six times and averaging 16 per season for his career. A patient power hitter, Bob Allison played right field for the Minnesota Twins in their early days after leaving Washington, and was integral in their climb to contention—with more than a little help from Harmon Killebrew and Tony Oliva. Hal Trosky is one of the greatest hitters no one has ever heard of. Playing first base for the Cleveland Indians in the 1930s, Trosky put up monster numbers from 1934 to 1939, knocking in 100 runs each season and 162 in 1936. Like Don Mattingly 50 years later, an injury kept Trosky from maintaining the pace. He finished his career with 1,500 hits, 200 home runs, and a .300 batting average. Wade Boggs has been playing twice as long as Trosky and is still trying to catch him in additional bases.

Northwest*

	Bases	Addl bases	Base avg	+/– vs. league
Harmon Killebrew, Idaho	5702	1526	.587	36%
Ken Williams, Oregon	3145	734	.580	30%
Earl Averill, Washington	4166	865	.584	26%
John Olerud, Washington	**3152**	**500**	**.558**	**20%**

*Washington, Oregon, Idaho, Montana, Wyoming, Alaska, British Columbia

The left fielder for the St. Louis Browns in the 1920s, Ken Williams holds the distinction of being the only non-Yankee to lead the league in home runs from 1920 through 1931. Williams hit 39 home runs and knocked in 155 runs in 1922, edging Ruth by four because the Yankees star played only 110 games due to a suspension for barnstorming in the off-season. He is also the only man other than Ruth to lead the league in slugging during the same time frame, slugging .613 in 1925 while Ruth missed time with a bellyache of mythic proportions. Earl Averill played alongside Iowa's Hal Trosky for the slugging Indians teams of the 1930s, retiring with 2,000 hits and a .318 batting average. John Olerud has regained his stroke in New York after fading badly in Toronto. In 1998, he topped 20 home runs and .350 for the second time. Olerud and Roberto Clemente are the only ones outside of Colorado to do that twice since the days of Stan Musial and Ted Williams.

Southwest*

	Bases	Addl bases	Base avg	+/– vs. league
Ted Williams, California	6903	2576	.710	59%
Barry Bonds, California	**5328**	**1577**	**.634**	**42%**
Mark McGwire, California	**4501**	**1334**	**.658**	**42%**

*New Mexico, Colorado, Utah, Arizona, Nevada, California, Hawaii

California, thanks to its population boom and 80-game little league seasons, has become the hitters' state in the second half of the century.

Caribbean

	Bases	Addl bases	Base avg	+/− vs. league
Orlando Cepeda, Puerto Rico	4547	866	.534	23%
Tony Perez, Cuba	5457	877	.510	19%
Juan Gonzalez, Puerto Rico	**3105**	**653**	**.600**	**27%**

Leading this list are two long-overdue Hall of Fame inductees: slugging first base-man for '60s pennant winners Orlando Cepeda, and slugging first baseman for '70s pennant winners Tony Perez. In 1961, Cepeda hit 46 home runs, knocked in 142 runs, and batted .311. Though he never produced that devastating a season again, he did finish his career with 379 home runs, 2,351 hits, and a .297 batting average. Perez was less spectacular but more consistent, knocking in 90 runs eleven years in a row. The very stats-conscious Juan Gonzalez of Puerto Rico should end up number 1 on this list before he's through.

When healthy, Juan Gonzalez is one of baseball's best hitters with men on base.

Greatest by Team and City

The top 50 seasons has its share of imbalance, too, most notably by team. The Yankees (19), Red Sox (9), and Cardinals (6) dominate the list. Of the original 16 teams, the Cleveland Indians, Washington/Minnesota Senators/Twins, Brooklyn/Los Angeles Dodgers, Cincinnati Reds, and Philadelphia Phillies go unrepresented. Of the expansion teams from 1993 or before, only the Colorado Rockies (big surprise) are represented.

Here's who has produced the biggest season for each team and in each of the 26 cities (other than Phoenix or Tampa Bay) that have hosted major league baseball in the twentieth century. No player has produced the best season for two different teams, though Hank Aaron did produce the best season for two different cities. If Angels fans are looking for a clue to their team's consistent inability to reach, or survive, the postseason, they can find it in Tim Salmon. He holds the dubious distinction of producing the worst "best" season on this list. Note also that the long-suffering fans of the original Washington Senators, who went on to become the Twins, saw their best hitting season produced in the second year of their existence (1902) and never exceeded for the remaining 58.

Team	Player	Year	Bases	Addl bases	Base avg	+/− vs. league
Angels	Tim Salmon	1995	410	107	.653	35%
Astros	Jeff Bagwell	1997	462	141	.667	44%
Athletics	Jimmie Foxx	1932	554	232	.790	72%
Blue Jays	John Olerud	1993	444	136	.668	44%
Braves	Hank Aaron	1971	402	165	.710	69%
Brewers	Robin Yount	1982	421	109	.611	35%
Browns	Ken Williams	1923	425	145	.670	52%
Cardinals	Mark McGwire	1998	545	235	.812	76%
Cubs	Hack Wilson	1930	528	189	.765	56%
Dodgers	Duke Snider	1954	462	152	.692	49%
Expos	Andres Galarraga	1988	368	99	.568	37%
Giants	Willie McCovey	1969	443	183	.724	70%
Indians	Albert Belle	1995	450	151	.727	50%
Mariners	Ken Griffey Jr.	1993	455	141	.671	45%
Marlins	Gary Sheffield	1996	466	162	.705	53%
Mets	Howard Johnson	1989	396	124	.611	45%
Orioles	Frank Robinson	1966	454	174	.685	62%
Padres	Fred McGriff	1992	391	127	.624	48%
Phillies	Mike Schmidt	1980	431	160	.677	59%
Pirates	Barry Bonds	1992	422	170	.703	67%
Rangers	Rafael Palmeiro	1999	453	127	.684	39%
Reds	Joe Morgan	1976	386	142	.659	58%
Red Sox	Ted Williams	1941	480	210	.799	78%
Rockies	Larry Walker	1997	487	188	.754	63%
Royals	George Brett	1980	356	128	.702	56%
Senators (01–60)	Ed Delahanty	1902	341	120	.637	55%
Senators (61–71)	Frank Howard	1969	442	143	.637	48%
Tigers	Norm Cash	1961	478	179	.725	60%
Twins	Harmon Killebrew	1967	436	161	.643	58%
White Sox	Dick Allen	1972	404	163	.668	67%
Yankees	Babe Ruth	1920	536	271	.884	102%

City	Player	Year	Bases	Addl bases	Base avg	+/– vs. league
Atlanta	Hank Aaron	1971	402	165	.710	69%
Baltimore	Frank Robinson	1966	454	174	.685	62%
Boston	Ted Williams	1941	480	210	.799	78%
Chicago	Dick Allen	1972	404	163	.668	67%
Cincinnati	Joe Morgan	1976	386	142	.659	58%
Cleveland	Albert Belle	1995	450	151	.727	50%
Dallas	Rafael Palmeiro	1999	453	127	.684	39%
Denver	Larry Walker	1997	487	188	.754	63%
Detroit	Norm Cash	1961	478	179	.725	60%
Houston	Jeff Bagwell	1997	462	141	.667	44%
Kansas City	George Brett	1980	356	128	.702	56%
Los Angeles	Mike Piazza	1997	424	134	.678	46%
Miami	Gary Sheffield	1996	466	162	.705	53%
Milwaukee	Hank Aaron	1963	448	155	.632	53%
Minneapolis	Harmon Killebrew	1967	436	161	.643	58%
Montreal	Andres Galarraga	1988	368	99	.568	37%
New York	Babe Ruth	1920	536	271	.884	102%
Oakland	Reggie Jackson	1969	448	163	.676	57%
Philadelphia	Jimmie Foxx	1932	554	232	.790	72%
Pittsburgh	Barry Bonds	1992	422	170	.703	67%
San Diego	Fred McGriff	1992	391	127	.624	48%
San Francisco	Willie McCovey	1969	443	183	.724	70%
Seattle	Ken Griffey Jr.	1993	455	141	.671	45%
St. Louis	Mark McGwire	1998	545	235	.812	76%
Toronto	John Olerud	1993	444	136	.668	44%
Washington	Frank Howard	1969	442	143	.637	48%

Greatest by Decade

Every decade since the 1880s, except one, has produced at least one hitter who has gone on to crack the top 25. The missing decade? The 1950s—ironic, considering that it was the height of the baby boom. The best hitters produced in the 1950s? Not 3,000-hit men Robin Yount, Dave Winfield, Eddie Murray, and George Brett. They don't even make the top three. Read on to find out who does—including a name you don't usually see alongside Cobb, Ruth, Gehrig, Williams, Musial, Mantle, Schmidt, and Bonds.

As for the '70s decades, Honus Wagner of the 1870s was just bumped out of the top 25 by Frank Thomas, and it remains to be seen what product of the 1970s will go to the head of the class. Vladimir Guerrero may be the best bet.

1870s:	Honus Wagner	1920s:	Stan Musial
1880s:	Ty Cobb	1930s:	Mickey Mantle
1890s:	Babe Ruth	1940s:	Mike Schmidt
1900s:	Lou Gehrig	1950s:	Jack Clark
1910s:	Ted Williams	1960s:	Barry Bonds

As for the 1950s, they didn't even place anyone in the top 50. Jack Clark was, in some ways, the Dick Allen of his day. Very patient at the plate, very well traveled, and very quietly the most productive hitter to come out of the 1950s. But that's not to say he was a *great* hitter—he topped 30 home runs only once, 100 RBI twice, and .300 twice. The best hitters born in the '50s hung on too long to pad their stats (Eddie Murray), were very good but never dominant (Dave Winfield), lost their bat speed too early (Jim Rice, Dale Murphy), lost too much time to injury (Andre Dawson) or personal issues (Dave Parker), made more outs than their batting averages suggest (George Brett), or hit more singles than their reputations suggest (Robin Yount).

With what he was able to accomplish in his rookie season alone, perhaps The Great One was supposed to be Fred Lynn. The only rookie to win the MVP award, Lynn nearly brought Boston a championship in 1975 before succumbing to a series of injuries that rendered him a mediocre player.

Although he had several good seasons with the New York Yankees, Dave Winfield had his best year in 1979 as a member of the San Diego Padres. Winfield hit .308, clubbed 34 homers, and led the National League with 118 RBI. It also marked the first time in his career that he accumulated more walks than strikeouts.

THE
NOTABLE
AND THE
MEMORABLE

8

Hitting the Ground Running

Great Rookie Seasons

Rookies Who Led the League (Modern Era)

We define rookies by today's primary standard, those players who have had fewer than 130 career at-bats.

Hits

> Tony Oliva 217 (1964—Minnesota)
> Dale Alexander 215 (1929—Detroit)
> Frank McCormick 209 (1938—New York Giants)
> Harvey Kuenn 209 (1953—Detroit)
> Nomar Garciaparra 209 (1997—Boston)
> Kevin Seitzer 207 (1987—Kansas City)
> Johnny Pesky 205 (1942—Boston)
> Dick Wakefield 200 (1943—Detroit)

Note: The rookie record for hits in a season is held by Lloyd Waner, with 223 (1927—Pittsburgh).

Home Runs

Mark McGwire 49 (1987—Oakland)
Al Rosen 37 (1950—Cleveland)
Ralph Kiner 23 (1946—Pittsburgh)

Note: The NL rookie record is 38, shared by Wally Berger (1930—Boston Braves) and Frank Robinson (1956—Cincinnati).

Batting Average

Tony Oliva .323 (1964—Minnesota)

Note: For those with 3.1 plate appearances per game, the highest batting average in the AL was .343 by Dale Alexander (1929—Detroit), while Lloyd Waner holds the NL record at .355 (1927—Pittsburgh).

Runs

Lloyd Waner 133 (1927—Pittsburgh)
Vada Pinson 131 (1959—Cincinnati)
Richie Allen 125 (1964—Philadelphia)
Frank Robinson 122 (1956—Cincinnati)
Tony Oliva 109 (1964—Minnesota)
Fred Lynn 103 (1975—Boston)

Note: The AL rookie record is 132 by Joe DiMaggio (1936—New York Yankees).

RBI

Ted Williams 145 (1939—Boston)
Walt Dropo 144 (1950—Boston)

Note: The NL rookie record is 119 by Wally Berger (1930—Boston Braves).

In his inaugural season, Lloyd "Little Poison" Waner set the rookie record for hits (223) and led the National League in runs scored (133). Waner played outfield for the Pittsburgh Pirates alongside his older brother, Paul "Big Poison" Waner.

If you're choosing up sides for a Rookie All-Star game in an Iowa cornfield, lining up with the immortals is no guarantee of victory. A squad of no-names could pound some of Cooperstown's finest into submission. Which of the following line-ups of rookies would you rather have going to bat for you?

Campanella, Cobb, Kaline, and Clemente . . . ?

		AB	H	2B	3B	HR	R	RBI	BA	SA
C	Roy Campanella	279	72	11	3	9	32	45	.258	.416
1B	George Sisler	274	78	10	2	3	28	29	.285	.369
1B	Bill Terry	163	39	7	2	5	26	24	.239	.399
2B	Eddie Collins	330	90	18	7	1	39	40	.273	.379
2B	Frankie Frisch	190	43	3	2	2	21	24	.226	.295
SS	Luke Appling	297	69	13	4	1	36	28	.232	.313
3B	Mike Schmidt	367	72	11	0	18	43	52	.196	.373
OF	Ed Delahanty	290	66	12	2	1	40	31	.228	.293
OF	Ty Cobb	150	36	6	0	1	19	15	.240	.300
OF	Harry Heilmann	182	41	8	1	2	25	22	.225	.313
OF	Al Kaline	504	139	18	3	4	42	43	.276	.347
OF	Roberto Clemente	474	121	23	11	5	48	47	.255	.382
OF	Willie Stargell	304	74	11	6	11	34	47	.243	.428

Honorable Mention: Harmon Killebrew, who had 254 at-bats over five seasons with the Senators before finally earning a full-time job in 1959; Brooks Robinson, who in his first season's worth of at-bats had 6 home runs, 48 RBI, and a .232 batting average (and 29 errors).

Or Benito, Buckshot, Smead, and Maurice?

		AB	H	2B	3B	HR	R	RBI	BA	SA
C	Earl Williams	497	129	14	1	33	64	87	.260	.491
C	Benito Santiago	546	164	33	2	18	64	79	.300	.467
1B	Del Bissonette	587	188	30	13	25	90	106	.320	.543
1B	Zeke Bonura	510	154	35	4	27	86	110	.302	.545
1B	Alvin Davis	567	161	34	3	27	80	116	.284	.497
2B	Riggs Stephenson	206	68	17	2	2	45	34	.330	.461
SS	Buckshot Wright	616	177	28	18	7	80	111	.287	.425
3B	Pinky Whitney	585	176	35	4	10	73	103	.301	.426
3B	Pinky Higgins	567	178	34	11	14	85	99	.314	.487
OF	Ike Boone	486	162	29	3	13	71	96	.333	.486
OF	Smead Jolley	616	193	38	12	16	76	114	.313	.492
OF	Joe Vosmik	591	189	36	14	7	80	117	.320	.464
OF	Taffy Wright	263	92	18	10	2	37	36	.350	.517
OF	Maurice VanRobays	572	156	27	7	11	82	116	.273	.402
OF	Mitchell Page	501	154	28	8	21	85	75	.307	.521
OF	Willie Montanez	599	153	27	6	30	78	99	.255	.471

ROOKIES YEAR AFTER YEAR

Much has been made of the Dodgers' string of Rookies of the Year: four in a row, three of them pitchers, from 1979 to 1982; and five in a row from 1992 to 1996. In 1997, half of their starting lineup consisted of recent winners: Mike Piazza, Eric Karros, Todd Hollandsworth, and Raul Mondesi.

But there are some other, less well-known strings of rookie hitters.

The Oakland Athletics produced three Rookies of the Year in a row (Jose Canseco, Mark McGwire, and Walt Weiss) from 1986 to 1988, with catcher Terry Steinbach a legitimate contender in 1987. It's no coincidence that the team ended up in the World Series in 1988, 1989, and 1990 after six consecutive seasons without a winning record.

The Pittsburgh Pirates of the mid-'20s produced even more talent than the Athletics of the late '80s, but ended up with fewer results. In 1924, Hall of Fame outfielder Kiki Cuyler finished fourth in the league in batting at .354 in his rookie season. In 1925, Glenn "Buckshot" Wright was given the shortstop job and knocked in 121 runs, also fourth in the league, as Pittsburgh won it all. In 1926, Hall of Fame outfielder Paul Waner hit .336, fifth in the league. And in 1927, Hall of Fame outfielder Lloyd Waner finished third in the league (behind his brother Paul) at .355. The 1927 Pirates, which already featured a fourth Hall of Famer in third baseman Pie Traynor, hit .305 and earned the right to face the Murderers' Row of the New York Yankees. But Babe Ruth had outhomered the entire Pirates team during the regular season, and he did so again in the World Series as the Yankees swept Pittsburgh. Cuyler had butted heads with manager Donie Bush during the 1927 season, and he was dealt to the Cubs in the off-season in one of the worst deals in baseball history. The Pirates, despite this remarkable string of rookie performances, would be on the outside looking in for the next 33 years.

But no team has rolled the dice as often and as effectively as the Senators/Twins of the late '50s and early '60s. In 1960, the original Washington Senators were playing their final season in the nation's capital. They finished in fifth place, 24 games out of first—and that was a good year! They'd finished dead last the past three seasons. They were on a 15-year run that featured one winning record (78–76 in 1952), one first-division finish (fourth place in 1946), and no closer than 17 games off the pace. But some funny things were happening in D.C. ("First in war, first in peace, last in the American League.") Rather than playing over-the-hill veterans, they were giving jobs to kids, and the rookies were producing. Center fielder Albie Pearson—all 5'5" and 140 pounds of him—had won the Rookie of the Year in 1958 (and promptly been traded). Outfielder Bob Allison had done the same in 1959 when he hit 30 home runs. Harmon Killebrew had finally nailed down a full-time job after five brief trials beginning when he was 18, and proceeded to lead the league with 42 home runs. Things only got better when the team moved to Minnesota in 1961. A 21-year-old named Zoilo Versalles was given the shortstop job and hit .280. In 1962, a 24-year-old third baseman named Rich Rollins knocked in 96 runs and batted .298. In 1963, the Twins found a spot for a 25-year-old named Jimmie Hall in the outfield and he hit 33 home runs. To cap it off in 1964, Tony Oliva had one of the greatest rookie seasons of all time. By 1965, these four, along with Killebrew and Allison, had taken the lowly once-Senators to Game 7 of the World Series before bowing to the Los Angeles Dodgers.

Earl Williams played for the 1971 Braves. Another big year in 1972 convinced the Orioles to give up four players for him—including their third starter (Pat Dobson), their second baseman (Davey Johnson, who would hit 43 home runs in 1973), and another future manager, catcher Johnny Oates. The Braves would be able to get him back in 1975 for a minor leaguer and $75,000.

Benito Santiago closed out his brilliant 1987 season for the Padres with a major league rookie record 34-game hitting streak. He has yet to hit .300 again, and his signing in 2000 by the Reds meant seven teams in nine years for Santiago.

Delphia Louis Bissonette debuted in 1928 with the Brooklyn Dodgers, but only lasted five seasons. The pride of New Orleans, **Henry John "Zeke" Bonura**, came up with the Chicago White Sox in 1934, knocked in 100 runs four of his first five seasons, but only lasted seven in the big leagues. With nine seasons in the majors, **Alvin Davis** of the 1984 Seattle Mariners lasted the longest of these slugging rookie first basemen. Without much protection in the order, Davis set the rookie record for intentional walks with 16. Ken Griffey Jr. removed just about every other mark Davis holds from the Seattle record book.

Despite hitting .337 in part-time play during his first six seasons, **Jackson Riggs "Old Hoss" Stephenson** remained a utility player for the 1921–25 Indians and 1926 Cubs. When he did get a chance to play full-time for the Cubs as an outfielder from 1927 to 1934, his average plummeted to .336.

Glenn "Buckshot" Wright, a rookie on the 1924 Pirates, knocked in 100 runs three of his first four seasons, and helped the Pirates win a world championship in 1925 (see "Rookies Year After Year," page 188). **Arthur "Pinky" Whitney** came up with the 1928 Phillies. He knocked in 100 runs four of his first five seasons, and may have been that club's finest third baseman prior to Mike Schmidt. **Michael "Pinky" Higgins** came up across town with the Philadelphia Athletics in 1933. While Connie Mack sold off his stars in the mid-'30s, Higgins stayed, and by 1936 was one of the best players on a last-place ballclub.

Ike Boone was a rookie on the 1924 Red Sox. He would manage only 13 home runs and 94 RBI over the next *five* seasons. **Maurice "Bomber" VanRobays** of the 1940 Pirates would hit only seven more home runs in his career. **Smead "Smudge" Jolley** would also fade fast. After his promising rookie campaign with the 1930 White Sox, he would last only three more seasons. **Joe Vosmik** debuted with the 1931 Indians, had a few more big seasons with Cleveland, the St. Louis Browns, and the Red Sox, and then retired with a .307 lifetime batting average.

Taffy Wright hit .350 in part-time play with the 1938 Senators, one point higher than league-leader Jimmie Foxx, but only had 263 at-bats. Wright went on to produce as a regular for Washington and the White Sox, flirting with the batting title again in 1947. (See "Great Rookie Half-Seasons," page 195, for other rookies who starred in brief call-ups, some who maintained that level over a full season, and others who proved to be flashes in the pan.)

ROOKIE DUOS

A team is fortunate enough to get production from one rookie hitter. Consider these teams that enjoyed spectacular offensive numbers from *two* rookies.

The 1975 Red Sox dropped rookie stars Fred Lynn and Jim Rice into a lineup already led by Hall of Famer Carl Yastrzemski and eventual Cooperstown resident Carlton Fisk. Lynn and Rice each topped 20 home runs, 100 RBI, and a .300 batting average. The Red Sox came agonizingly close to a world championship, losing in seven games to the Cincinnati Reds.

The Red Sox shouldn't feel ashamed to have come so close. The 1938 Indians finished 13 games off the pace despite a club-leading 113 RBI from rookie third baseman Ken Keltner and 112 RBI and a .343 batting average from rookie outfielder Jeff Heath. The 1929 Tigers hit .299 as a team, propelled by rookie first baseman Dale Alexander, who led the league in hits, and rookie outfielder Roy Johnson, who hit .314. These two joined a lineup that featured two Hall of Famers—Charlie Gehringer (.339 with 106 RBI) and Harry Heilmann (.344 with 120 RBI)—yet the Tigers still finished 36 games off the pace.

By 1977, after the Oakland A's dynasty was decimated by free agent defections and bad trades, **Mitchell Page** was supposed to be the cornerstone upon which they would be rebuilt. But after his sparkling rookie season, in which he also stole 42 bases, he managed to bat only .253 with diminished production. **Willie Montanez** holds the NL record for intentional walks issued to a rookie (14), as part of a 1971 Phillies last-place lineup that featured him, Deron Johnson, and *no one* else. Pitcher Rick Wise was one of the club's leaders in slugging average! Montanez would play for nine teams in his 14-year career, playing regularly for eight last-place teams. In fact, only 132 of his 1,632 big league games were spent on teams with winning records!

Obviously, not all Hall of Fame rookies take a back seat to Zeke, Riggs, Pinky 1, Pinky 2, and Taffy.

The original "Big Cat," **Johnny Mize**, batted .329 with 93 RBI for the 1936 Giants. The most consistent hitter in baseball history, **Eddie Murray** hit 27 home runs, knocked in 88 runs, and batted .283 for the 1977 Orioles. His yearly average through 1996? Not much different: twenty-five home runs, 95 RBI, and .288. **Tony Lazzeri** knocked in 114 runs for the 1926 Yankees. With the Astros in 1965, at the age of 21, **Joe Morgan** led the majors in walks with 97, the only time a rookie has ever done that—displaying the patience and batting eye that would make him a two-time MVP. Aloys Szymanski, a.k.a. **"Bucketfoot" Al Simmons**, hit .308 with 102 RBI for the 1924 Athletics. The **Waner** brothers, **Paul and Lloyd**, hit .336 and .355 for the 1926 and 1927 Pirates, respectively. **Earl Averill** hit .331 with 97 RBI for the 1929 Indians, and **"Ducky" Medwick** hit .306 with 98 RBI for the 1933 Cardinals. **Frank**

Robinson tied the NL record for home runs by a rookie with 38 for the 1956 Reds—getting plunked with pitches 20 times for his trouble, a major league rookie record. **Cal Ripken** hit 28 home runs and knocked in 93 runs for the 1982 Orioles—and, to much less fanfare, played in 160 consecutive games. Last, but not least, **Honus Wagner** hit .338 for Louisville in 1897.

The Greatest Rookie Seasons Ever

Mike Piazza, a player taken in the late rounds of the amateur draft as a favor to a family friend named Tom Lasorda, hit .318 with 35 home runs and 112 RBI. Many catchers have had productive rookie campaigns—perhaps because the position forces them to think more like a pitcher, accelerating their learning curve. But Piazza's, impressive as it is, is not the best.

Instead, that honor goes to Rudy York of the 1937 Tigers. York batted .307 with 35 home runs and 103 RBI—in only 104 games and 375 at-bats! Projected to Piazza's 149 games in 1993, that's 50 home runs and 148 RBI, both of which would be rookie records. York played some third base in his rookie year and eventually ended up at first base, but never again hit as many home runs as he did his first season.

The Tigers have placed two players on this list. In 1929, first baseman Dale "Moose" Alexander led the league in hits (215) on his way to a .343 batting average. He also had 25 home runs and 137 RBI. Done in by a leg injury, he would retire four years later with a lifetime batting average of .331 and a batting title to his credit when he hit .367 for the Tigers and Red Sox in 1932. He is the only American Leaguer to be traded during the season in which in he led the league in hitting.

The only rookie to lead the league in hitting during the modern era was Tony Oliva. He batted .323 for the 1964 Minnesota Twins, also leading the league in hits (217), doubles (43), and runs (109). He would win two more batting titles and would lead the league in hits four more times, but knee miseries ended his career prematurely, as he limped home with 1,917 hits and a .304 lifetime batting average.

Unfortunately, prematurely ending careers are not uncommon for the players on this list. Consider this man's first six seasons:

AB	H	HR	RBI	BA
625	206	35	142	.330
632	171	26	113	.271
629	216	42	162	.343
601	179	32	128	.298
554	185	19	110	.334
448	150	25	104	.335

ROOKIES IN OCTOBER

Rookie hitters have recently been in the middle of the World Series action quite often. Chipper Jones was batting in the pivotal third spot in the order for the 1995 Braves, the first rookie to do since Tom Tresh for the 1962 Yankees, Yogi Berra for the 1947 Yankees, and Jackie Robinson for the 1947 Dodgers. Andruw Jones—the youngest to play in the Series since Ken Brett in 1967—saw plenty of action in 1996. Chuck Knoblauch hit .308 for the Twins in the 1991 Series, midseason call-up Kevin Stocker was at shortstop for the Phillies in 1993, and Derek Jeter was at short for the Yankees in 1996. Of course, rookie shortstops in World Series play is a tradition in the Bronx—Frankie Crosetti in 1932, Phil Rizzuto in 1941, Tony Kubek in 1957, Tresh in 1962 (although he was in left field in October), and Jeter in '96. All but Kubek were on the winning side.

Who is it? Lou Gehrig? Jimmie Foxx? Hank Greenberg? No, a contemporary of theirs named **Hal Trosky**, who put up these numbers at first base for the Indians from 1934 to 1939. Despite those numbers, he led the league in RBI only once, and the Indians never got closer than 12 games back during this span. An injury sidelined him for half of 1941 and the war took two more years from him. After an unproductive 1946 season, he retired with a .302 lifetime batting average and 228 home runs.

The Indians produced another star-crossed rookie star in 1911. **Shoeless Joe Jackson** of Black Sox fame had 115 lifetime at-bats in 30 games from 1908 to 1910, which would make him a rookie by today's standards. Given a chance to play every day, Jackson hit .408—and didn't even win the batting title, as Ty Cobb hit .420 that year.

Joe Jackson isn't the only great hitter who is not in the Hall of Fame. Add **Vada Pinson** to that list. Pinson had 96 at-bats in 27 games for the Cincinnati Reds, then in 1959 the outfielder exploded for 20 home runs, 84 RBI, a league-leading 47 doubles and 131 runs scored, and a .316 batting average. But he was not eligible for the Rookie of the Year back then, and it went to Willie McCovey, who appeared in only 52 games—the fewest of any award winner (see "Great Rookie Half-Seasons," page 195).

Like Pinson, another rookie who led the league in both runs and doubles—as well as slugging average—was **Fred Lynn**. Lynn played center field for the 1975 Boston Red Sox and is the only rookie of the modern era to be the best player in his league. He batted .331 with 47 doubles, 21 home runs, 103 runs scored, and 105 RBI, enough to earn him MVP honors. He missed by about three feet hitting four home runs in a game against the Tigers, and he hit a three-run homer in the first inning of the legendary Game 6 of the World Series against the Reds. He would have one more big year in 1979, when he led the league in batting at .333, hit 39 home runs, and knocked in 122 runs. But nagging injuries robbed him of playing time most of his career, and he did not become one of the greatest players who ever lived, as was expected of him after his brilliant rookie campaign.

Lynn's rookie season might have been more than he could live up to, but it was nowhere near the aberration that 1950 was for Boston Red Sox first baseman **Walt Dropo**. "Moose" batted .322 with 34 home runs and a league-leading 144 RBI for one of the greatest hitting teams in recent history. He would play only 136 more games for the Sox. He lasted 13 years in the big leagues, but after 1950 his batting average would be just .263 and he would never again hit 30 home runs or knock in 100 runs in a season.

Nomar Garciaparra, however, appears to be the real deal. In 1997, he led the league in hits with 209, batting .306 with 30 home runs and 98 RBI at shortstop for Boston. Following that up with 35, 122, and .323 in 1998 was enough to convince the front office that they could let Mo Vaughn leave via free agency and give the team to Nomar.

The fourth Red Sox hitter on this list was the only other rookie to lead the league in RBI. In fact, he holds the rookie record. Unlike Dropo and Lynn, **Ted Williams** would fulfill the promise of his rookie season in 1939 (31 home runs, 131 runs, 145 RBI, and a .327 batting average). Williams slugged .609 that year, trailing only guys named DiMaggio, Foxx, and Greenberg. Using the criteria established in Chapter 2, this was the greatest rookie season of the twentieth century.

The rookie record for slugging average, however, is .618, set by **Mark McGwire** for the 1987 Athletics. He knocked in 118 runs and obliterated the rookie record for home runs when he hit 49.

The player whose rookie home run record McGwire shattered was **Wally Berger**, an outfielder for the Boston Braves in 1930. Berger hit .310 with 38 home runs and an NL rookie record 119 RBI. As magnificent as those numbers were, they were dwarfed by those put up by Hack Wilson and Chuck Klein during the greatest hitting season in history. It was so remarkable a year that we've dedicated Chapter 17 to it. When the league settled down, so did Berger. He would go on to have two more big seasons in 1934 and 1935, retiring in 1940 with a .300 lifetime batting average.

Another NL rookie who put up outrageous numbers in 1930 was a 29-year-old outfielder for the Cardinals named **George Watkins**. In 391 at-bats, he hit .373 with 17 home runs and 87 RBI. He was part of a lineup in which all eight regulars hit .300. In fact, all but one player on the team who came to bat 100 times batted .300. Watkins would manage to hit only .277 the rest of his seven-year career.

The National League's offensive explosion in 1930 was matched by the American League in 1936, when the league ERA was over 5. **Joe DiMaggio** certainly contributed to the damage, batting .323 with 29 home runs, 132 runs, and 125 RBI.

A youthful Babe Ruth as a member of the Boston Red Sox

But unlike Berger and Watkins, DiMaggio never did settle down. That's why you can find him on our short list of the greatest hitters who ever played the game.

So who had the greatest rookie season in history? Fred Lynn? Ted Williams? Joe DiMaggio? How about second baseman **Pete Browning**? Playing for Louisville in the American Association in 1882 at the age of 20, Browning led the league in both batting average and slugging average, something no one else has ever done. He hit .378 for the hometown team, earning him the nickname "the Louisville Slugger"!

GREAT ROOKIE HALF-SEASONS

A rookie is thrown into the batting order in midseason and proceeds to tear up the league. Is it the beginning of a great career? Or is it a fluke? Like most things in baseball, it could go either way.

Fred Haney of the 1922 Tigers proved to be a fluke. He hit .352 in 81 games, then .266 for the rest of his career. Haney's contemporary counterpart, Kevin Stocker, hit .324 in 70 games for the Phillies in 1993 and has been struggling to stay near .250 ever since. And then there is "Hurricane" Bob Hazle, who hit .403 in 41 games for the world champion Milwaukee Braves of 1957. He looked like the next superstar in a lineup that already featured Hank Aaron and Eddie Mathews, but he only played 20 more games in Milwaukee, hitting .179 before being sold to the Tigers. A year after hitting .403, he was out of baseball.

What will become of the modern Hurricane Hazle, **Shane Spencer**, remains to be seen. During the Yankees' record-setting 1998 season, Spencer stole the show in September, hitting three grand slams in 10 days. The left fielder from Key West, Florida, finished the season with 10 home runs and 27 RBI in 67 at-bats with a .373 average. He added two more home runs in the postseason, prompting comparisons to Roy Hobbs of *The Natural* and Joe Hardy of *Damn Yankees*. Whatever you want to call him, he was an unfair addition to an already overpowering Yankees lineup.

Bob Horner hit 23 home runs in 89 games for the 1978 Braves, coming to the team straight from college. He had 100 home runs before he turned 24, and he hit four in a game in 1986, but he ended up playing in Japan before he turned 30. What looked like a lock for a 500-homer career came to a close at *only* 218.

Dan Gladden hit .351 with 31 stolen bases in 86 games for the 1984 Giants. He never again hit .300—and only stole 30 bases one more time—but he did play a part in both Minnesota Twins titles in 1987 and 1991.

Willie McCovey did some damage immediately and never stopped. He hit 13 home runs, knocked in 38 runs, and batted .354 in 1959, winning the Rookie of the Year award despite playing in only 52 games. He would only hit .300 once more—in 1969, when he flirted with the Triple Crown—but he maintained the home run production until he retired in 1980.

Tim Raines had a record-setting season interrupted by the 1981 strike. The Expos left fielder was hitting .304 with 71 steals in 88 games. By the time he was through, "Rock" could lay claim to being one of the greatest leadoff men in baseball history.

Wade Boggs hit .349 in 104 games in 1982, and 17 years later he became the only man to enter the 3,000-hit club with a home run.

Boggs is just one of many Red Sox hitters who have had magical half-seasons, yet one of the few who were able to maintain that level. In 1987, the Sox thought they'd found their cleanup hitter of the future when big Sam Horn hit 14 home runs in 46 games—his production translating to 49 home runs and 120 RBI over 162 games. Horn had always had trouble against lefties, but then righties started to get to him, too. He went 17 for 115 (.148) over the next two seasons and was waived.

When Horn started to hit again for the Orioles in 1991, Sox fans were too busy gaping at Phil Plantier to notice. Plantier hit 11 home runs and batted .331 in 148 at-bats, his production projecting to 45 home runs and 142 RBI in a full season. But he hit out of a deep crouch with a pronounced uppercut, one of the most fundamentally unsound swings in the game. After batting .246 with less production in twice as many games in 1992, Plantier was dumped for a pitcher named Jose Melendez.

At the end of the 1996 season, all eyes were on Rudy Pemberton, who may have had the greatest rookie fortnight ever, batting .512 in his 13-game trial.

Sox fans with a sense of history may have wished that Pemberton had been traded immediately—as was done with **Ted Cox**, who went a rookie record 6 for 6 in his first at-bats in the big leagues in 1977. He hit .362 in his 13-game trial, then was dealt to the Indians for Dennis Eckersley. In the 700 or so at-bats that were the rest of his career, Cox hit .236 with 9 home runs.

But perhaps the most painful to remember for Boston fans are the 92 at-bats a rookie pitcher had in 1915. Projected to a full season, the pudgy southpaw hurler would have had 26 home runs and 137 RBI—in a league where someone named Braggo Roth took the home run title with 7 and only two players topped 100 RBI. But Babe Ruth only got the chance to play regularly for the Red Sox once, in 1919, before being sold to the Yankees to hit 662 of his 714 home runs.

9

1-2 Punches

Great Hitting Tandems

The 1-2 punch. Devastating in boxing, just as brutal in baseball. You will usually find them batting 3-4 in the lineup—the "meat of the order"—and no one goes to get a hot dog while they're coming up. When they stay together for an extended period of time, they begin to shape the identity of the entire team. No guarantees, but if they're supported by enough table-setters, glove men, and pitching, they may frequently find themselves taking hacks in October.

Some of the greatest 1-2 punches in baseball history have never been able to bring home a title, while others pretty much took up residence in the winner's circle. Some wreaked havoc over a fairly short period of time, while others sustained their fury for several years. And, as you'll see in the "No Protection" sidebar (page 200), some of the greatest "1"s have never had much of a "2" at all.

The greatest hitting tandems through the years are presented here, from Ty Cobb's exploits with another pair of Hall of Famers throughout his long career in Detroit, to the heyday of the 1-2 punch in the 1930s, to a *five*-headed monster in Brooklyn, to a pair of Willies in San Francisco, and on to the 1990s, where the economics of the game have made long-term hitting relationships a thing of the past.

Ty Cobb and Sam Crawford/Harry Heilmann

Ty Cobb was a part of two of the first great hitting tandems of the twentieth century. Yet from 1907 to 1925, with the greatest hitter of his time in his prime and ably supported by two Hall of Famers, the Tigers managed to win three pennants and no world championships. From 1907 to 1915, it was Cobb and Crawford in center and right. In 1907, they combined for 400 hits but were swept by the Cubs in the Series. In 1908, they finished 1-2 in batting again, but fell to the Cubs again. In 1909, they combined for 401 hits and fell to the Pirates in seven games.

From 1911 to 1913, they fell short each season to another pair of Hall of Famers—Eddie Collins and Home Run Baker, who combined to hit .340 to .350 each season. In 1911, Cobb and Crawford combined for 465 hits (a record at the time, but no longer—more tape-measure trivia if you know any of the three pairs of teammates to top that) and a .399 batting average with 256 runs scored between them. Thanks to one of the worst pitching staffs in the league, they finished 13½ games off the pace. In 1912, they topped 400 hits again and finished sixth, 36½ games back. In 1913, Cobb won the batting title and Crawford nearly led the league in hits, but they finished sixth, 30 games back. In 1914, they nearly combined for the Triple Crown, but climbed no higher than fourth. Between them in 1915, they led the league in runs, hits, triples, RBI, stolen bases, and batting average; they also had a pitching staff that season, winning 100 games but finishing behind the Red Sox.

By 1916, the 36-year-old Crawford had lost his job to 21-year-old Harry Heilmann. By 1919, Heilmann had established himself as one of the best hitters in the league, though it was Cobb and left fielder Bobby Veach who tied for the league lead with 191 hits as the Tigers finished fourth. In 1920, Cobb, Veach, and Heilmann all hit .300, but they finished seventh in the standings. In 1921, all three were in the outfield together, hitting .372 as a unit with 641 hits and 47 of the team's 58 home runs. The team finished sixth, 27 games back. In 1922, the outfield hit .360, but the team barely crept over .500. In 1923, Veach split time with 21-year-old Heinie Manush, another future Hall of Famer. The four men combined to hit .355, with Heilmann batting .403, but the Tigers finished 16 games behind the homer-hitting Yankees. In 1924, Cobb and Heilmann had 408 hits; the Tigers took third place. In 1925, Cobb and Heilmann hit .387; the Tigers finished in fourth place.

By 1926, Cobb was 39 years old and no longer a full-time player. Manush and Heilmann took the gold and bronze in the batting race—Manush denying Babe Ruth the Triple Crown he never won—but the Tigers finished sixth. But a 23-year-old had won the second-base job, though not in a fashion that suggested he would be one of the best to ever play the position, and the Tigers' years of hitting for naught were numbered. More on that later.

George Sisler and Friends

Babe Ruth ushered in the roaring '20s with 54 home runs in 1920. But he wasn't the only one setting records that season. A 27-year-old first baseman and part-time pitcher, George Sisler, collected 257 hits and batted .407 for the St. Louis Browns. He was the college boy to Ruth's street urchin, and for three seasons he and Ruth were the best in the American League. In 1920, Sisler and center fielder Baby Doll Jacobson combined for 473 hits to break the record held by Ty Cobb and Sam Crawford. They also combined for 234 runs and 244 RBI as the doormat Browns climbed all the way to fourth. Both Sisler and Ruth fell short of the Cleveland Indians, led by .388-hitting Tris Speaker and Jim Bagby, one of the most obscure 31-game winners of the post-deadball era. The Brownies made it all the way to third in 1923, as Sisler and Baby Doll combined for 433 hits and batted .360. A 31-year-old outfielder named Ken Williams turned himself into a power hitter, hitting 24 home runs and batting .347, while right fielder Jack Tobin led the team in hits with 236. The following season, the Browns actually stood on top of the AL as late as August. As a team, the Browns hit .313. Sisler batted .420 with 246 hits and 234 runs, while Williams blossomed into a league-leading slugger, hitting .332 with 39 home runs and 155 runs. Tobin collected 207 hits, Baby Doll hit .317 with 102 RBI, second baseman Marty McManus kicked in 109 RBI and a .312 average, and catcher Hank Severeid hit .321. They fell one game short of the more powerful Yankees. Sisler injured his shoulder down the stretch, then missed most of the 1923 season with eye problems. He was not the same hitter when he returned, and the Browns fell back to the bottom of the pack.

Rogers Hornsby and Jim Bottomley

The Browns shared a home field with the St. Louis Cardinals, and both teams also shared an inability to win a pennant. As Ruth and Sisler dominated the early '20s, Rogers Hornsby was their counterpart in the National League. Hornsby hit .370 in 1920, .397 in 1921, and .401 in 1922, but St. Louis could get no closer to first than seven games. It wasn't until first baseman "Sunny" Jim Bottomley arrived in 1923 that the Cardinals had another true power threat in their batting order. Bottomley hit .371 in his first full season, finishing second to Hornsby at .384. In 1924 they combined for 205 RBI, while in 1925 they exploded for 85 doubles, 60 home runs, 271 RBI, 430 hits, and a .380 batting average. Despite having the two best hitters in the league, the Cardinals still could get no higher than fourth place and 18 games back in the standings. In 1926, their offensive numbers weren't so gaudy—30 home runs, 213 RBI, and an average just over .300—but it was still the best duo in the league, leading them to the pennant and past the Yankees in the World Series. The dramatic Game 7 victory was their final game together, as Hornsby's reward for bringing St. Louis its first championship was to be traded to the New York Giants.

NO PROTECTION

Protection in the batting order is critical. If the pitcher is frightened by what he sees in the on-deck circle, he has to give in and put the ball over the plate. If he knows that the next man can't hurt him, he can nibble and hope the batter gets anxious. Lou Gehrig offered Babe Ruth plenty of protection, though the Babe still piled up a walk per game, and the Yankees won three championships with them in the lineup together. Were the other great hitters as fortunate?

Frank Thomas has put up huge numbers in Chicago despite a mediocre supporting cast. Ironically, one of Thomas's worst seasons as a pro came in 1998, when he had a true slugger in the lineup with him: Albert Belle. Thomas had won a batting title in 1997 when Belle had an off year, then saw his average drop 82 points the following year while Belle got it going.

Ralph Kiner led the NL in home runs in 1946 with 23 on a team that hit only 60. It was a situation he would have to get used to. In 1947, he teamed with an aging Hank Greenberg to hit 76. It was the only time that Kiner, in his prime, had anything close to a legitimate power threat in the lineup with him. This didn't stop him from leading the league in home runs seven times.

Tris Speaker won two championships with the Red Sox and one with the Indians during the deadball era. He was by far the best hitter on teams built around pitching and defense. Had Red Sox management not been so cheap, Boston's dynasty would likely have continued into the 1920s with Speaker playing alongside Babe Ruth in the outfield.

Dick Allen played with some good hitters during his travels—Johnny Callison, Bill White, and Joe Torre, for example—but it was usually a different partner each year (and sometimes none at all). In his best season, 1972, the best hitter on the team besides Allen was Carlos May, who hit a soft .308.

As hard as it is to comprehend how great a hitter Stan Musial was, it becomes even harder when you consider that he spent most of his career with little or no protection in the lineup. As a 21-year-old in 1942, he combined with future Hall of Famer Enos Slaughter to propel what there was of a Cardinals offense. That St. Louis team had pitching, though, and won the World Series in five games over the Yankees. Musial and Slaughter hooked up again in 1946, knocking in 233 runs as the Cardinals took the NL pennant and beat the Red Sox in seven. It was Musial's fourth Series and third championship in his five full seasons. He would

Frank Thomas struggled with the bat in 1998 despite the presence of Albert Belle in the White Sox lineup.

never return to the postseason, and would share the starting lineup with only two other men who hit .300 and knocked in 100 runs (third baseman Whitey Kurowski in 1947, and first baseman Bill White in 1962). Musial would play until 1960 before finding himself in the lineup with a 30-homer man (third baseman Ken Boyer, 32). No one else would manage to do it before Musial retired after the 1963 season.

What is hard to comprehend with Musial is virtually impossible to do with Ted Williams. The greatest hitter of his era, Williams enjoyed a rookie season in 1939 in which he teamed with Jimmie Foxx to hit 66 home runs and knock in 250 runs. Williams played until 1960, and it never got any better than that. His Boston teams always scored runs, but the only other 30-homer men he played with were Vern Stephens, Walt Dropo, and Jackie Jensen, three prototypical Fenway Park mirages. Others whose inflated stats couldn't match the output of Stephens, Dropo, and Jensen included Norm Zauchin, Frank Malzone, and Rudy York. During Williams's time, the Red Sox even had a 20-win lefty— Mel Parnell, one of only two for Boston in the 80 years since selling Babe Ruth—and they still couldn't win a World Series. The season in which he received his greatest offensive support was 1950, when Boston batted .302 and scored 1,027 runs (fourth all-time, and the last team to top 1,000). That was the year that Williams broke his elbow during the All-Star Game and missed half the season as the Red Sox lost the pennant by four games. Still don't believe in the Curse?

Babe Ruth and Lou Gehrig

Unquestionably the greatest 1-2 punch in baseball history, and possibly the greatest pair of teammates in any sport, Babe Ruth and Lou Gehrig laid waste to American League pitching for nearly 10 years, from the second half of the 1925 season through 1934. They weren't together as long as some other tandems, but they did more damage during their time together than anyone else, establishing marks that still stand today and have never even been seriously challenged in 68 years.

Their finest moments were in 1927 and 1928, when they led the Yankees to back-to-back World Series sweeps. They combined for 107 home runs in 1927, a record that stood for 34 years. They collected 410 hits and 247 walks, scored 307 runs, knocked in 339, and slugged nearly .770. In 1928, they tied for the league lead in RBI with 142, while again finishing 1-2 in home runs and slugging average. They again topped the 300 mark in runs, thanks to 383 hits and 230 walks. On and on it went: 81 home runs in 1929, 90 in 1930, and 92 in 1931, as they finished 1-2 in the league each season. In 1931, they broke their own marks with 312 runs scored and 347 RBI, records that still stand. They topped 60 home runs each season from 1932 to 1934, winning their final World Series together in 1932 in another sweep, victimizing the Cubs for 5 home runs, 14 hits, and 14 RBI in a mere four games.

So how could they fail to sweep the Series every season? It had something to do with these next two guys.

How was a pitcher rewarded when he retired New York Yankees legend Babe Ruth from 1925 to 1934? He was given the opportunity to face the next hitter, Lou Gehrig.

Jimmie Foxx and Al Simmons

The Philadelphia Athletics wrested control of the AL from the Yankees in 1929 and held it until 1931. The Athletics had better pitching, thanks to Hall of Famer Lefty Grove and George Earnshaw, and they also had enough hitting in first baseman Jimmie Foxx and left fielder Al Simmons to hold off Ruth and Gehrig. In 1929, they combined for 67 home runs and 274 RBI while batting .360. In 1930, they upped it to 73 home runs and 321 RBI. In 1931, they "slumped" to 52 and 248. They combined for 10 home runs in World Series play, winning in '29 and '30 and falling in seven in 1931. As the Depression hit, Athletics owner and manager Connie Mack began to break up his ballclub and sell off the pieces. Foxx and Simmons stayed together in 1932, finally outproducing Ruth and Gehrig with 93 home runs, 320 RBI, 429 hits, and 295 runs—only to fall short in the standings as the more powerful Ruth and Gehrig had done for the past three seasons. Simmons went to the White Sox in 1933, where the next-best power threat would be Zeke "Banana Nose" Bonura. Jimmie Foxx was the final holdover, lasting through the 1935 season. In 1936, he went to the Red Sox, where he wouldn't have anyone to swap home runs with until 1939, when

Ted Williams debuted with 31 home runs, 145 RBI, and a .327 batting average. Unfortunately for Sox fans, Foxx was an alcoholic who fell quickly after the 1939 season. Yet the fading Foxx would prove to be pretty much the best hitter the Sox could ever put in their lineup alongside Williams (see "No Protection," page 200).

Bill Terry and Mel Ott

While Ruth and Gehrig fought Foxx and Simmons in the AL, the best hitting duo in the National League was across the river from Yankee Stadium. When 19-year-old Mel Ott joined 29-year-old first baseman Bill Terry with the New York Giants in 1928, a poor man's Ruth and Gehrig was formed in Upper Manhattan. They played together for eight years, but only won one pennant—in 1933, when an injury limited Bill Terry to his worst season in the stretch. They each topped 100 RBI from 1929 through 1932, and were both over .300 in every season but two. Terry was Ott's manager through most of his career, until Ott took over the club himself in 1942. They went into the Hall of Fame only three years apart, Ott in 1951 and Terry in 1954.

Hank Greenberg and Charlie Gehringer

The Tigers of the mid- to late 1930s were offensive juggernauts led by these two Hall of Famers (as well as another Cooperstown G-man, Goose Goslin). They combined to top .300 in 1933, knocked in 266 runs in their pennant-winning '34 season, and both exceeded 200 hits in their first championship season of 1935. After missing most of 1936 with a wrist injury, Greenberg returned in 1937 to knock in 183 runs while Gehringer batted .371. Rookie catcher Rudy York added 35 home runs in 375 at-bats, while outfielders Gee Walker and Pete Fox both batted over .300. In 1938, Greenberg and Gehringer combined to score 277 runs and knock in 253. Gehringer began to fade, batting "only" .325 to Greenberg's .312 in 1939 and .313 to Greenberg's .340 in 1940, when they lost to the Cincinnati Reds in the World Series. In the end, it was seven seasons of Hall of Fame–caliber offense in the same lineup.

Lou Gehrig and Joe DiMaggio

The Tigers' stay at the top of the AL was a brief one, thanks to the emergence of 21-year-old rookie Joe DiMaggio in 1936. DiMaggio hit .323 with 29 home runs, 125 RBI, and 206 hits to give Lou Gehrig a replacement for Babe Ruth. Gehrig bounced back from what was a disappointing 1935 season by his standards to hit 49 home runs, knock in 152, and bat .354. They won their first of four consecutive World

Series that season. In 1937, DiMaggio erupted for 46 home runs, 167 RBI, and a .346 average, while Gehrig added 37 and 159, batting .351 and walking 127 times. In 1938, Gehrig began to fade, though he and DiMaggio still combined for 61 home runs and 254 RBI. In 1939, a rare neuromuscular disease forced Gehrig out of the game. The Yankees still managed to win the World Series that season, and DiMaggio would go on to win five more. In the future, his supporting cast would be under-rated clutch hitters such as Charlie Keller and Tommy Henrich, as the Yankees won with pitching and defense rather than explosive offensive numbers. In 1950, DiMaggio's last great season, he was briefly united with another Hall of Fame first baseman and left-handed slugger, who came by way of first St. Louis and then the Polo Grounds in Manhattan.

Johnny Mize and Joe Medwick, et al.

A pair of M&M boys before Mantle and Maris, 23-year-old first baseman Johnny Mize joined 24-year-old left fielder Joe Medwick on the 1936 Cardinals. Only two years removed from a world championship, the Cardinals would consistently con-tend—and fall short—during their time together. They combined to hit .340 with 231 RBI in '36, .370 with 56 home runs and 267 RBI in '37, .330 with 48 home runs and 224 RBI in '38, and .340 with 42 home runs and 225 RBI in '39. During Mize's best season, 1940, the Cardinals traded Medwick to the Dodgers. The Cardinals also moved Mize east to the Giants in 1942, where he combined with veteran Mel Ott for 56 home runs and 203 RBI. Mize then returned from the war to power the Giants to an unprecedented 221 home runs in 1947, a mark that stood for 14 years until the 1961 Yankees of Mantle and Maris blew past it with 240. The '47 Giants missed having four 30-homer men by only one, with Mize hitting 51, catcher Walker Cooper hitting 35, right fielder Willard Marshall hitting 36, and a center fielder named Bobby Thomson hitting 29. With one of the worst pitching staffs in the league, they managed only a fourth-place finish, 13 games behind a Dodgers team that hit only 83 home runs. In 1950, at the age of 37, Mize enjoyed his last big sea-son. While only getting 274 at-bats, Mize hit 25 home runs and knocked in 72 runs, joining with Joe DiMaggio in his last big season and Yogi Berra in his first big sea-son for 85 home runs to help lead the Yankees to the World Series. The MVP that season? Shortstop Phil Rizzuto, who hit seven.

Mickey Mantle and Yogi Berra

The Yankees won their third consecutive championship in 1951 without a 30-homer or 90-RBI man. Part-timer Gil McDougald was their only .300 hitter. But a

19-year-old center fielder named Mickey Mantle, who hit 13 home runs in a half-season, looked like he might be able to replace Joe DiMaggio in center field without embarrassing himself. From 1952 to 1964, Mickey Mantle was one of the league's most dangerous hitters, teaming first with catcher Yogi Berra and then with right fielder Roger Maris to power an offense that would help lead the Yankees to 11 pennants and six championships. Mantle and Berra combined for 53 home runs in 1952, 48 in 1953, 49 in 1954, and 64 in 1955, before the Mick came into his own in 1956. Mantle won the Triple Crown that year, hitting 52, while Berra added 30 as they combined for 235 RBI. They combined to hit at least 50 home runs a season for the rest of the decade. In 1960, a somewhat obscure young outfielder would come over from the Kansas City Athletics to replace Yogi as Mantle's home run partner. But more on him later.

Duke Snider, Gil Hodges, Roy Campanella, Carl Furillo, and Jackie Robinson

Mickey Mantle's most frequent date in the postseason would be with the Brooklyn Dodgers, whom he would help to beat four times in five years. Each of those four series featured these five hitters prominently.

One would be hard-pressed to find as fearsome a fivesome who played together as long as these Brooklyn Dodgers. In the age of free agency it would be virtually impossible to hold a group like this together for so long, but that's what the Dodgers were able to do—with all but Robinson on the team for its final 10 years in Brooklyn. It was an inauspicious beginning. A year after Jackie Robinson broke the color line, the Dodgers brought in 26-year-old Roy Campanella to catch for them. He enjoyed a mediocre half-season, as did 26-year-old center fielder Carl Furillo. The 24-year-old Gil Hodges hit .249 with 11 home runs, moving Jackie Robinson off first base. A 22-year-old outfielder named Duke Snider neither distinguished nor embarrassed himself in his first games in the majors. The 29-year-old Robinson was the best of the bunch, hitting .296 with 85 RBI as the Dodgers finished third in a tumultuous season that saw Leo Durocher replaced at midseason and promptly snagged by the rival Giants.

In 1949, all five blossomed at once. Campanella hit 22 home runs and knocked in 87. Snider took over center field and knocked in 92 runs. Furillo moved to right and hit .322 with 106 RBI. Hodges knocked in 115 runs. Robinson knocked in 124 while batting a league-leading .342 as the Dodgers won their first of five pennants in the next eight seasons (losing two others in the final game of the season). In 1950, the gang of five produced three 30-homer men, three 100-RBI men, and three .300 hitters. In 1951, they missed doing that again by one home run and five points. Furillo slumped in 1952, and their numbers dropped across the board, but they won the pennant for the first time since '49. With Robinson moving to left field in 1953, they enjoyed their greatest offensive season as the team scored 955 runs—18th all-time, a mark that wasn't topped for the next 43 years. Hodges knocked in 122 runs, Snider 126, and Campanella 142. Hodges hit 31 home runs, Campanella 41, and Snider 42. All five topped .300, with Furillo rebounding from the previous season to lead the league at .344. Campanella slumped in 1954 and the Dodgers fell 5 games short of the Giants, but Hodges and Snider combined for 82 home runs and 260 RBI. By 1955, Jackie Robinson was at third base and slowing down a bit. Campanella rebounded to hit 32 home runs, knock in 107, and bat .318 while Snider pretty much duplicated his run production of the season before. Furillo, now 33, was still hitting, going deep 26 times, knocking in 95 runs, and batting .314, while Hodges was his typical productive self. It was in the Series that they shone brightest, combining for 8 home runs and 20 RBI as they finally beat the Yankees and brought Brooklyn its only championship. They returned in 1956, though Campanella (34) and Robinson (37) were showing signs of slowing down. Hodges and Snider carried the offensive load, but they fell to the Yankees in seven, managing only one run and seven hits in the final three games of the Series.

By 1957, Jackie Robinson had been traded to the hated Giants, but he retired rather than report. Roy Campanella struggled through another difficult season, then broke his neck in a car accident after the season. Carl Furillo hit .306 in part-time duty, while Gil Hodges and Duke Snider both topped 90 RBI in Ebbets Field's final season. They finished 11 back, then landed in seventh place, 21 games back, in their first season in Los Angeles. Out of the friendly confines of Ebbets Field, Hodges, Furillo, and Snider managed only 55 home runs among them. Hodges and Snider were still in the lineup and still the Dodgers' biggest offensive weapons when they returned to the World Series in 1959, beating the White Sox in six. It was their last hurrah, and each, appropriately, hit a home run in the Series.

The future of the team, though no one realized it at the time, was 23-year-old Sandy Koufax and 22-year-old Don Drysdale. It would be pitching, not hitting, that the L.A. version of the Dodgers would be known for, especially when they moved to Dodger Stadium in Chavez Ravine, one of the greatest pitching parks in baseball history.

Hank Aaron and Eddie Mathews

In 1957, when the Dodgers fell from the top of the National League, it was the Milwaukee Braves who were there to take their place. They moved from Boston before the 1953 season, where 21-year-old third baseman Eddie Mathews immediately emerged as a dangerous power hitter, leading the league with 47 home runs while batting .302 and knocking in 135. The following season, another young star,

20-year-old Hank Aaron, showed some promise in an injury-abbreviated rookie season. With durable 33-year-old lefty Warren Spahn consistently winning 20 games, it was just a matter of time for Milwaukee. Aaron emerged in 1955, combining with Mathews for 68 home runs and 207 RBI as the Braves finished second. They fell only one game short in 1956 as Mathews and Aaron again combined for more than 60 home runs while big first baseman Joe Adcock topped both of them with 38 home runs and 103 RBI. They broke through in 1957 with Mathews and Aaron teaming up for 76 home runs and 226 RBI, adding four more home runs in a seven-game triumph over the Yankees. They returned to the Series in 1958, with Mathews and Aaron hitting 61 home runs. The Yankees kept both of them in the yard in the World Series, though, as they came back from a 3–1 deficit to take back the title.

In 1959, Eddie Mathews and Hank Aaron were at their best, combining for 85 home runs and 237 RBI while both topping .300. But the Braves were swept by the Dodgers in a best-of-three playoff, and would not return to postseason play for 10 years. In 1960, Mathews and Aaron hit 79 home runs and knocked in 250, but the Pirates beat them by 7 games. They topped 60 home runs again in 1961, with Joe Adcock adding 35 more, but Milwaukee fell to fourth, 10 games off the pace. In 1962, they hit 74 home runs and had 218 RBI, and the Braves took fifth place. In 1963, it was 67 home runs, 214 RBI, sixth place. They both had diminished seasons in 1964, combining for "only" 47 home runs, but each hit 32 in 1965 in the Braves' final season in Milwaukee. Nineteen sixty-six was their final season together, with Mathews fading to 16 home runs while Aaron came back better than ever with 44. It was their last of 13 seasons together, during which they hit a record 863 home runs as teammates.

Willie Mays and Orlando Cepeda/Willie McCovey

Unlike Hank Aaron, Willie Mays had to wait a few seasons before he had a consistent power threat alongside him in the Giants' lineup. It finally happened in 1958 in the Giants' first season in San Francisco. The 20-year-old "Baby Bull," first baseman Orlando Cepeda, hit 25 home runs and batted .312 as a rookie, matching Willie Mays's output of 96 RBI and winning the Rookie of the Year award. It only got better in 1959 when they combined for 62 home runs, 209 RBI, and a .315 average. Meanwhile, a precocious 21-year-old named Willie McCovey won the Rookie of the Year award in only 192 at-bats. He was so good he was able to move Cepeda to the outfield and third base, as he batted .354 with 13 home runs in one-third of a season.

McCovey fell victim to the sophomore jinx in 1960, but Mays and Cepeda continued to hit, with 53 home runs and 199 RBI between them. By 1961, McCovey had still not re-established himself, but Orlando Cepeda was staking a claim as the best hitter in the National League. He hit 46 home runs, knocked in 142, and batted .311 while Mays tried to keep pace with 40, 123, and .308. Still, the Giants continued to fall short in the standings. That changed in 1962 as McCovey returned to the form of his rookie season. While Mays and Cepeda combined for 85 home runs, 255 RBI, and a .305 average, McCovey added 20 home runs and 54 RBI in a half-season's worth of at-bats. Mays was the winning run on second with McCovey at bat and Cepeda on deck when the 1962 World Series came to a dramatic end (see Chapter 5).

The three enjoyed their best trio of seasons in 1963, combining for 116 home runs and 302 RBI, but the Giants fell back to third place, 11 back of the Dodgers. McCovey slumped badly in 1964, leaving Mays and Cepeda to hit 78 home runs, knock in 208, and bat .300 as San Francisco fell just 3 games short of the first-place Cardinals. A knee injury sidelined Cepeda for most of the 1965 season and he was never the same hitter again. Things might have been different in the standings if he had been in the Giants' lineup, as San Francisco fell only 2 games short of the Dodgers. It would be McCovey and Mays for the rest of the decade, as they combined to hit 90 home runs and knock in 204 in their best season as teammates.

Mays and McCovey would top 70 home runs in 1966 as the Giants again came agonizingly close, losing the pennant to the Dodgers by 1½ games. By now, McCovey was on the rise as an offensive threat and Mays was on the wane. They would manage to top only 50 home runs in 1967 as they finished second for the third consecutive season (to Orlando Cepeda and the St. Louis Cardinals). It was 59 more home runs for the pair and another second-place finish to Cepeda and the Cards in 1968. By 1969, 23-year-old Bobby Bonds emerged as the more dangerous hitting partner for McCovey as the Giants finished second in the NL West to the Braves of Hank Aaron, Orlando Cepeda, and another former Giant, Felipe Alou. Nineteen-seventy was Mays's last big season, as he hit 28 home runs and batted .291 while McCovey hit 39 and knocked in 126. In 1971, the Giants finally made it back to the postseason, though McCovey missed nearly half of the season with a knee injury, leaving first base to be filled by Willie Mays and a 6'6", 22-year-old slugger named Dave Kingman (who would go on to enjoy the dubious distinction of being the non–Hall of Famer with the most home runs).

The Giants pushed the Pirates to four games in the best-of-five NLCS in 1971, with Mays and McCovey leading the way for San Francisco with 3 home runs and 9 RBI. Willie Mays was traded to the New York Mets in 1972 and Willie McCovey went to the San Diego Padres before the 1974 season. Without them, the Giants would have to wait until 1987 before they would play in the postseason again—only this time there weren't even any second-place finishes along the way.

Mickey Mantle and Roger Maris

One year after Mays and McCovey came together, the most famous M&M combination was born. In 1960, Roger Maris come out of nowhere to hit 39 home runs to Mickey Mantle's 40, leading the league with 112 RBI and earning MVP honors. He earned the award the following season, as well, as he hit 61 home runs while Mantle added 54, their mark of 115 still standing as the all-time record. Four other Yankees topped 20 home runs as New York hit 240, a mark that stood for 35 years until three teams eclipsed it in the offensive explosion of 1996. Amazingly, Mantle and Maris were not the best hitting tandem in the league that season. (Do you know what pair topped them in RBI that season?) Mantle and Maris had to combine to top 60 again, in 1962 and 1964, in the last days of the Yankees' dynasty. They were knocked off the mountain by one of the most unlikely of teams.

Harmon Killebrew and Tony Oliva

The hapless Washington Senators moved to Minnesota to become the Twins in 1961 and began a slow climb to respectability. Harmon Killebrew and the underrated Bob Allison got them within 5 games of the Yankees in 1962, hitting 77 home runs and knocking in 228. But when the Twins reached the World Series in 1965, it was due in large part to the hitting of Killebrew and 24-year-old Tony Oliva. Oliva and Killebrew had come within 7 RBI of combining to take the Triple Crown in 1964, and would have done it in 1965 if not for an elbow injury that limited Killebrew to 401 at-bats. They appeared on the same lineup card until 1974, combining for 60 home runs five times, winning one pennant and two division titles, before age and injuries sapped their productivity.

Frank Robinson and Vada Pinson/Boog Powell

From 1965 through 1971, the Orioles and Twins were often battling at the top of the standings or in the ALCS while Frank Robinson and Harmon Killebrew battled at the top of the individual categories. Robinson has become associated so strongly with the Baltimore Orioles that many forget that he was a member of the Cincinnati Reds for 10 years. As a rookie in 1956, Robinson helped the Reds climb from 23½ back in '55 to within 2 games of first, combining for 73 home runs with the massive Ted Kluszewski. Kluszewski's biceps were so large that he had to cut the sleeves off his baseball jersey, but despite his pro wrestling appearance he was a consistent .300 hitter who regularly racked up more home runs than strikeouts. It was Robinson's only full season with Kluszewski, and he had to wait until 1959 to find another partner in crime. The vastly underrated Vada Pinson (try to find another man with 2,750-plus hits, 250-plus home runs, and 300-plus stolen bases who's not in the Hall of Fame) arrived to stay in the big leagues in 1959. They topped 50 home runs while hitting for average for six of the next seven years, reaching the

World Series in 1961. Robinson was traded while Pinson stayed and faded. In Baltimore, Robinson combined with beefy first baseman Boog Powell for 83 home runs and 231 RBI in Baltimore's '66 championship season, 69 home runs and 221 RBI for the '69 pennant winners, and 60 home runs and 192 RBI for the '70 champs.

Willie Stargell and Roberto Clemente/Dave Parker

While the Twins and Orioles dominated the American League in the late '60s and early '70s, the Pittsburgh Pirates were beginning a slow climb to the top of the heap in the National League East, where they would remain in contention throughout the 1970s. Back in 1965, the Pirates finished third in the NL, only three games behind the Dodgers. They were powered by the emergence of 26-year-old Willie Stargell, who combined with 31-year-old Roberto Clemente to hit 62 home runs, knock in 221, and bat .316. They played together for nine seasons in all, winning one World Series along the way. By 1975, Dave Parker had established himself as Clemente's replacement in right field. Stargell was nearing the end of his productive years, but had enough left in the tank to team with Parker to power the 1979 world champions. They combined to do some serious damage in the postseason, too, hitting .378 with 19 RBI between them. From 1965 to 1980, Stargell's Pirates never won fewer than 80 games. From 1969 to 1980, they never finished lower than third.

Johnny Bench and Tony Perez

While the Pirates dominated the NL East in the 1970s, the Big Red Machine did the same in the West. Though the best Cincinnati seasons of the decade belonged to Joe Morgan and George Foster, and the most enduring image of the team may be the headfirst slides of Pete Rose, year after year the consistent run production was delivered by catcher Johnny Bench and first baseman Tony Perez. The Reds won six division titles, four pennants, and two championships in the '70s. Perez and Bench led the 1970 pennant winners with 85 home runs and 277 RBI, enjoying their career years in the same season, though the team fell to the Orioles in the World Series. The Reds returned to the World Series in 1972, with Perez and Bench hitting 61 home runs and knocking in 215 runs. Bench and Perez each topped 100 RBI in 1973 and 1974, but the Reds fell to the Mets in the 1973 NLCS and fell short of the Dodgers in the Western Division in 1974. By 1975, second baseman Joe Morgan had emerged as a superstar, but it was Bench and Perez who drove in the runs, 219 between them. Perez delivered the big home run in Game 7 as the Reds won their first championship in 35 years that season, beating the Red Sox in one of the most dramatic

Dave Parker teamed with Willie Stargell to lead the Pittsburgh Pirates family to a World Series title in 1979.

World Series ever played. Cincinnati dominated in 1976, sweeping the Phillies in the NLCS and the Yankees in the Series, though Johnny Bench and Tony Perez were no longer the dominant forces in the lineup (Morgan and George Foster knocked in 232 runs that season). Despite a .234 average during the season, Bench dominated the World Series, batting .533 to take the MVP honors. Tony Perez was a member of the Montreal Expos in 1977, and the Big Red Machine would never win another postseason game. The dominant 1-2 power combination in the NL was no longer in Cincinnati but a few miles to the east in Philadelphia, where "the Beast" and "Bucketfoot" once did so much damage for the Athletics.

Mike Schmidt and Greg Luzinski

With 23-year-old Mike Schmidt and 22-year-old Greg "the Bull" Luzinski in the starting lineup together for the first time in 1973, the Phillies began their climb from baseball's depths. Since their epic collapse at the end of the 1964 season, Philadelphia had eroded to a perennial last-place club that had bottomed out with 95 losses in 1971 and 97 losses in 1972. As Schmidt and Luzinski developed as hitters—and the farm system began to produce a quality supporting cast—the Phillies improved to 71 wins in 1973, 80 wins in 1974, 86 wins in 1975, and back-to-back 101-win campaigns in 1976 and 1977, followed by a third consecutive Eastern Division championship in 1978. "Bullschmidt" hit their stride in 1975 with 72 home runs and 215 RBI, 59 and 202 in 1976, 77 and 231 in 1977. After a lesser year for Schmidt in 1978, the younger Luzinski had 186 home runs to Schmidt's 190. A pair of 500-homer men in Philadelphia? Not to be. Luzinski was a truly wretched left fielder even before his knees began to give out. When the Phillies finally won their first championship in 1980, Schmidt was a one-man gang. Luzinski watched Lonnie Smith play left field for most of the 1980 World Series and then moved over to Tony LaRussa's Chicago White Sox to be a very productive designated hitter until he retired in 1984 at 33. Between 1978 and the home run season of 1987, Schmidt would never have so much as a 20-homer man in the lineup to help swing the hammer.

Eddie Murray and Cal Ripken

Thanks to free agency and split-fingered fastballs, the 1980s was a weak decade for truly great hitting tandems. Eddie Murray and Cal Ripken enjoyed a long run as Hall of Fame teammates from 1982 to 1988. They hit 60 home runs and knocked in 203 in falling one game short of the Milwaukee Brewers in 1982. They hit 60 again the following season, knocking in 213 and both topping .300 as the Orioles won the World Series. They continued to put up individual numbers from that point forward, but

Eddie Murray and Cal Ripken Jr. provided plenty of punch in the Baltimore Orioles' lineup during the 1980s.

it was all downhill for the team. In 1984: 56 home runs and 196 RBI, fifth place. In 1985: 57 home runs, 234 RBI, fourth place. In 1986: 42 home runs, dead last. In 1987: 57 home runs, sixth place. In 1988: 51 home runs, 107 losses. Murray was in L.A. the following season, and the Orioles wouldn't buy themselves back into contention until 1996.

Dave Winfield and Don Mattingly

While Murray and Ripken were consistently good, Don Mattingly and Dave Winfield were briefly brilliant. In 1984, his first full season, Mattingly batted .343 to take the batting title. The race went down to the last game of the season, with Mattingly going 4 for 5 to beat out Winfield .343 to .340. They each reached 100 RBI along the way, but the Yankees finished 17 games behind the Tigers. They upped the ante in 1985. Though their batting averages fell, their production increased thanks to the presence of Rickey Henderson at the top of the order. Henderson scored 146 runs as Mattingly and Winfield combined for 61 home runs and 259 RBI. But with shades of Ruth and Gehrig in 1931, their offensive heroics weren't enough to win them a pennant. With owner George Steinbrenner deriding Dave Winfield as "Mr. May" during a Yankees slide in September, New York fell 2 games short of the better pitching of the Toronto Blue Jays.

They each topped 100 RBI in 1986 as Rickey Henderson again ignited the Yankees' offense, but this time they fell 5½ games short of the ill-fated Red Sox. Their hitting continued in 1987 as they topped 200 RBI again, but they were in fourth place, 9 games back when the season ended. They fell to fifth place in a tightly bunched division in 1988, though Mattingly and Winfield were both above .300 for the first time since 1984. Winfield sat out the 1989 season with a neck injury while Mattingly enjoyed his last big season. In 1990, Steinbrenner, not realizing that Winfield actually had more left in the tank than the much younger Mattingly, dealt the 38-year-old outfielder to the Angels for Claudell Washington. Hampered by injuries, Don Mattingly slumped badly, and the Yankees finished last.

Dave Winfield reached the postseason in 1993 with the Toronto Blue Jays, atoning for the awful fall performance in 1981 for which George Steinbrenner never forgave him. In his last season, Don Mattingly finally got to play meaningful games in October, showing flashes of his former brilliance in a losing cause against Ken Griffey and the Seattle Mariners.

Mark McGwire and Jose Canseco

Perhaps the most memorable of the 1980s hitting tandems was the Bash Brothers. Only 20 rookies in the game's history have ever topped 30 home runs, and

Oakland produced two of them in back-to-back seasons. (For the trivia equivalent of a tape-measure shot, can you name the other two rookies to top 30 home runs in back-to-back seasons for the same team?) Jose Canseco hit 33 home runs as a rookie in 1986, then McGwire topped him by hitting 49 as a rookie in 1987. The Bash Brothers played together for six seasons, combining for 60 home runs five times, three pennants, and one championship. In 1997, they were reunited and on their way to another 60 home runs together when McGwire was traded to the Cardinals.

The 1990s

Spiraling salaries have made it very difficult to keep hitting tandems together anymore. Trace the great hitters through the decades and watch the 1-2 punches get broken up and reassembled elsewhere. Barry Bonds teamed up with Bobby Bonilla in Pittsburgh, but the Pirates couldn't keep either of them. Bonds went to San Francisco in 1993 to team up with Matt Williams and Will Clark, but Clark signed with the Texas Rangers after the 1994 season, as the Rangers decided not to keep Rafael Palmeiro and Juan Gonzalez together. Meanwhile, back in San Francisco, Bonds and Williams stayed together for only four years, then Williams was traded to Cleveland after the 1996 season. Albert Belle and Carlos Baerga had been the dominant forces in Cleveland, but Baerga lost his bat speed and Belle left for more money to play with the White Sox. Belle joined Frank Thomas in Chicago, but they were together for two seasons with little to show for it.

When Belle left the Indians, it was just the beginning of the juggling in Cleveland, as they traded center fielder Kenny Lofton to acquire Dave Justice—who had been part of a powerful combination in Atlanta until Ron Gant broke his leg and was released—and Marquis Grissom, who had been part of a strong-hitting outfield in Montreal with Larry Walker and Moises Alou, who both left via free agency. Walker rejoined former Expo Andres Galarraga in Colorado, but only for a few seasons. The Braves signed Galarraga to replace Fred McGriff, whom Atlanta had acquired when the Padres could no longer afford to keep both McGriff and Gary Sheffield (who would later hook up with former Expo Moises Alou to help Florida win the World Series in 1997, before both of them would be traded the following year). Alou then joined Houston and Jeff Bagwell in 1998, only to blow out his knee before the 1999 season in a bizarre treadmill accident.

You get the idea. The longstanding hitting partnerships are few these days, with no obvious Hall of Fame pairings in evidence. Jim Thome and Manny Ramirez have been together since 1994, Paul O'Neill and Bernie Williams since 1993, Mark Grace and Sammy Sosa since 1992, Jeff Bagwell and Craig Biggio since 1991, and Jay Buhner and Junior Griffey from 1989 to 1999.

The trend is showing no sign of letting up. When Nomar Garciaparra debuted with the Red Sox in 1997, the Boston faithful pictured their young power-hitting shortstop hooked up with slugger Mo Vaughn at first for the next decade. The combination lasted exactly two seasons. When another phenom shortstop, Alex Rodriguez, had a huge year in 1996, Seattle fans assumed that with both Ken Griffey Jr. and A-Rod, it was just a matter of time before the World Series came to town. Four years later, Junior was in Cincinnati.

The tail-chasing continues.

TAPE-MEASURE TRIVIA

- Most hits by a pair of teammates: 473, George Sisler and Baby Doll Jacobson, 1920 St. Louis Browns; 473, Lefty O'Doul and Chuck Klein, 1929 Philadelphia Phillies (a team that featured four 200-hit men and finished fifth); 485, Bill Terry and Fred Lindstrom, 1930 New York Giants.
- Maris and Mantle's 270 RBI in 1961 were exceeded by a pair of Tigers boppers—Norm Cash and Rocky Colavito—who knocked in 272. They hit 86 home runs while outhitting Mantle and Maris .324 to .292, and walking 237 times to M&M's 220.
- 30-plus homers by rookies in consecutive seasons for the same team: Jimmie Hall, 33, 1963, and Tony Oliva, 32, for the Minnesota Twins in 1964.

10

Everybody Bats

THE MOST PRODUCTIVE GAMES AND INNINGS

S ome days the balls just hang higher and carry farther. Players and teams put up numbers they never thought possible, some having themselves a good week in one inning alone. If they could sustain it, they'd do irrevocable damage to the uneasy equilibrium between pitcher and hitter—but no one ever has for much longer than a week at a time. Sometimes it's a case of a great player unable to be contained; other times it's a flukish outburst by a man of modest abilities enjoying that one perfect afternoon.

You won't find any pennant-winning efforts here. Except for a few October outbursts, this chapter is unashamedly dedicated to the accumulation of personal recognition: from the four-homer club to the home-runs-in-eight-consecutive games club to a host of other clubs that only one man (or team) has ever joined.

In short, these are the biggest days that any player, or any team, has ever had.

Two Grand Slams in One Inning

Prior to the 1999 season, only eight players had ever hit two grand slams in one game: Tony Lazzeri in 1936, Jim Tabor in 1939, Rudy York in 1946, Jim Gentile in 1961, Frank Robinson in 1970, Robin Ventura in 1995, Chris Hoiles in 1998, and the lone National Leaguer, pitcher Tony Cloninger in 1966. Only 32 players had hit two home runs in an inning, with Willie McCovey and Jeff King doing it twice.

On April 23, 1999, in Los Angeles, Cardinals third baseman Fernando Tatis became the only player to do both—two grand slams in one inning. The major leagues have been in existence for 124 years and it's only happened once. Tatis did the work, but a number of other individuals deserve an assist.

First would be the Texas Rangers, for trading the young phenom to St. Louis before the trading deadline in 1998 for Royce Clayton and Todd Stottlemyre (whom they essentially rented for two months). The Rangers went on to lose to the Yankees in three straight in the first round of the playoffs. Tatis settled in at third in St. Louis for what right now looks to be a long time.

Then there's Mark McGwire, who hit in front of Tatis and left the bases loaded with a fly out in his second at-bat of the inning. Dodgers manager Davey Johnson gets an assist for keeping pitcher Chan Ho Park in to face 13 batters in the third inning. And a final assist to Chan Ho Park for being the first pitcher in 109 years to give up two grand slams in the same inning.

All Nine Runs

On September 2, 1996, near the end of a final, bittersweet season in Boston, left fielder Mike Greenwell—one of Boston's four left fielders in 58 years—drove in all nine of his team's runs in a 9–8, 10-inning victory over the Seattle Mariners. Batting eighth in the order between Tim Naehring and Bill Haselman, Greenwell singled in the winning run in the 10th off Rafael Carmona, capping off a night that saw him produce a two-run homer off Bob Wolcott in the fifth, a grand slam off Bobby Ayala in the seventh, a game-tying two-run double off Norm Charlton in the eighth, and four of his team's seven hits.

One of a Kind

Pete Milne.

Trot his name out and stump even the most hardcore baseball fan. What did Milne do that no other hitter in the history of the game has done? Let's set the situation and see if you can figure it out.

It's April 27, 1949. The Brooklyn Dodgers are leading the New York Giants 8–6 in the bottom of the seventh inning at the Polo Grounds—the dis-

Mike Greenwell was a one-man wrecking crew, knocking in all nine runs in a 9–8 Red Sox victory over the Mariners in 1996.

tinctively shaped old ballpark in Manhattan, with its short porches down each line and its spacious center field. There are three men on, no one out, and the pitcher is due to bat. Can you see it coming yet?

Called on to pinch hit—against Pat McGlothlin, for those of you scoring at home—lefty Pete Milne unloads on an outside fastball and drives it by Duke Snider in dead center, where it rolls and rolls and rolls. When Milne slid across home plate uncontested, he had a pinch-hit inside-the-park grand slam—the only one of its kind.

It would be the only home run of his 47-game career, and one of only 14 big-league hits.

Debuting with a Bang

More than 70 players have hit home runs in their first major league at-bat. More than a dozen have done it on the first pitch, including four pitchers (Bill Lefebvre, Don Rose, Clise Dudley, and Jim Bullinger). In fact, a dozen pitchers have homered in their first at-bat—quite a disproportionate number, including Hoyt Wilhelm, who played 21 years without hitting another one.

You'll find some very obscure names on this list, including Eddie Pellagrini, George Vico, Brant Alyea, Junior Felix, Bill Duggleby (the only man to hit a grand slam in his first at-bat), Emmett Mueller, Dan Bankhead (a Negro League pitcher who joined Jackie Robinson on the '47 Dodgers), Ed Sanicki, Frank Ernaga, Facundo Barragan, Benny Ayala, and Mitch Lyden.

A few players have gone on to have solid major league careers (Gary Gaetti, Terry Steinbach, Jay Bell, Bill White, Tim Wallach, for example). So did Will Clark, who hit a home run to dead center off Nolan Ryan in his first at-bat. So did Bert Campaneris, who hit two home runs in his first game. Yet Earl Averill is the only Hall of Famer to do it.

Only one man ever homered in his first *two* major league at-bats. The immortal Bob Nieman of the St. Louis Browns did it on September 14, 1951, in a 9–6 loss to the Red Sox in Fenway Park. Batting fifth and playing left field in a wretched, last-place Browns lineup between Ken Wood and Freddie Marsh, Nieman went deep off Mickey McDermott in the second with none on and added a two-run homer in the third off McDermott.

Nieman hit .372 in 12 games for St. Louis in 1951, but those were his only home runs. He played 12 years in the majors for the Browns, Tigers, White Sox, Orioles, Cardinals, Indians, and Giants, collecting 1,000 hits, 125 home runs, and a .295 average. He entered the record books again, as a footnote, when he contributed to a 29-run outburst by the White Sox in 1955, which you can read about later in this chapter (page 233).

Four Home Runs in a Game

Only a dozen men have hit four home runs in a game, and they range from flukes to legends.

May 30, 1894—Congress Street Grounds, Boston

The 1894 season was the first in which pitchers had to throw from 60 feet 6 inches. Batting leadoff and playing second base, Bobby Lowe hit four consecutive home runs in a nine-inning game against Cincinnati. Boston won 20–11 with Lowe taking Icebox Chamberlain deep all four times, including twice in the third inning alone. Only 25, Lowe enjoyed career highs in hits (212), doubles (34), triples (11), home runs (17), RBI (115), and batting average (.346) in 1894. As pitchers adapted to the new distance, Lowe's numbers returned to more normal levels. He finished a very respectable 18-year career in 1907 with the Tigers, having collected 1929 hits— but only 71 home runs.

July 13, 1896—West Side Grounds, Chicago

The notorious Big Ed Delahanty, cleanup hitter and first baseman for the Philadelphia Phillies in 1896, enjoys the distinction of having hit four inside-the-park home runs against the Chicago Colts (formerly the White Stockings and eventually the Cubs). Adonis Terry of the Colts gave up all four, but only five other hits, and Chicago ended up winning 9–8. These four home runs were more than 30 percent of Delahanty's league-leading 13 for the season. He also knocked in 126 runs in 123 games and batted .397 (down from his .400 seasons of 1894 and 1895).

June 3, 1932—Shibe Park, Philadelphia

> *"Largely because of Gehrig's quartet of tremendous smashes the Yankees outstripped the Athletics in a run-making marathon, winning 20 to 13, after twice losing the lead because of determined rallies by the American League champions."*
>
> —NEW YORK TIMES

The first player of the twentieth century to do it was Lou Gehrig on June 3, 1932, and at least one man has done it every decade since. Gehrig, overshadowed by Babe Ruth his entire career, found himself knocked out of the headlines by the retirement of legendary manager John McGraw after 31 years at the helm of the crosstown Giants.

Gehrig did his damage in Shibe Park against the Philadelphia Athletics, winners of three consecutive pennants from 1929 to 1931. A 20–13 victory for the Yankees, the wild game featured nine home runs in all—and all by Hall of Famers. In addition to Gehrig's four, Mickey Cochrane, Earle Combs, Babe Ruth, Tony Lazzeri, and Jimmie Foxx all went deep. Gehrig hit three solo home runs and one two-run homer, setting a record for the most games with at least three home runs. Gehrig's mark of four has since been eclipsed by Johnny Mize, who did it six times, and Joe Carter, who did it five times.

Gehrig had two tries to hit his fifth, grounding out and sending Al Simmons to the deepest part of the ballpark in center field to flag down a drive. Ironically, he would finish the season with a relatively low total (for him) of 34 home runs.

Batting cleanup between Babe Ruth and Ben Chapman:

- First inning, two-run home run off George Earnshaw
- Fourth inning, solo home run off George Earnshaw
- Fifth inning, solo home run off George Earnshaw (third of the inning, after Combs and Ruth)
- Seventh inning, solo home run off Roy Mahaffey

July 10, 1936—Forbes Field, Pittsburgh

Chuck Klein is in the Hall of Fame because he played in the hitter's paradise called the Baker Bowl in Philadelphia. But his finest game as a pro came in spacious Forbes Field in Pittsburgh.

By 1936, Klein was on the downside of his career. Returning to the Phillies early in the season after a disappointing stint with the Chicago Cubs, he was three years removed from his Triple-Crown season of 1933 and six years removed from knocking in 170 runs and batting .386 (and winning neither the batting crown nor the RBI title in the process). Klein would finish the season with 25 home runs and 104 RBI, his last big year at the plate.

Like Gehrig four years before, Klein narrowly missed a fifth home run. In his second time at bat, he pressed Paul Waner up against the wall in right to haul in his fly ball. Unlike any other four-homer game since, Klein's were the only home runs of the day.

Batting third between Johnny Moore and Dolph Camilli:

- First inning, three-run home run off Jim Weaver
- Fifth inning, solo home run off Jim Weaver
- Seventh inning, solo home run off Mace Brown
- Tenth inning, solo home run off Bill Swift

July 18, 1948—Shibe Park, Philadelphia

Sixteen years after the legendary Iron Horse pummeled the defending champion Athletics in Shibe Park, a flash in the pan named Pat Seerey did the same to a fourth-place Philadelphia squad. The 5'10", 200-pound Seerey, acquired early in the season by the White Sox after five undistinguished years with the Indians, would hit only 19 all season.

Seerey's outburst helped a White Sox team destined for 101 losses and last place to a 12–11 victory in 11 innings. He homered in three consecutive innings in the middle of the game as the Sox built an 11–7 lead, but a three-run homer by Eddie Joost in the seventh tied the game and gave Seerey a chance for his fourth. The left fielder delivered the game winner in the 11th. After providing the only punch in a lifeless Sox offense led by 41-year-old Luke Appling, Seerey would be unable to crack an outfield of Dave Philley, Herb Adams, and Catfish Metkovich, going 0 for 4 in 1949 before retiring at 26 with 86 home runs and a .224 batting average.

Batting fourth between Luke Appling and Aaron Robinson:

- Fourth inning, solo home run off Carl Scheib
- Fifth inning, two-run home run off Bob Savage
- Sixth inning, three-run home run off Charlie Harris
- Eleventh inning, solo home run off Lou Brissie

August 31, 1950—Ebbets Field, Brooklyn

"There were only 14,226 cash customers present to see Hodges' almost unprecedented feat—certainly unprecedented for a Dodger—but they enjoyed every minute of the entire performance by the Brooks, who hadn't beaten any team so humiliatingly in many a moon."

—NEW YORK TIMES

Ironically, only two of the four-homer crowd turned the trick in their home stadium. Gil Hodges was the first, sending four out of cozy Ebbets Field as the Dodgers beat the Boston Braves 19–3. Hodges was 26 at the time and establishing that his breakthrough season of 1949 was not a fluke. He would hit 32 home runs and knock in 113 in 1950, his second of seven consecutive 100-RBI seasons. Unlike Gehrig, Klein, and Seerey, Hodges would add a single, giving him 17 total bases for the game, tying the mark set by Lowe and Delahanty. He also became the third Dodger that season to hit three home runs in a game, establishing a new major league record.

Hodges is the only four-homer man to victimize a Hall of Famer in the process. Warren Spahn was uncharacteristically off that day, getting chased early. It didn't keep him from leading the league in wins with 21 and recording a 3.16 ERA.

Batting sixth between Carl Furillo and Roy Campanella:

- Second inning, two-run home run off Warren Spahn
- Third inning, three-run home run off Normie Roy
- Sixth inning, two-run home run off Bob Hall
- Eighth inning, two-run home run off Johnny Antonelli

July 31, 1954—Ebbets Field, Brooklyn

"Joe Adcock, first baseman for the Milwaukee Braves, was 'pictured' as a hero here tonight. A full color picture of Adcock . . . appeared on the front page of the Milwaukee Journal *. . . The caption in the journal had political over-tones. It read: 'This Joe Must Stay—Yes Sir!' It was an obvious reference to the 'Joe Must Go Club,' which made an unsuccessful bid for a recall move-ment against Senator Joseph R. McCarthy, Republican of Wisconsin."*

> —UPI

"I was using a borrowed bat all the time. I broke my regular bat last night, so today I used one belonging to Charley White. Boy, I could hardly lift the bat, it's the heaviest on the team. If I played for the Dodgers I'd hit thirty-five homers a year in this park."

> —JOE ADCOCK

Only Ebbets Field and Shibe Park have seen four home runs in a game more than once. Joe Adcock helped his Milwaukee Braves bury the Dodgers 15–7, piling up a record 18 total bases in the process—while seeing only seven pitches on the day. With a home run the night before, Adcock also tied the mark (which still stands) of five home runs in two consecutive games.

The slugging first baseman was only 26 and just beginning to establish him-self as a power threat in the National League—just as the long-suffering Braves, in only their second season in Milwaukee, were beginning to establish themselves as a pennant contender. A 20-year-old Hank Aaron and a 22-year-old Eddie Mathews had something to do with that. Adcock would go on to hit 336 home runs in the big leagues—including the home run that turned Harvey Haddix's 12-inning per-fect game into a heartbreaking loss, although it was ruled a double because Adcock passed Aaron on the bases—and Milwaukee would go on to win the 1957 World Series and narrowly miss repeating in 1958.

Adcock came to baseball late, not playing his first game until he was an 18-year-old at Louisiana State University. At 6'4" and 220 pounds, Adcock arrived at LSU to play center on the basketball team. He picked up baseball fast, and his power became legendary. He was the first to put a ball into the center-field bleachers at the Polo Grounds, 475 feet away—10 rows deep, no less—and the only player to clear the left-field roof at Ebbets Field. He became a huge target for enemy pitch-ers. Dodgers pitcher Clem Labine congratulated him on his four home runs by hitting him in the head the very next day. Six weeks later, Dodgers pitcher Don Newcombe ended his season with a pitch that broke Adcock's hand. And on the one-year anniversary of his four home runs, Jim Hearn of the Giants broke his forearm with a pitch. Perhaps that's why you can find a famous photo of a fed-up Joe Adcock charging the mound against Ruben Gomez, only to have the Giants pitcher turn tail and run.

Batting fifth between Hank Aaron and Andy Pafko:

- Second inning, solo home run off Don Newcombe
- Fifth inning, three-run home run off Erv Palica
- Seventh inning, two-run home run off Pete Wojey
- Ninth inning, solo home run off Johnny Podres

June 10, 1959—Memorial Stadium, Baltimore

It's been 40 years since an American Leaguer hit four home runs in a game. Rocky Colavito was the last to do it, leading the Indians past the Orioles 11–8 in the process. The Indians would finish only 5 games off the pace in 1959 as Colavito hit a league-leading 42 home runs and knocked in 111 runs. But after back-to-back 40-homer seasons, the Indians would trade the 26-year-old Colavito in the off-season for the older, slap-hitting Harvey Kuenn. The Indians would finish 21 games off the pace in 1960, and it would be 34 years before they even so much as contended again. Like many hitters of the era, Colavito would have his best year in the expansion season of 1961, when he hit 45 home runs, knocked in 140, and batted .290 for the Tigers. After hitting his 300th home run with the Kansas City Athletics in 1964, Colavito would return to Cleveland in 1965 for the first of his final two productive seasons. He would end his career with 374 home runs.

Colavito hit his four home runs in nine innings, consecutively, and at night. Batting cleanup between Tito Francona and Minnie Minoso:

- Third inning, two-run home run off Jerry Walker
- Fifth inning, solo home run off Arnie Portocarrero
- Sixth inning, two-run home run off Arnie Portocarrero
- Ninth inning, solo home run off Ernie Johnson

April 30, 1961—County Stadium, Milwaukee

"I could tell that something was bothering him. He looked like he was having trouble holding up his bat."

—WARREN SPAHN, AFTER NO-HITTING WILLIE
MAYS AND THE GIANTS ON APRIL 28, 1961

"I was just up there swinging."

—WILLIE MAYS, APRIL 30, 1961

In 1961, Mays became the fifth man in 14 years to hit four home runs in a game. By cranking out his four in April, he became the first to do it in the cooler days of spring, when the balls don't travel as far. (Mike Schmidt would also hit four home runs in April, but he benefited from a 20-MPH wind blowing out at Wrigley Field that day.)

Like all the others who preceded him, Mays put on his show in front of a fairly sparse attendance of 13,000. But the few Braves' fans on hand were cheering loudly in the top of the ninth when Mays reached the on-deck circle with two men out and a chance for a fifth home run if Jim Davenport could get on base. But George Brunet retired Davenport on a ground-out, and Mays had to settle for a mere four—all traveling over 400 feet, three off sliders, and one bomb off a sinker and traveling at least 450 to dead center.

Nineteen sixty-one was just another year at the office for Mays, his third of five consecutive .300-plus and 100-plus–RBI seasons and his third of six 40-plus–homer seasons. But on April 30, Mays had only two home runs for the season, and was riding an 0 for 7 and fearing an extended slump. His Giants team certainly wasn't in a slump. After being no-hit by Warren Spahn two days before, San Francisco responded with five home runs on the 29th and four others in addition to Mays's four on the 30th, tying the major league record of 13 in two consecutive games. Balls were flying out all over the yard as Milwaukee added 2 for an NL record of 10 in one game that has since been extended by 1.

Batting third between Jim Davenport and Willie McCovey:

- First inning, solo home run off Lew Burdette
- Third inning, two-run home run off Lew Burdette
- Sixth inning, three-run home run off Seth Morehead
- Eighth inning, two-run home run off Don McMahon

April 17, 1976—Wrigley Field, Chicago

"I was only trying to get a single to get Dick Allen into scoring position. I was not trying to get a home run because I wanted to win this game."

—MIKE SCHMIDT, ON HIS FOURTH HOME RUN IN THE 10TH INNING

Of all the four-homer games, this one was the wildest. Appropriate, given how many slugfests the Phillies and Cubs have had through the years. Mike Schmidt hit four consecutive home runs on a windy day in Chicago, with his first not coming until the fifth inning. With the Phillies down 13–2 at one point, Schmidt's third home run tied the game at 13–13 in the eighth and his fourth broke a 15–15 tie in

Mike Schmidt established himself as one of the premier power hitters in the National League with three straight home run crowns in 1974, 1975, and 1976.

the top of the tenth. The Phillies eventually won 18–16 in the largest comeback in National League history.

Schmidt went on to hit 38 home runs in 1976 for his third consecutive home run crown. He would add five more titles before he was finished.

Batting sixth between Dick Allen and Garry Maddox:

- Fifth inning, two-run home run off Rick Reuschel
- Seventh inning, solo home run off Rick Reuschel
- Eighth inning, three-run home run off Darold Knowles
- Tenth inning, two-run home run off Paul Reuschel

July 6, 1986—Fulton County Stadium, Atlanta

"I had a good week today."

—BOB HORNER

Like Ed Delahanty nearly 90 years to the day before him, Bob Horner hit four home runs in a losing cause. In the late '80s, the Braves themselves were a losing cause. When Horner walked off a college campus and into the Braves' lineup in 1978, hitting 23 home runs in a half season, Atlanta fans thought they were watching the next great home run hitter. But Horner never could play a full season; the closest he came was 1986 when he hit 27 home runs, including four in one game at the Launching Pad in Atlanta against the Montreal Expos.

Going into play that day, he was only 28 and had just passed the 200-homer mark. Four hundred was not an unreasonable goal, and four in one game certainly made it look like Horner's best days were in front of him. But he left to play in Japan the following year, missing the rabbitball 1987 season, and then returned to unproductive part-time duty in St. Louis in 1988 before retiring at 31.

Batting fourth between Dale Murphy and Ken Griffey Sr.:

- Second inning, solo home run off Andy McGaffigan
- Fourth inning, solo home run off Andy McGaffigan
- Fifth inning, three-run home run off Tim Burke
- Ninth inning, solo home run off Jeff Reardon

September 7, 1993—Riverfront Stadium, Cincinnati

"I don't even have words to explain it, just amazement I guess. Every time I hit it, I was, like, amazed."

—MARK WHITEN

There are some well-traveled players on this list, but none moreso than the overly talented, underachieving, switch-hittin' Mark Whiten. Whiten came up with Toronto, moved to Cleveland in 1991, was traded to St. Louis in 1993, was traded to Boston in 1995, lasted only 32 games before being traded to Philadelphia, was released and signed by the Braves in 1996, was released by them after a game-winning home run, was signed by Seattle, played for the Yankees the following season, and ended up back in Cleveland in 1998. Along the way, he played only two full seasons, one of those in 1993 with the Cardinals, when he hit 25 home runs and knocked in 99 runs.

Four of those home runs and 12 of those record-tying RBI came in one game—this from a player who had never hit 10 home runs or knocked in 50 runs in a *season*. Whiten propelled the Cardinals to a 15–2 win over the Reds, atoning for a misplayed fly ball that lost the opener of the doubleheader in the bottom of the ninth inning. He didn't exactly victimize a bumper crop of pitchers. Larry Luebbers wouldn't pitch in the big leagues for another six years after his 1993 rookie season. Mike Anderson, who was making his major league debut, would make only two more appearances. And the once unhittable Rob Dibble was at the tail end of a flame-out that saw him rip his uniform jersey off on national TV after yielding a game-winning home run to Bobby Bonilla; throw behind a batter's head; heave a ball from the pitcher's mound into the center-field bleachers, where it struck a female school teacher (and that was after a save); field a bunt and throw the ball at the batter's legs; and be wrestled to the locker room floor by his manager, Lou Piniella, who knows a thing or two about tantrums. Dibble would sit out the 1994 season with the inevitable arm injury that came from his wretched pitching mechanics, and would return in 1995 to walk 46 batters in 26 innings for the White Sox and Brewers.

Maybe that's what putting Mark Whiten in the record books will do to you. Batting sixth between Gerald Perry and Tom Pagnozzi:

- First inning, grand slam off Larry Luebbers
- Sixth inning, three-run home run off Mike Anderson
- Seventh inning, three-run home run off Mike Anderson
- Ninth inning, two-run home run off Rob Dibble

Greatest Rookie Game

In 1975, 23-year-old center fielder Fred Lynn won the Rookie of the Year award and the MVP as he led the Red Sox to the World Series. On June 18, 1975, he nearly became the only rookie to hit four home runs in a game. Instead, he had to settle for three home runs and 10 RBI in a 15–1 thrashing of the Detroit Tigers in Tiger Stadium. He went 5 for 6 on the night, upping his average to .352 and reaching 50 RBI barely two months into the season.

Lynn came within inches of hitting four home runs in the game and three home runs in the first three innings. In the first, he hit a two-run homer off Joe Coleman, then followed that up with a three-run shot in the second. In the third, he hit a two-run triple off the wall off Bob Reynolds. Lynn then returned in the ninth to hit a three-run home run off Tom Walker. At the time, only Tony Lazzeri (11) and Jim Bottomley (12) had knocked in more runs in one game.

Twelve RBI

> *"James Bottomley of the St. Louis Cardinals did some record batting at Ebbets Field yesterday afternoon that was entirely unappreciated by a crowd of about 8,000 spectators who had assembled for the sole purpose of seeing the Robins win a ball game and not Bottomley crack records by knocking baseballs all out of shape."*
>
> —NEW YORK TIMES

As hitting records go, Jim Bottomley's 12 RBI in one game has been one of the most enduring. It stood for 69 years before it was even tied, and has been matched only once in the 75 years since it was set. On September 16, 1924, "Sunny Jim" was only

24 and in the third year of a 16-year major league career. It was the first of six consecutive productive seasons at first base for the Cardinals that saw him knock in as many as 136 runs and bat as high as .367. But if a man ever made the Hall of Fame on the strength of one game, it was Bottomley.

He broke the mark of 11 RBI held by Wilbert Robinson—manager of the Brooklyn team and the Robins' namesake. Bottomley went 6 for 6 against Robinson's team with two home runs, a double, and three singles. He came to bat with 12 men on base and knocked in 10 of them. By scoring three runs himself, he had a hand in 13 of the Cards' 17 runs in their 17–3 victory.

Batting cleanup between Hall of Famers Rogers Hornsby and Chick Hafey:

- First inning, two-run single off Rube Ehrhardt
- Second inning, run-scoring double off Bonnie Hollingsworth
- Fourth inning, grand slam off Art Decatur
- Sixth inning, two-run home run off Art Decatur
- Seventh inning, two-run single off Tex Wilson
- Ninth inning, run-scoring single off Jim Roberts

Nine Hits

If marathon slugfests are your thing, you can't do much better than the extended pounding that the Philadelphia Athletics and Cleveland Indians administered to each other on July 10, 1932. The Athletics eventually won the game 18–17 in 18 innings as the teams combined for 58 hits. Jimmie Foxx made the headlines by hitting three home runs, knocking in eight, and scoring the winning run. In defeat, shortstop and number-2 hitter Johnny Burnett of the Indians went 9 for 11, a record for most hits in one game.

The modern record for hits in a nine-inning game is seven—held by second baseman Rennie Stennett, who contributed four singles, two doubles, and a triple to a 22–0 Pirate victory over the Cubs at Wrigley Field on September 16, 1975. He managed two hits in one inning *twice*.

Stennett matched the 7 for 7 of an even more obscure infielder, Cesar Gutierrez, who did it for the Tigers in 12 innings on June 21, 1970. Gutierrez hit .243 that season, a career high. He retired after the 1971 season with 128 hits in a full season's worth of at-bats spread across four seasons.

In the Zone: Home Run Streaks

From May 12 through May 18, 1968, 6′7″, 255-pound Frank "Hondo" or "the Capital Punisher" Howard hit 10 home runs for the Washington Senators in one week. He capped off his week against the eventual world champions, the Detroit Tigers, with two homers, including a three-run blast off Mickey Lolich over the left-field roof at Tiger Stadium. At the time, only Harmon Killebrew in 1962 had ever cleared the left-field roof.

Howard hit his 10 in only six games, obliterating the previous mark of seven home runs in six games held by, among others, Roger Maris and Willie Mays. His performance gave him 17 home runs, 34 RBI, and a .347 batting average, placing him at the top in all three categories in the American League. He was on pace for 82 home runs and 164 RBI. Not bad, considering that the rest of his team, the lowly Washington Senators, were batting .200 with 15 home runs. Frank Howard's lack of protection in the lineup would catch up to him, and he would bat only .255 the rest of the way, though he did finish with a league-leading 44 home runs during the Year of the Pitcher (see Chapter 17).

> *"I told them (his teammates) a long time ago, after I hit three in a row, 'One a day.' When you're in that streak, you feel like you're going to hit one every day. You really do. It usually doesn't happen. You just feel that way."*
>
> —DON MATTINGLY

> *"Amazed? No, I'm not amazed. Surprised? No, I'm not surprised. I know what he can do and it's just a matter of whether he wants it. We'll see how it works out."*
>
> —KEN GRIFFEY SR., MARINERS BATTING COACH,
> ON KEN GRIFFEY JR., JULY 1993

Three men have hit home runs in eight consecutive games. The first to do it was Dale Long from May 19 to May 28, 1956. The 30-year-old Pittsburgh first baseman—who would later gain trivial immortality by catching left-handed for the Chicago Cubs—in only his second full season went on a tear, going 15 for 28 with 8 home runs and 20 RBI. His record-breaking seventh came in his last at-bat with an 0–2 count against Ben Flowers of the Phillies; and his eighth, off Carl Erskine of the Dodgers, just cleared the right-field wall and proved to be the winning run in a 3–2 victory.

When Long's streak was finished, he got a raise (along with milk, beer, and cigarette endorsements), was ahead of Babe Ruth's 60-homer pace, was batting .420, and had the lowly Pirates contending for first place. By the time the season was over, his average had fallen to .263, he was being benched for a younger player, and the Pirates were in seventh place—in the second division, where they'd been every year but one since 1938, when they started printing World Series tickets and remodeling their press box a few weeks early.

Thirty-one years later, another lefty-swinging first baseman, New York Yankee Don Mattingly, matched Dale Long while hitting 10 home runs over the eight-game span. Mattingly's shot at tying the record helped the Rangers fill Arlington Stadium, a rare event in the days before Nolan Ryan came to pitch for Texas. In the fourth inning, when Mattingly drove a ball to left-center off Jose Guzman that just cleared the fence out of the reach of left fielder Pete Incaviglia, the crowd would not stop cheering until he reluctantly stuck his head out of the dugout and tipped his batting helmet.

Mattingly batted .459 during his stretch and had Yankees fans breathing easier. One of their few sources of pride during the dismal 1980s was Donnie Baseball, who put together the three greatest seasons at first base in New York since Lou Gehrig. He won a batting title on the last day of the 1984 season at .343, knocked in a league-leading 145 runs in 1985, and batted .352 with 238 hits in 1986. But early in 1987, after a clubhouse wrestling match with pitcher Bob Shirley, the 26-year-old Mattingly went on the disabled list with two damaged disks in his back. Rumors flew that his career might be over. When he returned to hit 30 home runs, knock in 115 runs, and bat .327, fans assumed that the worst was over.

Unfortunately, Mattingly had peaked early. His back plagued him for the rest of his career, eventually robbing him of his power and reducing him to a .280s slap hitter at a power position. He played until 1995—long enough to finally reach the postseason, where he flashed his old form, batting .417 with 6 RBI and a home run in the sixth inning of Game 2 at Yankee Stadium that sent the home crowd into hysterics. By then, Mattingly was 34 and a throwback, his home run drawing notice from the television announcers for the quickness of his trot and the absence of any bat-dropping self-admiration.

Don Mattingly kept Yankees fans cheering when times were tough in the Bronx.

Mattingly retired after the 1995 season with 2,153 hits and a .307 lifetime batting average. But a career that looked like a dead-solid lock for Cooperstown was heading downhill as soon as his home run streak ended.

A month before Mattingly's streak started, the Seattle Mariners drafted 17-year-old Ken Griffey Jr. with the first pick of the amateur draft. Only six years later, he had already established himself as one of the best players in the league, batting .300 in three consecutive seasons and knocking in 100 runs twice. But 1993 was his coming-out party. He hit 45 home runs and knocked in 109 runs, eight of them coming in a one-week stretch. Unlike Mattingly and Long, there was no doubt about his home run in game eight. It came on the first pitch of the seventh inning off Willie Banks of the Twins, who was working on a shutout, and it bounced off the facade of the third deck in right field in the Kingdome, triggering a three-minute standing ovation and two curtain calls.

And also unlike Mattingly and Long, the best for Griffey was still ahead of him. His home run in game eight was the 117th of a career that saw him hit 398 before he turned 30.

"He can do things other guys can't do. He's playing way above everybody else in baseball right now."

—TEAMMATE TINO MARTINEZ ON KEN GRIFFEY JR., 1993

Home Runs in 8 Consecutive Games: Day by Day

	Game 1	Game 2	Game 3	Game 4	Game 5	Game 6	Game 7	Game 8
Dale Long	5/19/56 Forbes Field, vs. Cubs	5/20/56 (Game 1) Forbes Field, vs. Braves	5/20/56 (Game 2) Forbes Field, vs. Braves	5/22/56 Forbes Field, vs. Cardinals	5/23/56 Forbes Field, vs. Cardinals	5/25/56 Forbes Field, vs. Phillies	5/26/56 Forbes Field, vs. Phillies	5/28/56 Forbes Field, vs. Dodgers
Don Mattingly	7/8/87 Metrodome, vs. Twins (2)	7/9/87 Comiskey Park, vs. White Sox	7/10/87 Comiskey Park, vs. White Sox	7/11/87 Comiskey Park, vs. White Sox	7/11/87 Comiskey Park, vs. White Sox	7/16/87 Arlington Stadium, vs. Rangers (2)	7/17/87 Arlington Stadium, vs. Rangers	7/18/87 Arlington Stadium, vs. Rangers
Ken Griffey Jr.	7/20/93 Yankee Stadium, vs. Yankees	7/21/93 Yankee Stadium, vs. Yankees	7/22/93 Municipal Stadium, vs. Indians	7/23/93 Municipal Stadium, vs. Indians	7/24/93 Municipal Stadium, vs. Indians	7/25/93 Municipal Stadium, vs. Indians	7/27/93 Kingdome, vs. Twins	7/28/93 Kingdome, vs. Twins

Everybody Bats: Team Hitting Records

The 1950 Boston Red Sox were very quietly one of the greatest hitting teams in baseball history. They finished in third place, 4 games behind the Yankees, though they scored 1,027 runs, or 6.7 per game. They scored 625 at Fenway Park alone, averaging 8 runs per game at home. The Sox did this while having the services of Ted Williams for only 89 games, as he fractured his elbow during the All-Star Game. Boston hit .302 as a team, the last team to do that. They had a pair of 144-RBI men (first baseman Walt "Moose" Dropo and shortstop Vern Stephens) and a batting champion (the 24-year-old Billy Goodman, .354, who did not have a regular position).

The Red Sox set a number of records that season, many at the expense of the hapless St. Louis Browns. They scored an AL-record 216 runs against them in 22 games, or an average of 10 per game. The Sox beat them 29–4 on June 8, a record for most runs in one game that has only been matched once since. The Browns held Boston to only 20 runs the day before, for a record 49 in two consecutive games, and 7 the following day, for a record 56 in three consecutive games. Three weeks later, the Red Sox and Philadelphia Athletics would hook up in a 22–14 battle, scoring an AL-record 36 runs between them.

A less auspicious hitting club, the 1955 White Sox, matched Boston on April 23 when they capitalized on 30-MPH winds in Kansas City to crush the Athletics 29–6. Fast-starting Bob Nieman (remember him?) did a lot of the damage with home runs in the first and second inning. Walt Dropo (remember him?), now with the White Sox, also homered as Chicago went deep a total of seven times. Leadoff man and shortstop Chico Carrasquel followed up his 4 for 5 the previous night with a 5 for 6 performance as the White Sox fell one short of the AL record for hits in a game with 29. The record, 30 by the Yankees in 1953, has since been topped by the Milwaukee Brewers, who banged out 31 against Toronto in 1992.

Chicago finished in third place in 1955, 5 games off the pace. They led the AL in batting at .268, but scored only 725 runs, good for fourth in an eight-team league.

Neither of these routs featured the biggest inning in twentieth-century baseball. That honor goes to the 1953 Boston Red Sox, who piled on the runs without the services of Ted Williams, who was flying fighter planes in Korea. Boston broke up a close 5–3 game with the Detroit Tigers in the bottom of the seventh at Fenway Park with 17 runs. The inning lasted 47 minutes and featured three pitchers and 23 batters, 14 of whom hit safely. Throw in a bases-loaded walk, two hits in one inning by the Boston pitcher, a wild pitch, and three hits by Vern Stephens. Two of the three outs were made by the only Hall of Famer in the lineup, George Kell. Only one Boston player homered in the outburst. If you were scoring at home, here's what the carnage looked like.

Billy Goodman, 2B	BB i	1B	
Ted Lepcio, PR			
Jimmy Piersall, RF	1B		
Al Zarilla, PH		BB	
Dick Gernert, 1B	HR	BB	
Ellis Kinder, P	1B	1B	
Sammy White, C	1B	BB	1B
Vern Stephens, LF	1B sb	2B	1B
Tommy Umphlett, CF	1B	BB	1B
Johnny Lipon, SS	K	1B	BB
George Kell, 3B	2B	FO	FO

Steve Gromek pitched one-third of an inning, yielding six hits and an intentional walk and being charged with seven runs. Dick Weik pitched one-third of an inning, yielding three hits and walking two and being charged with five runs. Earl Harrist was the Detroit stopper, giving up another three hits and another three walks, but getting touched for only four runs and leaving two runners on base once the madness finally stopped.

Oh, and by the way, Bob Nieman was in left field for the Tigers and Walt Dropo was at first base.

The Red Sox broke the modern record of 15 runs in one inning, set only one year before when the Dodgers erupted in the first at Ebbets Field against the Cincinnati Reds on May 21, 1952. The inning lasted 59 minutes and featured 21 hitters, 4 pitchers, 10 hits, 7 walks, 2 hit batsmen, another two-hit inning from the opposing pitcher, and only one home run. It could have been a lot worse if third baseman Bobby Adams had not robbed Billy Cox of a leadoff single and Andy Pafko not been thrown out trying to steal third. Here's how it happened, in a game that featured neither Bob Nieman nor Walt Dropo:

Billy Cox, 3B	5-3	1B	HBP
Pee Wee Reese, SS	BB	1B	BB
Duke Snider, CF	HR	BB	K
Jackie Robinson, 2B	2B	HBP	
Andy Pafko, LF	BB cs	1B	
George Shuba, RF	1B sb	BB	
Gil Hodges, 1B	BB	BB	
Rube Walker, C	1B	1B	
Chris VanCuyk, P	1B	1B	

Ewell Blackwell started for the Reds and faced the first five batters. Bud Byerly recorded one out when Pafko was caught stealing, yielding five hits and one walk. Herm Wehmeier, the league's wildest pitcher, did not disappoint. He faced three batters, walking one and hitting the other. Frank Smith walked three and hit another, two of these free passes coming with the bases loaded.

The Dodgers held on for a 19–1 victory.

Possibly the wildest game in baseball history took place on August 25, 1922, when the Cubs beat the Phillies 26–23 in a game that saw 51 hits in nine innings. Cubs right fielder Marty Callaghan became the first twentieth-century player to come to bat three times in one inning. Cubs center fielder Cliff Heathcote set a modern record by reaching base seven times, while Russell Wrightstone and Frank Parkinson of the Phillies became the first twentieth-century players to come to bat eight times in a nine-inning game. The Phillies fell behind 25–6, then came storming back despite having lifted their starters at several positions. They ended up leaving the bases loaded in the ninth inning.

Amazingly, that game saw only three home runs. And if it's home runs you want, you can't beat an 18–3 drubbing of the Baltimore Orioles by the Toronto Blue Jays on September 15 in the year of the home run, 1987. The Jays, whose 215 home runs were only good enough for second in the American League that year, went yard against the hapless Orioles' pitching 10 times, breaking the previous mark of 8.

Duke Snider—shown here in front of Ebbets Field's inviting right-field porch—contributed the only home run in Brooklyn's 15-run first inning in 1952.

Catcher Ernie Whitt hit three, MVP candidate George Bell hit two (his 44th and 45th), platoon man Rance Mulliniks hit two, and Lloyd Moseby, Rob Ducey (the first of his career), and a 23-year-old kid named Fred McGriff hit one. The second-leading home run man on the team, Jesse Barfield, was kept in the yard, as was a kid named Cecil Fielder. The game also saw the consecutive-inning streak of Cal Ripken stopped at 8,243.

Unfortunately for the Jays, this was one of the last high points of what looked to be a pennant-winning season. George Bell would hit only two more home runs from September 15 to October 4, slumping badly and losing the MVP to Alan Trammell of the Tigers in the process. Bell went 2 for 26 down the stretch and Toronto fell into a team hitting slump, while the ever-dramatic Kirk Gibson kept the Tigers from falling 4½ games behind with 6 to play when he hit a game-tying, ninth-inning home run off the Jays' dominant closer, Tom Henke, on September 27.

The Jays dropped three in a row to the Milwaukee Brewers, then the final three of the season in Detroit—the pennant clincher a 1–0 heartbreaker, the lone run coming on a Larry Herndon home run in the second inning off Jimmy Key that just barely cleared the wall in left, out of reach of a barely leaping George Bell.

Everybody Bats: World Series

"I stink. There is no other way to put it. I didn't get them out when I had to get them out."

—MITCH WILLIAMS

In 1993, it appeared that the Phillies would be evening up the World Series with the Blue Jays at 2–2 on a foggy, rainy night in Philadelphia. Down 3–0 in the first, they responded with four in the bottom of the inning as Todd Stottlemyre walked four, and then two more in the second on a two-run homer by center fielder Lenny Dykstra. When the Blue Jays took the lead back at 7–6 in the third, the Phillies countered with one in the fourth and five in the fifth—featuring another two-run shot by Dykstra—to make it 12–7. The Blue Jays pulled to within 12–9 in the sixth, but the Philadelphia lead was back up to 14–9 in the top of the eighth—setting a new record for highest-scoring Series game, breaking the 57-year-old mark set in a bloodbath in Game 2 of the 1936 Series when the Yankees unloaded on the Giants 18–4.

But the Blue Jays were about to put some distance between Game 4 1993 and Game 2 1936. Veteran Larry Andersen couldn't hold the Jays down in the eighth, yielding a run before exiting in favor of Mitch "Wild Thing" Williams. Manager Jim Fregosi was committed to Williams, though his reliever had already blown two saves in the NLCS. Wild Thing gave up a run-scoring single to Tony Fernandez, loaded the bases on walks, and gave up a two-run single to Rickey Henderson and a two-run triple to Devon White to put Toronto ahead. At two critical moments in the inning, the normally reckless Dykstra played balls timidly, allowing them to drop in front of him for hits or misjudging them and chasing them into the gap and back to the wall.

The Blue Jays would hold the Phillies scoreless in the eighth and ninth, after being able to do so only once in the first seven innings. When the dust finally cleared, a slew of records were set, including longest World Series game (4:14), most hits, most total bases, and most players to score a run for one team (*nine* for Toronto).

One record that was not broken was most runs in one inning. Fifteen batters came to bat for the Athletics in the bottom of the seventh in Game 4 of the 1929 World Series. It started with the Cubs up 8–0 on the Philadelphia Athletics and on their way to tying the Series at two games apiece. A home run by Al Simmons off Charlie Root was treated by the Philadelphia dugout as merely the avoidance of a shutout. Then Jimmie Foxx singled, and Hack Miller singled on a ball that Hack Wilson lost in the sun. Jimmy Dykes and Joe Boley singled, pinch hitter George Burns popped out, and Max Bishop singled, making the score 8–4 and chasing Root. Mule Haas greeted new pitcher Art Nehf with another fly ball that Hack Wilson lost in the sun. It went for an inside-the-park home run, and suddenly the score was 8–7 with only one man out. A walk to Mickey Cochrane took Nehf out of the game, and new pitcher Sheriff Blake was greeted with back-to-back singles by Al Simmons and Jimmie Foxx, Foxx's hit scoring Cochrane and tying the game. Pat Malone, Chicago's fourth pitcher of the inning, came on and promptly hit Hack Miller, loading the bases. Jimmy Dykes then followed with his second hit of the inning, a two-run double to left. The A's won 10–8, with 10 of their 15 hits and 10 of their runs all coming in one inning.

Refusing to Lose

"Faith. You gotta have faith. You know, they say time heals all wounds, and I don't quite agree with that a hundred percent. It gets you to cope with wounds. You carry them the rest of your life."

—PHIL RIZZUTO, AUGUST 3, 1979

"Our captain and leader has not left us—today, tomorrow, this year, next . . . our endeavors will reflect our love and admiration for him."

—TRIBUTE TO THURMAN MUNSON,
YANKEE STADIUM SCOREBOARD, AUGUST 6, 1979

By the numbers alone, what Bobby Murcer accomplished on August 6, 1979, doesn't stand up to the havoc wreaked by the hitters throughout this chapter. It wasn't even his own biggest day at the plate, having once homered in four consecutive at-bats in a doubleheader and homering twice on national TV for a child with cancer (while Howard Cosell informed the unsuspecting boy that the disease was in its final, fatal stages).

Murcer had come to the Yankees from Oklahoma as a 19-year-old shortstop in 1965, billed as the next Mickey Mantle. He didn't stick until 1969 as a center fielder, when he was given one of the few single-digit uniform numbers (1) that the Yankees had yet to retire. Despite the lofty expectations, Murcer managed to produce; in 1971 he batted .331 and slugged .543 with 91 walks during a pitchers' year, one of the greatest "unknown" seasons any hitter has ever had. Unfortunately for Murcer, the Yankees had to rebuild their dynasty by trading him away before the

1975 season. A role player by 1979, he returned from exile in midseason, after New York had won two consecutive championships and shortly before their captain, Thurman Munson, was killed in a plane crash on August 2.

On the 6th, the Yankees buried Munson. Murcer eulogized his friend and served as a pallbearer. The team returned to Yankee Stadium that night to play the division-leading Baltimore Orioles in a nationally televised Monday night game. Fans broke the moment of silence before the game to start a deafening chant of "THUR-MAN!" Reggie Jackson openly wept in right field. The team, which had been sleepwalking on the field since the tragedy, fell behind again, 4–0. In the bottom of the seventh, Bobby Murcer came up with two men on and hit a three-run homer. In the bottom of the ninth, down 4–3, he batted with the bases loaded and hit a two-run single to win the game.

The Yankees would finish fourth that season, 13½ games back, and wouldn't win another world championship for 17 years, the longest drought in Yankee Stadium history.

11

The Most Impressive Season and All-Time Records

"Babe Ruth always will be number one. Before I broke his record it was the greatest of all. Then I broke it, and suddenly the greatest record is Joe DiMaggio's hitting streak."

—HANK AARON

A record is a chronicle of achievement and circumstantial evidence of the extreme limit of possibility. In a sense, whenever a record is broken the range of what is possible increases and the context in which we view the past, present, and future shifts. Here are the current "outer limits" of what is possible, and how we got there.

The Single-Season Home Run Record

From the founding of the National League in 1876 until the end of World War I, the home run was the least common play in baseball. The poor quality of baseballs, combined with rules (or lack thereof) that allowed infielders and pitchers to scuff and discolor the ball, made swinging for the fences an unprofitable strategy. As a result, baseball was an inside game featuring place hitting, bunts, stolen bases, and hit and runs. From time to time a player would hit a significant number of home runs in a single season—like Ned Williamson, who hit 27 in 1884, Buck Freeman, who hit 25 in 1899, or Gavvy Cravath, who hit 24 in 1915—but these seasons were the result of stadium architecture rather than ability, and could not be sustained. In 1919, all of this would change. As William Curran points out in his book of 1920s baseball, *Big Sticks*, Babe Ruth asked to be relieved of his pitching duties and entered the Red Sox starting lineup during May 1919, the same month that Albert Einstein empirically tested the theory of relativity for the first time. In more ways than one, a revolution was afoot.

For many reasons, Ruth's 1919 season was muted. It was a short season of only 140 games, and Ruth played only 130. In 1918, major league baseball had shortened the season from 154 games to 140 games, partially in response to wartime shortages and requirements and partially due to poor attendance. In 1919, the season remained at 140 games due to poor attendance. It was also an extremely cold year, and the northeastern seaboard did not reach seasonable temperatures until July of that year. Finally, Fenway Park, as configured at that time, severely penalized left-handed power hitters. The right-field bullpens ("Williamsburg") and the right center-field bleachers had yet to be constructed. The net result of these differences from today's Fenway Park was that dead center was almost 100 feet deeper, the right-center power alley was 25 or more feet deeper, and the right-field foul pole was 12 feet deeper. The deepest point in the park, at 550 feet, was between dead center and the right-center power alley. Nevertheless, Ruth hit 29 home runs in 1919, shattering Ned Williamson's 1884 home run record of 27, by hitting 20 home runs on the road while managing a mere 9 home runs in Fenway Park. One wonders if Colonel Ruppert and Colonel Huston, the Yankees' owners who purchased Ruth's contract that winter, were Prohibition-era sabermetricians who understood the true meaning of Ruth's 1919 season and what was possible if he could only be freed from the shackles of Fenway Park. More likely, they knew that Ruth was a meal ticket. He broke the rules and drew huge crowds wherever he went.

Ruth played in the Polo Grounds in 1920, the Yankees' home stadium from 1913 to 1922. Finally playing in a hitter's park, Ruth exploded, hitting 29 home runs at home while adding 25 home runs on the road for a season total of 54. The enormity of Ruth's 54 home runs is hard to imagine today. He outhomered every team in the majors that year with the exception of the Phillies, and won the home run title by 35, a difference that exceeded his own single-season home run record of the previous year. Ruth increased his single-season home run record to 59 in 1921, and again in 1927 to 60. His singular dominance of power hitting during his heyday is unparalleled. During the 1920s, Ruth won the home run title in every full season in which he played, and, as shown here, easily outdistanced the runner-up in each year:

	BA	HR	RBI	SA		BA	HR	RBI	SA
Ruth, 1920	.376	54	137	.847	Sisler, 1920	.407	19	122	.632
Ruth, 1921	.378	59	171	.846	Williams, 1921	.347	24	117	.561
Ruth, 1923	.393	41	131	.764	Williams, 1923	.357	29	91	.623
Ruth, 1924	.378	46	121	.739	Hauser, 1924	.288	27	115	.516
Ruth, 1926	.372	47	145	.737	Simmons, 1926	.343	19	109	.566

	BA	HR	RBI	SA		BA	HR	RBI	SA
Ruth, 1927	.356	60	164	.772	Gehrig, 1927	.373	47	175	.765
Ruth, 1928	.323	54	142	.709	Gehrig, 1928	.374	27	142	.648
Ruth, 1929	.345	46	154	.697	Gehrig, 1929	.300	35	126	.582
	.365	407	1,165	.764		.350	227	997	.613

Ruth proved what was possible. He was the groundbreaker who took major league baseball from the place hitters and the spray hitters of its first 50 years and gave it to the power hitters. He swung from the heels, uppercutted, twisted his hips, and showed that the long ball could be hit with consistency. Others would follow—Gehrig, Foxx, Wilson, Greenberg—approaching Ruth's numbers in their career years, though none would hit so prodigiously with such regularity.

Ruth's home run standard of 60 stood for 33 seasons until it was broken by the wrong man. Roger Maris was a relatively unknown and unheralded left-handed power-hitting right fielder with the Kansas City Athletics in 1959 when he was packaged with Joe DeMaestri and Kent Hadley to the New York Yankees in return for Hank Bauer, Don Larsen, Norm Siebern, and Marv Throneberry. He was a shy and reticent man given to grousing when he did speak. He lacked the natural charisma and grace of a Willie Mays or an Ernie Banks that fans can love. He lacked the prodigious accomplishments and businesslike demeanor of a Ted Williams or a Henry Aaron that fans can come to respect. In short, he was meant to be in the supporting cast.

Maris's career statistics entering the 1960 season (his first MVP season) had a certain "Ron Kittle" ambience and gave no clue as to what was to follow.

	GP	BA	AB	2B	3B	HR	RBI	BA	SA
Indians, 1957	116	.235	358	9	5	14	51	.235	.405
Athletics, 1958	150	.240	583	19	4	28	80	.240	.431
Athletics, 1959	122	.273	433	21	7	16	72	.273	.464
	388	.249	1,374	49	16	58	203	.249	.434

Maris has been dismissed as a flash in the pan and a creation of Yankee Stadium. But his career years in 1960 and 1961, as well as the continuation of his career into the power pitcher's paradise of the mid- to late 1960s, dispel that notion. During his MVP seasons, Maris hit 26 of his 39 home runs on the road during 1960, and 31 of 61 on the road during 1961. This suggests that the development and maturation of Maris's skills played a much larger role in his improved production than his move to Yankee Stadium.

Maris's 1961 season and ultimate conquest of Ruth's record came in an expansion year in which two teams, the Los Angeles Angels and the Washington Senators, were added to the American League, increasing its membership to 10 teams. Home runs increased substantially during the year, rising to 1,534, or 128 per team—from 1,086, or 109 per team, during 1960. Adjusting for the 162-game schedule introduced in 1961, home runs increased by 12 percent over 1960. Moreover, Maris and the rest of the league faced expansion teams in approximately 15 percent of their games, though Maris does not appear to have benefited inordinately from facing the expansion pitching staffs of Los Angeles and Washington. He hit 13 of his 61 home runs off the two teams, which is exactly what would have been expected, all things being equal.

Maris was 27 years old when he broke Ruth's record, and seemed poised at the beginning of his prime years to become one of the all-time great home run hitters. It was not to be. The rest of his career became an attempt to avoid the limelight and exit stage left as soon as decently possible. After 1962, he would never play in more than 125 games in a season, never hit more than 26 home runs, shorten his swing to keep his batting average over .250, and retire from the game he endured at age 34. He is one of baseball's most intriguing and least understood players.

Surprisingly, Maris's record lasted longer than Ruth's record and rested more peacefully during its tenure. Whereas Ruth's record was seriously challenged by Hack Wilson in 1930, Jimmie Foxx in 1932, Hank Greenberg in 1938, Ralph Kiner in 1949, and Ernie Banks in 1958, Maris's mark remained relatively undisturbed until the post-strike home run explosion.

The latter half of the 1990s has seen home runs rise to an unprecedented level and remain there. Since 1994, major league teams have averaged in excess of one home run per game in every season. Over the entire history of baseball preceding 1994, this mark had only been reached once (during the 1987 season). Many theories have been advanced to explain this sudden and prolonged surge in power, but the most resonant are those that help explain why the pitchers and managers have been unable to adjust and rein in the long-ball hitters: smaller stadiums, larger players, and lighter bats (all the better to take into battle against hard-throwing relief pitchers and split-fingered fastballs).

In 1998, what became apparent as the attention of the baseball world drifted from the vapid wild-card races of poststrike baseball to the home run race of McGwire and Sosa was the tremendous equanimity and grace with which both men were dealing with the media circuses surrounding them. Sosa's joyful demeanor won the hearts of a cynical baseball world and established him as a worthy successor to Mr. Cub, Ernie Banks. His MVP award earned him a trip to the White House to light the nation's Christmas tree and a seat next to the First Lady at the State of the Union address. McGwire got a McDonald's commercial and a guest spot on the television show *Mad About You*.

Perhaps the most memorable aspect of McGwire's and Sosa's accomplishments in 1998 is not the magnitude of their home run numbers, but the manner with which they reached them. Neither McGwire nor Sosa reached 62 home runs on the last day of the season on the verge of exhaustion. Neither McGwire nor Sosa ever evinced a sense of desperation. They both reached 62 home runs with aplomb and assurance, with games to spare and the possibility of even better seasons to come.

The Career Home Run Record

The deadball-era home run king was Roger Connor, who hit 137 home runs in an 18-year career. Connor has been largely forgotten, but his offensive statistics stand up surprisingly well. When he retired in 1897, he not only held the career home run mark but also held the career triples mark at 227. His career slugging percentage was .486. By instructive comparison, Connor's career slugging percentage, compiled entirely in the deadball era, exceeds the career slugging percentages of Yogi Berra, Al Kaline, George Foster, and Roger Maris! Connor was not just a deadball-era slugger, but a slugger for any era.

Connor's career home run mark survived for 24 years until Babe Ruth smashed it in 1921, his fourth season as a regular player. Ruth joined the Boston Red Sox in 1914 at the age of 19 as a pitcher and quickly developed into one of the American League's premier hurlers. Ruth's long-ball abilities, however, did not go unnoticed by Ed Barrow, the Red Sox manager, or by American League baseball fans—so in 1918 he began to play outfield, winning his first home run title despite

Despite the stress of a wild-card race, a home run race, and a quest to make history, Sammy Sosa embraced the 1998 season as if it were a joyride in an amusement park.

playing only 95 games. Although there is no doubt that Ruth would have hit even more home runs had he not spent over three seasons as a pitcher, it is unlikely that he would have hit home runs at a Ruthian pace during those seasons. Fenway Park at that time was a very difficult park for left-handed power hitters, and Ruth was not immune, hitting only 9 of his 40 home runs during the 1918 and 1919 seasons at Fenway. In fact, during one three-year stretch between 1916 and 1918, Ruth managed only one home run in 108 consecutive games at Fenway Park!

After taking over the all-time home run lead at 138, Ruth proceeded to break his own record 576 times until he retired in 1935 with 714 home runs (holding a 336-homer lead over his nearest challenger). Ruth presided over baseball during the 1920s through his otherworldly and unparalleled dominance of all power-hitting statistics, including eight home run titles, five RBI crowns, and nine slugging-percentage titles during the decade. Ruth's exploits captured the imagination of America, and the 1920s became his movable feast. He appeared in movies, news-reels, advertisements, newspapers, periodicals, and books, and his celebrity extended so far beyond the world of baseball that he became a cultural icon. When we think of America in the 1920s, Ruth fits comfortably alongside F. Scott Fitzgerald, Charles Lindbergh, Jack Dempsey, and Al Capone.

It is interesting to speculate on how the course of baseball history might have been changed if Ruth had remained with the Red Sox, toiling in Fenway Park, hitting 25 to 35 home runs per year. We owe thanks to Harry Frazee and the clarion call of Broadway (he needed money to finance his production of "No, No, Nanette") that we do not know the answer.

Henry Aaron broke Babe Ruth's home run record in 1974, the 21st season of his career. Aaron, who was purchased by the Boston Braves from the Indianapolis Clowns of the Negro Leagues, is sometimes characterized as the last star of the Negro Leagues. Aaron suffered racism and abuse during his rise through the Braves' minor league system in the early '50s; and, perhaps as a result, he developed a hard exterior that, combined with his stern work ethic, made him a respected but not beloved hero. Aaron, like Maris, was not the 'Golden Boy' chosen to break the record. Like Ruth, he played right field; but unlike Ruth, he lacked the gaudy statistics and natural swagger. Playing through the pitcher's decade of the 1960s, Aaron's batting statistics did not seem to be those of an immortal. His highest season batting average of .355 was beaten by Ruth on eight occasions; his greatest season home run total of 47 was beaten by Ruth five times; his highest season RBI total of 132 was beaten by Ruth on eight occasions; and his highest single-season slugging percentage of .669 was below Ruth's career slugging percentage of .690. More important, Aaron was eclipsed in his own time by his contemporaries. Mantle, Robinson, and Yastrzemski won Triple Crowns during his career. Willie Mays was a living legend who twice hit 50 home runs. Ernie Banks won back-to-back MVP awards. It seemed that there was always somebody else to steal the spotlight and dim the public's perceptions of Aaron's talents.

So how could Aaron surmount Ruth's mark of 714 home runs? He was an extremely durable athlete who not only played many seasons, but did not miss games within seasons. Between 1955 and 1970, he never played less than 145 games in a season and never suffered a serious injury. Aaron, like Pete Rose, had an enormously long prime and he was able to post consistently productive seasons over a 19-year peak period that stretched from 1955 to 1973. A typical Aaron season was 1957, when he hit .327 with 44 home runs. He then duplicated that in 1962, 1963, 1969, 1971, and 1973. So although Aaron could never establish a period of obvious dominance when he was clearly the best hitter in baseball, he was intermittently at the top and always near the top over an extremely long time period. Aaron was not an overly large man at 6′ and 180 pounds, but he had a short, compact, aggressive swing that allowed him to pull the ball with great consistency. He was a purposeful man with fierce determination who once said his baseball career was business and he meant to keep business as good as possible for as long as possible.

Aaron's consistency and longevity as a player is a tribute to his conditioning, skill, and determination; from the perspective of his home run totals, it is primarily the result of two park illusions working in opposite directions. Aaron played the first 12 years of his career in Milwaukee County Stadium, which was a difficult home run park, and then played the next nine years in Atlanta–Fulton County Stadium, which was truly a "Launching Pad." These two park effects worked to suppress Aaron's home run numbers during the early part of his career and then to inflate them in the latter stages of his career, thus creating the false consistency of his power statistics:

	Home	Road	Total
Milwaukee County Stadium, 1954–65	185	213	398
Atlanta–Fulton County Stadium, 1966–74	190	145	335
Milwaukee County Stadium, 1975–76	10	12	22
	385	370	755

Although Milwaukee County Stadium has been the home park to Henry Aaron, Eddie Mathews, and Harvey's Wallbangers, it is a difficult home run park, reducing home runs by somewhere between 15 and 20 percent. Aaron's home-road home run statistics bear this out and indicate that he might have hit 50 home runs in 1957, 1962, or 1963 if he had played his home games in a neutral park. The Braves' franchise shift to Atlanta came at the perfect moment for Aaron and his pursuit of Ruth. Aaron was 32 in 1966 and was potentially entering the early stages of the decline phase of his career. Atlanta–Fulton County Stadium was a home run park extraordinaire that increased home runs by about 40 percent. Aaron would take advantage of this over his nine seasons in Atlanta and post his best power statistics during the twilight of his career. Aaron's road home run statistics during his stay in Atlanta are sufficiently impressive, however, to suggest that he would still have broken Ruth's record if the Launching Pad had been a neutral park.

Among active players, six have broken into the top 50 career home run list by the end of the 1999 season, including Mark McGwire (522—10th), Barry Bonds (445—22nd), Jose Canseco (431—24th), Cal Ripken Jr. (402—29th), Ken Griffey Jr. (398—31st), Fred McGriff (390—34th), Harold Baines (373—45th), Rafael Palmeiro (361—48th), and Gary Gaetti (360—50th). Albert Belle (358), Juan Gonzalez (340), Sammy Sosa (336), and Matt Williams (334) are poised to break through in 2000.

Based on his power surge over the past four seasons, Griffey is substantially ahead of Aaron's career home run pace. Other players such as Orlando Cepeda have been ahead of Aaron's pace in the early stages of their careers, but no one has been ahead of Aaron at such a developed stage in his career. Compare his year-by-year totals with Aaron's, Ruth's, McGwire's, and Foxx's.

	Ruth		Aaron		Foxx		Griffey Jr.		McGwire	
Age	Season	Career	Season	Career	Season	Career	Season	Career	Season	Career
19					3	3	16	16		
20	4	4	13	13	13	16	22	38		
21	3	7	27	40	33	49	22	60		
22	2	9	26	66	37	86	27	87	3	3
23	11	20	44	110	30	116	45	132	49	52
24	29	49	30	140	58	174	40	172	32	84
25	54	103	39	179	48	222	17	189	33	117
26	59	162	40	219	44	266	49	238	39	156
27	35	197	34	253	36	302	56	294	22	178
28	41	238	45	298	41	343	56	350	42	220
29	46	284	44	342	36	379	48	398	9	229
30	25	309	24	366	50	429			9	238
31	47	356	32	398	35	464			39	277
32	60	416	44	442	36	500			52	329
33	54	470	39	481	19	519			58	387
34	46	516	29	510	5	524			70	457
35	49	565	44	554	3	527			65	522
36	46	611	38	592	0	527				
37	41	652	47	639	7	534				
38	34	686	34	673						
39	22	708	40	713						
40	6	714	20	733						
41			12	745						
42			10	755						

Griffey's career trajectory will become crucial if he is to break Aaron's record. Jimmie Foxx, the preeminent slugger on Connie Mack's awesome Athletics teams of the late '20s and early '30s, had 429 home runs at the age of 30—the most ever by a player before the age of 31—but finished with "only" 534 career home runs due to a variety of factors, including alcoholism, which severely diminished his effectiveness over the latter stages of his career.

Mark McGwire's position is a more difficult one. Despite sporting the best career home run percentage in baseball history, he was still 31 behind Aaron's career home run pace at the end of 1999. Persistent heel injuries during 1993 and 1994 cost McGwire over 200 games during what should have been the prime of his career. If we assume that McGwire, absent the injuries, would have hit at least as many home runs during 1993 and 1994 as he hit in 1991 and 1992, then his career home run total would rise to 568 and pull ahead with Aaron's career total of 510 at age 34. On the positive side of the ledger, McGwire is healthy and seemingly at the height of his powers, having hit 245 home runs during the past four seasons. Also, McGwire's midcareer shift from the Oakland Coliseum to Busch Stadium, which parallels Aaron's midcareer shift from Milwaukee County Stadium to Atlanta–Fulton County Stadium, has benefited and will continue to benefit him.

The many factors that have led to the substantial increase in home runs over the latter half of the 1990s—primarily stadium architecture and the improved strength and conditioning of players—should continue to exist for the foreseeable future. As such, Aaron's career home run mark is now in permanent jeopardy and should be challenged and broken early in the twenty-first century.

Cal Ripken Jr. is much more than a guy who came to play every day. He was the 1982 American League Rookie of the Year, earned two American League MVP awards, and will finish his career as a rare member of both the 3,000-hit and 400-home-run clubs.

Triples

The single-season triples record of 36, set by Owen Wilson of the Pittsburgh Pirates in 1912, is perhaps the most unusual and inexplicable record in baseball history. It is an "outlier" in the true sense of the word, not just in terms of Wilson's mediocre nine-year career (.269 batting average with 59 home runs in 1,280 games) but also in terms of the many seasons and players that have followed. Since 1900, no player in the majors or high minors (other than Wilson) has hit more than 26 triples in a season.

The time and place of Wilson's record makes sense. Several factors made the triple a much more common hit at that time than it is today. The place-hitting ethic of the day that made the home run the least common play dictated that outfielders position themselves much closer to the infield than they do today. When a ball was hit into the gap, the outfielders had to run farther to track it down, and the question wasn't Will he try for three? It was Can they hold him to three? The "one-run-at-a-time" inside game that all teams practiced encouraged aggressive baserunning. Baseball stadiums of the day featured at least one deep field, as stadiums lacked outfield bleachers, and home run fences merely delineated the boundaries of the city block on which the stadium was built. Forbes Field, Wilson's home park, followed this pattern with extremely generous dimensions (360 feet to left field, 406 feet to left-center, 462 feet to just left of dead center, 422 feet to center field, 408 feet to right-center, and 376 feet to right field) that no doubt helped him in amassing his improbable total of three-baggers.

The same factors that helped Wilson in 1912 prevailed throughout the dead-ball era, and just about all of the career triples leaders played the majority of their careers before 1920.

1. Sam Crawford, 1890–1917	312
2. Ty Cobb, 1905–28	298
3. Honus Wagner, 1897–1917	252
4. Jake Beckley, 1888–1907	248
5. Roger Connor, 1880–97	227
6. Tris Speaker, 1907–28	223
7. Fred Clarke, 1894–1915	219
8. Dan Brouthers, 1879–1904	212
9. Paul Waner, 1926–47	190
10. Joe Kelley, 1889–1908	189

The inverse of these factors, however, have existed since 1920, with outfielders playing deeper, runners becoming less prone to taking risks to move from second base to third base, and stadium architecture becoming more uniform with distances to the outfield fences shortened. As such, the triple truly has become the least common play in baseball. Since the end of World War II, only two players have reached career totals of 150 triples—Stan Musial with 177 (19th on the all-time list) and Roberto Clemente with 166 (29th on the all-time list).

Hits

The single-season hits record of 257 was set in 1920 by Gorgeous George Sisler, the left-handed–hitting first baseman and team leader of a powerful St. Louis Browns team that featured such professional hitters as Ken Williams, Baby Doll Jacobson, and Jack Tobin. Sisler was an established American League star in 1920 and had hit over .340 in each of his three prior seasons with good extra-base power and excellent speed. While the 1919–20 rule changes that provided all hitters with a newer and cleaner ball raised American League batting averages from .268 in 1919 to .283 in 1920, the biggest beneficiaries were the line-drive power hitters like Sisler, who were now able to propel the resilient unadulterated baseballs into the power alleys with much greater regularity. Extra-base hits increased significantly in 1920 with doubles rising by 25 percent, triples by 17 percent, and home runs by 53 percent. Sisler was also helped by his home park, Sportsman's Park, whose cozy right-field dimensions (350 feet to left field, 379 feet to left-center, 430 feet to center field, 354 feet to right-center, and 325 feet to right field) became more important as more and more hits were aimed to its power alleys and home run fences. Sisler's home-road split in 1920 shows that he hit an astounding .473 in Sportsman's Park with 150 hits, including 50 extra-base hits, while only managing a "paltry" .341 on the road with 107 hits, including 36 extra-base hits.

Sisler would go on to post excellent seasons in 1921 and 1922, almost duplicating his 1920 season in 1922 when he collected 246 hits and set a then American League record by hitting in 41 consecutive games. For the three-year period of 1920 to 1922, Sisler was as great a hitter as anyone in baseball and a stylistic counterpoint to Babe Ruth. Sisler, however, developed a sinus infection during the 1922 off-season that ultimately affected his optic nerve and forced him to sit out the entire 1923 season. When he returned in 1924, he was a better-than-average hitter but was never again great.

	GP	AB	H	2B	3B	HR	RBI	BA	OBP	SP
Sisler, 1915–22	1047	4155	1498	242	100	59	612	.361	.400	.510
Sisler, 1924–30	1008	4112	1314	183	65	41	563	.320	.351	.426

The hitter-friendly conditions of 1920 continued through the decade and into the early 1930s as baseball determined for perhaps the first time that fans like offense. The introduction of the "cushioned cork center" baseball in 1926, which was more resilient than its predecessor, further increased the speed and distance with which baseballs flew off bats. Under such conditions, and with night baseball not yet having arrived, it is no surprise that all of the top 10 season hit totals (with the exception of Ty Cobb's 1911 campaign) occurred during this period of unbridled offense.

1. George Sisler, 1920	257
2. Lefty O'Doul, 1929	254
2. Bill Terry, 1930	254
4. Al Simmons, 1925	253
5. Chuck Klein, 1930	250
5. Rogers Hornsby, 1922	250
7. Ty Cobb, 1911	248
8. George Sisler, 1922	246
9. Babe Herman, 1930	241
9. Heinie Manush, 1928	241

Between the mid-1930s and the late 1980s, hitting conditions primarily moved against hitters as night baseball became the norm and the older bandboxes were torn down. After World War II, players such as Wade Boggs (240 hits in 1985), Rod Carew (239 hits in 1977), Don Mattingly (238 hits in 1986), and Kirby Puckett (234 hits in 1988) have posted season hit totals that place in the top 20 of all time.

Career Hits

Pete Rose holds the all-time hit record with 4,256. Rose, a.k.a. "Charlie Hustle," was an intense, combative contact hitter who battled on every pitch of every at-bat. He played for 24 seasons, posting interchangeable season after interchangeable season with metronome consistency in a prime that lasted for over 15 years. Rose collected 200 hits on 10 occasions, posted over 600 plate appearances in 16 consecutive seasons, and won four batting titles, including his last in 1981 at age 40.

1. Pete Rose, 1963–86	4,256
2. Ty Cobb, 1905–28	4,190
3. Hank Aaron, 1954–76	3,771
4. Stan Musial, 1941–63	3,630
5. Tris Speaker, 1907–28	3,514
6. Honus Wagner, 1897–1917	3,430
7. Carl Yastrzemski, 1961–83	3,419
8. Paul Molitor, 1978–98	3,319
9. Eddie Collins, 1906–30	3,313
10. Willie Mays, 1951–73	3,283

The top 10 on the all-time career hits list include players from all eras of baseball history, but the players on the list share some characteristics. The key factor in amassing an exceptional career hits total (besides being able to hit) is the ability to sustain a level of excellence or competence over an extremely long period. This ability is directly linked to desire and physical fitness, and, as such, the players at the top of the career hits list are determined ballplayers who were known in their time for their dedication to practice and training. A secondary characteristic shared by these players is an aggressiveness at the plate coupled with a good strikeout-to-walk ratio. So whether they were power hitters or place hitters, more often than not they put the ball in play. Paul Molitor, who recently retired at number 8 on the all-time hits list, fits the mold perfectly.

That Tony Gwynn, going into the 2000 season with 18 years in the majors and eight batting titles, is still seven or so good seasons from the career hits record highlights the magnificence of Rose's accomplishment.

Paul Molitor became the first player ever to reach 3,000 career hits with a triple.

Batting Average

Since 1903, when the American League adopted the foul-strike rule, the rules of the pitcher-hitter confrontation have remained relatively unchanged, and variations in league batting average have been driven by other factors such as stadium architecture and the size and position of the strike zone, which have varied and created hitter's and pitcher's eras from time to time. In general, the highest single-season batting averages have been posted during hitters' years, such as the period immediately following the introduction of the cork-centered baseball in 1911 or the hitter-friendly years between 1920 and 1930.

	BA	Relative BA
1. Rogers Hornsby, 1924	.424	149.8
2. George Sisler, 1922	.420	147.4
3. Ty Cobb, 1911	.420	153.8
4. Ty Cobb, 1912	.409	154.3
5. Joe Jackson, 1911	.408	149.5
6. George Sisler, 1920	.407	143.3
7. Ted Williams, 1941	.406	152.6
8. Rogers Hornsby, 1925	.403	138.0
9. Harry Heilmann, 1923	.403	142.9
10. Rogers Hornsby, 1922	.402	137.3

The highest single-season batting average since the foul strike was established in 1903 belongs to Rogers Hornsby, who hit .424 in 1924. Hornsby, a right-handed–hitting second baseman who played the majority of his career with the St. Louis Cardinals, stood well off the plate and dove into the ball, generating excellent line-drive power. Between 1920 and 1925, Hornsby was the National League's answer to Babe Ruth, pacing the senior circuit in batting average, on-base percentage, and slugging percentage in each year.

Ty Cobb, who played from 1907 to 1928, holds the all-time career batting average record with an eye-popping mark of .366. Cobb, who has been characterized as the meanest man ever to play baseball, was the dominant player in the American League during the deadball era. He personified the hardnosed take-no-prisoners ethic of that era, slapping the ball to all fields with his split-handed batting grip and running hard at all times with his steel showing. He led the American League in batting 12 times, slugging 8 times, and RBI 4 times, and won the Triple Crown in 1907, the sole year he captured the home run title. Given the circumstances under which baseball is now played, Cobb's career batting average may well qualify as one of the unbreakable records now on the books. Since Cobb's retirement, the introduction of night baseball, bigger and better gloves, travel, the development of the slider, increased use of relief pitchers, and the improved positioning of fielders have all conspired to restrain batting averages. If you consider that the difference between a .300 hitter and a .270 hitter over 500 at-bats is about 14 hits, or about two hits per month, over the course of a season, it becomes apparent that in batting averages, small differences make all the difference. Since World War II, only nine players (Stan Musial, Ted Williams twice, Rod Carew, George Brett, Wade Boggs, Tony Gwynn three times, Andres Galarraga, Larry Walker, and Jeff Bagwell) have exceeded Cobb's career mark in a single season.

The closest challengers to Cobb were Rogers Hornsby (.358), George Sisler (.340), and Shoeless Joe Jackson (.356). Hornsby, who played the prime of his career

In 1999, Wade Boggs became the first player in baseball history to earn his 3,000th career hit with a home run.

through the high-average decade of the 1920s, peaked in career batting average at .363 after the 1929 season. A foot injury in 1930 ended his career as a regular and any realistic chance of surpassing Cobb. George Sisler was also sidetracked by ailments. His lifetime batting average reached .361 after the 1922 season, but he was forced to sit out the 1923 season with sinus problems that ultimately damaged his eyesight. Upon his return in 1924, his batting average fell precipitously over the remainder of his career, and he finished up with a .340 lifetime mark. Jackson is a more interesting case. His career was truncated in 1920 when he was banned from baseball for his role in the Black Sox scandal. This had the effect of both potentially inflating his career average by removing the decline phase from his career and potentially lowering his career batting average by removing him from baseball on the cusp of the great hitting decade of the 1920s. Jackson was born in 1899 and would have been 31 years old on Opening Day in 1921. Jackson was a big man for his time, standing 6'1" and weighing 200 pounds, and he used a 40-ounce bat he called "Black Betsy." He showed excellent extra-base power throughout the 1910s and would in all likelihood have thrived during the 1920s. Also in their 30s in the 1920s, Zack Wheat and Jack Fournier saw their career batting averages go up significantly during the decade. Would Jackson have been able to raise his already stratospheric career batting average sufficiently to match Cobb's career mark? For the worst of all reasons, we will never know.

Cobb played the majority of his career (and all of his prime years) for the Detroit Tigers in what was the heyday of the spitball and the scuffball, when American League batting averages hovered in the .240s and .250s. As a result, Cobb not only holds the record for the highest batting average in baseball history but holds the highest relative batting average (which compares a player's batting average to the league average during his career) with a 134.8 career mark.

	BA		Relative BA
1. Ty Cobb, 1905–28	.366	1. Ty Cobb, 1905–28	134.8
2. Rogers Hornsby, 1915–37	.358	2. Joe Jackson, 1908–20	133.1
3. Joe Jackson, 1908–20	.356	3. Pete Browning, 1882–94	131.6
4. Ed Delahanty, 1888–1903	.346	4. Tony Gwynn, 1982–	128.1
5. Tris Speaker, 1907–28	.345	5. Ted Williams, 1939–60	128.1
6. Ted Williams, 1939–60	.344	6. Dan Brouthers, 1879–96	127.8
7. Billy Hamilton, 1888–1901	.344	7. Napoleon Lajoie, 1896–1916	127.3
8. Dan Brouthers, 1879–96	.342	8. Rod Carew, 1967–85	127.0
9. Babe Ruth, 1914–35	.342	9. Rogers Hornsby, 1915–37	126.2
10. Harry Heilmann, 1914–32	.342	10. Tris Speaker, 1907–28	125.4

From World War II to the end of the 1998 season, the highest lifetime batting averages have been posted by Ted Williams at .344 (6 on the all-time list), Tony Gwynn at .339 (16), Wade Boggs at .328 (29), and Rod Carew at .328 (30). In rela-

Dating back to 1983, Tony Gwynn has batted .309 or better for 17 consecutive seasons.

tive batting average, all of these players improve their rankings, with Gwynn (4), Williams (5), and Carew (8) entering the top 10 of all time. Although the great-average hitters of the postwar era have varying styles, they share a thoughtful and incisive understanding of their craft and an obsessive work ethic to counteract and adopt to the ever-changing pitchers and pitching strategies they have faced.

RBI

RBI are tabulated on an individual basis, and in some general way are thought to reflect a player's ability to deliver in the clutch. This is only partially true, because more than any other hitting statistic, RBI are generated in a team context and are affected by a player's spot in the batting order and the number of men on base when he comes to bat. All other things being equal, a player on a good hitting team will drive in more runs than a similar player on a poor hitting team because he will have more RBI opportunities over the course of the season.

This difficulty in evaluating a player's RBI ability is highlighted by the single-season RBI record held by Hack Wilson, who drove in an incredible 190 runs for the Chicago Cubs during the 1930 season. The 1930 season was the hitter's year to end all hitter's years. The National League hitters batted .303 while the league's pitchers posted a 4.97 ERA. It would not be an exaggeration to say that the base paths were clogged around the league that year and that Wilson's outstanding RBI season was completely in context with a season in which 16 other National Leaguers drove in 100 or more runs. By comparison, Wilson's 190 RBI were responsible for plating 19 percent of the Cubbies' 998 runs during 1930, while Wally Berger's 130 RBI for the hapless 1935 Boston Braves represented 23 percent of that team's 575 runs. So despite Wilson's awesome RBI total, we can still debate whether Wilson in 1930 or Berger in 1935 was the better RBI man.

	RBI	GP	RBI/game
1. Sam Thompson, 1894	141	99	1.424
2. Sam Thompson, 1895	165	119	1.387
3. Sam Thompson, 1887	166	127	1.307
4. Hack Wilson, 1930	190	154	1.234
5. Al Simmons, 1930	165	138	1.196
6. Hank Greenberg, 1937	183	154	1.188
7. Lou Gehrig, 1931	184	155	1.187
8. Cap Anson, 1886	147	125	1.176
9. Jimmie Foxx, 1938	175	149	1.174
10. Hugh Duffy, 1894	145	125	1.160

Wilson's 190 RBI in 154 games during the 1930 season represents the fourth-best season on an RBI per game basis in major league history. All three of the top RBI per game seasons were recorded by Big Sam Thompson, who played outfield between 1885 and 1898 with the Detroit Wolverines and the Philadelphia Phillies of the National League. Thompson was the preeminent RBI man of his time, driving in 100 or more runs on eight occasions. RBI were not kept as an official statistic in Thompson's era, and we can only wonder if Thompson's prowess was widely known among managers, players, and fans. Thompson's 1887 season, in which he drove in 166 runs and won the RBI crown by 62 over Roger Connor, is particularly notable. This is the largest margin for an RBI crown in baseball history and has only been approached by Hank Greenberg's 51-RBI margin over Lou Gehrig in copping the 1935 title.

The career RBI record is held by Henry Aaron, with 2,297. He passed Babe Ruth with 2,009 RBI during 1975, one year after he broke Ruth's career home run record. Aaron is the only man in baseball history to have driven in 1,000 runs on home runs and 1,000 runs on other hits.

1. Hank Aaron, 1954–76	2,297
2. Babe Ruth, 1914–35	2,212
3. Lou Gehrig, 1923–39	1,995

4. Stan Musial, 1941–63	1,951
5. Ty Cobb, 1905–28	1,939
6. Jimmie Foxx, 1925–45	1,921
7. Eddie Murray, 1977–97	1,917
8. Willie Mays, 1951–73	1,907
9. Cap Anson, 1876–97	1,879
10. Mel Ott, 1926–47	1,860

The top 10 career RBI list is diverse and shows a mix in styles and eras. Not surprisingly, both the legendary sluggers of the '20s and '30s (Ruth, Gehrig, and Foxx) and the multitalented stars of the postwar era (Aaron, Mays, and Musial) are represented. They are joined by deadball-era stars like Ty Cobb and Cap Anson, who hit only 214 home runs between them, proving that there is more than one way to get the job done.

Mel Ott is perhaps the most interesting player to break the top 10 list. Despite playing his entire career for the New York Giants and retiring with 511 career home runs, his image, like that of many other National League stars of the 1930s and 1940s such as Johnny Mize and Ralph Kiner, has dimmed to the point of obscurity in the public's perception. This is sad, but his position among the top RBI producers of all time provides a reminder of his greatness. Ott was a small man at 5′9″ and 170 pounds, who combined power with excellent strike zone judgment and the ability to take advantage of the Polo Grounds' short foul lines by pulling fly balls into its short right-field porch. Surprisingly, Ott's home-road RBI split (945 RBI at home, 915 on the road) does not show a pronounced home park effect, perhaps because he became less home run conscious on the road and hit for a significantly higher batting average (.311 career road batting average over 1,362 games, .297 career home average over 1,368 games).

As of the end of the 1999 season, Harold Baines (!) had the most RBI of any current player with 1,583, which was good for 27th on the all-time list and placed him 26 RBI away from the top 20. With 1,152 and just turning 30, Ken Griffey Jr. has a great shot at top 3 status. Seven more 120-RBI seasons will leave him behind only Aaron and Ruth.

Slugging Percentage

Babe Ruth holds the record for the highest career slugging percentage at .690. Like many of Ruth's slugging accomplishments, this is a standard that is in a class by itself. Only four other players (Williams at .643, Gehrig at .632, Foxx at .609, and Greenberg at .605) in the history of baseball have compiled career slugging percentages above .600, and none have seriously challenged Ruth's mark. To put in perspective how difficult matching Ruth's career slugging percentage mark would be, consider that Sammy Sosa's slugging percentage during 1998, a season in which he batted .308 with 66 home runs, was "only" .647!

Babe Ruth has posted the only single-season slugging percentages in the history of baseball to exceed .800, .847 in 1920 and .846 in 1921. The Yankees were tenants of the Polo Grounds during 1920 and 1921, and Ruth recorded astonishing home slugging percentages of .985 in 1920 and .929 in 1921. It is fascinating to consider what numbers Ruth might have thrown on the board if John McGraw had not evicted the Yankees from the Polo Grounds and the "House That Ruth Built" had never been built. For although Yankee Stadium was constructed with Ruth in mind, it would never have the pronounced positive effect on Ruth's power statistics that the Polo Grounds did.

1. Babe Ruth, 1920	.847
2. Babe Ruth, 1921	.846
3. Babe Ruth, 1927	.772
4. Lou Gehrig, 1927	.765
5. Babe Ruth, 1923	.764
6. Rogers Hornsby, 1925	.756
7. Mark McGwire, 1998	.752
8. Jeff Bagwell, 1994	.750
9. Jimmie Foxx, 1932	.749
10. Babe Ruth, 1924	.739
11. Babe Ruth, 1926	.737
12. Ted Williams, 1941	.735
13. Babe Ruth, 1930	.732
14. Ted Williams, 1957	.731
15. Mark McGwire, 1996	.730
16. Frank Thomas, 1994	.729
17. Hack Wilson, 1930	.723
18. Rogers Hornsby, 1922	.722
19. Lou Gehrig, 1930	.721
20. Larry Walker, 1997	.720

Until recently, the top 20 single-season slugging percentages were the exclusive preserve of the sluggers of the 1920s and Ted Williams. However, over the past five seasons there has been an explosion of standout seasons that compare with the greatest slugging seasons of all time. With Mark McGwire (1998) and Jeff Bagwell (1994) posting slugging percentages in excess of .750 in neutral to negative hitter's parks like Busch Stadium and the Astrodome, the possibility of the .800 barrier being reached is once again realistic.

Hitting Streaks

The confluence of skill, endurance, and luck necessary to create and maintain a long hitting streak seems to occur no more than once in a generation and sometimes not at all. For this reason, there is an aura of magic associated with each hitting streak. We intuitively know that something unique is occurring, and the player involved is performing something akin to an act of levitation—floating when the forces of gravity argue that he should fall, carrying out an improbable task that becomes more improbable with each passing game.

The first hitting streak to garner public attention was Bad Bill Dahlen's 42-gamer in 1894. Dahlen was an above-average–hitting shortstop who rung up a .272 career batting average in 21 seasons between 1891 and 1911. Although he hit better early in his career, topping the .350 mark in both 1894 and 1896, Dahlen was not the kind of player who seemed to be earmarked for immortality. What is most notable about Dahlen's streak is that except for one bad game, DiMaggio's "unbreakable" record might never have been set. Dahlen's streak was ended on August 7, 1894, in a 13–11 slugfest won by his Chicago Colts over the Cincinnati Reds. The Colts had 17 hits that day, but Dahlen went 0 for 6 and was the only member of the Colts' starting lineup not to get a hit. Dahlen would immediately follow his 42-game streak with a 28-game streak to hit in 70 of 71 games in a row!

Dahlen's streak was overshadowed three years later when Wee Willie Keeler of the Baltimore Orioles put together a 44-game hitting streak running from Opening Day of the 1897 season until June 18. Keeler batted leadoff for the fine Orioles teams of the 1890s and was an established star. Perhaps for this reason, his streak captured public attention and was widely remembered as evidence of his great hitting abilities. Keeler was a consistent high-average hitter, gathering over 200 hits in eight consecutive seasons between 1894 and 1901 while posting a .345 lifetime batting average. Keeler, known for his "hit 'em where they ain't" adage, was the poster child for the place-hitting era with singles representing over 85 percent of his 2,932 career hits. Keeler's 44-game mark stood as the major league record until Joe DiMaggio's 56-game streak in 1941, and still stands as the National League mark, tied with Pete Rose's 44-game streak in 1978.

Between 1920 and 1922, George Sisler batted .400, averaging 141 runs, 255 hits, 78 extra-base hits, and 117 RBI per 154-game season, marking him as the only American Leaguer in the early '20s who could be compared with Ruth as a hitter without looking ridiculous. In 1922, the year in which Sisler's St. Louis Browns challenged the New York Yankees for the American League pennant, Sisler put together a 41-game hitting streak that played a pivotal role in the down-to-the-wire pennant race. Sisler's streak began on July 27 and carried into September. In early September,

Sisler injured his shoulder, and because of the closeness of the pennant race continued to play, aggravating his injury. After running the streak to 39 games, Sisler's shoulder became so bad that he was forced to sit out a four-game series with the Red Sox. Despite the seriousness of his injury, Sisler returned for a crucial mid-September three-game set with the Yankees, who led the Browns by a half-game. He could not lift his right arm and could only swing one-handed; but in the first two games of the series, which the Browns and Yankees split, he managed two bloop singles, stretching his streak to 41 games. In the finale, Sisler was held hitless and the Browns lost. Over the remainder of the season, Sisler would play intermittently and ineffectively while the Yankees would hold on to win the 1922 American League pennant by a single game.

Despite the high league batting averages of the late 1920s and 1930s, baseball would not see another long hitting streak until the 1940s. Entering the 1941 season, Joe DiMaggio was an established superstar, having won the American League home run crown in 1937, batting title in 1939 and 1940, and MVP award in 1939. Yet these achievements and all his success in the seasons to follow would be overshadowed by his 56-game hitting streak, which occurred in a two-month period between May 15 and July 17 of 1941. For unlike any of DiMaggio's other accomplishments, the 56-game hitting streak entered American lore and placed him with Ruth and Cobb and the other legends of the game.

Uncharacteristically, the Yankees and DiMaggio were struggling early in the 1941 season. DiMaggio was hitting below .300 with little power on May 15, when the streak was started with a bloop single off Cotton Ed Smith of the Chicago White Sox. As the streak began with little press or public attention, there were several close calls in games in which DiMaggio could only manage a single hit. On May 29, game 14 of the streak, DiMaggio's sole hit in a five-inning rain-shortened contest was a Baltimore chop off home plate that he managed to beat out by a step. In a portent of things to come, on June 1, game 18, he extended the streak with an eighth-inning smash off the glove of Ken Keltner, the Cleveland Indians third baseman. Interestingly, DiMaggio did go hitless in a game during the streak when he went 0–2 with a walk on May 26 in an exhibition game against the Norfolk Tars, a Yankees farm team. Jimmy Halperin, a southpaw who would never make it to the majors, was the pitcher who shut DiMaggio down.

As the streak passed 20 games, it became widely reported nationwide. Targets like Rogers Hornsby's right-handed batter's mark of 33 games, George Sisler's American League mark of 41 games, and Wee Willie Keeler's major league mark of 44 games were mentioned. As each of these marks was approached and passed, the intensity of public attention and support grew. During this period of the streak, the Les Brown Orchestra rushed out a novelty tune, "Joltin' Joe DiMaggio," which was the kind of song that proves crass commercialism wasn't invented in the 1950s. DiMaggio would later say he didn't really take his chances of setting the major league mark seriously until he reached Hornsby's mark of 33 games on June 20. In his mind, this was the first point during the streak when he started to feel good at the plate!

The streak's closest call came in game 38 on June 26. DiMaggio was hitless going into the home half of the eighth inning with the Yankees leading the visiting St. Louis Browns by a 3–1 score. Moreover, DiMaggio was scheduled to bat fourth. So the Yankees needed a baserunner to ensure that he got another chance to extend the streak. With one out, the Yankee Stadium faithful got their wish when Red Rolfe worked Browns pitcher Eldon Auker for a walk. Joe McCarthy then had Tommy Henrich bunt to stay out of the double play. With Henrich out of the way, DiMaggio faced Auker and lined his first pitch into the left-field corner for a double. Dan Daniel of the *New York World-Telegram* wrote: "When DiMag finally got his hit, the Yankees rushed out on the field and put on a bigger demonstration than their 1927 predecessors did when Babe Ruth hit his sixtieth home run."

DiMaggio began to hit with more authority as the streak lengthened. His bat was stolen from the bat rack in the Yankees' dugout at Yankee Stadium during a rain delay on July 1, game 44. As a result, DiMaggio was forced to use Tommy Henrich's bat—a 36-inch, 36-ounce stick that was identical to DiMaggio's—to break Keeler's all-time mark, which he did with a home run off Dick Newsome on July 2. The streak would come to an end on July 17 at Municipal Stadium after 56 games when Al Smith and Jim Bagby shut out DiMaggio with help from Ken Keltner, who made two backhanded stops on hot shots down the third-base line.

Joe DiMaggio captured the imagination of America when he hit safely in 56 straight games in 1941.

During his 56-game streak, DiMaggio hit .408 with 91 hits, 56 runs, 15 home runs, and 55 RBI. Such was the public interest in DiMaggio's streak that the other great baseball story of 1941, Ted Williams's quest to bat .400, was all but hidden during the streak. Williams actually outhit DiMaggio during the time period of the streak, batting .412. DiMaggio continued to hit after the streak and put together another 16-game streak to hit safely in 72 of 73 games, topping Bad Bill Dahlen's mark of hitting in 70 of 71 games.

The records that did not fall to DiMaggio in 1941 were his own high minors consecutive hit streak of 61 games, set in 1933 with the San Francisco Seals of the Pacific Coast League, and Joe Wilhoit's professional baseball mark of 69 games, set in 1919 with Wichita of the Class A Western Association. Since DiMaggio's 56-game streak, only Pete Rose with 44 games in 1978 and Paul Molitor with 39 games in 1987 have mounted determined challenges to the mark. Like Ruth's 60-homer mark, DiMaggio's 56-game standard has taken its place in baseball myth, becoming more and more intimidating and unreachable with each passing year. It is often mentioned as—and surely is—one of the most unbreakable records in professional sports.

12

All in the Family

FATHERS, BROTHERS, AND SONS

Psychologists and sociologists have long debated the relative importance of heredity and environment in predicting the abilities and other characteristics that children will exhibit in later life.

The heredity theory suggests that people inherit most of their abilities from their parents. Undoubtedly, they do inherit some abilities. But what abilities? A major league ballplayer may marry a lady whose genes tend toward Supreme Court justices. Their child may be a lawyer who plays a great game of softball in the annual office tournament, or perhaps a professional umpire. The odds are against the meeting of two people with an established "baseball gene."

In the history of the majors from 1876 until now, there have been only 356 brother acts and 149 father-son combinations (many of them pitchers, such as the Deans, the Niekros, or the Bagbys), with some overlap in families like the Alomars, the Boones, or the Hairstons. These are pretty small numbers when compared to the many thousands of players who have been active in the 123 years of major league baseball. Moreover, in many of these family acts there are substantial differences in achievement. Only trivia junkies remember the brothers of Bill Dickey, Honus Wagner, Dick Allen, or Jose Canseco. Similarly, Earl Averill, Yogi Berra, and Eddie Collins were Hall of Famers in large measure due to their prowess with the bat, but their sons struggled through undistinguished careers and were mediocre hitters at best.

This look at the greatest hitting families steers away from those such as the Aaron family (Hank and Tommie) or the Murray family (Eddie and Rich), who would rank high on a composite basis, but whose record would essentially be that

American League slugger Jose Canseco was born on July 2, 1964, in Havana, Cuba, as was his twin brother, Ozzie Canseco, who had brief stints in the major leagues with the Oakland A's and St. Louis Cardinals.

of one family member. Instead, we have focused on those rare instances in which the "hitting gene" has been more or less evenly distributed among the family. The exception that proves the rule are families like the DiMaggios or the Alous. Joe, Dom, and Vince DiMaggio were all successful major leaguers and had long careers. Likewise, Felipe, Matty, and Jesus Alou were high-caliber players during the 1960s and 1970s.

The proponents of the heredity argument would say it doesn't matter what the level of achievement was, the mere fact that the lesser family member made the majors at all is proof that heredity is a factor, since even the most marginal player in the major leagues is by definition one of the better hitters in the world. They are right. These marginal family members are unquestionably outstanding ballplayers, and their skill might well be inherited. For example, Hank Aaron's brother Tommie was an International League batting champion and MVP, which marks him as an extremely talented player by anyone's standards. It is only in comparison to outstanding major leaguers like Hank that his accomplishments pale.

If heredity is the key, then it is surprising that there are as many or more quality father-son hitting combinations than quality brother hitting combinations since brothers have 80 percent or more DNA factors in common whereas fathers and sons only have about 50 percent. This suggests that environment may play a stronger role than heredity. Joe, Dominic, and Vince DiMaggio's father was a fisherman, and no one ever threw a 90 MPH fastball at him. Maybe if someone had, he would have drilled it right back at them. The environmental factor that encouraged the DiMaggios' success was most likely the unusually good minor baseball programs that the Bay area had during their childhoods and a love of the game that kept them practicing and playing whenever possible.

A review of baseball's great hitting families does nothing to resolve the question of heredity and environment, but merely adds more fuel to the fire.

Top Brother Combinations

	GP	BA	R	H	HR	RBI	BB	SB
Joe DiMaggio, 1936–51	1736	.325	1390	2214	361	1537	790	30
Dom DiMaggio, 1940–53	1399	.298	1046	1680	87	618	750	100
Vince DiMaggio, 1937–46	1110	.249	491	959	125	584	412	79
	4245	.298	2927	4853	573	2739	1952	179
Paul Waner, 1926–45	2549	.333	1627	3152	113	1309	1091	104
Lloyd Waner, 1927–45	1993	.316	1201	2459	27	598	420	67
	4542	.326	2828	5611	140	1907	1511	171
Felipe Alou, 1958–74	2082	.286	985	2101	206	852	423	107
Matty Alou, 1960–74	1667	.307	780	1777	31	427	311	156
Jesus Alou, 1963–79	1380	.280	448	1216	32	377	138	31
	5129	.292	2213	5094	269	1656	872	294
Ed Delahanty, 1888-1903	1835	.346	1599	2596	101	1464	741	455
Jim Delahanty, 1901–15	1186	.283	520	1159	19	489	378	151
Frank Delahanty, 1905–15	287	.226	109	223	5	94	66	50
Joe Delahanty, 1907–09	270	.238	68	222	4	100	74	24
Tom Delahanty, 1894–97	19	.239	13	16	0	6	8	4
	3597	.310	2309	4216	129	2153	1267	684
Irish Meusel, 1914–27	1289	.310	701	1521	106	819	269	113
Bob Meusel, 1920–30	1407	.309	826	1693	156	1067	375	142
	2696	.310	1527	3214	262	1886	644	255
Roy Johnson, 1929–38	1155	.296	717	1292	58	556	489	135
Bob Johnson, 1933–45	1863	.296	1239	2051	288	1283	1075	96
	3018	.296	1956	3343	346	1839	1564	231

Based upon their combination of offensive skills, the DiMaggios rank as the greatest hitting brothers. Jolting Joe is, of course, the best remembered of the brothers, given his 56-game hitting streak, his marriage to Marilyn Monroe, and a Paul Simon namecheck. Joe's career was the stuff of legend—leader of the Yankees from the late 1930s to the early 1950s, 10 World Series championships, three MVP awards, two batting titles, two home run titles, and perhaps the single most impressive individual record in baseball history. While Joe was the best player of the brothers, Dom and Vince were also outstanding, both being selected on more than one occasion to play in the All-Star Game. Dom was smaller than his brothers and was noteworthy for being the only player in major league baseball at the time to wear eyeglasses, hence his nickname, "the Little Professor." Nevertheless, he was an excellent leadoff hitter, pacing the American League in runs scored twice and finishing his career with a lifetime batting average of .298. People thought it amazing that Dom could hit at all since he couldn't see. Far fewer people wore corrective lenses in those days, and there was not a general appreciation that lenses could give the wearer better-than-normal eyesight à la Ted Williams. Dom was faster than his brothers, stealing 100 bases over his career. Vince was a composite of his brothers, hitting with more power than Dom but less than Joe and similarly fitting into the middle in terms of speed.

Paul "Big Poison" Waner's and Lloyd "Little Poison" Waner's careers have a fairy-tale quality about them. Paul was spotted in 1922 playing for his Harrah, Oklahoma, town team by a San Francisco Seals scout on a 10-day drunk. The scout needed an excuse for why he was two weeks late getting back to the coast, and Paul (whom he had never seen play) was his alibi. Like many of the greats, Paul was drafted as a pitcher but switched to the outfield when he hurt his arm. After two seasons with the Seals, including one in which he batted .401, his contract was sold to the Pittsburgh Pirates for $100,000 and he was a major leaguer. Upon arriving in Pittsburgh for the 1926 season, Paul promptly announced to Barney Dreyfus, the Pirates' owner, that he had a younger brother who was a better ballplayer than he was. He lied, but Lloyd was a pretty good player himself and joined the Pirates for the 1927 season. Paul and Lloyd would play as teammates on the Pirates for 14 seasons, lead their team to the 1927 World Series, and both assemble Hall of Fame careers. Paul was a line-drive hitter who used the whole park and collected boatloads of doubles and triples. His strikeout-to-walk ratio was excellent and he led the National League in 13 different offensive categories during his career, including three batting titles. Lloyd, while not the equal of Paul as an offensive player, was a high-average contact hitter who neither walked nor struck out. Together they amassed 5,611 career hits, the all-time mark for a brother combination.

The Alou brothers from Haina in the Dominican Republic were all scouted and signed by the San Francisco Giants as outfielders, with Felipe joining the big club in 1958, Matty in 1960, and Jesus in 1963. All three were teammates with the Giants for the 1963 season, and on September 15 that year shared the San Francisco outfield for one inning in a game against the Pittsburgh Pirates. The reason this event did not occur more often during 1963 was that the Giants were pennant contenders and Willie Mays had to be benched for the trick to be carried out.

Felipe, the eldest, was a free-swinging line-drive power hitter who had the misfortune to peak as a hitter during the mid-1960s when strikeouts and shutouts were plentiful. In a three-year period between 1966 and 1968, Felipe would bat .308 with 57 home runs and lead the National League in runs scored once and hits twice. Over his career, Felipe would bat a deceiving .286 with 206 home runs.

Matty was a struggling free-swinging slap hitter with the Giants, but in 1966 he was traded to the Pittsburgh Pirates, where Harry "the Hat" Walker taught him to chop down on the ball. Matty learned well and garnered over 30 infield singles en route to winning the 1966 National League batting title. Over the next six seasons, Matty would reach the .300 mark five times and establish himself as one of the most highly regarded contact hitters in the game. He would finish his career with a .307 mark.

Jesus, the youngest, had a similar skill set to Matty with his abilities pitched at a lower level. He would assemble a .280 lifetime batting average during a 15-year career with five major league teams. Perhaps Jesus's most exceptional accomplishment was to take the family trait of swinging at everything to extremes and only walk 138 times during his career!

The Delahanty brothers are often discounted as a true brother combination on the grounds that Ed, with his .346 lifetime batting average, two batting titles, two home run crowns, and three RBI titles, stands head and shoulders above his four brothers. While it is true that Frank, Joe, and Tom were fringe players, Jim had a substantial and successful 13-year major league career as an infielder and outfielder. Playing through the heart of the deadball era, Jim was an above-average offensive player whose .283 career batting mark was significantly above the league average. Jim's best season was 1911, when he batted .339 and drove in 94 runs for the Detroit Tigers.

Irish and Bob Meusel had mirror image careers as star players in the Big Apple during the 1920s. They would face each other in three consecutive World Series between 1921 and 1923, with Bob driving home the championship-deciding run in Game 6 of the 1923 Series. While Irish generally took the ball to the opposite field and Bob hit with more power, both were line-drive power hitters who played for perennial pennant-contending clubs.

After a cup of coffee in 1914 with the Washington Senators, Irish broke into the majors for good in 1918 with the Philadelphia Phillies. Traded to John McGraw's New York Giants in 1921, he made his mark, driving in more than 100 runs in four straight seasons between 1922 and 1925 and helping the Giants to four consecutive World Series appearances between 1921 and 1924.

Bob broke in with the Yankees in 1920 and became one of the important cogs in Murderers' Row, helping the Yankees to three straight World Series appearances between 1921 and 1923 and three more between 1926 and 1928. Like his brother, Bob was a reliable RBI man and drove in 100 runs on five occasions during his 11-year career, leading the American League in both home runs and RBI in 1925.

While most of the families in the chart are well known to those who follow baseball, Bob and Roy Johnson tend to be forgotten when one speaks of great-hitting brothers. Their records, however, speak for themselves. They were full-blooded Indians and played most of their careers during the 1930s, well before the full integration of major league baseball.

Other strong-hitting brother combinations include Ken and Clete Boyer and Lee and Carlos May. Both sets of brothers combined for 444 roundtrippers each. Also notable are Joe and Luke Sewell, contact hitters who compiled over 3,500 hits during the hitter's era of the late 1920s and early 1930s, as well as Dixie and Harry Walker, who both won National League batting titles during the 1940s.

Top Father-Son Combinations

	GP	BA	R	H	HR	RBI	BB	SB
Bobby Bonds, 1968–81	1849	.268	1258	1886	332	1024	914	461
Barry Bonds, 1986–	2000	.288	1455	2010	445	1299	1430	460
	3849	.278	2713	3896	777	2323	2344	921
Ken Griffey Sr., 1973–91	2090	.296	1129	2143	152	859	719	200
Ken Griffey Jr., 1989–	1535	.299	1063	1752	398	1152	747	167
	3625	.297	2192	3885	550	2011	1466	367
Gus Bell, 1950–64	1741	.281	865	1823	206	942	470	30
Buddy Bell, 1972–89	2405	.279	1150	2514	201	1106	836	55
David Bell, 1995–	458	.256	174	374	35	167	109	10
	4604	.278	2180	4711	442	2215	1415	95
Sandy Alomar Sr., 1964–78	1481	.245	588	1168	13	282	302	227
Sandy Alomar Jr., 1988–	896	.275	373	845	86	417	152	22
Roberto Alomar, 1988–	1722	.304	1117	2067	151	829	758	377
	4099	.278	2078	4020	250	1528	1212	626
Felipe Alou, 1958–74	2082	.286	985	2101	206	852	423	107
Moises Alou, 1990–	919	.295	535	966	145	612	337	73
	3001	.289	1520	3067	351	1464	760	180
Ray Boone, 1948–60	1373	.275	645	1260	151	737	608	21
Bob Boone, 1972–90	2264	.254	679	1838	105	826	663	38
Bret Boone, 1992–	945	.255	442	880	106	462	257	39
Aaron Boone, 1997–	213	.274	85	195	16	105	47	24
	4795	.261	1851	4173	378	2130	1575	122

The four top father-son hitting combinations in the history of baseball are currently active. The Bondses (Bobby and Barry) and the Griffeys (Ken Sr. and Ken Jr.) are, of course, on a level all by themselves. But they are joined by the Alomars (Sandy Sr., Sandy Jr., and Roberto) and Alous (Felipe and Moises), who are moving up on the all-time list.

Based upon their mix of speed, power, and on-base percentage, the Bondses are the greatest hitting father-son combination (although the Griffeys are not far behind). Bobby was labeled as a problem during his playing career primarily due to his incongruent skill set. He broke into the majors with the San Francisco Giants as a very effective leadoff hitter, using his ability to propel himself into scoring position with extra-base hits and stolen bases. Managers and coaches, however, had difficulty seeing him as a leadoff hitter because of his awesome power and high strikeout totals. As a result, Bobby's swing was tinkered with and he was moved around in the batting order. Despite this, Bobby scored runs, crossing the plate over 100 times in five consecutive seasons between 1969 and 1973 and reaching the 30/30 club on five occasions. Bobby's career had a rapid decline phase that colors people's perception of what a good ballplayer he was, but he did end up with eye-catching career statistics, including 332 home runs and 461 stolen bases.

Despite the lofty standards set by Bobby, Barry has exceeded his father in every offensive category and has been the dominant offensive player in the National League during the 1990s, winning three MVP awards. With his mix of power-hitting and base-stealing abilities, Barry is a unique player and has set new standards for power-speed statistics, reaching the 30/30 club five times, the 40/40 club once, and, on August 23, 1998, becoming the first player in major league history to hit 400 home runs and steal 400 bases in his career. At age 35, Barry has a legitimate shot at 500 home runs and a potentially matchless career record of 500 home runs and 500 stolen bases.

Patience at the plate and a shorter (but still vicious) stroke have allowed Barry Bonds to surpass his father's career numbers.

Ken Griffey Jr. had yet to turn 30 at the end of the 1999 season and was already only two short of the 400 mark in home runs. He has led the American League in homers on four occasions, including back-to-back 56-homer seasons in 1997 and 1998. If the rest of his career goes as expected, Ken Jr. will not only vault the Griffey family to the top of the list of best father-son combinations, but will be personally challenging Hank Aaron for all-time home-run honors. Ken Sr., who is best remembered for his years with the Big Red Machine in the mid-1970s, played until he was 41 to allow himself to play alongside Ken Jr. Late in the 1990 season, Ken Sr. (40) joined his son Ken Jr. (20) in the outfield of the Seattle Mariners. They played 21 games together that season and 30 more in 1991, and even managed to hit back-to-back home runs. This was no one-inning publicity stunt, as Ken Sr. pulled his weight, hitting .377 and .282 in each of his partial seasons with the Mariners.

In the Alomar family, the hitting talent is concentrated in Roberto, who is a high-average spray hitter with good speed. Over the past few seasons, Roberto has added a little pop to his bat and, at age 31, has a reasonable shot at reaching the 3,000-hit plateau. If Roberto is able to continue to perform as expected, the Alomars should vault past the Bells into third place among father-son combinations.

The hitting talent is more evenly distributed in the Alou family, with both Felipe and Moises having very similar offensive capabilities. If he can recover from the knee injury that kept him out all of 1999, Moises should have several more productive seasons that may allow the Alous to also surpass the Bells.

There are too many father-son combinations in major league history to more than scratch the surface in one chapter. The Hegans, the Hundleys, the Kennedys, the McRaes, the Schofields, and the Smalleys are all examples of families in which both a father and a son had useful major league careers. The Bells and the Boones carry the banner for this group, with Gus and Buddy Bell and Ray and Bob Boone all having solid if unspectacular careers with moments of glory thrown in here and there. Interestingly, both the Bells and Boones have now added a third generation to the majors. When Bret Boone was called up from Calgary of the Pacific Coast League in 1992 and inserted into a late-season game at second base for the Seattle Mariners, he became the first third-generation player in baseball history. He is now firmly established as a productive albeit well-traveled second baseman, while his brother Aaron, who plays third for the Reds, and David Bell are becoming full-time players.

This sudden upsurge in great hitting father-son combinations has been matched by a dramatic increase in the number of all types of father-son combinations in the major leagues. In the past 20 years, over 40 percent of the total father-son combinations in the history of major league baseball have been added. Heredity, coupled with a wealthy father who can install a pitching cage in the backyard, may have something to do with that.

13

What Might Have Been

GREAT HITTERS WHOSE CAREERS WERE CUT TRAGICALLY SHORT

It is no exaggeration to say that, but for the absence of one lucky break (or the presence of one too many unlucky ones), the ranks of the greatest to ever play the game could easily swell by a dozen or more. Some great hitters never could get it done out of the minor leagues, while others were kept out of the majors by prejudice. Still others had their careers tragically or foolishly abbreviated.

If only Pete Reiser could have kept from running into walls.

If only Joe Hauser could have played in the major leagues during the age of the designated hitter (or at least the age of the slow-footed first baseman).

If only Josh Gibson could have played in the major leagues during any age at all.

Though the numbers in the Big Book may not say so, these are some of the greatest hitters to ever swing a bat: the unfortunate ones whose careers were derailed by anything from love to death, the unknown legends of the minors, and the underappreciated superstars of the Negro Leagues.

The best of each group get their turn at bat.

Star-Crossed

Dale Alexander

Dale "Moose" Alexander broke into the majors in 1929 playing first base with the Detroit Tigers. He played in 155 games that year, hitting .343 with 25 home runs and leading the American League with 215 hits. If there had been a Rookie of the Year award in 1929, Alexander would have gotten it. He followed up his 1929 season with two more excellent years, batting over .300 in both seasons and establishing himself as one of the top hitters in the game.

Early in the 1932 season, Alexander was traded by the Tigers to the Boston Red Sox to make way for Harry Davis, a slick-fielding first baseman who ultimately flopped and lost the Tigers' first-base job to Hank Greenberg in 1933. Alexander had a monster season with the BoSox in 1932, batting .367 and winning the American League batting title. But then fate took a hand. Midway through the 1933 season, Alexander suffered a minor ankle sprain in a game at Fenway Park against the Philadelphia A's and left the game for treatment. The Red Sox team physician, Doc Woods, put Alexander's leg in a diathermy machine and then forgot about him. By the time Doc Woods returned, Alexander had suffered third-degree burns to his leg. The burns developed into gangrene and Alexander almost lost his leg. Alexander, who was slow-footed to begin with, could not recover from the accident, and his major league career was over at the age of 30. He finished up with a lifetime batting average of .331 in his five-season career.

Lyman Bostock

The most violent ending to a young star's major league career was the murder of 27-year-old Lyman Bostock. A victim of mistaken identity, Bostock was shot in a car in Gary, Indiana, in September 1978. He was hitting .296 at the time, and .311 for his career. Having joined the Angels as a free agent in 1978, Bostock started slow and offered to forgo his first month's salary. The Angels wouldn't let him do it, so he donated it to charity.

Tony Conigliaro

Tony Conigliaro was a tall, strong right-handed slugger from Revere, Massachusetts, who broke in with the Boston Red Sox in 1964 at the age of 19. Fenway Park was made to order for Conigliaro and he hit the ground running, slamming 24, 32, and 28 home runs in his first three seasons.

Conigliaro was putting together another fine year in 1967 with 20 home runs and 67 RBI when he was struck in the face by a Jack Hamilton pitch on August 18. The pitch nearly killed Conigliaro, caving in his face and forcing him to miss over a year and a half. He returned in 1969 and played two more seasons, having perhaps the best year of his career in 1970, when he hit 36 home runs and drove in 116 runs. Unfortunately, the damage to his eye from the beaning in 1967 started to affect his vision, and he was out of baseball in 1971 at the age of 26. He would make one more futile attempt to return in 1975, but his reflexes were gone. As the Red Sox played Game 7 of the World Series in Fenway Park, few remembered that Conigliaro had been in their Opening Day lineup.

Playing in Fenway Park, Conigliaro was conservatively a 300- to 400-homer man. As it was, his career never reached its peak, and he never reached maturity as a baseball player. Still, he managed to hit 166 home runs and average .264 with 28 home runs and 86 RBI per season in the equivalent of six full major league campaigns.

Ray Chapman

Ray Chapman is the only player to die as a result of an injury received during a major league baseball game. Chapman was struck on the temple by a submarine delivery from Carl Mays on August 16, 1920, at the Polo Grounds during a game between Chapman's Cleveland Indians and the New York Yankees. He died the next day at St. Lawrence Hospital when emergency surgery was unable to save him. What is not often said about Ray Chapman is that he was the best shortstop in the American League during the late 1910s and was potentially destined for the Hall of Fame before his untimely death.

After just 12 major league seasons, Kirby Puckett rapped out 2,304 hits before glaucoma prematurely ended his career.

Chapman joined the Indians in 1912 and beat out Ivy Olson and Roger Peckinpaugh for the shortstop job based upon his strong defense. Olson was the incumbent and a good major league shortstop. He would go on to play over 1,000 games at shortstop during a 14-year career spent primarily with Brooklyn. Peckinpaugh, who was a rookie, like Chapman would end up with the Yankees, establishing himself as one of baseball's stars in the early 1920s and winning an MVP award in 1925 with the Washington Senators.

Chapman played during a strong pitcher's era, so his career batting statistics do not appear to be impressive. But he was a strong hitter, putting together a career .278 batting average during a period when major league batting averages were in the .240s and .250s. In 1915, when Chapman batted .270, the major league batting average was .248. In 1917, he batted .302, stole 52 bases, and scored 98 runs when the major league batting average was .249. In 1918, he led the American League in runs scored and walks, and in 1919 he hit over .300 again. In addition to his high batting average, Chapman showed decent punch, excellent speed, and good strike zone judgment. He was also considered to be the best or second-best defensive shortstop in the majors along with Rabbit Maranville.

Chapman was having the best season of his career in 1920, batting .303 with 97 runs scored in only 111 games, when tragedy struck. Given Chapman's ability to outhit the league and post .300 batting averages prior to the rule changes of 1920, there can be little doubt that he would have prospered in the hitter's era of the early 1920s. Ironically, many of the rule changes that helped the hitters in the 1921 season and beyond came about directly as a result of Chapman's death.

Charlie Ferguson

Charlie Ferguson was one of the most promising young pitchers in the National League during the mid-1880s. He broke in with the Philadelphia Phillies at the age of 21 in 1884 and proceeded to win 20 games in each of his first four seasons, compiling a 99–64 record with a 2.67 ERA.

Ferguson was also fairly adept with the bat. After taking his first three seasons (in which he batted .269) to get comfortable, he exploded in 1887, batting .337 and driving in 85 runs in only 264 at-bats. Projecting his RBI output to a 600 at-bat season, Ferguson was on pace to drive in 193 runs and set the all-time major league single-season RBI record! His hitting excellence was, of course, noticed by Phillies manager Harry Wright, who moved Ferguson to second base for the last eight weeks of the 1887 season.

So why haven't you heard of Charlie Ferguson before? Because 1887 was the last season of his major league career. In the spring of 1888, Ferguson contracted typhoid fever and died a few weeks after his 25th birthday.

Bo Jackson

One of the greatest athletes to ever play the game, football star Bo Jackson had established himself as a legitimate baseball player in the late 1980s. He hit 32 home runs and knocked in 105 runs for the Royals in 1988 and was on his way to eclipsing those numbers when he separated his shoulder diving for a ball at Yankee Stadium (in a game in which he'd already hit three home runs). Jackson's career was ruined when he injured his hip after an apparently harmless tackle in an L.A. Raiders playoff game. He tried to play for the Chicago White Sox in 1991, but it was too painful to even watch. Jackson resorted to hip replacement surgery, then defied everyone's expectations when he returned to the big leagues in 1993. Facing live pitching for the first time in nearly two years, Bo Jackson came to the plate on Opening Day and hit a home run in his first at-bat. A part-time player for two years, the one-legged Jackson would hit 28 more before hanging it up after only scratching the surface of his potential.

Bill Lange

Playing for the Chicago Colts, forerunner of the Chicago Cubs, Bill Lange was one of the best outfielders and all-around athletes in baseball during the 1890s. He combined power and speed with spectacular defensive work in a seven-year career between 1893 and 1899. He was a big man for the time at 6′2″ and 195 pounds, but unlike most big men of his era he had blinding speed, stealing 399 bases. As a hitter, Lange finished in the top 10 several times, compiling a .330 lifetime batting average.

Lange's career came to a lurching halt in 1899 when he got married. His bride was the daughter of a wealthy businessman, and because she wanted Lange to go into business with her father, he did. Baseball, of course, was not as respectable in the 1890s as it is today, and society had more barriers of class, ethnicity, and occupation. Lange was crossing the tracks with his marriage, and to be accepted in his new world he had to leave his old world behind.

As it turned out, Lange's marriage was unsuccessful and ended in divorce. He never returned to baseball, and he remains perhaps the only man who gave up a Hall of Fame baseball career for love and a position in the family business.

Pete Reiser

"You're better with one leg and one eye than anybody else I got."

—LEO DUROCHER

"And that's the way I'll end up—on one leg with one eye."

—PETE REISER

Pistol Pete Reiser is perhaps the greatest hitter who never was. In 1941, he led the Brooklyn Dodgers to the World Series with an MVP-type season, winning the National League batting crown and pacing the senior circuit in runs scored, doubles, triples, and slugging percentage. Reiser was a slashing line-drive hitter who ran well and played with reckless abandon on both offense and defense. Unfortunately, he was never able to repeat his 1941 season—in part due to World War II, which took the 1943, 1944, and 1945 seasons from him, and in the main because of his propensity for injuries.

When Reiser returned from military service in 1946, he was still a productive player, hitting over .300 in both 1946 and 1947 and leading the National League in stolen bases in both seasons. However, he had a problem with outfield walls—he couldn't stop running into them. He was carried off the field suffering concussions on at least 10 occasions during his career and several times was near death as a result of his headlong defensive play.

His first beaning came only five days into his great 1941 season. He woke up in the hospital with his uniform on, and was told to stay put for a week. Reiser checked right out instead and went to the ballpark the following day. With the score tied 7–7 in the eighth, the bases loaded, and the same pitcher who'd hit him in the head the day before coming on in relief, Leo Durocher sent Reiser up to pinch hit. He hit a grand slam to dead center.

In 1942, he ended up in the hospital again after hitting the wall in St. Louis, though he had the presence of mind to throw the ball back in before he collapsed. This time he stayed for two days, though his doctor advised him to take the rest of the season off. Reiser met the Dodgers in Pittsburgh, where the game went 14 innings and Leo Durocher called on him to pinch hit yet again. He scored both runners with what should have been a triple, except he collapsed after rounding first.

After returning from the war in 1946, Reiser came back to an Ebbets Field that had been remodeled, with the center field brought in 30 feet. Reiser forgot about the new distance on June 5, when he ran into the wall at full speed chasing a drive by Culley Rikard of the Pirates. The umpire who had to run out to the fallen Reiser discovered that he had held onto the ball. He was then carried off the field on a stretcher, and a priest administered him the Last Rites in the clubhouse. He regained consciousness and returned to the Dodgers, only to collide with another player in the outfield during warm-ups and wind up back in the hospital with a golf-ball–sized blood clot in his head. He fought through double vision and dizzy spells to return to the team, only to collapse in the Polo Grounds outfield after another diving catch. They carried him off again. He was conscious in the clubhouse this time, but unable to recognize anyone in the room.

After 1947, Reiser was unable to play regularly, and he retired in 1952 after 10 major league seasons with a .295 lifetime batting average compiled in the equivalent of only four full seasons of at-bats. He stayed in baseball, first as a manager in the minors, returning to the big leagues as a coach for Leo Durocher's Cubs.

How good could Pete Reiser have been? Paul Molitor is probably a good comparison. Molitor and Reiser had similar offensive capabilities—high-average hitters with line-drive power and excellent speed, hampered by strings of injuries. Molitor took a lot fewer shots to the head, so his injuries were less serious. Molitor also had the option of playing designated hitter to avoid the wear and tear of defense, becoming a full-time DH in 1991. Maybe Reiser could have been a great designated hitter, or maybe the role would have just doused the competitive fire that sent him into all of those walls in the first place.

Ross Youngs

Ross Youngs took over the New York Giants right-field spot from Dave Robertson, the two-time National League home run champion, in 1918. During a seven-year period between 1918 and 1924, Youngs established himself as one of the top offensive players in the National League and a fan favorite in New York. He was a high-average contact hitter who could take a pitch. This, coupled with his hustling, aggressive style of play, allowed Youngs to be consistently among the league leaders in batting average, runs scored, hits, walks, and on-base percentage. He had his best year in 1924, batting .355 and pushing his slugging percentage above .500 for the only time in his career.

In 1925, Youngs's batting average plummeted to .264 and his fielding suffered. Just prior to spring training for the 1926 season, he was diagnosed with Bright's disease—or in modern parlance, nephritis, an inflammation of the kidney that ultimately leads to kidney failure. Somehow he was able to play in 95 games during the 1926 season. The Giants paid to have a nurse care for Youngs on road trips, and amazingly he returned to form and lifted his batting average to .307. But Youngs was bedridden after the 1926 season and passed away on October 22, 1927, at the age of 30.

Despite his short career, Youngs was inducted into the Hall of Fame. In his seven seasons prior to the onset of his illness, Youngs batted .333, averaging 104 runs, 194 hits, and 70 walks per 154-game season while helping the New York Giants to four straight National League pennants between 1921 and 1924. In addition to his offensive capabilities, he was an excellent fielder whom John McGraw called the greatest outfielder he had ever seen.

Mike Piazza will undoubtedly go down as the greatest 62nd-round draft pick in baseball history. Might there have been another who could hit like him but was passed over completely?

Beating the Bushes

The minor leagues, as they were organized in the nineteenth century and the first third of the twentieth century, were independent. Minor league teams were owned by individuals who were trying to make a profit either by drawing fans to the park or by selling their players' contracts to teams in other professional baseball leagues. This created a tension that kept some players out of the majors for many years or for whole careers. For example, Buzz Arlett, "the Babe Ruth of the Pacific Coast League," was a fan favorite and drawing card for the Oakland Oaks of the Pacific Coast League and thus had an economic value to the owners of the Oakland Oaks that was in some ways independent of his playing abilities. To major league owners who might be willing to purchase Arlett's contract, he was a potentially good hitter with obvious defensive weaknesses. As such, the major league owners put a much different and lower value on Arlett than the owners of the Oakland Oaks did. For this reason, it was extremely difficult for Arlett to move from the Pacific Coast League to the major leagues.

It should also be noted that in some cases, players like Arlett were just as happy to stay in the minors. The location of the major league franchises and the number of teams in the major leagues was arbitrary. So Baltimore had the Orioles in the International League, Milwaukee had the Brewers in the American Association, and San Francisco had the Seals and the Missions in the Pacific Coast League, not because they were bush league cities but because that's just how things worked out. In the pre-television pre-radio world, minor league teams playing in major league cities were free to make as much money as major league teams by drawing at the gate, and some did. The star players of the American Association, the International League, and the Pacific Coast League were paid on a par with major leaguers and were the heroes of their cities. Their exploits were reported on the front page of the sports section, and they were the talk of the town because they were the only game in town.

Joe Hauser ("Unser Choe")

Joe Hauser, born in Milwaukee in 1899, broke in with Providence of the Eastern League in 1918 and played two years for them. Although he didn't set the world on fire (7 home runs with a batting average in the .270s), he was signed by his home-town Milwaukee Brewers of the American Association in 1920. He immediately began the rampage that would make him the best home run hitter in minor league history. Over the next two years, he hit 35 homers with the Brewers while batting about .300.

The fans in Milwaukee loved him and gave him the nickname "Unser Choe" (Our Joe), which stuck with him thereafter. A German lad and a hometown boy to boot! Milwaukee is a major place of settlement for Americans of German extraction, and Unser Choe is a sort of fractured German term. Unser means "our" in German, but Choe doesn't mean anything. Phonetically, that was the best a German speaker could come up with in approximating "Joe," since there are no English "J" sounds in the German language. Such adulation from his fellow Milwaukeeans undoubtedly contributed to his success at the plate.

Hauser's performance in Milwaukee earned him a shot at the majors, where he played for the Philadelphia Athletics for five years and the Cleveland Indians for one. In 1922, his first year in the majors, Hauser batted .323 with 9 homers in 111 games. In the next two years, he proved that he was no flash in the pan. In 1923, he raised his home run output to 16 while batting .307 in 146 games, and in 1924 Joe had his "career year." In that year he played in 149 games and hit 27 home runs, which was second in the American League only to Babe Ruth, who hit 46. His batting average slipped to .288, but he knocked in 115 runs, fourth-highest in the league, and posted a slugging average of .516.

At the end of the season, he was 26 years old and the world should have been his oyster. Imagine the contract he would have signed today with those stats. But fate intervened. During spring training, he suffered a broken kneecap on a non-contact play in a game against the Philadelphia Phillies and missed the entire 1925 season. He tried to come back the next year, but the magic was gone. The knee never really healed. He batted only .192 in 92 games and was farmed out to the Kansas City Blues of the American Association for the 1927 season. Joe had an excellent year in Kansas City, .352 with 20 homers, and was brought back to Philadelphia in 1928. He did well, batting .260 with 16 homers and a .517 slugging percentage in 95 games.

Connie Mack had paid big money to acquire Hauser from Milwaukee and didn't give up easily, but by 1928 Jimmie Foxx was coming into his own and was ready to play full-time. Hauser's lack of mobility as a result of his bad knee meant that first base was his only feasible position. Unfortunately, first base was also Foxx's best position. Mack decided to make room for Foxx and traded Joe to the Cleveland Indians, with whom he played in the 1929 season. He had shown signs of getting his batting eye back in 1928, but he needed to play every day. Cleveland played him in only 37 games, almost exclusively as a pinch hitter, and he batted only .250 with 3 home runs. Cleveland wasn't disposed to change this, and Hauser quit in midseason.

While his fielding percentage slipped by less than 10 points, only the coaches, who saw him play day to day, were in a position to make an objective judgment as to how many grounders, pop-ups, and foul balls he couldn't get into position to handle. The judgment seems to have been universally negative since no other major league team was willing to accept Joe's defensive shortcomings in order to get his bat into the lineup on an everyday basis, and that was the end of his major league career. His lifetime major league stats are more than respectable: .284 batting average (.304 before his injury), .478 slugging average, and 79 home runs. If there had been designated hitters in those days, Joe Hauser would probably have played a full major-league career à la Jose Canseco or Chili Davis and would be well known today as a fine major league hitter.

Hauser might well have packed it in at this stage, although he was only 30. Instead, he re-embarked on his minor league career and in seven seasons, between 1930 to 1936, astonished the baseball world. He joined the Baltimore Orioles of the International League in 1930 and hit 63 home runs while driving in 175 runs and batting .313.

After the 1931 season, Hauser joined the Minneapolis Millers of the American Association, where in 1933 he hit 69 homers with 182 RBI. Over the seven years he batted .297, drove in 860 runs, and slugged 302 roundtrippers. He led the league in home runs in four years out of the seven, runs scored twice, and RBI once. His home runs during this period, combined with those he had previously hit in the minors and those he hit when he played from 1937 to 1942 as player-manager of Sheboygan in the Class D Wisconsin League, gave him a minor league total of 399. Adding in his 79 major league homers, you have a grand total of 478, the second-highest total in minor league history.

Ike Boone

Isaac Morgan "Ike" Boone's baseball career was essentially a series of movements upward, downward, and sideways. In a 17-year career in the majors and high minors, he played in 14 different cities and changed teams 16 times. He played during eight different seasons in the majors between 1922 and 1932, but regularly in only two seasons with the Boston Red Sox. He played 261 games in those two seasons (1924 and 1925), during which he batted .331 with 22 home runs and 163 RBI. His lifetime batting average in 1,145 major league at-bats was .319 with 26 home runs. In 6,807 minor league at-bats, he averaged an impressive .370, the highest lifetime batting average in minor league history.

How could a hitter of such skill be unable to establish himself in the majors? A clue is provided in contemporary reports that described Boone's glove as being purely "ornamental." Add to this that he was slow-footed and considered to have poor range, and you have a player that no major league team was prepared to play on a regular basis.

The minor leagues were not so particular, and Ike got to play every day—perhaps more than he really wanted. The Pacific Coast League went in for marathon seasons in those days, and in 1929 he played 198 games with Mission (San Francisco). Home run totals in lengthy seasons such as these are not always meaningful. The same can be said of any cumulative statistic such as RBI, hits, or runs scored on a single-season basis. However, relative statistics like batting average may be even more meaningful given the grueling nature of so long a season. Ike batted a league-leading .407 and was batting .448 after 83 games the following season when he went to the Brooklyn Dodgers. There he languished on the bench, getting only 101 at-bats during the remainder of the 1930 season but turning in a very credible .297 batting average.

The 1930 Dodgers had a pretty tough outfield to break into—Babe Herman (.393), Johnny Frederick (.334), and Rube Bressler (.299). It was Bressler, then nearing the end of his career, whom Ike spelled from time to time in the outfield and reasonably expected to replace to an even greater extent in the following year, 1931.

Unfortunately for Ike, the Dodgers acquired Lefty O'Doul from the Phillies in the off-season. Lefty was an established star and was coming off a season in which he had batted .383. That was all she wrote as far as Ike's major league career was concerned. The Dodgers had the outfield they wanted, and Ike got a ticket to Newark in the International League (IL). Fourteen miles by road, but a different planet by baseball standards.

Ike obviously didn't let it get him down as he won the IL batting title with an average of .356. The following year he played for Jersey City, also in the IL, where he hit .320. But in 1933, he was off to Toronto, again of the IL, where he found the only relative stability in his career. He spent the final four years of his career (1933–36) with Toronto, his longest stint anywhere. His batting average over the period was .349. During the final three years he was also player-manager.

In 1934, at age 37, Ike won the batting title with an average of .372, was named MVP, and managed the Maple Leafs to the International League championship. In 1957, he was inducted into the International League's Hall of Fame. Over his career, Ike won batting titles in the Southern Association, the Texas League, two in the Pacific Coast League, and two in the International League.

Rocky Nelson

Glenn "Rocky" Nelson's career started in 1942 and ended in 1962. He played a total of 18 seasons of major and minor league ball with three seasons lost to military service in World War II. Rocky played in nine major league seasons for five different teams: the St. Louis Cardinals, the Pittsburgh Pirates, the Chicago White Sox, the Brooklyn Dodgers, and the Cleveland Indians. Brooklyn, after trading him away, reacquired him twice, as did Pittsburgh. St. Louis did it once. In 1951, Rocky played for three different major league teams. Everyone seemed to agree that such a great minor league hitter belonged in the majors somewhere, but no one could ever find exactly where.

The problem was that Rocky just didn't hit very well at the major league level. Bill James has developed formulas to predict major league performance based on minor league records, but Rocky didn't come close to his "predicted" performance. Yet whenever he was demoted to the minors, he immediately began to knock the cover off the ball.

Nobody can say that Rocky didn't get a fair shot at the bigs. It is ironic that when he finally had the kind of major league season that was close to what everyone had been expecting all along, he was 36 years old and it was too late. In 1960, he hit .300 in 93 games for the World Series champion Pittsburgh Pirates. His slugging average was .470 with 7 homers and 35 RBI. In the seven-game World Series, Rocky hit .333 in nine appearances at the plate, hitting a homer and driving in 2 runs.

It was Nelson's last hurrah. In 1961, he hit below .200 and was released by Pittsburgh. His career statistics in the majors were a .249 batting average with 31 home runs and 173 RBI. He had an excellent control of the strike zone, striking out only 94 times in 1,394 times at bat while walking on 130 occasions. This suggests that he was a defensive hitter at the major league level and a more aggressive hitter in the minors. He finished his career the following year with the Toronto Maple Leafs of the International League, where he had recorded some of his finest years. The local fans loved him and speculated that perhaps he tried too hard when he had a shot at the majors. Unlike most of the others reviewed in this chapter, he was not a defensive liability.

In any case, the fact is that in between disappointing major league assignments, he put together a fabulous minor league career, leading the International League in batting twice, home runs four times, and RBI three times, including Triple-Crown titles in 1955 for the Montreal Royals and 1958 for the Toronto Maple Leafs. Between 1953 and 1958, Rocky played in five full International League seasons, averaging 36 home runs and 120 RBI per season. His lifetime minor league batting average was .319 in 5,032 at-bats with 234 home runs and 1,009 RBI. He was selected International League MVP three times, a feat no one else has accomplished.

Buzz Arlett

Russell "Buzz" Arlett broke into professional baseball as a pitcher with the Oakland Oaks in 1918. He was a big right-handed spitballer standing 6'3" and weighing north of 225 pounds, and between 1918 and 1922 he would establish himself as one of the better pitchers in the PCL, compiling a 99–80 record. While Arlett never hit over .300 as a full-time pitcher, he did hit with authority, and in 1923, after suffering arm trouble, he moved to the outfield.

Given the opportunity to hit on a full-time basis, Arlett thrived at the plate. He was a switch-hitter who hit with power and had an excellent strikeout-to-walk ratio. In his first season as an outfielder, he batted .330 and drove in 101 runs in 149 games. Arlett, however, did not take to his outfield duties with such alacrity, and developed a reputation as a lackadaisical fielder with poor range. Because of the long PCL season, Arlett's home run and run production statistics are sometimes discounted, but his hitting statistics stand scrutiny. During his eight seasons as a full-time outfielder with the Oaks, Arlett batted .355 and averaged 103 runs scored, 192 hits, 44 doubles, 8 triples, 25 home runs, and 126 RBI per 154-game season. Notwithstanding Arlett's fine hitting statistics, it must be pointed out that the PCL was a hitter's league, and during his eight-year stint as an outfielder he would only lead the PCL in doubles twice, triples once, and RBI once.

Arlett finally got to the majors in 1931 at the age of 32 when his contract was purchased by the Philadelphia Phillies. Sharing the Baker Bowl outfield with Chuck

Klein, Arlett had a good season for the Phillies, batting .313 with 18 home runs and finishing in the National League's top five in both home runs and slugging percentage. Despite this success, the Phillies did not renew Arlett's contract and he was forced back to the minors after a single season.

Arlett would split the next five seasons between the Baltimore Orioles of the International League (1932 to 1933) and the Minneapolis Millers of the American Association (1934 to 1936), experiencing a renaissance as a power hitter. During his two seasons in Baltimore, Arlett won back-to-back home run titles, stroking 93 roundtrippers and driving home 290 runs. Upon moving to Minneapolis in 1934, Arlett would capture another home run title, hitting 41 home runs in only 116 games. Over the five-year swan song of his minor league career, Arlett hit .337 while averaging 43 home runs and 141 RBI per 154-game season.

Curiously, Arlett's post–major league career path exactly parallels that of Joe Hauser. Both played for the Baltimore Orioles for two seasons upon leaving the majors and both won back-to-back IL home run titles during those seasons— Hauser in 1930 and 1931, Arlett in 1932 and 1933. Both went to the Minneapolis Millers following Baltimore. Hauser won the AA home run title in his first two seasons in Minneapolis, 1932 and 1933, while Arlett won the AA home run crown in his first season in Minneapolis, 1934. Arlett and Hauser, who were both born in January 1899, would play as teammates on the Millers between 1934 and 1936 and both end their AAA careers in 1936.

After his career, Arlett managed unsuccessfully in the low minors for several years and then returned to Minneapolis to continue with the rest of his life. He was a major league–caliber hitter who never got a fair shot at the majors. His major league career was held ransom by the gap between what the owners of the Oakland Oaks wanted for their drawing card and what the major leagues were willing to pay for another weak-fielding PCL phenom. By the time Arlett got to the majors, he was 32 years old, overweight, and had lost any chance to be considered a prospect. His minor league career, however, stands on its own merit. Arlett was the best ballplayer in Oakland, Baltimore, and Minneapolis over a 16-year period, and that's not too bad.

Smead Jolley

Smead "Smudge" Jolley was a counterpoint to Ike Boone—a baseball-playing gypsy who carried a magic bat while playing for 14 different teams in 11 different leagues. Like Boone, Jolley won batting titles, winning three in the Pacific Coast League, one in the International League, and two in the Class B Western International League. Like Boone, Jolley was a terrible fielder.

Jolley was a tall, awkward country boy who between 1922 and 1925 worked his way from the Cotton States League to the San Francisco Seals of the Pacific Coast

League as a pitcher-outfielder. While Jolley was a mediocre pitcher, winning as many as he lost, he was a terrific hitter, and after the 1926 season the hitting finally won out. Upon becoming a full-time outfielder, Jolley terrorized PCL pitching between 1927 and 1929, batting .396 while averaging 116 runs scored, 240 hits, 41 doubles, 31 home runs, and 141 RBI per 154-game season. During that three-year period, he would lead the PCL in hits twice, batting average twice, home runs once, and RBI twice, and win the Triple Crown in 1928.

After the 1929 season, Jolley's contract was bought by the Chicago White Sox. During his four-year major league career, his defensive ineptitude became the stuff of legend; however, both the White Sox and later the Boston Red Sox struggled to find a way to keep his bat in the lineup. Chicago, after watching him struggle in the outfield for more than two seasons, attempted to convert him into a catcher on the basis that his lack of range wouldn't be a factor, but gave up the experiment when it became apparent that he might be seriously hurt trying to catch a pitched ball. A repeated story asserts that Jolley made three errors on a single play during his final season in Boston. As the story goes, while playing outfield Jolley let a single roll through his legs, muffed the ball off the wall, and then threw wildly when sending the ball back to the infield. Despite his misadventures in the field, Jolley hit well during his four years in the majors, batting .305 and averaging 15 home runs and 102 RBI per 154-game season.

After his major league career, Jolley played six more years in the Pacific Coast League and the International League, winning batting titles in 1936 for Albany in the IL and in 1938 for Hollywood in the PCL. In 1940, he dropped down to Class B ball and won back-to-back batting titles for Spokane in the Western International League. Like Boone, Jolley was a one-dimensional player who couldn't stick in the majors despite solid hitting statistics. He finished his minor league career with a .366 lifetime batting average, the third-highest in minor league history.

Lou Novikoff

Novikoff played harmonica, was fluent in Russian, fed his Russian wolfhound caviar while he fed himself cabbage, and won four consecutive minor league batting titles: .367 for Moline of the Three-I League in 1938, .368 for Tulsa of the Texas League in 1939, a Triple Crown for L.A. of the Pacific Coast League in 1940 (41 home runs, 171 RBI, and .363 with 259 hits), and .370 for Milwaukee of the American Association in 1941.

But the Mad Russian was wrapped a bit too tight for the big leagues when he arrived in 1941. In fact, he blamed his troubles with the Cubs on tight-fitting uniforms, crooked foul lines, and the ivy on the outfield wall. He stole third base with the bases loaded, and struck out on a pitch over his head with the bases loaded to avoid being fined for a called third strike.

Novikoff lasted until 1946 in the big leagues, then found his true calling when he started playing softball. You'll find him in *that* sport's Hall of Fame.

Other great minor league hitters include Ox Eckhardt, a tall slap-hitting Texan who, besides playing in the National Football League, compiled a .367 career minor league batting average in 14 seasons; Bunny Brief, a slick-fielding eight-time minor league home run champion who was consistently unimpressive in his opportunities to make the majors; Nick Cullop, who slammed 420 career minor league home runs but struck out too often in his brief trials in the majors; and the 5′7″, 150-pound Jigger Statz, who collected 3,356 hits in the minors and another 737 in the majors—including 209 in 1923 for the Cubs — good for 4,093 for his career.

Finally, no dissertation on the subject of minor league hitters would be complete without mention of Joe Bauman. He was not in the same category as the group we've discussed, playing almost exclusively in the low minors—but see what you think.

Joe Bauman

In July of 1947, something occurred near Roswell, New Mexico, that has come to be known as the "Roswell incident." It is alleged that an extraterrestrial vehicle and its alien occupants crashed and were recovered. The Air Force denies this and provides evidence that it never happened. Nevertheless, the controversy rages, and Roswell continues to cash in on its notoriety by hosting get-togethers for UFO fans, Trekkies, and other conspiracy theorists.

In the summer of 1954, another incident occurred in Roswell that was a little more down to earth. Joe Bauman, playing for the Roswell Rockets in the Longhorn League (Class C), had probably the greatest season in the history of professional baseball. Joe hit 72 homers. Not only that, but he batted .400 and knocked in 224 runs while scoring 188 runs himself. He walked 150 times and had an awesome slugging average of .916. This stupendous feat was achieved in only 138 games.

Joe had played AAA ball in the American Association in 1948, but that was the highest level he ever achieved. Maybe if he hadn't lost four years of his career to World War II, things might have been different. He was and is a big man (6′5″, 235 pounds) and is still alive and well and living in Roswell. He is now the only person in professional baseball, living or dead, to have hit more home runs in a season than Mark McGwire.

Other minor league players whose records fell to McGwire's onslaught were Joe Hauser, who hit 69 homers with Minneapolis of the American Association (1933) and 63 with Baltimore of the International League (1930); Bob Crues, 69 with Amarillo of the West Texas–New Mexico League (1948); Dick Stuart, 66, with Lincoln of the Western League (1956); Bob Lennon, 64, with Nashville of the

Southern Association (1954); and Ken Guettler, 62, with Shreveport of the Texas League (1956).

It is interesting to note that when Roger Maris hit his 61st homer out of the ballpark, he not only erased the Babe's record but also the Pacific Coast League record of Tony Lazzeri, who hit 60 for Salt Lake City in 1925. Two of Murderers' Row in one stroke of the bat. A good day's work!

OTHER INTERESTING MINOR LEAGUE HITTING PERFORMANCES

The Yankee Clipper's record for hitting safely in 56 consecutive games is often described as the safest record in baseball. Many feel it will never be broken, and it has never been seriously challenged at the major league level. It should, however, be pointed out that it has already been broken at the minor league level. In 1933, a player with the San Francisco Seals of the Pacific Coast League had a hitting streak that ran for 61 games. The 18-year-old ballplayer's name . . . Joe DiMaggio.

Another young player, 19-year-old Babe Ruth, played only one year in the minors. In that one year, 1914, he distinguished himself as a fine pitcher (22–9) and led the International League in winning percentage with .710. The Red Sox called him up to the majors for a month in midsummer and again for good in September, so his minor league career wasn't even a full season. During the season, his team, the Providence Grays, had noticed that the Babe handled the bat rather well and they gave him a few starts in the outfield and at first base. He only hit one home run for the Grays, but it was his first in organized baseball.

That home run was hit in Toronto against the Maple Leafs, and the ball (or what was purported to be the ball) many years later wound up in the Canadian Sports Hall of Fame. That anyone had the prescience to save a pitcher's first and only homer is questionable. It wouldn't have been the first piece of fake baseball memorabilia, but it was autographed and could have been authentic. More likely it was a foul ball that Ruth, who hurled a one-hit shutout, was asked to sign as the winning pitcher. The issue was rendered academic during the '60s when someone stole the ball and reputedly threw it into Lake Ontario. The Babe's widow donated one of his authentic home run balls to the Hall as a substitute.

Another interesting fact is that the minor leagues integrated before the majors. In 1946, Branch Rickey's Brooklyn Dodgers farmed out a newly signed player to the Montreal Royals of the International League. He was Jackie Robinson, the first black man to play in organized baseball since the turn of the century. Rickey knew that the pressures on Robinson would be intense and reckoned that in Canada, the terminus of the Underground Railroad, he would not face the stress of racism in home games at least. His other purpose in sending him to Montreal was to assure that he had the character and ability to succeed in the majors. He amply showed both, as he ignored overt racism from other teams and led the league in batting at .349.

Baseball Before 1947

Major league baseball was not "major league" baseball until 1947 (and given the slowness of the integration process, probably not even that until sometime in the 1960s or 1970s). The systematic exclusion of black players from the major leagues prior to 1947 substantially weakened the quality of play and lowered the competitive balance. This is not to say that prior to integration the American League and the National League were not the two best baseball leagues going—they were—but they were not as good as they could be or as good as they would be. The exclusion of black players meant that a portion of each major league team's roster was filled by players who were AAA-caliber at best and whose true calling was to chase fly balls for the Oakland Oaks or bat leadoff for the Newark Bears or be the number-2 starter for the Sacramento Solons. The inclusion of black players in the major leagues would have sent this bottom quartile packing and improved the competitive balance by eliminating the easy outs and punching bags that the major leaguers fattened their statistics against.

In his 10 major league seasons, Jackie Robinson led the Brooklyn Dodgers to six World Series appearances.

The stars of the all-white major leagues would in most cases still have been stars in an integrated league. The inclusion of black players would not have prevented Babe Ruth from hitting an astounding number of home runs. The pitching he faced would have improved somewhat with Bill Foster, Jose Mendez, Bullet Joe Rogan, and others joining the professional hurlers' fraternity; however, Ruth would still have hit home runs in bunches. The exclusion of black players, however, certainly prevented the power hitters of the Negro Leagues from having the opportunity to be prolific home run hitters at the major league level.

On April 15, 1947, major league baseball was truly born as Jackie Robinson made his debut at first base with the Brooklyn Dodgers and became the first black man to play in the major leagues since Moses and Welday Walker toiled for the Toledo Blue Stockings of the American Association in 1884.

Following in the wake of Jackie Robinson, Negro League stars like Monte Irvin, Sam Jethroe, and Roy Campanella were able to join the major leagues for short careers. Unfortunately, integration did not come soon enough for most. The lack of reliable statistical information regarding the careers of Negro League players has made direct comparisons with major league players difficult. As time passes and memories fade, players are defined more and more by their statistical legacy. In the absence of a statistical legacy, Negro League players have become shadowy figures excluded from discussions or lists of the all-time greats because of a lack of evidence. What empirical evidence does exist, however, weighs heavily on the side of the Negro League stars. Since integration, black players have excelled in the major leagues, providing the game with many of its brightest stars. There can be little doubt that given the opportunity to play in the major leagues, Josh Gibson, Buck Leonard, Mule Suttles, Turkey Stearnes, Oscar Charleston, and the other stars of the Negro Leagues would have stood shoulder to shoulder with the likes of Babe Ruth, Lou Gehrig, Jimmie Foxx, and Hank Greenberg.

John Henry Lloyd

The dominant hitter in Negro League baseball in the early twentieth century was a tall, rangy shortstop named John Henry Lloyd. In the practice of his time, Lloyd was a line-drive hitter with excellent bat control who "'hit 'em where they ain't." In the white press, he was referred to as the "black Honus Wagner" to give a shorthand description of his skill set and talent level; however, to the black fans he was simply "Pop," while to Cuban fans he was "Cuchara" or "Scoop." As the quality of baseballs improved, Lloyd became more of a power hitter and actually led the Negro National League in home runs in 1928 at the age of 44!

While Lloyd was the top hitter in Negro League baseball, the most influential man was a pitcher, Rube Foster. Foster, a player-manager, entered the ownership ranks by founding the Chicago American Giants in 1911 with financial backing from Charles Comiskey's son-in-law. He then became a league builder in 1920 by founding the Negro National League, a Midwest loop that featured teams in such cities as Chicago, St. Louis, Detroit, and Kansas City. Foster's goal was to put black baseball on an organized footing and raise its standing in order to speed the process of integration. The success of the Negro National League, however, gave birth to imitators, and the Eastern Colored League formed in the Northeast, followed by the Negro Southern League.

The organized black leagues in the 1920s were somewhat haphazard affairs with uneven schedules and short seasons. Due to the impoverished nature of their clientele, most teams continued to rely on barnstorming as their main source of income. Despite this, the organized black leagues served their primary purpose as many young players were developed and the leagues' top players garnered national reputations. The great hitters of black baseball during the 1920s included Oscar

Charleston and Turkey Stearnes, along with such notables as Martin Dihigo, Judy Johnson, Dick Lundy, Biz Mackey, and Cristobal Torriente.

Oscar Charleston

Oscar Charleston, the "Hoosier Comet," was a stocky left-handed–hitting outfielder who combined power and speed. He was a forerunner of Albert Belle and intimidated opponents with his strength and famous mean streak that revealed itself in a penchant for running over middle infielders. Charleston hit for a high average, winning several batting titles, and was also a consistent power hitter, leading the Negro National League in home runs on several occasions.

Turkey Stearnes

Like Joe Morgan or Mel Ott, Turkey Stearnes was a small man who hit home runs. Stearnes, who batted with an odd open stance, won seven home run crowns and is the holder of the all-time Negro League career home run mark with 171 roundtrippers. Despite his excellent power, Stearnes, who also led the Negro Leagues in batting on four occasions, spent much of his career in the leadoff spot due to his speed and ability to get on base.

With the advent of the 1930s and the Depression, organized black baseball collapsed with only the financially sound traveling teams like the Homestead Grays, the Cuban Stars, and the Kansas City Monarchs remaining solvent. The center of black baseball shifted to Pittsburgh, where Cumberland Posey's Homestead Grays and Gus Greenlee's Pittsburgh Crawfords began to accumulate talent. The Negro National League reemerged in 1933 under Greenlee's guidance, with the Negro American League forming in 1937. This structure remained stable until the integration of major league baseball took fan interest away from the Negro Leagues.

The 1930s and 1940s saw a renaissance of sorts occur within black baseball, with many great hitters taking the field. Among the greatest players who never donned major league uniforms were Cool Papa Bell, Josh Gibson, and Buck Leonard, along with other celebrated performers such as Ray Dandridge, Mule Suttles, and Willie Wells.

Cool Papa Bell

Cool Papa Bell was a forerunner of the artificial turf players of the 1970s. A stringbean at 5'11" and 150 pounds, Bell switch-hit and used his blinding speed both to get on base and to steal bases. Bell had extremely good bat control and was able to compile one of the highest career batting averages in Negro League history.

Josh Gibson

Josh Gibson was a natural home run hitter with awesome Mark McGwire–type power. He joined the Homestead Grays at age 17 and immediately began to hit tape-measure shots while maintaining an exceptionally high batting average. Gibson was a broad and powerful man, standing 6′1″ and weighing over 200 pounds. A right-handed batter, he stood flat-footed in the batter's box and generated his power from the hips with a no-step swing. It is clear that Gibson's contemporaries were in awe of his abilities. Between 1937 and 1945, Gibson would team with Buck Leonard as the Negro Leagues' "Ruth-Gehrig" combination, bringing nine straight Negro National League pennants to the Homestead Grays.

Buck Leonard

Buck Leonard, the second half of the Homestead Grays' "Ruth-Gehrig" combination, was a fearsome line-drive hitter who consistently batted over .320. Leonard, a left-handed hitter, batted cleanup, protecting Gibson in the batting order, and had his best year in 1939 when he led the Negro National League in both batting average and home runs.

With the breaking of the color barrier by Jackie Robinson in 1947, fan interest in the Negro Leagues began to wane as young black players were scouted by the major leagues and drafted into the minor leagues. By the early 1950s, a few traveling teams like the Indianapolis Clowns were the only vestiges of "Jim Crow" baseball. Unfortunately, the integration of the major leagues did not result in a torrent of black players entering the big leagues. With second-division franchises like the Philadelphia Athletics, St. Louis Browns, and Washington Senators seemingly consigned to mediocrity, this new talent pool was a golden opportunity for these teams to reverse the tides of history, but major league baseball did not act boldly. Instead, teams moved timidly, with a few exceptions, such that by the end of 1953 half of the major league teams had yet to sign a black player to a major league contract.

Ray Dandridge

Perhaps the saddest tale in this regard is Ray Dandridge, the smooth-fielding and fine-hitting third baseman of the Newark Eagles who was drafted in 1949 at age 36 by the New York Giants and assigned to their Minneapolis Millers farm team in the American Association. Dandridge would win the American Association's Rookie of the Year award in 1949 and cop its MVP award in 1950, and would struggle on until 1955 but would never merit a call-up to the big club.

Mo Vaughn, who won the American League MVP award in 1995, is one of the last major leaguers to wear Jackie Robinson's number 44, retired by baseball in 1997.

Since 1947, black players have more than proven their competitive abilities and provided the major leagues with roughly half of its great hitters, including 7 of 13 500-homer men, 8 of 16 3,000-hit men, and 17 of 33 lifetime .300 batting averages. Black players have starred on many of baseball's top teams such as the Toronto Blue Jays of the early 1990s who won back-to-back World Series championships with Roberto Alomar, Devon White, Joe Carter, and Dave Winfield playing key roles, or the New York Yankees of the late 1970s, who won back-to-back World Series championships featuring Chris Chambliss, Willie Randolph, Roy White, Mickey Rivers, and Reggie Jackson.

Given the proportion of black players among post–World War II baseball's elite, the worm turns and the question is no longer whether or not Josh Gibson and Cool Papa Bell belong among the all-time greats. Instead, the question becomes just how weak were the pre–World War II major leagues as a result of the color barrier? Try to imagine post–World War II baseball without Willie Mays, Hank Aaron, Frank Robinson, Willie McCovey, Ernie Banks, Joe Morgan, Reggie Jackson, Willie Stargell, Roberto Clemente, Eddie Murray, Rod Carew, Tony Gwynn, Dave Winfield, Barry Bonds, Rickey Henderson, Lou Brock, Andre Dawson, Frank Thomas, Sammy Sosa, Juan Gonzalez, Albert Belle, Mo Vaughan, Ken Griffey Jr., and hundreds of other black athletes who have played in the major leagues over the past 50 years, and you will begin to suspect that the answer is "much weaker."

THE HOW AND THE WHY

14

Walk Softly and Carry a Big Stick

The Evolution of the Bat

"The first step in hitting is to find the right bat."

—MICKEY MANTLE

Throughout its history, baseball has undergone many changes. Rules, for example, have been adjusted to alter the balance of pitching and hitting. Up until 1887, pitchers could throw seven balls before a batter was issued a base on balls. In 1969, the mound was lowered from 15 inches to 10 inches after Boston's Carl Yastrzemski won the American League batting title with a .301 average. And in 1973, the AL adopted the designated hitter rule in hopes of generating more offense for fans.

Other changes have made an impact on the game as well. The beloved Brooklyn Dodgers packed their bags and moved to Los Angeles. An artificial playing surface called Astroturf was installed in several major league stadiums and had an enormous effect on game play and strategy. The New York Yankees, arguably the most revered organization in the history of American sports, changed managers 21 times from 1973 to 1996 under the ownership of "the Boss," George Steinbrenner.

One aspect of the game—at least at the professional level—that has remained relatively unchanged is the baseball bat. Or has it? Hitters have walked up to the plate carrying a bat since the game began in the mid-1800s, but today's bats are not made with the hewn hunks of hickory that they first swung. Bats have been subject to ceaseless experimentation—flattened, rounded, lengthened, shortened, end-loaded, balanced, lightened, thickened, thinned, darkened, boned, and corked. Some hitters, such as major league outfielder Ellis Burks, even change bats depending on the pitcher they're facing. "If I'm facing a pitcher who throws hard, I'll use a lighter bat," says Burks. "If it's a guy who throws a lot of offspeed junk like a knuckleballer, I think it's better to have a bat that's a little heavier."

Hitting a Round Ball with a Flat Bat?

In 1885, a rule stated, "A portion of one side of the bat may be flat instead of round." Think of how easy it must have been to make square contact back in those days. The rule changed in 1893 to, "The bat must be completely round."

Players have done everything from sleeping with their bats to hammering nails in the barrel. Through it all, one element has remained consistent: the type of wood used to make a bat. White ash has always been the predominant material used in wooden baseball bats. It has the ideal combination of strength, resiliency, and density. Early on, some bats were made of hickory because its density yields heavier bats. But players soon realized that it was often difficult to maintain an efficient swing with a heavy piece of lumber. Other woods were also tested in an experimental phase, but white ash has never been unseated as the best wood for bats.

Browning's Broken Bat Baits Bradsby

The first Hillerich & Bradsby Louisville Slugger bat was made for Pete "the Gladiator" Browning. Browning was a star for Louisville's Eclipse team of the old American Association in 1884. He was hitting .341 when his favorite bat broke. John Andrew "Bud" Hillerich was at the game and invited Browning to his father's woodworking shop.

Browning and Hillerich picked out a piece of white ash and began fashioning the bat to Browning's specifications. Throughout the night, Hillerich had Browning take practice swings until he proclaimed the bat just right. The Hillerich bat business was born.

Despite the protestations of his father, J. Frederich Hillerich, Bud Hillerich continued making bats. It became a major part of the business after the turn of the century. On September 5, 1905, Honus Wagner signed a contract giving the J. F. Hillerich and Son company permission to use his autograph on Louisville Slugger bats.

Heavy Bats Produce Heavy Swings

Bats used in the early 1900s were longer and heavier than those used today. Handles were thicker to help lengthen the life of the bat. A player could go through an entire season using just a few bats. In an average season today, major league teams purchase approximately seven dozen bats per player.

Thicker handles also forced hitters to swing the bat in a more conservative manner, rather than whipping it through the strike zone. Swings were generated by the hitter's hands and arms, and did not fully engage the hip and shoulder (rotation) or back and abdomen (coiling and uncoiling).

Hitting styles were much different during the deadball era (1900–19) than today: contact was king. Hitting the ball for power by swinging the bat aggressively was taken as a sign of stupidity. Swinging and missing a pitch was considered embarrassing, and strikeouts were perceived as humiliating events. The approach of Ty Cobb epitomized the hitting technique during this period. Cobb used a big bat, choked up, and focused on making contact. Bat control was the skill that separated great hitters from mediocre hitters. As Wee Willie Keeler said, "Hit 'em where they ain't."

A young pitcher-outfielder named George Herman Ruth spun Keeler's famous quote a bit differently. Ruth's response to Keeler was, "Well, they ain't on the other side of the fence." The player's approach to hitting a baseball changed forever with the emergence of Ruth; he introduced the power game to baseball. Ruth was said to have used a 54-ounce bat early in his career. When he hit 60 home runs in 1927, Ruth wielded a 36-inch, 40-ounce bat. More important, Ruth presented a new hitting style and different type of swing. He took violent, thunderous cuts at the ball, sending it great distances. Hitters around the league were enamored with Ruth's new approach at the plate (not to mention his paycheck). Bats with big barrels and thinner handles allowed hitters to more easily copy Ruth's swing. Bats soon became more personalized than ever before.

Anything for a Few Extra Knocks

Through the years, players have attempted to treat their bats to gain an advantage. Old-timers often "boned" their bats by rubbing the barrel with ham bones. Sometimes hitters would illegally hammer nails into the hitting area so that the ball would strike "iron."

Then there is "corking": Players drill a half-inch–diameter hole anywhere from 8 to 14 inches deep into the flat end of the bat. The hole is then filled with cork or a free-floating drop of mercury or superballs to deaden the hollow sound that would otherwise result. According to physicists, corking is a waste of a hitter's time. A hollowed-out bat may be lighter, but it won't help you hit the ball farther or with greater consistency.

Different wood finishes have been developed. Some give the bat more durability. Others influence the color of the bat and provide a psychological advantage. Darker bats are popular under lights because the bat is less visible to the fielders as well as umpires (for check swings).

According to the rules, bats must be no longer than 42 inches in length with a maximum diameter of 2¾ inches. While hitters during Cobb's and Ruth's playing days swung bats in the range of 36 to 42 ounces, players today use 31- to 33-ounce bats. Lighter bats are easier to control. Better bat control equates to more consistent contact and makes a better all-around hitter. Some argue that the loss in bat mass (weight) reduces power. But the loss in mass is offset by the increased bat speed. The player is able to hit the ball just as far, and with greater consistency.

The only drawback is that bats break or crack with greater frequency today. Although the wood remains strong, the design of the bat decreases life span. Lighter bats with thinner handles are weaker and less likely to survive a Roger Clemens heater that misses the sweet spot.

The Aluminum Bat

Anytime baseball bats are discussed, the aluminum bat works its way into the conversation. Aluminum bats were developed in the 1970s to replace wooden bats in amateur baseball leagues. They are used from Little League levels right up through college baseball. Professional leagues still only use wooden bats.

Aluminum bats were first developed because of their durability. A metal bat can last over a few seasons, where a wood bat may last only a day. Although one aluminum bat is much more expensive than one wood bat, the long-term economics still weigh heavily in favor of metal. Unfortunately, the combination of technology and competing bat companies has created a controversy.

Cost of Aluminum Versus Wood for a Collegiate Baseball Team (One Season)

Bat	Cost of bat	Bats per season	Total cost
Aluminum	$200	8	$1600
Wood	$30	15 dozen	$5400

Why Baseball Purists Despise Aluminum

The intentions behind developing aluminum bats were good. As some see it, the problem came to pass when technology became too good. Baseball purists adamantly argue that aluminum bats have had an adverse effect on the game.

Aluminum bats are typically lighter than wood bats. They are hollow inside and are made from a lightweight alloy. This allows for a wide (2¾-inch barrel), lightweight bat. Typical aluminum bat specifications may be 2¾-inch barrel, 33 inches, 28 ounces. The sweet spot can be made larger, which grants larger room for error. In other words, a ball that hits below the sweet spot on a wood bat may result in a weak fly ball to the outfield. Hit the same pitch on the same location of the bat using aluminum (plus add in the increased bat speed), and the ball might sail out of the park.

In a nutshell, the aluminum bat is lighter than wood, made of a stronger material, has the same size barrel, but owns a larger sweet spot. Advantage number one.

The other factor is known as the *trampoline effect.* Because aluminum bats are hollow, the barrel actually gives during impact with the ball, then springs back to shape like a trampoline, propelling the ball at higher speeds and for longer distances.

WHAT THE BASEBALL PURISTS SAY

1. The ball travels farther off an aluminum bat.
2. Because of the larger sweet spot, the ball jumps off the bat even when not ideally struck.
3. Pitchers are afraid to throw inside. Because aluminum bats are so light, hitters are able to whip the bat at high speeds and get the barrel to the ball in time.
4. The trampoline effect allows routine ground balls to shoot through the infield because they are propelled off the bat at higher speeds.
5. The trampoline effect can make it impossible for the pitcher to defend himself from 60 feet away when a line drive is hit off an aluminum bat.

Composite Bats

Taking the safety and the integrity of the game into account, bat companies have begun to develop a new type of bat. "Composite" bats mirror the performance of wooden bats, yet possess the durability of aluminum. They are made with ceramic or Kevlar fibers that are compression molded and said to dampen vibration and add strength . One problem: after repeated impacts, the brittle fibers break down, resulting in inferior performance. Stronger bonding of the fibers would help extend the life (and high-grade performance) of the bat. Because composite bats are even more expensive than aluminum, it is important to the bat companies (and, of course, the consumer) that they possess greater durability.

BAT RACK TRIVIA

1. What was Shoeless Joe Jackson's special nickname for his bat?
2. Hall of Famer George Brett hit a ninth-inning home run off Yankee reliever Goose Gossage in New York. After a protest by New York manager Billy Martin, the homer was disallowed, causing Brett to charge screaming from his dugout. Why was the home run disallowed?
3. What happened to the bat Joe DiMaggio used to tie Wee Willie Keeler's mark of hitting safely in 44 straight games?
4. What former major league player carried a heavy bat around with him everywhere he went in the off-season to help strengthen his wrists?
5. In the 1985 film *The Natural*, Roy Hobbs carried a special bat labeled "Wonderboy." In the final game, Hobbs hits a long foul in the ninth inning. He returns to the plate only to find his bat is broken in two pieces. What is the name of his replacement bat?

Answers
1. Black Betsy
2. The pine tar on his bat was deemed too high according to league specifications.
3. His bat was stolen.
4. Ted Williams
5. Savoy Special

15

Newton at the Bat
The Science of Hitting

All-time baseball slugger Babe Ruth ruminated not at all about the science of hitting a baseball with a wood bat. His approach, reflected in his remark, "All I want to do is give that thing a ride, anywhere," was to simply attack any pitch he thought he could reach with his R-43 model Louisville Slugger.

The Babe, because of his extraordinary strength, actually favored mass over bat speed in his long-ball slugging approach. The Babe's bats, made from the finest Northern white ash, weighed 40 to 54 ounces and measured 36 inches in length. Today's major league sluggers favor bats weighing 31 to 33 ounces, tapered at the handle, all the better to whip the barrel into the approaching ball. Slugging Sammy (Sosa) and Big Mac (McGwire) employ speed where the Babe used mass, or weight, to "give that thing a ride."

Bat + Fast Swing = Long Balls; Heavier Bat + Fast Swing = Longer Balls

If a heavier bat is swung at the same velocity as a light bat and they both hit the ball on the sweet spot, or *center of percussion* (that spot on the bat that gives you most energy exchange into the ball), the heavy bat will hit the ball farther than a light bat.

However, because most people cannot swing a heavier bat as fast, there is a limitation to each batter's ability to generate this type of energy. College players swing their bats at an average swing speed of 65 MPH. Major league players average a bat swing speed of 85 MPH. No one ever recorded the speed of Ruth's swing, but it has been estimated at more than 80 MPH.

The Babe may have been successful at hitting long balls, but he was literally doing a lot of heavy lifting when he needn't have. Because the mass of the bat is so much greater than the mass of the ball, the velocity is a much more significant factor than the mass of the bat. For maximum power, players should use a lighter bat that can be swung faster.

This is the applicable law of physics that can be put to work for you: The more you increase the velocity, the more you increase the effect of the mass. For example, an object that weighs 30 ounces and is swung at 50 MPH is going to be more potent than if it is swung at 40 MPH. The lightest wood bat, made by Louisville Slugger for the Cincinnati Reds' Joe Morgan and the Boston Red Sox's Billy Goodman, weighed 30 ounces. Future baseball Hall of Famer Tony Gwynn has used a Louisville Slugger wood bat weighing 30.5 ounces or 31 ounces. He calls it his "pea-shooter"; in this millennium Tony has shot more than 3,000 peas with his Louisville Slugger model C-263. Bats made any lighter than 30 ounces simply do not have the strength, resiliency, and density that is necessary to hold up against the force of 90-MPH fastballs. They splinter and break too easily.

Trial and error is the best method that a player can use to discover what weight of bat works best—that is, allows for control and sufficient speed of the swing, upwards of at least 80 MPH for those who aspire to play professional baseball. Each athlete is different in size of hands and strength of arms, torso, and lower body, so each must experiment to match the weight and length of the bat to his individual abilities.

The Ball-Bat Collision

Extraordinary things happen to a baseball when it undergoes a collision with the bat. Robert Adair, Yale University physicist, explains:

> A baseball hitting a bat gets severely compressed. It may be flattened to about half its original size. As it is leaving the bat, however, it instantly springs back into shape. The energy generated by this adds speed to the ball. If the pitch comes in at 90 MPH, the hit will go back out at about 110 MPH.

The collision is not entirely elastic. Much of the energy of the colliding ball and bat is dissipated in frictional heat. However, significantly large forces, reaching as high as 8,000 pounds, are required to change the motion of a 5⅛-ounce baseball from a speed of 90 MPH toward the plate to a speed of more than 100 MPH toward the center-field bleachers, all in the one-thousandth of a second that the ball makes contact with a wood bat. In this millisecond, the ball is compressed to one-half of its original diameter, pancaked on the bat, while the bat, which also has properties of elasticity, is compressed to about one-fiftieth as much.

The speed of the pitched ball is also significant in determining the distance of a batted ball. Its role is demonstrated in the adage, "The harder they come in, the harder they go out." Consider this: according to tests conducted by the makers of Louisville Slugger bats, one would have to hit a stationary ball off a tee 50 percent faster with a bat in order to get the same distance as one would if that ball were coming in at 90 MPH.

Weathering the Hits

Heat can definitely give a batted ball more air time, and thus turn a gapper off the wall into a four-bagger. If two different balls reach a velocity of 147 feet per second after impact, and each leaves the bat at a 30-degree angle to the horizontal plane, but one is hit on a warm 95-degree (Fahrenheit—F) day and the other is struck at night when the air has chilled to 50 degrees F, the results will be different.

In the first scenario, the air density would be 0.071 pounds per cubic foot. After 1 second of flight time, the velocity of the ball decreases to 120 feet per second (ft/sec). After 4 seconds in the air, the ball is going 78 ft/sec. It completes its arc and hits the bleachers 360 feet from home plate (in one of Camden Yards' short-porch power alleys)—a homer.

In the second scenario, the air density is thick—0.077 pounds per cubic foot. The ball starts out at the same velocity, 147 ft/sec, but gravity and drag quickly take hold, and after 1 second it slows to 117 ft/sec.

When the ball hits terra firma, if not the glove of a pursuing outfielder, the ball is only 345 feet from home plate, 15 feet short of the daytime blast. Clearly, temperature and air density can dramatically affect the outcome of a well-struck ball. So can changes in humidity and atmospheric pressure.

Moist air is lighter than dry air. When the weather is dry, barometric pressure rises (more pressure); when stormy, the barometer falls (lower pressure). As air pressure increases and the air gets drier, it contracts and allows more air molecules per cubic foot; hence the air is denser. Altitude makes a big difference in air density. Atmospheric pressure results from the aggregate weight of the air above an object. Therefore, the higher an object, the less "weight" bearing down on it. The density of air in Denver (at 5,200 feet) would be 0.0597 pound per cubic foot at 95 degrees F and 0.0650 at 50 degrees F. Ken Griffey Jr., take note: At either of these temperatures the ball will travel farther in Denver than it does in Seattle (even on a hot day).

Grooved Bat Surface, Increased Backspin, Longer Flight?

The golf community is familiar with this idea: a grooved bat, like a grooved golf club, imparts backspin when it makes contact with the bottom half of the ball.

There is no question that backspin helps a fly ball carry farther, but there is a difference of opinion on whether a grooved bat can impart the necessary backspin. Peter Brancazio, a professor of physics at Brooklyn College, postulates: "I imagine it could add 20 to 30 feet to a 350-foot hit." However, George Manning, a mechanical engineer and vice president of technical services for Hillerich & Bradsby Co., which makes the Louisville Slugger, disagrees. He says that the duration of contact (1.0 to 1.5 milliseconds) between the bat and the ball is insufficient time to increase the backspin and thus alter the flight distance of the ball.

Coefficient of Restitution (COR)

The coefficient of restitution (COR) of a baseball plays a major role in determining how far a ball will travel. This is the ratio of the ball's velocity after a collision (bat striking a pitched ball) to its velocity before a collision. For major league baseballs, this ratio must be between 0.514 and 0.578, plus or minus 3.2 percent, which means that the rebound speed must be 51.5 percent to 57.8 percent of the original speed, plus or minus 3.2 percent. (By comparison, a tennis ball has a COR of 0.67 and a basketball 0.76.)

Here's a simplified look at COR. Assume the number 1 is the maximum capability that you can possibly achieve. If you drop a ball from head height, and it bounces back up to that exact height, then you have achieved the maximum capability, which is 1. There would be no loss of energy in the ball. You might call it the perfect rebound, which is the coefficient of 1.

However, COR never really measures the perfect 1. For a baseball, a more common coefficient would be somewhere around 0.5. Even if you could achieve the perfect rebound of 1, it would never come higher than the height from which you dropped it, assuming it was a free-fall drop and not propelled in any manner.

If you had a ball of putty and you dropped it on the ground, it would just stop as a glob and not rebound; you would have a coefficient of restitution of 0 (zero). If you had something perfectly elastic, it would measure as 1. These are the two extremes.

If you put any additional energy whatsoever on the ball, then you have changed the scenario. For example, if you throw the ball against the ground instead of just dropping it, it will bounce higher. Likewise, a ball can come off the bat faster than it came onto the bat because you are putting energy in from the bat itself (the speed of the swing and mass of the bat). You added something—it is no longer a simple rebound.

Physicists describe a simple rebound as a ball put in play that has been minimally distorted or compressed. Fans would know it as a bunt, the shortest hit in the game of baseball. The Babe, Sammy, and Mac wouldn't be familiar with it at all.

16

From the Baker Bowl to the Green Monster

The Effect of the Ballpark on Hitting

Of the many elements of baseball that make it unique among team sports, the most intriguing is the playing field itself. No other sport allows so much variation in where the lines in the playing surface are drawn. One park can turn fly balls into home runs; another can turn home runs into dazzling running catches; and some parks can do both, depending on whether the ball is pulled or hit the other way.

Such distortions can dramatically skew the numbers put up by a team's offense, change how a lineup goes about its business in *all* of the parks in which it plays, and can delude entire front offices, press corps, and most of a team's fans into thinking it has an offensive juggernaut on its hands.

Though it all begins with dimensions, the distance to the outfield walls is not the only effect a ballpark can have. Each stadium has unique characteristics that influence the outcome of the pitcher versus hitter battle. We routinely use the terms *hitter's park* or *pitcher's park* with an intuitive sense as to their meaning, but the variety of factors that can play a role in creating a hitter's park or a pitcher's park are many and complex—and they are all covered here.

Dimensions

The dimensions of the playing field have a clear impact. Obviously it was easier for a right-handed batter to hit a home run at the Polo Grounds, which measured 258 feet to the left-field foul pole, than it was at Griffiths Stadium, which measured 402 feet down the left-field foul line. Similarly, Camden Yards' 7-foot–high left-field fence attracts more home runs than the Metrodome's 23-foot–high right-field fence. What is often less understood is that small dimensions also reduce the area that must be covered by the outfielders and therefore reduce the number of hits that drop between them. This is why some smaller ballparks that have a substantial positive impact on home runs have a much less profound effect on runs scored. A good example of this was Sportsman's Park in St. Louis, which increased home runs by about 40 percent over a neutral park but only increased runs scored by about 12 percent. The converse of this is a large park, which reduces home runs but because of its expansive outfield becomes a happy hunting ground for line-drive hitters. Forbes Field in Pittsburgh is a good example of a park that favored slap hitters and line-drive hitters. Perhaps the most important factor, however, is the size of foul territory, which is inversely related to hitting. A small foul territory like Fenway Park's or Wrigley Field's will allow many foul balls that might have been caught in other parks to fall harmlessly into the seats and provide the batter with another opportunity to hit safely.

Visibility

Visibility plays a large role in a hitter's ability to pick up the ball out of the pitcher's hand. This is the primary reason why hitting during day games is consistently superior to hitting during night games. No matter how bright or focused the lighting provided for night games, it will create shadows and affect the acuity of the batter's vision. The key factor in determining visibility at a ballpark is the *hitter's background*, which is roughly defined as what is in the batter's field of vision when he looks at the pitcher. During the 1920s, players complained that they couldn't hit in Ebbets Field on Mondays because of the laundry hanging on the balconies of the apartments beyond the center-field fence. During the late '60s and early '70s, many baseball parks addressed the issue of hitter's background by cordoning off the center-field bleacher seats and covering them with a dark tarpaulin. Today, the park with the worst hitter's background is probably Shea Stadium, which has been a long-term home to numerous successful power pitchers like Tom Seaver and Dwight Gooden over its history, but no batting champions.

Climate

Climate factors affect a ballpark's friendliness to hitters. Warm air is less dense than cold air, providing less resistance to fly balls. For this reason, the ball has always carried well at the Big A in Anaheim. Prevailing winds also play a role. Wrigley Field is famous for its changeable winds, which can vary from a cold damp bluster off Lake Michigan to a warm summer breeze blowing out toward its ivy-covered walls. When the winds are blowing in at Wrigley, the park becomes favorable to pitchers and 2–1 scores are not uncommon. With the wind blowing out, Wrigley is a bandbox with extremely reachable power alleys, and high scores become the norm.

Altitude

The admission of the Colorado Rockies to the National League in 1993 has brought into the open one of the most important factors in creating a positive environment for hitting: altitude. As altitude increases, the air thins and reduces the resistance that a baseball encounters when hit or thrown. This effect is much more substantive than the same effect created by warmer air, and has the twin effect of increasing the distance that a hit ball travels and reducing the snap on breaking pitches. So not only does the ball travel better when contacted at altitude, but it is also easier to contact. Prior to the Rockies' first game at Mile High Stadium, Atlanta–Fulton County Stadium (the Launching Pad) at 1,000 feet above sea level was the highest park in major league baseball history and was estimated to have increased home runs by 40 percent over a neutral park during its history.

THE MOST INEFFECTUAL EFFECT

An Italian engineer—let's call him DiMaggio—did the definitive studies of ballistic trajectory back in the fifteenth century. DiMaggio's problem was that city walls could easily be destroyed by cannon fire at point-blank range, but since the defenders also had cannons it was impossible to get into point-blank range without sustaining unacceptable casualties. A way had to be found to lob cannon balls in from a safe distance with reasonable accuracy. These studies are the basis of modern artillery manuals, and on your sightseeing tours of forts you will note that the long-distance cannons are usually set at about 45 degrees, which gives optimal distance.

So what's that mean for baseballs? When a ball leaves a bat at 45 degrees, the horizontal and vertical vectors of velocity are equal. The vertical thrust begins to decrease immediately due to gravity and air friction, while the horizontal thrust is less subject to gravity. Eventually the force of gravity totally overcomes the vertical thrust and the ball accelerates downward, eventually achieving almost the same velocity it had when it left the bat. On the other hand, the horizontal thrust has been steadily slowing. The end result is that the ball is traveling almost straight down at the end of its flight.

The implication: Increasing the height of the outfield fence has relatively little effect on decreasing traditional home runs. Higher fences will reduce the relatively rare line-drive home run. But moving the fence back 5 feet will have a greater effect on fly-ball home runs than increasing the height of the fence from 10 to 60 feet. As any pitcher knows, they call it the Green Monster not because it's so tall, but because it's so close. Red Sox lefty Bill Lee felt it was so close that if it fell down it would crush Rico Petrocelli at short.

So both DiMaggio the engineer and DiMaggio the right-handed slugger would tell you that they can build the fences as high as they like in even Coors Field, but it will do very little to keep the ball in play.

Home Run Parks

The most egregious example of a home run park in the history of baseball is the Victorian folly, Lakefront Park, which was constructed in 1883 by Albert Spalding, the owner of the Chicago White Stockings of the National League.

Lakefront Park was considered the finest park of its time. It could seat 5,000 fans, had 18 private boxes with armchairs and curtains, featured 41 uniformed attendants, and included a pagoda over the main entrance that was occupied by the First Cavalry band during games. But the park was located on a tiny parcel of land next to Lake Michigan, and as a result had the smallest playing field of any major league park ever built. On Opening Day of the 1883 season, its measurements were 186 feet to left field, 280 feet to left-center, 300 feet to dead center, 252 feet to right-center, and 196 feet to right field. To compensate for its small size, Lakefront Park's right-field fence was 37 feet high, and any ball hit over the 6-foot–high left-field fence was a ground rule double. The 1883 White Stockings were an impressive hitting team, including such notables as Cap Anson, Abner Dalrymple, George Gore, King Kelly, Fred Pfeffer, and Ned Williamson; however, the high right-field fence, the left-field ground rule, and the dead 1880s baseball conspired to check their efforts. Despite hitting a league-leading 277 doubles, the White Stockings could only manage 13 home runs during 1883, including 11 home runs in 49 games at Lakefront Park.

Prior to the 1884 season, Spalding eliminated the left-field ground rule, and a ball hit over the left-field fence was counted as a home run. The White Stockings exploded, hitting 131 home runs in 56 games at Lakefront Park to tally 142 home runs for the season, a record that stood until Ruth, Gehrig, and company hit 158 roundtrippers in 1927. The White Stockings outscored the league by a huge margin, averaging 7.4 runs per game compared to a league average of 5.2 runs per game. White Stockings players dominated the season-ending individual hitting statistics, taking the top four spots in the home run derby and the top five spots in the RBI chase while the team finished an ignominious fourth, 22 games out of first place. Ned Williamson, the White Stockings' third baseman, led the league in home runs with 27 dingers, which easily shattered Harry Stovey's existing single-season record of 14 and lasted as the major league mark until 1919, when Babe Ruth slammed 29 homers.

The home run statistics of the White Stockings and its big four of Williamson, Pfeffer, Anson, and Dalrymple was entirely the result of Lakefront Park's tiny dimensions. Home-road splits were as follows:

	Home	Road	Total
Ned Williamson	25	2	27
Fred Pfeffer	25	0	25
Abner Dalrymple	18	4	22
Cap Anson	20	1	21
Rest of the team	43	4	47
Total	131	11	142

It is estimated that Lakefront Park increased home runs by 380 percent over a neutral park. This is a figure that has never been approached by any other major league ballpark, and makes anything that has happened or might happen at Coors Field seem positively restrained. Interestingly, because of its small playing surface, Lakefront Park cut down on singles, doubles, and triples to such a degree that it only increased runs scored by approximately 20 percent over neutral parks. After the 1884 season the White Stockings moved to West Side Park, with a capacity of 10,000, and Lakefront Park became a footnote to baseball history.

After the demise of Lakefront Park, the Baker Bowl was the next great hitter's park to be built for major league baseball. The Baker Bowl, a wood and concrete stadium, was constructed in 1895 by William Baker, the owner of the Philadelphia Phillies, to house his National League club, which it did until July of 1938. Like many urban ballparks, the Baker Bowl was constrained by the city block on which it was built. Located north of Penn Square, the prominent features of the Baker Bowl were its extremely short right-field power alley and a hump that ran through center field to accommodate a Pennsylvania & Reading Railroad tunnel that ran under the ballpark. The Baker Bowl's dimensions were 335 feet up the left-field foul line, 408 feet to dead center, 300 feet to right-center field, and 280 feet up the right-field foul line. In an attempt to prevent cheap home runs, the right-field fence, made of tin over brick, was 40 feet high from the right-field foul line to right-center and 35 feet high from right-center to center field. Later, in 1915, when Gavvy Cravath began to regularly lob fly balls over the right-field fence, William Baker became alarmed that his Phillies might begin to hit too many home runs and ask for salary increases. So he raised the height of the right-field fence to 60 feet from the right-field foul line to right-center and 47 feet from right-center to center field.

Over its 43-year history, the Baker Bowl increased home runs by 60 percent and runs scored by 15 percent over a neutral park. The Phillies, despite being a generally mediocre second-division club, appeared to be hitting terrors, copping 13 team home run titles and 15 individual home run titles during their tenancy. A breakdown of the home-road splits of the Phillies' individual home run champions shows that the vast majority of their home run titles were directly attributable to the Baker Bowl.

	Home	Road	Total
Sam Thompson, 1895	13	5	18
Ed Delahanty, 1896	5	8	13
Gavvy Cravath, 1913	14	5	19
Gavvy Cravath, 1914	19	0	19
Gavvy Cravath, 1915	19	5	24
Gavvy Cravath, 1917	8	4	12
Gavvy Cravath, 1918	8	0	8
Gavvy Cravath, 1919	10	2	12
Cy Williams, 1920	12	3	15
Cy Williams, 1923	26	15	41
Cy Williams, 1927	15	15	30
Chuck Klein, 1929	25	18	43
Chuck Klein, 1931	22	9	31
Chuck Klein, 1932	29	9	38
Chuck Klein, 1933	20	8	28

The player most closely associated with the Baker Bowl is Chuck Klein. Klein, a tall, lanky left-handed batter, played the first six years of his career in the Baker Bowl, posting astounding offensive numbers—leading the National League in hits twice, doubles twice, home runs four times, RBI four times, and batting average once. He would garner over 200 hits in five of those seasons, including 250 or more hits in two seasons, and win the Triple Crown in 1933. Over the six-year period, his home-road splits were enormous.

Home

	GP	BA	AB	R	2B	3B	HR	RBI	OBP	SA
1928	37	.386	145	28	6	3	9	26	.422	.655
1929	71	.391	304	65	25	2	25	78	.434	.734
1930	77	.439	326	91	32	3	26	109	.483	.794
1931	74	.407	297	79	22	7	22	78	.470	.751
1932	77	.423	338	92	26	7	29	97	.469	.799
1933	72	.467	285	62	28	2	20	81	.516	.789
	408	.422	1695	417	139	24	131	469	.470	.764

Road

	GP	BA	AB	R	2B	3B	HR	RBI	OBP	SA
1928	27	.324	108	13	8	1	2	8	.360	.472
1929	78	.321	312	61	20	4	18	67	.382	.583
1930	79	.332	322	67	27	5	14	61	.389	.578
1931	74	.266	297	42	12	3	9	43	.323	.418
1932	77	.266	312	60	24	8	9	40	.334	.481
1933	80	.280	321	39	16	5	8	39	.338	.436
	415	.295	1672	282	107	26	60	258	.354	.498

It should be noted that even Klein's road numbers are somewhat inflated, as the National League batting average was .283 between 1928 and 1933. In 1934, Klein was traded to the Chicago Cubs, and his overall statistics began to look like his road statistics when he played for the Phillies. Klein would return to the Phillies in 1936 and play out the string in both the Baker Bowl and Shibe Park. Over his 17-year career, Klein's 154-game Baker Bowl season was .397 with 44 home runs and 158 RBI, while his 154-game neutral park season was .277 with 18 home runs and 80 RBI. His home-road differential is so stark that it is hard to believe the home and road statistics were generated by the same player. In the Baker Bowl, Klein was the greatest hitter who had ever lived. In neutral parks, he was a medium-range power hitter whose numbers looked a lot like those of Al Cowens or Joe Rudi.

Fenway Park, perhaps the most celebrated ballpark in the world, is renowned as one of the best hitter's parks in the American League. Interestingly, when it was constructed in 1912, Fenway Park was essentially a pitcher's park, but then underwent a significant reconfiguration in 1934 that converted it into an extreme hitter's park. As originally laid out in 1912, Fenway Park had a spacious outfield featuring a right field that outdid the "Death Valley" that would later be constructed in Yankee Stadium. Fenway Park's original dimensions were 324 feet down the left-field foul line, 488 feet to center field, 550 feet to just right of center field, and 313 feet down the right-field foul line. Under this configuration between 1912 and 1933, Fenway Park reduced home runs by almost 50 percent and runs scored by 5 percent when compared to a neutral park.

In 1934, Fenway Park's wooden bleachers on the left- and right-field lines were replaced with concrete and steel grandstands, and home plate and the outfield fences were moved, making the park's new measurements 312 feet down the left-field foul line, 379 feet to left-center field, 389 feet to center field, 420 feet to just right of center field, 380 feet to right-center field, and 334 feet to right field. Additionally, the foul territory was reduced. These changes echoed changes that

The Green Monster at Fenway Park affects the approach of both hitters and pitchers.

had occurred in Forbes Field, Shibe Park, and other parks as major league baseball added to the capacity of its stadiums in the late 1920s and early 1930s. Fenway Park, constrained as it was by Brookline Avenue, Jersey Street, Lansdowne Street, and Van Ness Street, could only reduce the size of its playing surface as amenities and capacity were added.

It is estimated that the reconfigured Fenway Park has increased home runs by 12 percent and runs scored by 14 percent over a neutral park. In the 66 seasons since 1934, the Red Sox have led the league in batting 22 times while Red Sox players, including Jimmie Foxx, Ted Williams, Billy Goodman, Pete Runnels, Carl Yastrzemski, Fred Lynn, Carney Lansford, and Wade Boggs, have grabbed 20 individual batting crowns.

THE FENWAY EFFECT

The two players who most personified the unfortunate glory of the Red Sox during the years since Fenway Park became Fenway Park are Ted Williams and Carl Yastrzemski. Both were tall left-handed batters who played left field and spent their entire careers with the Red Sox. Williams was the Boston left fielder from 1939 to 1960 and passed the torch to Yastrzemski, who played in the shadow of the Green Monster from 1961 to 1983.

Williams, the nonpareil hitter, came up in 1939 from the San Diego Padres in the Pacific Coast League and tore the cover off the ball from day one. Williams hit for high average with excellent power and had awesome strike zone judgment. Over his career, he led the American League in runs scored six times, doubles twice, home runs four times, RBI four times, bases on balls eight times, batting average six times, on-base percentage twelve times, and slugging percentage eight times. He won the Triple Crown twice and is the last player to hit over .400, batting .406 in 1941. Williams's home-road splits show that he hit .361 with 248 home runs and 965 RBI over his career at Fenway Park while batting .328 with 273 home runs and 874 RBI on the road. This works out to a 154-game Fenway Park season of .361 with 33 home runs and 128 RBI and a 154-game neutral park season of .328 with 37 home runs and 119 RBI. Play the games in a parking lot, and he'd put up the same numbers.

Yastrzemski, who debuted in 1961, started more slowly than Williams and did not become a bona fide home run hitter until 1967, when his power statistics surged at the age of 28. He led the American League in runs scored three times, hits twice, doubles three times, home runs once, RBI once, bases on balls twice, batting average three times, on-base percentage five times, and slugging percentage three times, and he was the last American Leaguer to win the Triple Crown. Yastrzemski's home-road splits, however, show a decided home park advantage. Over his career, his 162-game Fenway Park season was .306 with 23 home runs and 103 RBI, while his 162-game neutral park season was .264 with 21 home runs and 78 RBI. Don't play the games at Fenway, and Yastrzemski might not make the Hall of Fame.

Some ballparks increase home runs. Some ballparks increase extra-base hits. Some ballparks increase batting averages. Coors Field, constructed in 1995 as the permanent home of the Colorado Rockies, increases everything, raising home runs by 40 percent, hits by 35 percent, and runs scored by 55 percent over a neutral park. At 5,000 feet above sea level, Coors Field is subject to an enormous altitude effect. Scientists have estimated that the ball carries approximately 11 percent farther in the rarefied air of Denver than it does at sea level. Put another way, a 300-foot fly ball hit in Yankee Stadium would travel 333 feet in Coors Field. To compensate for this effect, Coors Field is a big park and has the largest outfield in the major leagues. It is not, however, nearly large enough (as shown in the following table), and therefore it has a large positive impact on home runs.

	Left Field	Left-Center Field	Center Field	Right-Center Field	Right Field
Neutral park at sea level	330	380	400	380	330
Neutral park at 5,000 feet	366	422	444	422	366
Coors Field	347	390	415	375	350

As a result of Coors Field's spacious dimensions, outfielders have more room to cover, and more balls reach the power alleys, increasing doubles and triples. Also, the outfielders must play deeper because the ball carries well, and therefore more bloop singles are allowed to drop. Finally, as if all this weren't enough to help hitters, the thin air at Coors Field takes the snap out of breaking pitches, robbing hurlers of their major league stuff and making them very hittable.

In Coors Field's short four-year history, the Rockies have put on awesome hitting displays at home, while struggling on the road. Dante Bichette, the poster child for what Coors Field can do, has posted Ruthian numbers at home, hitting .369 with 43 home runs and 168 RBI per 162-game Coors Field season over the past three years, while batting .265 with 19 home runs and 88 RBI per 162-game neutral park season. This pattern of enormous home-road differentials is repeated among all the Colorado regulars. Between 1996 and 1998, the Rockies as a team have hit .330 with 361 home runs at Coors Field while batting only .245 with 245 home runs on the road. In their four seasons at Coors Field, the Rockies have led the National League in batting four times, home runs three times, and runs scored three times. Individually, Rockies players have led the league in batting once, home runs three times, and RBI three times. These numbers suggest that Coors Field is the most extreme hitter's park in the modern era and is only waiting for the right player to don a Rockies uniform before Bob Beamon–type hitting records begin to be set.

The history of the great hitter's parks like the Baker Bowl, Fenway Park, and Wrigley Field—and now Coors Field—has been one of individual heroics and team failure. In its 43-year history, the Baker Bowl was home to one pennant and no world champions. Fenway Park, in the 66 seasons since its reconfiguration, has been the home of four pennants and no world champions. Perhaps saddest of all, Wrigley Field, in its 84 years, has hosted six pennant winners and no world champions. There are many factors suggesting that extreme hitter's parks may ultimately hurt the home side. An extreme hitter's park gives a batter who can take advantage of it superficially impressive statistics. This causes the home team to systematically overrate its hitting talent and not make personnel changes as quickly as required. The converse will occur with respect to its pitching staff, as the home team consistently underestimates its pitching talent and makes many unwarranted personnel changes. The home team's players will develop abilities and strategies that lead to success in the home park, even if these abilities or strategies have a negative impact in a neutral park. For example, a Dante Bichette will learn to hit fly balls in Coors Field because they are likely to carry for home runs. But he may be unable to adjust and effectively swing down on the ball at Pro Player Park or the Astrodome. Finally, because runs are plentiful at the home park, the home team will not be fluent practitioners of offensive or defensive one-run strategies such as base stealing, sacrificing, or squeeze plays and will not be tournament tough when it comes to win a big series on the road. Whatever the reasons, over the history of baseball the paper tigers created by the great hitter's parks have been unable to carry their teams to postseason glory.

There's no place like home for Dante Bichette and the other Colorado Rockies' hitters.

ARTIFICIAL TURF

In response to the exodus of the Giants and Dodgers from New York in the late '50s, a wave of municipally-owned multipurpose sports facilities were built in Cincinnati, Pittsburgh, Philadelphia, and other American cities during the '60s and '70s. The multipurpose stadiums were built to retain each city's professional sports franchises, and as a result were not tailored to baseball. They tended to be oversized with large foul territories and distant outfield fences that favored pitchers by lowering batting averages and reducing home runs. As a cost-saving measure, the multipurpose stadiums featured artificial turf, which required no groundskeeping in the true sense of the word. Artificial turf caused ground balls to travel more quickly and bounce more consistently than on grass.

The multipurpose stadiums, with their large dimensions and fast carpets, created the need for speed on defense. Additionally, because of their large dimensions, one-run strategies became prevalent in the multipurpose stadiums and speed became an important offensive weapon. As such, artificial turf changed baseball by defining the type of player who was likely to be successful. The National League, which had many more artificial turf stadiums than the American League during the 1970s, began to play a much more aggressive brand of baseball based around speed. Whitey Herzog's St. Louis Cardinals of the 1980s were the archetypal artificial turf team, with players like Vince Coleman, Willie McGee, and Tom Herr. The 1982 World Series that featured the St. Louis Cardinals against Harvey's Wallbangers, who had hit 216 home runs, showed the philosophical and stylistic differences that had arisen between the Senior and Junior Circuits as a result of the artificial turf stadiums.

The effect of artificial turf on overall hitting has been moot at best. While ground balls will travel through the infield or to the outfield wall more quickly on artificial turf, the bounce is truer and fielders are able to position themselves more deeply and still make the play. The top hitter's ballparks in the major leagues like Fenway Park and Wrigley Field have grass fields, suggesting that factors other than the type of playing surface play a much larger role in determining a ballpark's friendliness to hitters or pitchers.

The recent trend toward classic ballparks such as Camden Yards, Jacobs Field, and The Ballpark in Arlington has resulted in a number of artificial-turf ballparks such as Busch Stadium and Kauffman Stadium switching to natural grass and suggests that there will be fewer artificial-turf ballparks in the major leagues in the foreseeable future. This, coupled with the increasing importance of home runs in creating offense, has swung the pendulum away from the "artificial turf" players of the 1970s and 1980s and back toward the muscle-bound "grip it and rip it" sluggers of the 1950s.

Whether playing at home or away, Boston's Jim Rice could flat-out hit.

17

1930 and 1968

WHEN EVERYONE HIT AND
NO ONE HIT—AND WHY

Baseball is a game of subtle battles whose delicate competitive balance is created by an exquisite geometry. The pitcher's rubber is 60 feet 6 inches from home plate, which is 17 inches wide, measurements that make both pitching and hitting extremely daunting tasks. At these measurements, dominating pitchers like Randy Johnson or Sandy Koufax are both intimidating and virtually unhittable, while punching bags like Randy Lerch or Steve Trachsel have utility infielders sprinting to the bat rack and begging their managers for a couple of swings.

The bases are 90 feet apart, which is exactly the right distance to make infield hits and stolen bases possible but rare. A ground ball rockets into the hole between shortstop and third, but the shortstop ranges to his right, makes a backhanded stop, plants his back foot, and fires a laser beam to the first baseman just in time to nip the runner by half a step.

This equilibrium did not arise through serendipity or alchemy, but rather through trial and error and experimentation during the nineteenth century, when the game was not yet the "grand old game" and its rules were malleable.

During the twentieth century, baseball has twice seemingly spun out of control and tested the equilibrium the rulemakers had so painstakingly sought to establish. Simply put, 1930 was the year that everybody hit, while 1968 was the year that nobody hit. In 1930, the National League (including pitchers) batted a collective .303 while the American League chipped in with a healthy mark of .288. In 1968, the National League hit .243 while the American League rung up a shockingly anemic .230 league batting average. So 1930 and 1968 were watershed years in the evolution of hitting and thus baseball. In any season, league batting averages will move up and down within a range of expected outcomes based upon short-term influences such as individual talent or climate, while in the background longer-term influences will move performance levels upward or downward over the course of a decade or quarter-century. For baseball's hitters, 1930 was the high tide of such long-term influences and 1968 was the ebb.

1900–29

The first twenty years of the twentieth century are often and perhaps incorrectly characterized as the deadball era. During this time period, the game belonged to the pitchers who delivered the same dirtied, doctored, lifeless ball throughout each game to hitters who had little or no chance of taking them deep. Most hitters swung with their forearms and simply attempted to put the ball into play and get on base. The inside game of bunts and stolen bases was practiced by all teams, as each run was extremely valuable.

The first development to increase offense in baseball occurred in 1911—the introduction of the "lively ball" in both the American League and the National League. Reach Company, which supplied baseballs to the American League, developed the cork-centered baseball in 1909 as a replacement for the India rubber center baseball then in use. Both leagues adopted the new baseball for the 1911 season, and a huge surge in offensive production occurred as runs per game increased by 26.6 percent in the American League and 9.7 percent in the National League. Hitting improved substantially in 1911 as the number of .300 hitters in the American League increased from 8 in 1910 to 27 and from 8 to 16 in the National League. Both Ty Cobb and Joe Jackson hit over .400 during the season, becoming the first major leaguers to hit over .400 since 1901 when Nap Lajoie hit .426 in the last days before foul balls became strikes.

	BA	Runs per game	HR	SA	ERA
1910 National	.256	4.03	214	.338	3.02
1910 American	.243	3.64	147	.313	2.52
1911 National	.260	4.42	316	.356	3.39
1911 American	.273	4.61	198	.358	3.34

The ball didn't stay lively for long. The hitters' improved performance was not sustained, and the pitchers regained the upper hand by 1913. Pitchers began to rely even more on trickery—spitballs, as well as other efforts to doctor or discolor the baseball during games. Runs came back down, and so did attendance. While other nonessential industries were being shut down during World War I, major league

In 1911, a season in which the collective American League batting average was .273, Ty Cobb out-classed his contemporaries by hitting at a .420 clip.

baseball continued on and was roundly criticized in the press for it. Though not the sole reason, all those empty seats at the ballpark contributed to the decision to play shortened seasons in both 1918 and 1919.

Not coincidentally, between the 1919 and 1920 seasons the spitball and other doctored pitches were banned (although each team was allowed to nominate two spitballers who could continue to throw the pitch for the remainder of their careers). These pitches were considered to be disgusting from a sanitary point of view—the country was in the throes of the Spanish influenza—and it was feared that "trick" pitches were more dangerous than other pitches because of their irregular and unpredictable flight. This rule change effectively disarmed the pitchers by taking away the most powerful out pitch in their repertoire.

On August 16, 1920, one of the saddest and most influential events in baseball history occurred when Ray Chapman of the Cleveland Indians was killed by a pitched ball at the Polo Grounds. Chapman, a right-handed batter who crowded the plate, froze on an inside pitch from submariner Carl Mays of the New York Yankees and was struck on the temple, dying the next day. The ball hit Chapman so solidly that Mays actually fielded it when it rolled out to the pitcher's mound and threw to first, thinking it had come off Chapman's bat. The ball that struck Chapman was gray with dirt, and many felt that Chapman had been unable to pick it up out of Mays's hand. Major league baseball reacted quickly and during the 1920 off-season outlawed the deliberate discoloration of the baseball and instituted a "clean ball" directive that enjoined umpires to remove dirty or damaged balls from play and replace them with new, clean baseballs.

The unadulterated baseball was much lighter and flew farther and faster when hit because it did not have many innings of accumulated spit, mud, and tobacco absorbed into its cover. Position players noted how much easier the clean ball was to throw because it was "so much lighter." Not surprisingly, offense improved dramatically in both leagues as runs per game increased by 16.4 percent in the American League and 8.8 percent in the National League.

These rule changes substantially and obviously aided the hitters' cause by improving the visibility of the baseball. Two less obvious side effects of the rule changes were that new baseballs carried much better than older baseballs and that the pitchers had difficulty gripping the new baseballs. During the 1920s, *Scientific American*, at the behest of John McGraw, tested baseballs then in use and determined that the slightest use of a baseball reduced its resiliency. As such, the continual introduction of new baseballs into each game was a boon to the hitters. The introduction of the resin bag and the practice of the umpires rubbing game balls in Chesapeake Bay sand prior to the game came as a result of pitchers' complaints that they couldn't get enough purchase on the clean baseballs to make their breaking pitches break. The result of the 1920 rule changes was that the hitters were now dominant and runs per game increased by 12.9 percent in the American League and 20.8 percent in the National League.

	BA	Runs per game	HR	SA	ERA
1919 National	.258	3.65	207	.337	2.91
1919 American	.268	4.09	240	.359	3.22
1920 National	.270	3.97	261	.357	3.13
1920 American	.284	4.76	369	.387	3.79
1921 National	.289	4.59	460	.397	3.78
1921 American	.292	5.12	477	.408	4.28

The final element in the chemical reaction that triggered the offensive explosion of the 1920s was Babe Ruth. Ruth was the trailblazer who changed the style of hitting from the place hitters of the deadball era like Ty Cobb and Eddie Collins to the sluggers of the 1920s like Ken Williams and Hack Wilson. Ruth showed that swinging with your whole body and uppercutting the ball paid big dividends. His example spread through his Yankees teammates and American League foes during 1920 and then to the National League during 1921. Throughout the 1920s, league batting averages would remain at historically high levels, fluctuating between .280 and .292, while power statistics improved throughout the decade as more and more players became practiced in the art of the long ball. The crescendo came in 1930.

1930

The 1930 season opened on April 17 with President Herbert Hoover throwing the opening pitch and the hapless Boston Red Sox edging the hometown Washington Senators 4–3. As banal as Opening Day may have been, it quickly became apparent that something was afoot as almost every game seemed to feature multiple-run innings, clogged base paths, and long home runs. On April 29, 123 runs were scored in seven major league games. On May 12, the New York Giants carried a 14–1 lead into the sixth inning against the Chicago Cubs and barely held on for a 14–12 triumph. In four straight games against the New York Yankees during late May, the World Series–champion Philadelphia Athletics' pitching staff, featuring Lefty Grove and George Earnshaw, surrendered 51 runs. The baseball press, led by *The Sporting News*, began to express its concern, and John McGraw, the longtime manager of the New York Giants (who played shortstop for the Baltimore Orioles in 1893 when the pitchers were moved back to 60 feet 6 inches), made a forceful case in a *New York Sun* article arguing that the pitching distance should be reduced to 58 feet to give the pitchers a chance. It was even suggested by New York Yankees owner Jacob Ruppert that the spitball be restored.

The summer of 1930 was remarkably hot and included heat waves across the U.S. that killed many people in America's major cities. These extremely high temperatures no doubt helped the hitters, who continued to pound pitchers through the dog days. On June 23, the Brooklyn Dodgers recorded 12 straight hits with two out in the sixth inning against Heinie Meine of the Pittsburgh Pirates. On July 21, the Brooklyn Dodgers and St. Louis Cardinals split a twin bill that featured 44 runs. In back-to-back games on July 23 and 24, the Philadelphia Phillies succumbed 16–15 to the Pittsburgh Pirates and 19–15 to the Chicago Cubs, wasting 44 hits in the process, but did themselves one better by losing 19–16 to the St. Louis Cardinals in late September in the height of the pennant race.

	BA	Runs per game	HR	SP	ERA
1930 National	.303	5.68	892	.448	4.97
1930 American	.288	5.41	673	.421	4.65

The concerns of the baseball press and baseball traditionalists were well founded, as the offensive numbers posted during 1930 were staggering. The National League hit .303 collectively (.312 if the pitchers' at-bats are not counted) with six of eight teams batting over .300, including the New York Giants at .319, the Philadelphia Phillies at .315, and the St. Louis Cardinals at .314, which represented three of the four highest team batting averages of the twentieth century. Forty-three of 64 starting regulars batted over .300 with 17 players driving in more than 100 runs and 17 players scoring more than 100 runs. Additionally, many players experienced career years during 1930, recording astonishing personal achievements like Hack Wilson's all-time RBI record of 190 or Bill Terry's .401 batting average.

Almost every team was able to field a batting order that looked like Murderers' Row. The pennant-winning St. Louis Cardinals featured a balanced lineup that led the National League in runs scored with 1,004. All eight of its starters batted over .300, and its bench was extremely deep, including aberrant production from Showboat Fisher (.374), Gus Mancuso (.366), Ernie Orsatti (.321), and Ray Blades (.396). The top of the second-place Chicago Cubs' batting order was perhaps the most intimidating and productive in the National League, anchored by Hall of Famers Hack Wilson and Gabby Hartnett.

	H	R	HR	RBI	BA	SA
Woody English, SS	214	152	14	59	.335	.511
Kiki Cuyler, RF	228	155	13	134	.355	.547
Hack Wilson, CF	208	146	56	190	.309	.723
Gabby Hartnett, C	172	84	37	122	.339	.630

The New York Giants, who set the all-time twentieth-century team batting average mark of .319 during the 1930 season, featured players in the 3, 4, and 5 slots who each hit more than 20 home runs, drove in more than 100 runs, and scored more than 120 runs:

	H	R	HR	RBI	BA	SA
Fred Lindstrom, 3B	231	127	22	106	.379	.575
Bill Terry, 1B	254	139	23	129	.401	.619
Mel Ott, RF	182	122	25	119	.349	.578

The Brooklyn Dodgers, who led the National League for most of the 1930 season before fading down the stretch, hit .304 as a team, receiving career years from Del Bissonette, Johnny Frederick, and Babe Herman. Herman, who hit .393 with 241 hits, 143 runs, 35 home runs, 130 RBI, and a .678 slugging percentage, recorded perhaps the greatest season ever by a player who did not lead the league in a single offensive category. Herman, who was the clown prince of Wilbert Robinson's "Daffiness Boys," was overrun twice during 1930 on home runs and also hit the famous bases-loaded double that season that resulted in three Dodgers standing on third base.

The Pittsburgh Pirates, who were also-rans during 1930, managed to bat .303 as a team with Pie Traynor, Paul Waner, and one-year wonder Adam Comorosky carrying the offensive load. The last-place Philadelphia Phillies, tenanted in the claustrophobic confines of the Baker Bowl, hit .315, led by Chuck Klein and Lefty O'Doul, and set the all-time major league team record for hits in a season with 1,783—more than *11* per game. Unfortunately, their pitching staff gave up 1,993 hits—nearly *13* every game—and recorded a putrid team ERA of 6.71 while allowing opposing teams to bat an eye-popping .346 against them over the course of the season. It was seasons like this that gave truth to the refrain that the Phillies were a better-hitting team than every team in baseball except the one they were playing.

The American League batted "only" .288 during 1930. This was probably the result of a disparity in talent between the two leagues, as the first division of the junior circuit held its own in comparison to its National League colleagues while the second division lagged badly. Three of the eight American League squads batted over .300—the New York Yankees, Washington Senators, and Cleveland Indians. Surprisingly, the world champion Philadelphia Athletics hit a "paltry" .294 as a team but compensated with good power and strong pitching to coast to the American League pennant. Their lineup did, however, include three legendary Hall of Famers and was intimidating in its own right.

	H	R	HR	RBI	BA	SA
Al Simmons, LF	211	152	36	165	.381	.708
Jimmie Foxx, 1B	188	127	37	156	.335	.637
Mickey Cochrane, C	174	110	10	85	.357	.526

The 1930 New York Yankees averaged an astronomical 6.9 runs per game over the course of the season, scoring 1,062 runs, a total that has been surpassed only one time, when the same Yankees' lineup tallied 1,067 runs in 1931. Despite their hitting heroics, the Yankees finished a disappointing third in 1930 and were never a factor in the pennant race. Their batting order featured Babe Ruth and Lou Gehrig, the most fearsome slugging combination ever, along with two other Hall of Famers in the 1 through 4 slots.

	H	R	HR	RBI	BA	SA
Earle Combs, CF	183	129	7	82	.344	.523
Tony Lazzeri, 2B	173	109	9	121	.303	.462
Babe Ruth, RF	186	150	49	153	.359	.732
Lou Gehrig, 1B	220	143	41	174	.379	.721

The 1930 Washington Senators, who provided the main challenge to the Athletics, broke the mold for Washington baseball, which had generally been good pitching and so-so hitting. During 1930, the Senators, true to form, did pace the American League in pitching with a 3.96 team ERA, but also stroked the ball at a .302 clip with Joe Cronin (.346), Sam Rice (.349), and Heinie Manush (.362) leading the way. The 1930 Cleveland Indians assembled perhaps the most awesome collection of career years ever concentrated in a single team and posted a .304 team batting mark. Such unremembered immortals as Eddie Morgan (.349 with 26 home runs and 136 RBI), Johnny Hodapp (.354 with 225 hits), and Dick Porter (.350) keyed the Indians' attack.

1931–67

In the aftermath of the 1930 season, the American League and National League held meetings in December to determine the best method to reestablish the competitive balance between the pitchers and the hitters. No course of action was agreed upon at these meetings, but before the start of the 1931 season the National League introduced a baseball with a thicker cover and raised seams (instead of the traditional countersunk seams). The American League adopted the raised seams prior to the 1931 season but would not embrace the thicker cover until 1934. So the two leagues used demonstrably different baseballs during the early 1930s with the junior circuit's the livelier.

	BA	Runs per game	HR	SA	ERA
1930 National	.303	5.68	892	.448	4.97
1930 American	.288	5.41	673	.421	4.65
1931 National	.277	4.48	493	.387	3.86
1931 American	.278	5.14	576	.396	4.38

The effect of the new baseball was immediate and dramatic. The heavier National League baseball did not carry as well. Home runs plummeted by 44.7 percent and runs per game fell by 21.1 percent. Players complained that hits that were home runs the year before were just easy fly-outs in 1931. Hack Wilson's home runs fell from 56 to 13. Additionally, the raised seams gave the pitchers better purchase on the ball and allowed them to get more movement on their breaking pitches. Carl Hubbel, the New York Giants' ace screwballer, said: "The ball just plain felt bigger in your hand. It was easier to grip."

The journey from 1930, the year everybody hit, to 1968, the year nobody hit, is the story of an inexorable downward drift in batting averages as each significant development in major league baseball seemed to work against the hitters.

Night baseball was introduced to the major leagues in 1935 when the Cincinnati Reds installed lights at Crosley Field. Over the next six years, lights were installed in more and more parks—Ebbets Field in 1938, Shibe Park in 1939, the Polo Grounds in 1940, Comiskey Park in 1940, Municipal Stadium in 1940, Sportsman's Park in 1940, and Griffiths Stadium in 1941—as owners realized the economic boom that would result from night baseball. Major league baseball, however, still had a prejudice against night baseball, and a strict limit was imposed on the number of night games each team could schedule. As such, the impact of night baseball on hitting was muted in the pre–World War II era. After World War II, the limit on night games was lifted and the number of night games continued to rise. Hitters were negatively affected as more and more of their at-bats occurred under the lights, where the ball was harder to pick up out of the pitcher's hand.

The increasing size and improving quality of baseball gloves during the 1940s, 1950s, and 1960s worked against the hitters. Better gloves not only made fielders more surehanded on balls hit to them, but gave them better range to either side by making one-handed catches possible. In 1930, the National League and American League averaged 2.40 and 2.53 errors per game, respectively. By 1968, errors per game had declined by 29 percent to 1.71 in the National League and by 33 percent to 1.69 in the American League. This reduction in errors was no doubt matched by an unquantifiable decrease in "seeing-eye" ground balls and infield hits as fielders were able to make a play on more and more hits that had been previously unplayable.

Perhaps the most important long-term trend working against the hitters was the abandonment of the urban ballparks that had been built in the early decades of the twentieth century. In almost every instance when a franchise shifted or a new facility was built, the new ballpark was more favorable to pitchers than its predecessor, and as such made the hitters' lot a more difficult one. In 1938 the Philadelphia Phillies abandoned the Baker Bowl, the best hitter's park in the major leagues with its extremely short right-field power alley, to become tenants of Shibe Park, a normally proportioned ballpark. In 1948 the Cleveland Indians closed cozy League Park with its short porch in right field that had been the sight of their weekday games since 1932 in favor of cavernous Municipal Stadium. In 1954 and 1966, respectively, the St. Louis Browns and St. Louis Cardinals traded Sportsman's Park, an excellent hitter's park with short power alleys, for modern ballparks with deep power alleys. In 1958 the Brooklyn Dodgers and New York Giants fled to the left coast, ultimately exchanging Ebbets Field and the Polo Grounds for Dodger Stadium and Candlestick Park. In both cases, the Dodgers and Giants moved from ballparks with short home run porches to facilities with expansive foul territories and distant power alleys.

The net effect of these ballpark changes was to make the task of hitting in the major leagues more difficult. The new stadiums were suburban stadiums and not constrained by a city block. Outfields were more spacious and home run porches became a thing of the past. Many of the new stadiums were multipurpose facilities intended for football as well as baseball. This meant that the seating was pushed back to accommodate the football field, thereby substantially increasing the amount of foul territory over that which was common in the baseball-only urban ballparks. When the major leagues expanded in 1961 and 1962, the trend toward ballparks with more spacious outfields and larger foul territories accelerated as each of the expansion teams ultimately built large multipurpose facilities, including the Astrodome and Shea Stadium, two of the better pitcher's parks in the majors.

But it wasn't all about lights and dimensions. A major development in pitching during the period 1930 to 1968 was the rise of the relief pitcher. Through the 1930s, most teams used their ace starter as a spot closer, but this began to change after World War II with the emergence of Joe Page of the Yankees, Ted Wilks of the Cardinals, and Ellis Kinder of the Red Sox. The career relievers like Hoyt Wilhelm and Elroy Face began to appear during the 1950s, and by the 1960s nearly every team had a modern bullpen including a closer, a setup man, and a mop-up man. The development of the modern bullpen gave managers greater ability to substitute their pitchers at any point during a game and thereby reduced the number of at-bats per season that a hitter would have against tired or ineffective pitchers. Another important development in pitching was the popularization and proliferation of the slider. The slider had great impact because it was relatively easy to master and could be used as an out pitch. Prior to the advent of the slider, pitchers primarily threw fastballs and curves, which are relatively easy to discern from one another. The slider was not as easy to pick up as the curveball, and therefore could be used to great effect by hard-throwing pitchers.

The baseball world was changing, but—as the Lamarckian evolutionists on PBS will tell you—organisms under environmental stress will develop the necessary characteristics to survive in that challenging environment. With batting averages declining and strikeouts rising through the 1950s, offenses became increasingly dependent on the home run as major league teams inevitably adopted the strategy necessary to win in a low-average era when serial offenses were difficult to sustain. The zenith of the home run ethos was reached in the expansion season of 1961, when the major leagues combined for a record 2,730 home runs and the New York Yankees, led by Roger Maris and Mickey Mantle, hit a then all-time team record 240 home runs.

Ford Frick, the commissioner of Major League Baseball and a friend of Babe Ruth, was alarmed at the increase in home runs and the threat to Ruth's record. In 1961, when it became apparent that Maris and Mantle had legitimate chances to hit more than 60 home runs, Frick brought out the "asterisk" that was used to diminish Maris's achievement. In the off-season between 1962 and 1963, Frick was in a near panic that the asterisk might not be enough and was quoted as saying: "I would even like the spitball to come back. Take a look at the batting, home run and slugging records for recent seasons, and you become convinced that the pitchers need help urgently." In actuality, an analysis of the hitting records showed no such thing.

	BA	Runs per game	HR	SA	ERA
1927 National	.282	4.58	483	.386	3.91
1927 American	.285	4.92	439	.399	4.14
1961 National	.262	4.52	1196	.405	4.03
1961 American*	.256	4.53	1534	.395	4.02

*AL expanded to 10 teams

Nineteen sixty-one hitting records were basically comparable to those of 1927 from the point of view of runs scored. In both 1927 and 1961, the average team scored approximately 4.5 runs per game. The difference was in how they got those runs. In 1927, teams hit for a higher average and bunched singles and extra-base hits to generate runs. In 1961, teams swung for the fences and used the long ball to propel their offenses. Frick, however, only saw the increase in home runs and the threat to Ruth's record.

Between the 1962 and 1963 seasons, Frick pressed for rule changes to restrain home run hitting and got his wish when the Official Baseball Playing Rules Committee increased the size of the strike zone both at the top and bottom, changing the definition from "between the armpits and the top of the knees" to "between the shoulders and the bottom of the knees." This change, coming in what was already a period of declining batting averages, was akin to throwing a millstone to a drowning man.

	BA	Runs per game	HR	SP	ERA
1962 National*	.261	4.48	1449	.393	3.94
1962 American	.255	4.44	1552	.394	3.97
1963 National	.245	3.81	1215	.364	3.29
1963 American	.247	4.08	1489	.380	3.63

*NL expanded to 10 teams

Even though it had been 27 years since Babe Ruth last stood in the batter's box, Commissioner Ford Frick's "asterisk" decision was convincing evidence that the Bambino's presence was little diminished.

The immediate effect of the new strike zone was to enormously improve the lot of power pitchers by allowing the high hard one to become the higher hard one. It is a rare hitter who can handle a Nolan Ryan or a Tom Seaver up in the strike zone. As such, every team's pitching staff was soon populated by tall, hard-throwing pitchers like Don Drysdale, Bob Veale, Jim Maloney, Sam McDowell, and Bob Gibson who challenged and overpowered hitters high in the strike zone. Exacerbating the situation was an unregulated increase in the height of pitcher's mounds that occurred during the 1960s as ballpark groundskeepers adjusted the height of pitcher's mounds to the liking of the home team pitching staffs. This again aided the power pitchers by allowing them to more easily keep their pitches high in the strike zone. League batting averages and power statistics eroded noticeably over the next five seasons as no check to the pitcher's dominance was found.

1968

Portentously, the 1968 season opened with a shutout as Dean Chance of the Minnesota Twins (previously the Washington Senators) beat the "new" Washington Senators 2–0 at D.C. Stadium. Five days later, the New York Mets and Houston Astros broke three National League records, including most consecutive scoreless innings, by playing a 24-inning 1–0 game that the Astros broke open with an unearned run in the 24th. Tommie Agee and Ron Swoboda of the Mets both went 0 for 10 in the game to set some sort of record for futility while Bob Aspromonte of the Astros made a valiant bid for immortality by going 0 for 9 in the six-hour marathon. From the beginning of the 1968 season, it was evident that the hitters were struggling as game after game was a low-hit pitchers' duel with over 20 percent of games ending in shutouts. Stellar pitching performances like Catfish Hunter's perfect game and Luis Tiant's 19-strikeout performance were the talk of the baseball world. As early as June, National League president Warren Giles asked the league's general managers to suggest ways that scoring could be increased.

Consecutive scoreless innings streaks entered the public consciousness during 1968 as long-forgotten deadball-era marks were challenged. In early June, Don Drysdale broke Walter Johnson's consecutive scoreless innings streak, which had been set in 1913, by stringing together 59 innings (or 5½ complete games) without giving up a run. Drysdale's mark was immediately challenged as Bob Gibson accumulated 48 scoreless innings in early July before giving up a run on a wild pitch. With pitchers putting up goose eggs with such regularity, it is not surprising that the team record for consecutive scoreless innings also fell. The Chicago Cubs were shut out in four consecutive games, including an 11-inning 1–0 loss to the Atlanta Braves en route to establishing a major league mark of 48 consecutive scoreless innings. The previous mark for polite behavior had been held by the 1906 Philadelphia Athletics.

With both leagues playing low-scoring games of catch and neither league providing an exciting pennant race, attendance fell to 1965 levels. Baseball's showcase, the All-Star Game, only served to put an exclamation point on baseball's dilemma. In the most somnolent Midseason Classic ever, the sluggers of the American and National Leagues combined for 8 hits and 1 run while striking out 20 times. Willie Mays singled to lead off the bottom of the first inning, went to second on a misplayed pickoff attempt, moved up to third on a wild pitch, and scored when Willie McCovey grounded into a double play. After that offensive flurry the pitchers took over, and neither the American League nor the National League could score a run. Willie Mays was named the game's MVP, ostensibly for scoring the game's only run but more likely because the baseball writers could not determine which of the National League's six pitchers who combined on the three-hit no-walk shutout should get the award.

As the season progressed, 1968 became known as the year of the pitcher, with Bob Gibson and Denny McLain as the standard bearers. Gibson was virtually unhittable all year and posted an astounding 1.12 ERA, the lowest since the deadball era, while McLain became the first 30-game winner in the majors since Dizzy Dean in 1934. Fittingly, both Gibson and McLain were awarded their league's Cy Young and MVP awards.

	BA	Runs per game	HR	SA	ERA
1968 National	.243	3.43	891	.341	2.99
1968 American	.230	3.41	1104	.339	2.98

The hitting statistics of 1968 were a source of great concern to Major League Baseball. Not only were runs down by more than one per game since 1962, but home runs, the traditional crowd pleaser, had decreased by 34 percent, from 3,001 to 1,995. Ford Frick had gotten his wish. The American League hit .230 overall with its top hitting team, the Oakland Athletics, posting an underwhelming .240 average. Among its 80 starting regulars, only one player hit over .300, two players drove in over 100 runs, and no one scored 100 runs. Carl Yastrzemski's .301 batting average was the lowest mark for a batting champion in the history of major league baseball, and it took a late-season surge on Yaz's part to top .300 at all. The story in the National League was little better. Among its 80 starters, five players managed to hit .300, one player drove in over 100 runs, and no one scored 100 runs. Offense had fallen in both leagues to levels not seen since the deadball era. To put this into perspective, the 1906 Chicago White Sox, the original hitless wonders who averaged 3.77 runs per game, would have outscored 16 of 20 major league teams in 1968.

	BA	Runs per game	HR	SB	SA
1906 White Sox	.230	3.77	6	214	.286
1968 White Sox	.228	3.05	71	90	.311

It seemed that a significant portion of the hitters were completely overmatched as every team started one or two players whose offensive contributions were almost nonexistent. The world champion Detroit Tigers featured a shortstop troika of Ray Oyler (.135), Dick Tracewski (.156), and Tom Matchick (.203), who combined for 8 homers and 41 RBI over the season. Third base was patrolled by Don Wert, who hit a tepid .200 in 150 games while chipping in with 12 homers and 37 RBI. Mayo Smith's decision to put Al Kaline in the starting lineup for the World Series by playing Mickey Stanley, the team's center fielder, at shortstop was driven by the complete lack of production from the left side of the infield.

The second-place Baltimore Orioles, despite having in place the batting order that would lead them to five pennants over the next six seasons, hit at a .225 clip. The Orioles' team batting average was pulled down by three regulars, Mark Belanger (.208 in 472 AB), Paul Blair (.211 in 421 AB), and Curt Blefary (.200 in 451 AB), and a weak hitting bench that included Dave May (.191 in 84 games), Curt Motton (.198 in 83 games), and Elrod Hendricks (.202 in 79 games).

The Boston Red Sox, one of the American League's better hitting teams in 1968, let George Scott rack up 350 at-bats and 112 games at first base while hitting .171 with 3 homers and 25 RBI. This was probably the result of loyalty on the part of Red Sox manager Dick Williams to a player who had performed well the year before—however, Scott's backup, Dalton Jones, provided the same production (5 homers and 29 RBI in 354 at-bats), albeit with a higher batting average (.234).

The fabled Yankees hit an ignominious .214 as a team during 1968 to set an all-time franchise low. Tom Tresh, the everyday shortstop, hit .195 with 11 homers in 152 games but stayed in the lineup because he was significantly more productive than the team's backup middle infielders, who included Dick Howser (.153), Gene Michaels (.198), and Ruben Amaro (.122).

The Dodgers, despite having a starting rotation of Don Drysdale, Bill Singer, Claude Osteen, and Don Sutton—and only two years removed from a World Series appearance—managed to finish firmly in the National League's second division on the strength of their extraordinarily weak hitting. The Dodgers' batting order, which generated little power, featured five players who hit below .240, including the entire infield of Wes Parker (.239), Paul Popovich (.232), Zoilo Versalles (.196), and Bob Bailey (.227). The team leader in home runs with 10 was Len Gabrielson, a part-time outfielder, while Tom Haller, the team's backstop, led the club in RBI with 53.

Ironically, the two hitting highlights of 1968 were nostalgic reminders of the not-too-distant past when home runs were plentiful and the sluggers were dominant. On September 15, Roger Maris hit his 275th and final home run, while Mickey Mantle slammed his 535th and last home run on September 18 off Denny McLain at Tiger Stadium—as McLain intentionally grooved a batting practice fastball that the Mick hit out to pass Jimmie Foxx on the all-time list.

	BA	HR	RBI	BB	SA
1968 Mickey Mantle	.237	18	54	106	.398
1961 Mickey Mantle	.317	54	128	126	.687
1968 Roger Maris	.255	5	45	24	.374
1961 Roger Maris	.269	61	142	94	.620

Both Maris's and Mantle's 1968 statistics pale in comparison to their glorious accomplishments of 1961, but when one considers their numbers in the context of the 1968 season, a different picture emerges. Both Maris and Mantle exceeded their respective leagues' hitting and slugging averages, suggesting that, as far as they'd fallen, both retired while they were still net contributors to their teams' success.

In the aftermath of the 1968 season, major league baseball returned the strike zone to its 1962 size, between the armpits and the top of the knees. Additionally, the maximum height of the pitcher's mound was set at 10 inches. These changes, in concert with the expansion to 24 teams, led to a significant increase in runs and home runs during 1969. The ripples from 1968 would continue through the 1970s and 1980s with such developments as the designated hitter rule, improved hitting backgrounds, and the lower strike zone as Major League Baseball remembered that fans like offense and took steps to ensure that a season like 1968 would never happen again.

18

Different Strokes for Different Folks

Hitting Styles and the Gurus Who Taught Them

*D*ifferent strokes for different folks. There's more than one way to skin a cat. *Variety is the spice of life.* Any one of these familiar clichés most definitely applies to hitting a baseball, because there's no one right path to success. Each hitter has to find what works best for him.

For example, 5′9″ Chuck Knoblauch would be foolish to swing the bat like Babe Ruth did, and it's hard to imagine the physically imposing slugger Mark McGwire choking the bat like Ty Cobb and punching the ball through the infield for singles. Picture Mr. October, Reggie Jackson, a man who would nearly corkscrew himself into the ground when he swung and missed, hitting off a stiff front leg and slashing doubles into the power alleys. It's hard to imagine, isn't it? Nevertheless, through the years baseball's landscape has been dotted by hitting gurus who theorized that one hitting style was superior over all others, no matter who was swinging the bat.

The Deadball Era

The predominant hitting styles in baseball over the last 80 years have always evolved as the result of some precipitating event rather than a brilliant theoretical discovery. Before 1920, in the so-called deadball era, the single was king. Controlling the bat and the swing was of paramount importance. There were several reasons why batters preferred to choke the bat and punch singles into the outfield.

For one, the deadball era was appropriately named because the ball was "dead." That is, it didn't travel very far or fast when hit. Also, balls weren't replaced very often. Many games were finished using only one or two balls. By the middle and late innings, a ball was in pretty bad shape and few players had the strength or technique to drive it any great distance.

Another factor in the early days of baseball (pre-1900) was the configuration of the playing fields. Many didn't have outfield fences. Therefore, the outfielders played deep in order to keep balls from getting between them or over their heads for home runs. With the outfielders playing deep, it was only logical for hitters to develop a hitting style that produced ground balls and line drives. The king of ground balls, bunts, and line drives was an outfielder for the Detroit Tigers whose batting style was the standard during the deadball era.

Ty Cobb still holds the record for the highest career batting average (.367), and his career total of 4,191 hits is second-best all-time. Cobb accomplished his batting feats by choking up, holding his hands three to four inches apart, and punching, slapping, and stroking the ball into the outfield. He was indisputably the greatest hitter of his time, and it was only natural that his contemporaries would emulate his technique. That is, until one George Herman Ruth arrived on the scene and changed baseball—and hitting, in particular—forever.

The Sultan of Swat

In 1918, as a pitcher and part-time outfielder for the Boston Red Sox, Babe Ruth led the American League in home runs—with 11! By the time he had finished the 1920 season as a full-time outfielder for the New York Yankees, he had revolutionized the game.

Babe Ruth mashed 54 home runs in 1920, more than any other *team* in the American League, and more than all but one team (Philadelphia) in the National League. His prodigious wallops captured the imagination of baseball fans everywhere—and, just as important, most baseball owners, managers, and players were equally captivated by the long ball. A new style of hitting was born, and its father was named Ruth.

The Babe was a big, strong man, much bigger and stronger than most players of his time. He used a huge bat—long and heavy—that he held by the end with the last two fingers of his right hand draped over the knob. The combination of his strength and big bat enabled Ruth to generate the optimal mix of bat speed and mass to propel the ball great distances.

Ruth would coil back away from the pitcher, then powerfully and quickly rotate his hips forward toward the playing field as he swung at the pitch. This powerful hip rotation would cause his hips to actually change places from beginning to end of his swing. When he swung and missed, Ruth would nearly corkscrew himself into the ground. His style was quickly copied by many in the game, so quickly in fact, that by 1922, Ruth would finish only third in the AL in homers, and all but one team in the league hit more home runs than he did.

The most obvious benefit of Ruth's new style was power. There were, however, some drawbacks to this rotational approach—namely, less frequent contact (more strikeouts) and less use of the whole field (more pitches were pulled). Nevertheless, the rotational style of hitting gained widespread acceptance, most notably by a young Red Sox outfielder who would refine Ruth's technique.

The Spendid Splinter

Ted Williams played baseball for the Boston Red Sox for all or part of 19 seasons. For his career he batted .344, sixth-best all-time, rocked 521 home runs, and walked 2,019 times while striking out only 709 times.

Williams played during the era directly following Ruth, Gehrig, Foxx, and other great sluggers. If Ruth was a swaggering, bare-knuckles heavyweight, Williams was a patient technician. Power was still the most coveted attribute a hitter could have, and Williams developed a style that produced plenty of pop. He rotated his hips through the hitting area in much the same way Ruth had, and his propensity to pull the ball to right field was perhaps even greater than Babe's. But the biggest differences between them were Williams's patience and his incredibly keen vision.

Ted Williams had great eyesight, even better than the 20/20 vision that is the standard of excellence for most human beings. Physicians confirmed that Williams's vision was 20/15, so it was no surprise that he usually made solid contact with the ball and that he infrequently swung at pitches out of the strike zone. In fact, Williams's most often quoted mantra for great hitting had nothing to do with the rotational swing he is famous for. Williams's cornerstone for success at the plate was to "get a good ball to hit." He understood that if you wanted to hit the ball with great power like Ruth, it was paramount that the pitch must be in a location that would allow the batter to pull the ball—into the air—with authority. This is the number-one tenet of modern rotational hitting: get a pitch from the middle of the plate in with enough elevation to allow the batter to hit a fly ball to the pull side. This was still the hitting theory that Williams promulgated as he managed the 1969 Washington Senators to their first winning season since their inaugural campaign of 1961. Even as Williams enjoyed his success with the customarily anemic Senators, the game of baseball was undergoing fundamental change, and a light-hitting backup catcher was formulating a new, dramatically different hitting approach.

New Ballparks, Charlie Lau, and the Modern Weight-Shift System

When Houston's Astrodome opened for business in 1965, it signaled the beginning of a dramatic shift in the design of major league ballparks. Between 1965 and 1980, new ballparks including the Astrodome, Veterans Stadium, Riverfront Stadium, Three Rivers Stadium, Busch Memorial Stadium, and Royals Stadium were fitted with Astroturf, a hard, slick, fast surface that put a premium on hitters who could slash the ball into the outfield gaps and fast outfielders who could cut those balls off. Offensive baseball became more a game of speed than power. Charlie Lau, a savvy student of the game, especially hitting, was paying close attention, and he developed a new theory of hitting that was markedly different from what Ruth and Williams had espoused.

As a journeyman catcher for the Tigers, Braves, and Orioles, Charlie Lau had an ideal vantage point for observing what did and didn't work for major league hitters. Lau saw the bigger, faster ballparks and theorized that the best way to attack them was to hit fewer fly balls and strike out less often. The result would be ground balls and line drives that would scoot past infielders and outfielders and run across the fast turf to the outfield walls. To do this, he would jettison the high-power, low-contact rotational style of hitting in favor of something that generated more consistent contact and lower ball flight. A new style of hitting was born.

Lau's new technique became known as the modern weight-shift style. Its fundamental principles were a stance deep in the box, facilitating a longer look at the pitch, weight heavily on the back side during the prelaunch phase, then a marked shifting of weight to the front foot during the stride. Lau believed that you must first go back in order to go forward.

Lau instructed hitters such as George Brett and Harold Baines to stand with a bent waist and a square stance, and to land on a stiff front leg. The head stayed down well past impact, and because they allowed the ball to get well back into the hitting zone, Lau's disciples hit the ball back through the middle and to the opposite field, pulling the ball only on inside pitches.

Another hallmark of the modern weight-shift theory is the releasing of the top hand after impact. This is a result of the bat staying through the hitting zone for so long, with the result being such great extension that it's nearly impossible for the top hand to remain on the bat. This releasing of the top hand reduced the premature rolling over of the hands and resulted in few balls being pulled and more of the field being used.

As hitting coach, Lau brought his method to a Kansas City Royals team led by George Brett and Hal McRae. The Royals played in a large stadium with fast Astroturf. Their lineup was loaded with line-drive hitters who would drive the ball into the gaps for extra-base hits. The Royals became the model for teams that played in similar ballparks, and Lau's system was employed with great success by hitters who made consistent contact and hit for higher averages. The one negative aspect of the weight-shift style was a reduction in home runs. Lau, however, believed that more consistent contact and using what your ballpark gave you was more than an even tradeoff for fewer home runs. Ted Williams, still a man everyone respected when the topic was hitting, did not agree.

Today's Game

Today, hitting has come full circle, and once again the home run is king. The reasons given for the long-ball renaissance are many: expansion (fewer quality pitchers); a livelier ball; bigger, stronger players; smaller ballparks; smaller strike zone. Pundits argue that in the aftermath of the catastrophic 1994 baseball strike, major league baseball has made a concerted multipronged effort to generate more offense in the game, because surveys have indicated that fans prefer slugfests to pitching duels.

One interesting piece of the modern long-ball revival is *how* the home run hitters are getting it done. No particular hitting style is dominant. Rotational swingers such as Jose Canseco, Jim Thome, and Larry Walker are routinely knocking the ball out of the park, while weight-shift hitters such as Alex Rodriguez, Frank Thomas, and Manny Ramirez go deep with equal frequency. Hybrid-type hitters such as Mark McGwire and Rafael Palmeiro, whose swings contain components of both the rotational and weight-shift styles, reach the fences with remarkable consistency. It seems that both Lau and Williams have been proven right, confirming what we surely should have known all along: there is no singularly correct style of hitting.

With apologies to all hitting gurus, well known and otherwise, batting is an individual exercise and you should stick with what works for you.

19

The Impact of Expansion on Offense

The conventional wisdom regarding expansion is that it dilutes the league talent base by allowing players into the majors who could not have otherwise made the grade. In general, most attention focuses on the dilution in pitching talents; however, it stands to reason that hitting talent is also diluted. Both pitchers and hitters who "do not belong" are added to team rosters during an expansion season and the number of "unfair" matchups increases over that which would occur in a normal season. Exceptional hitters like Mark McGwire and Tony Gwynn have more opportunities to feast on "minor league" pitchers masquerading as major leaguers while dominating pitchers like Roger Clemens and Curt Schilling have more opportunities to blow their best pitches past the overmatched hitters filling out the bottom of teams' batting orders. In this way, the league is weakened and the level of competition is diminished. Under such circumstances, the variability of individual performances within the major leagues increases and individual records become more reachable. Overall hitting does not necessarily increase, because just as the top players' career-year statistics will be inflated by the weakened competition, so the overall league results will be deflated by the weaker hitters and their below-average offensive contributions.

The temporal impact of expansion, however, raises questions. The out-of-context hitting performances that tend to occur during expansion seasons do not carry forward into the seasons that follow. This argues that the weakened competition the top players exploited during the expansion season strengthens over time, and in fact strengthens rather quickly. For expansion to weaken major league baseball over an extended period of time, two things would have to be true: The population pool from which players are drawn would have to be invariant or shrinking, and the player selection process would have to be efficient. The history of baseball argues forcibly that neither condition is true.

Between 1901, the year that the American League was recognized as a major league, and 1961, the year that major league baseball finally expanded, the population of the U.S. more than tripled. Thinking linearly, one would expect three times as many American baseball-aged males to be available in 1961 as compared to 1901—and yet there were only 18 major league teams in 1961, as compared to 16 in 1901. During the 1950s, the period that some see as the golden era of baseball, the population of the U.S. was approximately 150 million and there were 16 major league teams, or a team for every 9.4 million people. In the late 1990s, the population of the U.S. is approximately 250 million and there are 30 major league teams, or a team for every 8.3 million people.

But the comparison is not fair for several reasons. Prior to 1947, major league baseball did not permit the recruitment of black players, and full integration of both major leagues was not accomplished until many years later. The internationalization of baseball that began in the 1950s with Latin American players like Chico Carrasquel from Venezuela and Minnie Minoso from Cuba has increased dramatically during the 1980s and 1990s with more and more players coming from Latin American and Asian countries. Given this substantial growth in the population pool from which major leaguers can be drawn, it has been possible for the major leagues to expand the number of teams while keeping the quality of baseball at a uniformly high level.

If the major league player selection process were efficient, we would expect the players in the major leagues to be the best players available. So in 1961, when the major leagues expanded from 16 teams to 18 teams, the 128 starting players for the existing 16 teams were the best 128 players available and the expansion Los Angeles Angels and Washington Senators necessarily stocked themselves with weaker players because they were what was available. This is, of course, patently absurd, since inefficiencies exist. Strong teams will have bench players who could start on other teams. Teams that are deep in a certain position will have players buried in their minor league system who have major league talent. Team front offices have varying abilities in identifying and developing talent. Scouting is a sometimes random process with certain parts of the U.S. and the world more heavily scouted than others, which can lead to extremely talented players never receiving the opportunity to progress. Finally, it is difficult to predict which players will excel as they move up each rung of the ladder to the major leagues, and, as such, trial and error is the rule. In reality, teams will try several or many players at a position before settling on the player they feel can play at a major league level consistently.

What this suggests is that the quality of major league baseball is weakened during an expansion season not because there are more players in the league but because the task of staffing a major league baseball club is a difficult one. Sufficient numbers of major league–caliber players are available to fill each team's rosters, but the process takes time. The problem of identifying major league–caliber players is of course especially visited upon the expansion teams themselves, who not only must staff an entire 25-man roster but must also establish a working farm system. In recent expansion seasons, player moves prompted by high salaries have improved the lot of expansion teams like the Florida Marlins, Arizona Diamondbacks, and Tampa Bay Devil Rays by allowing them access to high-quality major league players like Gary Sheffield, Matt Williams, and Fred McGriff. This does not change the number of new players who will be entering the league as a result of expansion, but helps to more evenly distribute talent within the major leagues and put some of the onus to identify new players upon nonexpansion teams. In any event, over the course of the 162-game season expansion teams are able to improve themselves at many positions, such that the gap between the league's top players and its weakest players is reduced, and the likelihood of career years falls dramatically in the seasons that follow.

A review of baseball's expansion seasons supports this line of reasoning, as many of baseball's most famous career years have occurred in expansion seasons—yet variations in overall league batting averages and power statistics between expansion seasons and the seasons immediately before and after are erratic and best explained by others factors such as ballpark effects and rule changes.

	BA	R/G	HR	HR/G
1960	.255	4.31	2128	0.86
1961	.258	4.53	2730	0.95
1962	.258	4.46	3001	0.93
1963	.246	3.95	2704	0.84

In 1961, major league baseball's first official expansion season since 1879 when the National League expanded from six to eight franchises, the American League added franchises in Los Angeles and Washington and saw offense and home runs surge. The increases in both home runs and runs per game over 1960 were, however, completely within normal ranges and did not suggest any significant changes were occurring. Fans were treated to extraordinary individual hitting performances the likes of which had not been seen since the 1930 season. The increase in runs and home runs experienced during 1961 is primarily attributable to Wrigley Field, the Los Angeles Angels' home park, and Metropolitan Stadium, the Minnesota Twins' home park, which were introduced to major league baseball that year. Wrigley Field, the former home of the Los Angeles Angels of the Pacific Coast League, was a bandbox that measured only 345 feet to the power alleys. Wrigley Field increased runs scored by 25 percent and home runs by 100 percent over a neutral park during 1961 and was the scene of 248 home runs during the season.

Metropolitan Stadium, the scene of 181 home runs in 1961, was also a strong hitter's park, increasing runs and home runs by approximately 10 percent over a neutral park during its 21-year history.

In 1962, the National League awarded two new franchises to Houston and New York. Although players such as Willie Mays, Frank Robinson, and Hank Aaron had fine seasons, only Tommy Davis of the Los Angeles Dodgers had an out-of-context season, batting .346 and driving in 153 runs. Flying in the face of the expectation that expansion leads to higher levels of offense, runs per game and home runs per game actually declined in the majors during 1962. This was due in part to the addition of two strong pitcher's parks, Colt Stadium and Dodger Stadium, to the roster of major league stadiums that year. Colt Stadium, the new home of the Houston Colt 45's, had deep power alleys that were made all the more difficult to reach because the wind consistently blew in from right field. Over its history, Colt Stadium would reduce runs by 15 percent and home runs by 35 percent compared to a neutral park. In 1962, both the Dodgers and Angels moved from terrific hitter's parks, the Los Angeles Coliseum and Wrigley Field respectively, to pitcher-friendly Dodger Stadium, taking a substantial number of runs and home runs out of the league. By 1963, any lingering impact of the 1962 expansion was buried by Ford Frick's rule changes that expanded the strike zone and began the era of the high hard one.

The major leagues next expanded in 1969 when the American League admitted the Kansas City Royals and the Seattle Pilots and the National League added the Montreal Expos and the San Diego Padres, bringing the total number of major league franchises to 24.

	BA	R/G	HR	HR/G
1968	.237	3.42	1995	0.61
1969	.248	4.07	3119	0.80
1970	.254	4.34	3429	0.88

During the 1969 season, major league offensive statistics improved dramatically, with home runs per game and runs per game increasing by 31 percent and 19 percent, respectively. This increase in offense was not attributable to expansion, but was the result of concerted steps on the part of baseball to help the hitters in the aftermath of the 1968 season; that season had represented the nadir for hitters in the twentieth century with both the major league batting average and runs per game falling to historically low levels. More troubling to Major League Baseball, attendance fell for the second year in a row in 1968 to 9 percent below the all-time attendance record of 25.2 million set in 1966.

Following the dictum that pitching and defense win pennants but offense puts fannies in the seats, the Official Baseball Playing Rules Committee set about helping its hitters during the off-season leading up to the 1969 season. The strike zone was squeezed at the top and bottom to include only the area between the top of the knees and the armpits. This represented a return to the definition of the strike zone used prior to 1963. Additionally, the maximum height of the pitcher's mound was set at 10 inches, which represented a de facto 5-inch lowering of the mound. Individual teams also took steps to increase offense by moving in home run fences and reducing foul territory. In Chicago, the White Sox moved the home run fences at Comiskey Park in by 15 feet, which resulted in the number of home runs hit at Comiskey Park jumping from 76 in 1968 to 141 in 1969. The Atlanta Braves moved Atlanta–Fulton County Stadium's fences in by 10 feet, increasing the number of home runs hit at the Launching Pad from 85 in 1968 to 159 in 1969. Similarly, the Los Angeles Dodgers moved Dodger Stadium's fences in by 10 feet and saw home runs double from 48 in 1968 to 96 in 1969. Finally, in Oakland the Athletics moved the fences in by 3 feet on the foul lines and 10 feet in dead center; but, more important, substantially reduced the foul territory behind home plate. As a result, the Oakland "Mausoleum" saw 143 home runs in 1969 as compared to 96 the year before.

Baseball expanded to 26 teams in 1977 with the addition of the Seattle Mariners and the Toronto Blue Jays to the American League. Home runs and scoring jumped during 1977 but fell back to pre-expansion levels in the following season. Two extraordinary individual seasons occurred in 1977. Rod Carew had the best season of his Hall of Fame career, gathering 239 hits and batting .388, while George Foster came close to copping a National League Triple Crown by hammering 52 home runs and driving in 149 runs while batting .320.

In 1993, the National League expanded to 14 teams, bringing the major league total to 28, with the addition of the Colorado Rockies and the Florida Marlins. As with many expansion seasons, home runs and runs per game jumped in 1993. This, however, was just the first season in a trend of ever-increasing runs per game and home runs that has continued throughout the 1990s and peaked in 1996, with runs per game exceeding 5.00 for the first time since 1936.

	BA	R/G	HR	HR/G
1992	.256	4.12	3038	0.72
1993	.265	4.60	4030	0.89
1994	.270	4.92	3306	1.03

As noted in this chart, the increase in offense experienced in 1993 was part of a trend that continued throughout the 1990s. Stadium architecture has moved strongly toward a revival of the baseball-only urban parks of the early twentieth century through the construction of retro facilities like Camden Yards, Jacobs Field, The Ballpark at Arlington, and Coors Field, or the reconfiguration of existing multipurpose stadiums like the Astrodome, Busch Stadium, or Candlestick Park to create a more intimate baseball setting. For hitters, the primary advantage of these developments has been smaller foul territories and more reachable home run fences, resulting in higher batting averages and increased power statistics. The admission of Denver, located at 5,000 feet above sea level, has also helped hitters by adding a hitter's paradise to the majors.

The latest expansion of the major leagues occurred in 1998 with the addition of the Arizona Diamondbacks to the National League and the Tampa Bay Devil Rays to the American League.

	BA	R/G	HR	HR/G
1997	.267	4.77	4640	1.02
1998	.266	4.79	5064	1.04

The 1998 season was perhaps the quintessential expansion season as league offensive statistics were basically identical to the year before, yet baseball fans were treated to a number of extraordinary individual hitting accomplishments. It was the season of Mark McGwire and Sammy Sosa's neck-and-neck race to the all-time single-season home run record that transfixed baseball fans over the last two months of the season, overshadowing the mock pennant races of wild-card baseball. McGwire's and Sosa's seasons were so exceptional that many other extraordinary slugging seasons that also occurred in 1998 were overshadowed. Both Ken Griffey Jr. and Greg Vaughn reached the 50-homer mark, and both Juan Gonzalez and Albert Belle surpassed the 150-RBI mark during the season.

Further expansion of major league baseball seems likely. Many baseball markets remain untapped, and on this one issue the economic interests of the players and the owners should be aligned. To date, expansion has not weakened the quality of baseball played in the major leagues, as the pool of available baseball players has kept pace with the growth of the majors. Expansion does create a state of flux in the major leagues during which the consistency and quality of competition is diminished for a short period of time. During this period of change, the competitive balance shifts and certain players are better equipped than others to take advantage of the new equilibrium.

The exact role of expansion in creating career seasons may be difficult to quantify, but it is real, as has been shown again and again throughout baseball history. The top batting average (.361), home run total (61), and RBI total (153) of the 1960s all occurred in expansion seasons. The top batting average (.388), home run total (52), and RBI total (149) of the 1970s all occurred in the expansion year of 1977. The top home run total (70) and RBI total (158) of the 1990s both occurred in an expansion year.

The extraordinary individual accomplishments of expansion seasons definitely require scrutiny. This is not to say that Mark McGwire and Sammy Sosa could not have broken Roger Maris's single-season home run record in a nonexpansion season, but expansion certainly made their task a bit easier.

20

The Left-Hander's Advantage and Switch-Hitters

Ask baseball fans who's the greatest hitter of all time, and chances are you'll hear the names Babe Ruth, Ty Cobb, Ted Williams, Joe Jackson, Lou Gehrig, or—from the devout National Leaguers—Stan Musial. All lefties. Lefties may be discriminated against when it comes to driving a stick-shift car or trying to write in a looseleaf notebook, but they have a huge advantage when it comes to hitting a baseball.

The 30 Best: Lifetime Batting Average

10 years and 4,000 at-bats
(left-handed hitters in boldface)

.366	**Ty Cobb**	.342	**Jesse Burkett**	.333	Cap Anson
.358	Rogers Hornsby	.342	**Babe Ruth**	.333	**Paul Waner**
.356	**Joe Jackson**	.342	Harry Heilmann	.333	**Eddie Collins**
.347	Pete Browning	.341	**Bill Terry**	.332	Sam Thompson
.346	Ed Delahanty	.340	**George Sisler**	.331	**Stan Musial**
.345	**Willie Keeler**	.340	**Lou Gehrig**	.330	**Heine Manush**
.345	**Tris Speaker**	.339	Nap Lajoie	.329	**Wade Boggs**
.344	**Billy Hamilton**	.339	**Tony Gwynn**	.329	Hugh Duffy
.344	**Ted Williams**	.336	Riggs Stephenson	.329	Honus Wagner
.342	**Dan Brouthers**	.334	Al Simmons	.328	**Rod Carew**

The Recent Best: Lifetime .300 Hitters

4,000 at-bats, active 1980 or later
(left-handed and switch-hitters in boldface)

.339	Tony Gwynn	.305	**George Brett**
.329	**Wade Boggs**	.305	Bill Madlock
.328	**Rod Carew**	.304	Jeff Bagwell
.320	Frank Thomas	.304	**Bernie Williams** (SH)
.320	Edgar Martinez	.304	**Roberto Alomar** (SH)
.318	Kirby Puckett	.303	**Al Oliver**
.312	**Larry Walker**	.303	**Pete Rose** (SH)
.310	**Mark Grace**	.303	**Mike Greenwell**
.308	Paul Molitor	.302	**Will Clark**
.307	**Don Mattingly**	.301	**Mo Vaughn**
.306	**Ralph Garr**	.301	Julio Franco
		.301	John Olerud

Left-Handers

Three out of 10 major league hitters are left-handed. Nearly 5 out of 10 Hall of Fame hitters are left-handed. Seven out of 10 of the great ones in terms of career batting average are left-handed. True, the list of highest lifetime batting averages is heavy on the early years—25 of the top 30 played their last game no later than 1945, and 12 played their last game in 1920 or earlier. But the list of recent hitters with a .300 lifetime average is also skewed to the left—13 of 20 are either left-handers or switch-hitters.

One more way to demonstrate the left-hander's advantage is to look at batting titles. Of the 198 major league batting titles from 1901 through 1999, 124 (63 percent) have been won by lefties and another 8 by switch-hitters (4 percent); only 33 percent have been won by pure righties. A list of right-handers who have won more than one title in the past 25 years? It's pretty short: Edgar Martinez and Bill Madlock combined to win 6. The lefties: Larry Walker, Tony Gwynn, Wade Boggs, George Brett, Dave Parker, and Rod Carew have won 26, with Willie McGee doing it twice as a switch-hitter.

Shoeless Joe Jackson of the Chicago White Sox. A young Babe Ruth admitted he patterned his swing after Jackson's.

Many great hitters are born with natural talent and are physically superior to others. They can swing a bat as effortlessly as Junior Griffey, or pick up pitches by watching how the seams spin as those with the 20/15 vision of a Ted Williams can do. It's not that the baseball gods have been dispensing these gifts to left-handers more often than right-handers. It's a function, ironically, of how rare it is to be left-handed in the first place. And like most things about hitting, it comes back to pitching—right-handed pitching, to be specific.

For example, during the 1996 season, only 28 percent of the pitchers who took the mound in the major leagues were left-handed. In the National League, only 24 starting pitchers were southpaws. It wasn't much different in 1956 or 1916. Down through the years, roughly 3 in 10 pitchers and hitters have been left-handed. Because only one in 10 human beings is left-handed, this means that, all else being equal, a left-handed man is three times more likely to make it to the big leagues than a righty.

Today, every baseball fan knows that playing it by "the book" means putting lefties in the lineup when a righty is pitching. Yankees manager Casey Stengel introduced platooning in the 1950s, having a lefty and righty share the same position. Success is always imitated, and Stengel's Yankees went to the World Series 10 times during his 12-year tenure.

Platooning enables a manager to get the best out of the hitters on his team, and often results in some hidden weapons. The 1955 Yankees had only two individuals with more than 70 RBI, but the two-headed monster at first base (Moose Skowron and Joe Collins) knocked in 106 runs, while outfielders Elston Howard and Irv Noren combined for 102 RBI. Earl Weaver's 1979 AL champion Orioles were eerily similar to the '55 Yankees in many ways, including the production hidden in left field (Gary Roenicke and John Lowenstein combining to hit 36 home runs and knock in 98 runs) and at designated hitter (Lee May and Pat Kelly hitting 28 home runs and knocking in 94 runs).

But what does the platoon system look like from inside the batter's box? Why is it easier for a lefty to hit a righty, a righty to hit a lefty?

When a hitter faces a pitcher who throws from the same side as he hits, nearly every pitch moves away from him. This makes it much more difficult for the hitter to put the bat on the ball. The path of a fastball moves slighty away from the batter. Curveballs drop down and away, and sliders cut across the hitting zone. If the batter commits to a pitch early and is fooled, he has no way to recover because it's moving away from him. Best case, he lunges to foul it off. Worst case, a sick-looking swing or a called strike.

A pitcher throwing from the opposite side is much easier to hit. All the pitches are coming in to the hitter. Fastballs come slightly toward the hitter. Curveballs and sliders sweep into the batter's hitting zone. A ball coming in toward a hitter is much easier to judge and handle than one that runs away.

There are several other advantages that help the hitter from the opposite side:

Vision. Both of the batter's eyes can focus on the pitcher's release point. Because of this, the batter has an easier time keeping his front shoulder closed, which helps him avoid pulling out on the pitch.

Time. The hitter can see the ball a split-second longer when it's thrown from the opposite side, because it takes a few inches longer to reach the plate. And when it comes to hitting a baseball, a few inches can mean several hundred feet by the time the ball lands. This is why sidearmers frequently get eaten up by opposite-hand hitters; their pitches travel an even longer distance to reach the plate. The hitter is less likely to get fooled if he can wait to recognize the pitch type and location. And even if he does get fooled, the path of the ball is moving into his swing. The hitter can adjust his swing and increase his chances of making contact.

Plate coverage. The opposite-hand hitter can look for the pitch on the outside part of the plate and try to hit it up the middle or to the opposite field. He doesn't have to worry so much about the inside pitch, because if he gets one, turning on it will be a natural reaction. Many pitchers don't even try, choosing to nibble on the outside corner instead. Go back to Tom Glavine's two starts in the 1995 World Series and watch how this left-hander pitched to Cleveland's right-handed sluggers—away, away, away. Those pitchers who do try to come inside do so at their own peril, knowing that it will be a lot easier for the opposite-hand hitter to get his bat through the hitting zone and turn on the ball. In a righty-righty or lefty-lefty situation, the pitch can get in on the hitter's hands quicker, and that gives him more to think about. If the hitter looks for the inside pitch and gets something outside, he's in big trouble. If the hitter looks for the pitch away and it's thrown inside, he has less time to react.

Fear. Imagine being a right-handed hitter facing a Nolan Ryan curveball that starts out at your head, and then breaks over the plate for a strike. If you guess correctly that it's a curveball and step into the pitch, you have a chance of making contact. If you guess incorrectly, you could get killed. You may remember John Kruk's helpless lefty-lefty at-bat against Randy Johnson during the 1993 All-Star Game. It was obvious that sheer terror had quite an effect on his performance. When a pitch is coming at you from the opposite side, you immediately know to get out of the way. A Greg Maddux tailing fastball thrown to a lefty, and a Fernando Valenzuela screwball to a righty, are exceptions to the rule—and one of the secrets to their success.

There are some hitters who couldn't care less what arm the pitcher throws with, feeling that once the ball is released it's simply the batter against the ball. Rogers Hornsby and Honus Wagner won seven National League batting titles from the right side of the plate, and Bill Madlock and Roberto Clemente won four. In fact, Hornsby won seven batting titles in a row and has the second-highest lifetime batting average. Considering the left-hander's advantage, maybe *he's* the greatest hitter in baseball history.

> *"There are advantages to switch-hitting. Any batter will tell you that the toughest pitch to hit is the one that moves away from him. Every successful pitcher has a curve or slider. Most of them have both pitches. I didn't have to swing at a Bob Gibson slider or a Jim Bunning curve from the right side of the plate."*

— PETE ROSE

> *"One of the scariest things I ever did was when I got my first hit off of Nolan Ryan. He can be a very intimidating figure because besides throwing so hard, he'll put one right in your ear. The one hit that I can remember was a curveball with two strikes. I had a 1–2 count, and he threw one right at my head, purposely up and in to get me off the plate. And I said to myself, OK, he's setting me up for the curveball. He's going to throw that one where he starts it off at my head and it just breaks right over the plate, and he wants me to flinch. [Hanging in] was not an easy thing to do because if I read the pitch wrong, I'd have a hard time getting out of the way. But I saw the pitch and stayed with it and lined a base hit to left field."*

—DAVE GALLAGHER, MAJOR LEAGUER 1987–95

Bill Madlock won four batting titles in the National League. He won back-to-back hitting crowns with the Chicago Cubs in 1975 and 1976, and won two more as a Pittsburgh Pirate in 1981 and 1983.

Switch-Hitters

When did today's switch-hitters decide to become switch-hitters? Usually the moment of truth came as early as the teen years, when they started seeing their first really good breaking balls. Most of us persevere and learn to cope as best we can. But some say to themselves "I don't have to put up with this" and teach themselves to hit from both sides. For the fleet-of-foot, right-handed batter, there is an added incentive in trying to switch-hit. By moving to the other side of the plate, he is one step closer to first base. A few extra infield singles or safe bunts can make a major difference in batting average over the course of a season.

Surprisingly, anecdotal evidence of switch-hitting predates the development of the breaking ball in the early 1870s. In the famous game at the Capitoline

Grounds on June 14, 1870, in which the Brooklyn Atlantics ended the Cincinnati Red Stockings' 91-game winning streak, Bob "Death to Flying Things" Ferguson, the Brooklyn captain and a right-handed batter, surprised teammates, opponents, and onlookers alike when he turned around and batted left-handed during the Atlantics' decisive 11th inning rally. The explanation given by Ferguson for his switch-hitting was that he wanted to avoid hitting the ball to the Red Stockings' shortstop, George Wright, who was their best fielder!

In 1872, the National Association made it legal for a pitcher to "jerk his arm, snap his wrist or bend his elbow" when he delivered the ball as long as he kept his hand below his hip at the point of release. This rule change allowed pitchers such as Candy Cummings, Phoney Martin, and Bobby Mathews to throw sidearm or submarine curveballs, thereby creating a more pressing reason for batters to switch-hit.

Switch-hitting remained a relatively rare skill in the 1870s and early 1880s, with only a handful of everyday players doing it. By the late 1880s, a number of quality switch-hitters entered the game, including such players as Tommy Tucker, Duke Farrell, Walt Wilmot, Kid Gleason, Candy LaChance, and Dan McGann. Switch-hitting became so pronounced by 1887 that *Sporting Life* complained about the increasing number of switch-hitters who moved from one side of the plate to the other while the pitcher was in his motion! Interestingly, at this same time, a switch-pitching fad occurred with right-handed pitchers, Tony Mullane, Larry Corcoran, and Icebox Chamberlain trying to pitch a few innings from the port side.

Tommy Tucker of the American Association's Baltimore Orioles became the first switch-hitter to win a major league batting title when he hit .372 in 1889, while Walt Wilmot of the National League's Chicago Colts became the first switch-hitter to win a major league home run title when he stroked 13 in 1890. The reason for this influx of switch-hitters in the 1880s was a concomitant increase in left-handed pitchers. Prior to the mid-1880s, there had been a prejudice against left-handed pitchers. Once this foolish prejudice was dropped and curveballing left-handed pitchers began to take to the mound, switch-hitting became an extremely attractive option.

The prevalence of switch-hitting receded during the twentieth century as teams experimented with platooning, which first came into use during the 1900s and was popularized by George Stallings and the Miracle Braves in 1914. The drift from switch-hitting to platooning may have been a result of the increasing size of major league rosters after the turn of the century. Prior to 1900, teams carried 15 to 18 players who generally were comprised of 7 position players, a pitching staff, and 2 or 3 catchers. As such, there were no viable platooning options except at the catcher's spot. By 1910, rosters had expanded to 25 players, providing managers with a flexibility they had previously not been afforded.

Through the first half of the twentieth century, the top switch-hitters in major league baseball were George Davis, Max Carey, and Frankie Frisch. Notably, no

Many major league switch-hitters have hit home runs from both sides of the plate in one game. During the 1995 season, Ken Caminiti turned the trick three times in one week.

switch-hitter won a major league batting title or a home run crown during the twentieth century until the "Commerce Comet," Mickey Mantle, came to the Bronx in the 1950s. The Negro Leagues did, however, feature a number of great switch-hitters through the 1930s and 1940s, including such players as Cool Papa Bell and Biz Mackey. Perhaps as a result of the return of the running game after the integration of the major leagues, or the impact of a generation of Americans growing up watching Mickey Mantle hit, switch-hitting began to return to prominence in the 1960s with the emergence of star-quality switch-hitters like Maury Wills, Pete Rose, Reggie Smith, and Roy White. The number of switch-hitters continued to increase through the 1970s as the multipurpose artificial turf stadiums of the National League shaped baseball and every team seemed to have a slap-hitting switch-hitting speedster at the top of its lineup.

Today, switch-hitting is as popular as it has been at any time. Many minor league organizations focus on switch-hitting as a means of improving the offensive value of light-hitting middle infielders or speedy outfielders, and many players are eager to learn a skill that might be the difference between earning lunch money in the minors or hitting the jackpot in the major leagues.

Eddie Murray is the only switch-hitter in base-ball history to accumulate more than 3,000 hits and 500 home runs.

Despite the obvious benefits to a player, becoming a switch-hitter is very difficult, since by the age of 10 or 12 most people are firmly established as left- or right-handers. This is why Little League coaches can play a critical role in introducing the concept while there is still time for young players to absorb it with relative ease. Changing from one side to the other involves using the opposite side of the brain, which does not normally deal with precision motor skills. (Pete Reiser, the Brooklyn Dodgers' star of the 1940s, was one of the few totally ambidextrous major leaguers; although he threw right-handed and batted left-handed at the major league level, he could hit and throw with proficiency from either side.)

Bringing the sweet spot of a round bat to precisely the right place, at the instant required to make contact near enough to the center of gravity of a spinning baseball traveling at 90-plus MPH in a nonlinear direction, is amazing. But then driving it forward within the boundaries of a 90-degree sector while avoiding eight fielders strategically placed to prevent you from getting safely on base is one of the most remarkable achievements in all of sports.

It makes blowing away Scud missiles seem like child's play. Radar and other tracking systems, supported by powerful computers, pick up the incoming Scud at a considerable distance, predict its invariable course, plot an interception vector, and fire a missile or two. Usually the Scud is history. On the other hand, a major league batter has less than half a second to do the same thing, using his eyesight as radar, and his brain, experience, and intuition to predict the variable course of the ball. Even the best hitters are only successful in about 30 percent of their at-bats.

Learning to perform this feat later in life from the unnatural side is almost impossible. Yet quite a few players attempt it. Natural left-handers generally have an easier time becoming switch-hitters because they live in a right-handed world and are forced to do many things with their "wrong" hand. This sets up lines of communication between the left and right sides of the brain that righties do not have. For example, the heavy doors on public buildings or shopping centers are almost always set up for right-handers. Scissors, hand tools, can openers, the flush handles on urinals, four-on-the-floor gearshifts, computer mice—you name it, they are all right-handed. There are of course left-handed versions of some of these, but stores don't always stock them—and anyway, what's the point? If you set up your mouse to run left-handed, then you won't develop the dexterity to operate almost all of the other computers in the world.

On the other hand, if the training occurs early enough, it is, to use a computer analogy, part of the formatting of the brain. For example, we all learn to walk, run, and tie our shoelaces at a very young age. But wait a minute—walking and running are common and natural to every human being, while tying shoelaces is a learned and somewhat unnatural skill. Walking and running are proof that both sides of the brain can cooperate to operate the legs, else we could not walk or run. Tying shoelaces likewise confirms that the left and right hands can cooperate on a complex task. How did civilized knowledge get mixed in with instinctual knowledge? Simple—the brain was still "formatting" and took in any knowledge acquired during that period and made it part of hard-wired memory.

The importance of early training in switch-hitting is best exemplified by Mickey Mantle, the greatest switch-hitter in major league history. He has a lifetime batting average of .298, a slugging average of .557, and, most important, a total of 536 home runs. As the table indicates, no other switch-hitter has hit more home runs. Mantle hit tape-measure shots from both sides while maintaining a high batting average. The Mick's dad and his grandfather, one pitching left and the other right, taught him to switch-hit before he was in the second grade. In fact, they started when he was four. Motor skills learned as early as Mickey acquired them are as totally ingrained as knowing how to tie your shoelaces. He was a perfectly comfortable switch-hitter by the time he was eight. While Mickey was a natural right-hander in most everything else, when it came to hitting he was neither left nor right; he was both.

Switch-Hitters: Home Runs

1. Mickey Mantle, 1951–68	536	11. Ken Caminiti, 1987–	209
2. Eddie Murray, 1977–97	504	12. Devon White, 1986–	190
3. Chili Davis, 1981–	350	13. Tim Raines, 1979–	168
4. Reggie Smith, 1966–82	314	14. Roy Smalley Jr., 1975–87	163
5. Bobby Bonilla, 1986–	277	15. Pete Rose, 1963–86	160
6. Ted Simmons, 1968–88	248	16. Roy White, 1965–79	160
7. Ken Singleton, 1970–84	246	17. Tony Phillips, 1982–	160
8. Mickey Tettleton, 1984–97	245	18. Tom Tresh, 1961–69	153
9. Ruben Sierra, 1986–98	239	19. Bernie Williams, 1991–	151
10. Howard Johnson, 1982–95	228	20. Roberto Alomar, 1988–	151

The only switch-hitters in recent years with a shot at Mantle's record have fallen by the wayside as they ran out of time and career. Switch-hitters don't, as a rule, hit with much power; note how few have even reached the 200-homer plateau.

As much as Mantle dominated the power side of switch-hitting, another switch-hitter totally dominated the area of little hits, amassing a total that may never be matched: Pete Rose. Ty Cobb, the former record holder, who was not a switch-hitter, had 4,191 hits in 24 seasons. Rose trumped this with 4,256 hits, the most any player has ever hit, also in 24 seasons.

Switch-Hitters: Hits

1.	Pete Rose, 1963–86	4256	11.	Chili Davis, 1981–1999	2380
2.	Eddie Murray, 1977–97	3255	12.	Willie McGee, 1982–1999	2254
3.	Frankie Frisch, 1919–37	2880	13.	Tony Fernandez, 1983–	2240
4.	George Davis, 1890–1909	2688	14.	Willie Wilson, 1976–1994	2207
5.	Max Carey, 1910–29	2665	15.	Larry Bowa, 1970–1985	2191
6.	Tim Raines, 1979–	2561	16.	Maury Wills, 1959–1972	2134
7.	Ted Simmons, 1968–88	2472	17.	Garry Templeton, 1976–1991	2096
8.	Ozzie Smith, 1978–96	2460	18.	Ken Singleton, 1970–1984	2029
9.	Red Schoendienst, 1945–63	2449	19.	Tony Phillips, 1982–	2023
10.	Mickey Mantle, 1951–68	2415	20.	Roberto Alomar, 1988–	2007

Rose hit 160 homers in his 24 seasons, and of his hits, 3,215 were singles, which means that only 24 percent of his total hits went for extra bases. To put it into perspective, Mantle's lifetime batting average was about the same as Rose's, but extra-base hits accounted for 39 percent of his output.

Like Mantle, Pete acquired the skill when he was quite young. His younger brother, Dave, recalls, "I don't know how many hours of batting practice I threw to him. At night, he'd come home from a date and swing a heavy leaded bat Uncle Buddy gave him, swing 150 times right-handed and 150 times left-handed in front of a mirror, and not for ego. He was perfecting his swing. He'd say 'low outside' . . . swing . . . 'high inside' . . . swing . . . and move the bat, like he was hitting the ball where it was pitched."

An interesting thing about the all-time hit list for switch-hitters is that it is possible for a 22-year-old from a city with both a National and an American League team to say in all honesty that since age 6, he or she has personally seen the vast majority of the game's most prolific switch-hitters in live action. Obviously something is going on, and the increasing focus on switch-hitting in the minors and player development has not only led to more switch-hitters playing in the majors, but to more great switch-hitters.

Appendix:

Hitting Leaders and Highlights, 1901–99

Season	HR	RBI	BA	SA	Bases	Highlights
1901 NL	16 Sam Crawford	126 Honus Wagner	.376 Jesse Burkett	.534 Jimmy Sheckard	365 Jesse Burkett	Napoleon Lajoie of the Philadelphia Athletics wins Triple Crown, legitimizes fledgling outfit called the American League.
1901 AL	14 Napoleon Lajoie	125 Napoleon Lajoie	.426 Napoleon Lajoie	.643 Napoleon Lajoie	369 Napoleon Lajoie	
1902 NL	6 Tommy Leach	91 Honus Wagner	.357 Ginger Beaumont	.463 Honus Wagner	303 Sam Crawford	Standing only 5'6" and weighing only 150, Tommy Leach of the Pittsburgh Pirates is an unlikely home run champ. Appropriately, his will be the lowest league-leading total of the century.
1902 AL	16 Socks Seybold	121 Buck Freeman	.378 Napoleon Lajoie	.590 Ed Delahanty	341 Ed Delahanty	
1903 NL	9 Jimmy Sheckard	104 Sam Mertes	.355 Honus Wagner	.532 Fred Clarke	320 Jimmy Sheckard	On July 2, Washington Nationals slugger Big Ed Delahanty disappears.
1903 AL	13 Buck Freeman	104 Buck Freeman	.344 Napoleon Lajoie	.518 Napoleon Lajoie	311 Buck Freeman	
1904 NL	9 Harry Lumley	80 Bill Dahlen	.349 Honus Wagner	.520 Honus Wagner	314 Honus Wagner	On May 30, Frank Chance of the Chicago Cubs is hit by pitches five times in a doubleheader. He never leaves either game despite losing consciousness at one point.
1904 AL	10 Harry Davis	102 Napoleon Lajoie	.376 Napoleon Lajoie	.552 Napoleon Lajoie	334 Napoleon Lajoie	
1905 NL	9 Fred Odwell	121 Cy Seymour	.377 Cy Seymour	.559 Cy Seymour	376 Cy Seymour	Cy Seymour of the Cincinnati Reds misses the Triple Crown by one home run. Teammate Fred Odwell leads the league but will never hit another home run in the big leagues.
1905 AL	8 Harry Davis	83 Harry Davis	.308 Elmer Flick	.462 Elmer Flick	303 George Stone	
1906 NL	12 Tim Jordan	83 Harry Steinfeldt/ Jim Nealon	.339 Honus Wagner	.477 Harry Lumley	295 Honus Wagner	Bouncing back from an injury-shortened 1905 season, Napoleon Lajoie narrowly misses his fifth batting title in six years. Second-year man George Stone of the St. Louis Browns bests him with a career year.
1906 AL	12 Harry Davis	96 Harry Davis	.358 George Stone	.501 George Stone	343 George Stone	
1907 NL	10 Dave Brain	85 Sherry Magee	.350 Honus Wagner	.513 Honus Wagner	310 Honus Wagner	Ty Cobb and Detroit Tigers teammate Sam Crawford finish in the top 3 in runs, hits, triples, total bases, batting average, and slugging average, but Detroit is swept by the Cubs in the World Series.
1907 AL	8 Harry Davis	119 Ty Cobb	.350 Ty Cobb	.468 Ty Cobb	310 Ty Cobb	
1908 NL	12 Tim Jordan	109 Honus Wagner	.354 Honus Wagner	.542 Honus Wagner	362 Honus Wagner	Sam Crawford becomes the first man to win home run crowns in both the AL and NL.
1908 AL	7 Sam Crawford	108 Ty Cobb	.324 Ty Cobb	.475 Ty Cobb	310 Ty Cobb	

Season	HR	RBI	BA	SA	Bases	Highlights
1909 NL	7 Red Murray	100 Honus Wagner	.339 Honus Wagner	.489 Honus Wagner	308 Honus Wagner	Ty Cobb wins his only home run title, and does so without hitting a ball over the fence all season.
1909 AL	9 Ty Cobb	107 Ty Cobb	.377 Ty Cobb	.517 Ty Cobb	344 Ty Cobb	
1910 NL	10 Wildfire Schulte/ Fred Beck	123 Sherry Magee	.331 Sherry Magee	.507 Sherry Magee	357 Sherry Magee	Rather than see the despised Ty Cobb win the batting title, the St. Louis Browns allow Napoleon Lajoie to go 8 for 8 in the season-ending doubleheader. He collects six bunt singles against a pulled-back infield.
1910 AL	10 Jake Stahl	120 Sam Crawford	.385 Napoleon Lajoie	.551 Ty Cobb	364 Napoleon Lajoie	
1911 NL	21 Wildfire Schulte	107 Wildfire Schulte / Owen Wilson	.334 Honus Wagner	.534 Wildfire Schulte	384 Wildfire Schulte	In the first-ever rabbitball season, Wildfire Schulte of the Cubs has a career year, topping 20 in doubles, triples, and home runs. In the AL, Shoeless Joe Jackson finds that batting .408 is no guarantee of a batting title.
1911 AL	11 Home Run Baker	127 Ty Cobb	.420 Ty Cobb	.621 Ty Cobb	411 Ty Cobb	
1912 NL	14 Heinie Zimmerman	102 Heinie Zimmerman/ Honus Wagner	.372 Heinie Zimmerman/	.571 Heinie Zimmerman	356 Heinie Zimmerman	Longtime reserve Heinie Zimmerman explodes with a Triple-Crown season, though baseball researchers later provide evidence that he had only 99 RBI. Shoeless Joe hits .395 but again finishes second to Ty Cobb in batting.
1912 AL	10 Tris Speaker/ Home Run Baker	130 Home Run Baker	.409 Ty Cobb	.584 Ty Cobb	411 Tris Speaker	
1913 NL	19 Gavvy Cravath	128 Gavvy Cravath	.350 Jake Daubert	.568 Gavvy Cravath	353 Gavvy Cravath	Baker Bowl slugger Gavvy Cravath of the Phillies misses a Triple Crown by five base hits. Shoeless Joe finishes second to Cobb yet again, this time at .373.
1913 AL	12 Home Run Baker	117 Home Run Baker	.390 Ty Cobb	.551 Joe Jackson	371 Joe Jackson	
1914 NL	19 Gavvy Cravath	103 Sherry Magee	.329 Jake Daubert	.509 Sherry Magee	332 Gavvy Cravath	Cobb is credited with another batting crown, though he appears in only 98 games. The Miracle Braves go from last to first and sweep the Series with only one .300 hitter. On July 11, Babe Ruth comes to bat for the first time—and strikes out.
1914 AL	9 Home Run Baker	104 Sam Crawford	.368 Ty Cobb	.513 Ty Cobb	364 Tris Speaker	
1915 NL	24 Gavvy Cravath	115 Gavvy Cravath	.320 Larry Doyle	.510 Gavvy Cravath	352 Gavvy Cravath	A 41-year-old Honus Wagner hits an inside-the-park grand slam on July 29. On May 6, pitcher Babe Ruth hits his first home run—against the Yankees. On August 29, pitcher George Sisler outduels Walter Johnson 2–1.
1915 AL	7 Braggo Roth	112 Bobby Veach/ Sam Crawford	.369 Ty Cobb	.491 Jack Fournier	392 Ty Cobb	

Season	HR	RBI	BA	SA	Bases	Highlights
1916 NL	12 Cy Williams/Dave Robertson	83 Heinie Zimmerman	.339 Hal Chase	.461 Zach Wheat	305 Zach Wheat	In July, a 42-year-old Honus Wagner hits an inside-the-park home run. Rogers Hornsby hits his first home run in May. The Red Sox repeat as world champs, despite hitting only one home run at Fenway Park all season.
1916 AL	12 Wally Pipp	103 Del Pratt	.386 Tris Speaker	.502 Tris Speaker	356 Tris Speaker	
1917 NL	12 Gavvy Cravath/Dave Robertson	102 Heinie Zimmerman	.341 Edd Roush	.484 Rogers Hornsby	321 George Burns	Olympic legend Jim Thorpe of the Reds collects the most famous of his 176 major league hits—a swinging bunt single in the 10th that is the only hit off Hippo Vaughn in the "double no-hitter" thrown by Vaughn and Fred Toney.
1917 AL	9 Wally Pipp	103 Bobby Veach	.383 Ty Cobb	.570 Ty Cobb	397 Ty Cobb	
1918 NL	8 Gavvy Cravath	76 Sherry Magee	.335 Zach Wheat	.455 Edd Roush	249 Heinie Groh/Charlie Hollocher	In a season shortened to 140 games by World War I, the Red Sox dabble with using Babe Ruth as a regular in half of their games. He leads the league in home runs and ties for third in RBI with former Boston pitching ace Smokey Joe Wood.
1918 AL	11 Tilly Walker/Babe Ruth	78 Bobby Veach	.382 Ty Cobb	.555 Babe Ruth	269 Tris Speaker	
1919 NL	12 Gavvy Cravath	73 Hy Myers	.321 Edd Roush	.436 Hy Myers	298 George Burns	On September 20, Babe Ruth establishes a new single-season home run record with his 28th. A month ago to the day, minor leaguer Joe Wilhoit's 69-game hitting streak comes to an end.
1919 AL	29 Babe Ruth	114 Babe Ruth	.384 Ty Cobb	.657 Babe Ruth	385 Babe Ruth	
1920 NL	15 Cy Williams	94 George Kelly/Rogers Hornsby	.370 Rogers Hornsby	.559 Rogers Hornsby	389 Rogers Hornsby	Ruth obliterates the single-season home run and slugging average records while also setting a modern record for RBI. George Sisler of the St. Louis Browns sets a record of his own: 257 hits in a season, a mark that still stands.
1920 AL	54 Babe Ruth	137 Babe Ruth	.407 George Sisler	.847 Babe Ruth	536 Babe Ruth	
1921 NL	23 George Kelly	126 Rogers Hornsby	.397 Rogers Hornsby	.639 Rogers Hornsby	438 Rogers Hornsby	On July 12, Babe Ruth becomes the all-time home run champ with 137, passing Roger Connor. He will go on to break his own single-season home run, RBI, and bases marks. On August 19, Ty Cobb gets his 3,000th hit.
1921 AL	59 Babe Ruth	171 Babe Ruth	.394 Harry Heilmann	.846 Babe Ruth	601 Babe Ruth	
1922 NL	42 Rogers Hornsby	152 Rogers Hornsby	.401 Rogers Hornsby	.722 Rogers Hornsby	515 Rogers Hornsby	Rogers Hornsby establishes new NL standards in these five offensive categories as well as hits, doubles, total bases, and on-base percentage. On August 25, the Cubs go up 25–6 on the Phillies and hold on to win 26–23. George Sisler hits in 41 consecutive games.
1922 AL	39 Ken Williams	155 Ken Williams	.420 George Sisler	.672 Babe Ruth	441 Ken Williams	

Season	HR	RBI	BA	SA	Bases	Highlights
1923 NL	41 Cy Williams	125 Irish Meusel	.384 Rogers Hornsby	.627 Rogers Hornsby	367 Cy Williams	Babe Ruth hits a home run in the first game ever played at Yankee Stadium. On July 7, pitcher Lefty O'Doul is tagged for 16 runs in three innings; he will return to the majors five years later as a hitter and will go on to win two batting titles.
1923 AL	41 Babe Ruth	131 Babe Ruth	.403 Harry Heilmann	.764 Babe Ruth	569 Babe Ruth	
1924 NL	27 Jack Fournier	136 George Kelly	.424 Rogers Hornsby	.696 Rogers Hornsby	462 Rogers Hornsby	Hornsby sets the single-season batting average record and comes within two home runs of another Triple Crown. Jim Bottomley knocks in 12 runs against the Dodgers.
1924 AL	46 Babe Ruth	129 Goose Goslin	.378 Babe Ruth	.739 Babe Ruth	533 Babe Ruth	
1925 NL	39 Rogers Hornsby	143 Rogers Hornsby	.403 Rogers Hornsby	.756 Rogers Hornsby	464 Rogers Hornsby	Hornsby wins another Triple Crown and sets an NL slugging average mark that even withstood McGwire's onslaught. On June 2, Lou Gehrig replaces Wally Pipp at first base. On May 17, Tris Speaker collects his 3,000th hit. On June 3, Eddie Collins collects his 3,000th hit. On May 5, 38-year-old Ty Cobb hits 3 home runs and goes 6 for 6 against the Browns.
1925 AL	33 Bob Meusel	138 Bob Meusel	.393 Harry Heilmann	.613 Ken Williams	427 Al Simmons	
1926 NL	21 Hack Wilson	120 Jim Bottomley	.336 Paul Waner	.568 Cy Williams	363 Jim Bottomley	Ruth returns from a suspension- and injury-shortened 1925 to dominate the league again, missing a Triple Crown by six points. On June 8, he hits the first "tape-measure" home run—a 626-foot bomb that lands two blocks away from Tiger Stadium. After the season, Ty Cobb and Tris Speaker are accused of throwing games in 1919—charges that are later dropped. By today's rules for minimum plate appearances, Paul Waner would have been the first rookie to win a batting title.
1926 AL	47 Babe Ruth	146 Babe Ruth	.378 Heinie Manush	.737 Babe Ruth	509 Babe Ruth	
1927 NL	30 Hack Wilson/Cy Williams	131 Paul Waner	.380 Paul Waner	.590 Chick Hafey	419 Rogers Hornsby	Mel Ott hits his first home run at 18. Babe Ruth breaks his own record with 60 home runs. More quietly, Lou Gehrig breaks Ruth's record for RBI in a season with 175. On July 18, Ty Cobb, now with the Athletics, reaches 4,000 hits against the Tigers.
1927 AL	60 Babe Ruth	175 Lou Gehrig	.398 Harry Heilmann	.772 Babe Ruth	556 Lou Gehrig	
1928 NL	31 Hack Wilson/Jim Bottomley	136 Jim Bottomley	.387 Rogers Hornsby	.632 Rogers Hornsby	433 Jim Bottomley	On September 3, Ty Cobb doubles against Washington for the 4,191st and final hit of his career. Goose Goslin of Washington finishes fast to take the batting title from the Browns' Heinie Manush by one point in a final-day, head-to-head showdown between the two teams.
1928 AL	54 Babe Ruth	142 Babe Ruth/Lou Gehrig	.379 Goose Goslin	.709 Babe Ruth	515 Babe Ruth	

Season	HR	RBI	BA	SA	Bases	Highlights
1929 NL	43 Chuck Klein	159 Hack Wilson	.398 Lefty O'Doul	.679 Rogers Hornsby	496 Rogers Hornsby	On July 6, the Cardinals establish a modern record by scoring 28 runs against the Phillies.
1929 AL	46 Babe Ruth	157 Al Simmons	.369 Lew Fonseca	.697 Babe Ruth	444 Lou Gehrig	Chuck Klein sets a new NL mark for home runs in a season with 43. Mel Ott is at 42, but Phillies pitchers intentionally walk him five times on the final day of the season, once with the bases loaded.
1930 NL	56 Hack Wilson	190 Hack Wilson	.401 Bill Terry	.723 Hack Wilson	528 Hack Wilson	Hack Wilson sets a new NL record for home runs, and does so before the end of August. On May 21, Babe Ruth passes up a shot at four home runs in a game by batting right-handed and striking out in the ninth inning against the A's.
1930 AL	49 Babe Ruth	174 Lou Gehrig	.381 Al Simmons	.732 Babe Ruth	520 Lou Gehrig	
1931 NL	31 Chuck Klein	121 Chuck Klein	.349 Chick Hafey	.584 Chuck Klein	406 Chuck Klein	32 doubles are hit in a Cards–Cubs double-header, as an overflow crowd of 45,000 spills into the outfield in St. Louis. In the AL, Earl Webb of the Red Sox hits a major league record 67 doubles.
1931 AL	46 Babe Ruth/ Lou Gehrig	184 Lou Gehrig	.390 Al Simmons	.700 Babe Ruth	527 Lou Gehrig	
1932 NL	38 Mel Ott/ Chuck Klein	143 Don Hurst	.368 Lefty O'Doul	.646 Chuck Klein	480 Chuck Klein	Dale Alexander wins the batting crown, though under present scoring rules he would not have enough plate appearances to qualify. It costs Jimmie Foxx, who hit .364, a Triple Crown. Foxx is only the third man to top 50 home runs in a season.
1932 AL	58 Jimmie Foxx	169 Jimmie Foxx	.367 Dale Alexander	.749 Jimmie Foxx	554 Jimmie Foxx	
1933 NL	28 Chuck Klein	120 Chuck Klein	.368 Chuck Klein	.602 Chuck Klein	421 Chuck Klein	Though it's Chuck Klein and Jimmie Foxx who dominate their leagues all season, it's Babe Ruth who steals the show at the first All-Star Game with a home run.
1933 AL	48 Jimmie Foxx	163 Jimmie Foxx	.356 Jimmie Foxx	.703 Jimmie Foxx	499 Jimmie Foxx	
1934 NL	35 Mel Ott/ Ripper Collins	135 Mel Ott	.362 Paul Waner	.615 Ripper Collins	429 Mel Ott	On July 5, Lou Gehrig hits his 17th grand slam to pass Babe Ruth for most all-time, on his way to a record 23. On July 13, Ruth hits his 700th home run.
1934 AL	49 Lou Gehrig	165 Lou Gehrig	.363 Lou Gehrig	.706 Lou Gehrig	518 Lou Gehrig	
1935 NL	34 Wally Berger	130 Wally Berger	.385 Arky Vaughan	.607 Arky Vaughan	411 Mel Ott	On May 25, Babe Ruth hits three home runs in a game, the final three of his career.
1935 AL	36 Hank Greenberg/ Jimmie Foxx	170 Hank Greenberg	.349 Buddy Myer	.636 Jimmie Foxx	476 Hank Greenberg	

Season	HR	RBI	BA	SA	Bases	Highlights
1936 NL	33 Mel Ott	138 Joe Medwick	.373 Paul Waner	.588 Mel Ott	425 Mel Ott	Joe Medwick establishes an NL record for doubles that still stands (64). On May 3, Joe DiMaggio breaks in with the Yankees with three hits. Three weeks later, teammate Tony Lazzeri knocks in an AL-record 11 runs in one game.
1936 AL	49 Lou Gehrig	162 Hal Trosky	.388 Luke Appling	.696 Lou Gehrig	533 Lou Gehrig	
1937 NL	31 Mel Ott/ Joe Medwick	154 Joe Medwick	.374 Joe Medwick	.641 Joe Medwick	447 Joe Medwick	On June 3, Negro League legend Josh Gibson nearly hits a ball out of Yankee Stadium. Tigers rookie catcher Rudy York hits a record 18 home runs in one month. Mickey Cochrane has his skull fractured by a pitched ball after homering in what proves to be his last at-bat in the major leagues.
1937 AL	46 Joe DiMaggio	183 Hank Greenberg	.371 Charlie Gehringer	.673 Joe DiMaggio	499 Hank Greenberg	
1938 NL	36 Mel Ott	122 Joe Medwick	.342 Ernie Lombardi	.614 Johnny Mize	425 Mel Ott	On August 2, the Dodgers use yellow baseballs in a game against the Cardinals at Ebbets Field.
1938 AL	58 Hank Greenberg	175 Jimmie Foxx	.349 Jimmie Foxx	.704 Jimmie Foxx	517 Jimmie Foxx	Jimmie Foxx sets a record with nine multihomer games, yet falls five short of the league lead in home runs. On June 21, Red Sox third baseman Pinky Higgins gets 12 consecutive hits over two days.
1939 NL	28 Johnny Mize	128 Frank McCormick	.349 Johnny Mize	.626 Johnny Mize	445 Johnny Mize	On April 20, Ted Williams debuts against the Yankees with consecutive strikeouts before doubling. He will go on to have the greatest rookie season in history. On May 2, Lou Gehrig pulls himself from the Yankees' starting lineup. He retires on June 21 and on July 4 becomes the first man to have his uniform number retired.
1939 AL	35 Jimmie Foxx	145 Ted Williams	.381 Joe DiMaggio	.694 Jimmie Foxx	451 Ted Williams	
1940 NL	43 Johnny Mize	137 Johnny Mize	.317 Stan Hack	.636 Johnny Mize	450 Johnny Mize	The top four hitters in the NL fail to have enough plate appearances to qualify for the batting title by today's standards. Today, the winner would be Cubs third baseman Stan Hack at a distant .317.
1940 AL	41 Hank Greenberg	150 Hank Greenberg	.352 Joe DiMaggio	.670 Hank Greenberg	477 Hank Greenberg	On September 24, Jimmie Foxx becomes the second man to hit 500 home runs.
1941 NL	34 Dolph Camilli	120 Dolph Camilli	.343 Pete Reiser	.558 Pete Reiser	398 Dolph Camilli	On July 17, Joe DiMaggio's hitting streak is stopped by the Cleveland Indians at 56 games.
1941 AL	37 Ted Williams	125 Joe DiMaggio	.406 Ted Williams	.735 Ted Williams	480 Ted Williams	Ted Williams goes 6 for 8 on the final day of the season to finish the season at .406, the last man to top the .400 mark. On September 17, Stan Musial goes 2 for 4 in his first big league game. On June 6, the New York Giants introduce the batting helmet to the major leagues.

Season	HR	RBI	BA	SA	Bases	Highlights
1942 NL	30 Mel Ott	110 Johnny Mize	.318 Enos Slaughter	.521 Johnny Mize	382 Mel Ott	On May 19, Paul Waner joins the 3,000-hit club with a single against the Pirates, his former team.
1942 AL	36 Ted Williams	137 Ted Williams	.356 Ted Williams	.648 Ted Williams	483 Ted Williams	Fans jam Yankee Stadium for a Yankees–Senators game, though the main attraction is a pregame batting matchup between Babe Ruth and Walter Johnson. Ruth hits a home run.
1943 NL	29 Bill Nicholson	128 Bill Nicholson	.357 Stan Musial	.562 Stan Musial	419 Stan Musial	With 29, Bill Nicholson of the Cubs hits more home runs than the rest of his teammates combined. On June 17, manager Joe Cronin of the
1943 AL	34 Rudy York	118 Rudy York	.328 Luke Appling	.527 Rudy York	385 Rudy York	Boston Red Sox clubs pinch-hit three-run homers in both ends of a doubleheader. For the season he bats .429 as a pinch-hitter with 5 home runs.
1944 NL	33 Bill Nicholson	122 Bill Nicholson	.357 Dixie Walker	.549 Stan Musial	410 Bill Nicholson	The St. Louis Browns reach their only World Series, taking the pennant on the final day of the season as .234-hitting Chet Laabs hits 2 of his 5
1944 AL	22 Nick Etten	109 Vern Stephens	.327 Lou Boudreau	.528 Bobby Doerr	372 Bob Johnson	home runs for the season.
1945 NL	28 Tommy Holmes	124 Dixie Walker	.355 Phil Cavaretta	.577 Tommy Holmes	437 Tommy Holmes	On August 1, Mel Ott hits his 500th home run. Braves outfielder Tommy Holmes hits in 37 consecutive games; he finishes the season at the top of the league in home runs, though he only fans
1945 AL	24 Vern Stephens	111 Nick Etten	.309 Snuffy Stirnweiss	.476 Snuffy Stirnweiss	379 Snuffy Stirnweiss	*nine* times all season. Hank Greenberg returns from the war to hit a ninth-inning grand slam that wins the pennant for the Tigers.
1946 NL	23 Ralph Kiner	130 Enos Slaughter	.365 Stan Musial	.587 Stan Musial	439 Stan Musial	Carvel Rowell of the Braves shatters the Ebbets Field clock with a home run on May 30. On July 14, Lou Boudreau, player-manager of the
1946 AL	44 Hank Greenberg	127 Hank Greenberg	.353 Mickey Vernon	.667 Ted Williams	499 Ted Williams	Cleveland Indians, debuts the Ted Williams shift, in which only the third baseman and left fielder play to the left of second base.
1947 NL	51 Johnny Mize/Ralph Kiner	138 Johnny Mize	.363 Harry Walker	.639 Ralph Kiner	459 Ralph Kiner	On April 15, Jackie Robinson of the Brooklyn Dodgers breaks the color line in the National League. On July 5, Larry Doby of the Cleveland Indians does the same in the American League.
1947 AL	32 Ted Williams	114 Ted Williams	.343 Ted Williams	.634 Ted Williams	497 Ted Williams	Despite winning the Triple Crown, Ted Williams narrowly misses winning the AL MVP as one Boston sportswriter leaves him off his ballot completely.

Season	HR	RBI	BA	SA	Bases	Highlights
1948 NL	40 Johnny Mize/ Ralph Kiner	131 Stan Musial	.376 Stan Musial	.702 Stan Musial	508 Stan Musial	On June 13, Babe Ruth's uniform number is retired by the Yankees. He dies two months later, and tens of thousands of mourners file past his casket in Yankee Stadium. Hack Wilson quietly dies a pauper a few months later.
1948 AL	39 Joe DiMaggio	155 Joe DiMaggio	.369 Ted Williams	.615 Ted Williams	439 Ted Williams	
1949 NL	54 Ralph Kiner	127 Ralph Kiner	.342 Jackie Robinson	.658 Ralph Kiner	489 Stan Musial	A hitless final game of the season against the Yankees costs Ted Williams a batting title and a Triple Crown, and helps cost the Red Sox the pennant. Monuments to Lou Gehrig and Babe Ruth are erected in center field in Yankee Stadium.
1949 AL	43 Ted Williams	159 Ted Williams/ Vern Stephens	.343 George Kell	.650 Ted Williams	530 Ted Williams	
1950 NL	47 Ralph Kiner	126 Del Ennis	.346 Stan Musial	.596 Stan Musial	445 Ralph Kiner	On August 11, Yankees manager Casey Stengel benches a slumping Joe DiMaggio. A month later, DiMaggio responds to the unprecedented action with three home runs at Griffith Stadium in D.C. Billy Goodman wins the batting title for the Red Sox despite not having a regular position
1950 AL	37 Al Rosen	144 Vern Stephens/ Walt Dropo	.354 Billy Goodman	.585 Joe DiMaggio	414 Joe DiMaggio	
1951 NL	42 Ralph Kiner	121 Monte Irvin	.355 Stan Musial	.627 Ralph Kiner	470 Ralph Kiner	Mickey Mantle debuts on April 18, going 1 for 4. His first home run comes 13 days later against the White Sox. Rookie Willie Mays goes 0 for 12 before homering off Warren Spahn on May 28. The man Willie Mays moved out of center field, Bobby Thomson, homers in the bottom of the ninth against the Dodgers to win a three-game playoff and send the Giants to the World Series.
1951 AL	33 Gus Zernial	129 Gus Zernial	.344 Ferris Fain	.556 Ted Williams	439 Ted Williams	
1952 NL	37 Ralph Kiner/ Hank Sauer	121 Hank Sauer	.336 Stan Musial	.538 Stan Musial	407 Stan Musial	In the heat of a batting race on the last day of the season, Stan Musial is the starting pitcher against the Cubs so that he can face his rival, leadoff man Frankie Baumholtz. Ted Williams hits a game-winning home run against the Tigers in his last at-bat before joining the Marines as a fighter pilot in Korea. Ralph Kiner wins his seventh home run title in his seventh season in the league. Boston first baseman Walt Dropo ties the major league record with 12 consecutive hits.
1952 AL	32 Larry Doby	105 Al Rosen	.327 Ferris Fain	.541 Larry Doby	372 Al Rosen	

Season	HR	RBI	BA	SA	Bases	Highlights
1953 NL	47 Eddie Mathews	142 Roy Campanella	.344 Carl Furillo	.627 Duke Snider	466 Stan Musial	Joe Adcock becomes the first man to hit a home run into the center-field bleachers at the Polo Grounds, 475 feet from home plate. Twelve days earlier, Mickey Mantle's legend is born with a 565-foot home run at Griffith Stadium in Washington. On June 18, Gene Stephens gets three hits in one inning for the Red Sox in a 17-run seventh. Indians third baseman Al Rosen misses a Triple Crown by .0011 points.
1953 AL	43 Al Rosen	145 Al Rosen	.337 Mickey Vernon	.613 Al Rosen	452 Al Rosen	
1954 NL	49 Ted Kluszewski	141 Ted Kluszewski	.345 Willie Mays	.667 Willie Mays	462 Stan Musial	Bobby Thomson loses his job again, this time to Henry Aaron. Aaron hits his first home run in St. Louis on April 23. On May 2, Stan Musial hits five home runs in a doubleheader.
1954 AL	32 Larry Doby	126 Larry Doby	.341 Bobby Avila	.535 Minnie Minoso	387 Mickey Mantle	
1955 NL	51 Willie Mays	136 Duke Snider	.338 Richie Ashburn	.659 Willie Mays	461 Willie Mays	On September 19, Ernie Banks hits his record fifth grand slam in one season. Willie Mays becomes the seventh man to hit 50 home runs in a season. Al Kaline wins the batting title at 20, the youngest to ever do so. Under present rules, the highly selective Ted Williams would have won—but they went by at-bats, not plate appearances, back then.
1955 AL	37 Mickey Mantle	116 Jackie Jensen/ Ray Boone	.340 Al Kaline	.611 Mickey Mantle	429 Mickey Mantle	
1956 NL	43 Duke Snider	109 Stan Musial	.328 Hank Aaron	.598 Duke Snider	423 Duke Snider	Dale Long hits home runs in eight consecutive games. Frank Robinson ties the rookie record with 38 home runs. Mickey Mantle sets a new mark for home runs from both sides of the plate in the same game with three, a mark he would break seven more times. On May 30, his 20th home run comes within 1½ feet of leaving Yankee Stadium.
1956 AL	52 Mickey Mantle	130 Mickey Mantle	.353 Mickey Mantle	.705 Mickey Mantle	488 Mickey Mantle	
1957 NL	44 Hank Aaron	132 Hank Aaron	.351 Stan Musial	.626 Willie Mays	442 Willie Mays	Sixteen years after hitting .406 and slugging .735, Ted Williams comes the closest to meeting those numbers again.
1957 AL	42 Roy Sievers	114 Roy Sievers	.388 Ted Williams	.731 Ted Williams	461 Mickey Mantle	
1958 NL	47 Ernie Banks	129 Ernie Banks	.350 Richie Ashburn	.614 Ernie Banks	431 Ernie Banks	On May 13, Stan Musial becomes the eighth member of the 3,000-hit club. Ernie Banks's unprecedented power surge for a shortstop wins him MVP honors, despite a sixth-place finish by the Cubs.
1958 AL	42 Mickey Mantle	122 Jackie Jensen	.328 Ted Williams	.620 Rocky Colavito	436 Mickey Mantle	

Season	HR	RBI	BA	SA	Bases	Highlights
1959 NL	46 Eddie Mathews	143 Ernie Banks	.355 Hank Aaron	.636 Hank Aaron	451 Hank Aaron	Willie McCovey makes his debut on July 30, going 4 for 4 against future Hall of Famer Robin Roberts. The majors' shift from rail to air travel claims a victim: three-time RBI champ Jackie Jensen, the Red Sox 32-year-old right fielder retires from the game after the '59 season due to fear of flying.
1959 AL	42 Harmon Killebrew/ Rocky Colavito	112 Jackie Jensen	.353 Harvey Kuenn	.530 Al Kaline	372 Mickey Mantle/ Harmon Killebrew/ Rocky Colavito	
1960 NL	41 Ernie Banks	126 Hank Aaron	.325 Dick Groat	.595 Frank Robinson	413 Eddie Mathews	On June 17, Ted Williams becomes the fourth member of the 500-homer club. His 521st and final home run comes on September 26 in his last at-bat.
1960 AL	40 Mickey Mantle	112 Roger Maris	.320 Pete Runnels	.581 Roger Maris	405 Mickey Mantle	
1961 NL	46 Orlando Cepeda	142 Orlando Cepeda	.351 Roberto Clemente	.611 Frank Robinson	415 Willie Mays	On May 9, Jim Gentile becomes the first man to hit grand slams in consecutive at-bats; he will finish the season with five to tie the record. On July 17, Ty Cobb dies of cancer. On October 1, Roger Maris hits his 61st home run in the final game of the season. Only 14 years after Jackie Robinson breaks the color barrier, black and Latino players in the NL sweep all five of these offensive categories. Players of color will dominate the National League for the rest of the decade.
1961 AL	61 Roger Maris	142 Roger Maris	.361 Norm Cash	.687 Mickey Mantle	479 Mickey Mantle	
1962 NL	49 Willie Mays	153 Tommy Davis	.346 Tommy Davis	.624 Frank Robinson	460 Willie Mays	On May 19, Stan Musial becomes the all-time NL hits leader with 3,431, passing Honus Wagner. Harmon Killebrew ends Mickey Mantle's eight-year run as AL bases leader.
1962 AL	48 Harmon Killebrew	126 Harmon Killebrew	.326 Pete Runnels	.605 Mickey Mantle	407 Harmon Killebrew	
1963 NL	44 Willie McCovey/ Hank Aaron	130 Hank Aaron	.326 Tommy Davis	.586 Hank Aaron	448 Hank Aaron	The strike zone is expanded, from the top of the shoulders to the bottom of the knees. Stan Musial, already a grandfather, retires at season's end with 3,630 base hits.
1963 AL	45 Harmon Killebrew	118 Dick Stuart	.321 Carl Yastrzemski	.555 Harmon Killebrew	371 Bob Allison	
1964 NL	47 Willie Mays	119 Ken Boyer	.339 Roberto Clemente	.607 Willie Mays	433 Willie Mays	Members of the once-lowly Washington Senators, now known as the Minnesota Twins, lead the AL in seven offensive categories: runs, hits, doubles, triples, home runs, total bases, and batting average. It's a feat matched only by the 1908 Tigers of Ty Cobb and Sam Crawford.
1964 AL	49 Harmon Killebrew	118 Brooks Robinson	.323 Tony Oliva	.606 Boog Powell	409 Harmon Killebrew	

Season	HR	RBI	BA	SA	Bases	Highlights
1965 NL	52 Willie Mays	130 Deron Johnson	.329 Roberto Clemente	.645 Willie Mays	436 Willie Mays	On September 13, Willie Mays becomes the fifth member of the 500-homer club. On August 20, Eddie Mathews hits a home run that propels Aaron and Mathews past Ruth and Gehrig as the all-time home run tandem.
1965 AL	32 Tony Conigliaro	108 Rocky Colavito	.321 Tony Oliva	.536 Carl Yastrzemski	370 Rocky Colavito	
1966 NL	44 Hank Aaron	127 Hank Aaron	.342 Matty Alou	.632 Dick Allen	401 Hank Aaron	Tony Cloninger–a pitcher–hits 2 grand slams and knocks in 9 runs in a 17–3 victory over the Giants. Frank Robinson's Triple Crown performance makes him the only man to win the MVP in both leagues.
1966 AL	49 Frank Robinson	122 Frank Robinson	.316 Frank Robinson	.637 Frank Robinson	454 Frank Robinson	
1967 NL	39 Hank Aaron	111 Orlando Cepeda	.357 Roberto Clemente	.573 Hank Aaron	407 Hank Aaron	On May 14, Mickey Mantle becomes the sixth player to hit 500 home runs. Two months later, Eddie Mathews becomes the seventh. A player en route to 500, Tony Conigliaro, has his career ruined when he is hit in the eye with a pitched ball.
1967 AL	44 Carl Yastrzemski/ Harmon Killebrew	121 Carl Yastrzemski	.326 Carl Yastrzemski	.622 Carl Yastrzemski	451 Carl Yastrzemski	
1968 NL	36 Willie McCovey	105 Willie McCovey	.335 Pete Rose	.545 Willie McCovey	369 Billy Williams	Thirty-one-game winner Denny McLain throws batting practice fastballs to Mickey Mantle, allowing Mantle to hit home run 535 and move into third place on the all-time list. In a year dominated by pitching, Carl Yastrzemski is the AL's only .300 hitter. Hank Aaron joins the 500-homer club.
1968 AL	44 Frank Howard	109 Ken Harrelson	.301 Carl Yastrzemski	.552 Frank Howard	386 Carl Yastrzemski	
1969 NL	45 Willie McCovey	126 Willie McCovey	.348 Pete Rose	.656 Willie McCovey	443 Willie McCovey	On September 22, Willie Mays becomes the second man to hit 600 home runs.
1969 AL	49 Harmon Killebrew	140 Harmon Killebrew	.332 Rod Carew	.608 Reggie Jackson	469 Harmon Killebrew	
1970 NL	45 Johnny Bench	148 Johnny Bench	.366 Rico Carty	.612 Willie McCovey	445 Billy Williams	On May 12, Ernie Banks becomes the ninth member of the 500-homer club. Five days later, Hank Aaron becomes the first man to have both 3,000 hits and 500 home runs. Two months later, Willie Mays joins Hank Aaron on that short list.
1970 AL	44 Frank Howard	126 Frank Howard	.329 Alex Johnson	.592 Carl Yastrzemski	463 Carl Yastrzemski	
1971 NL	48 Willie Stargell	137 Joe Torre	.363 Joe Torre	.669 Hank Aaron	415 Joe Torre	On April 27, Hank Aaron joins the 600-homer club, though a Willie Mays single in the 10th wins the game for the Giants. A month later, Willie Mays hits his 22nd extra-inning home run, which remains a record. Harmon Killebrew and Frank Robinson enter the 500-homer club as members 10 and 11. Reigning AL batting champion Alex Johnson is suspended by the Angels and eventually ruled emotionally incapacitated.
1971 AL	33 Bill Melton	119 Harmon Killebrew	.337 Tony Oliva	.546 Tony Oliva	378 Bobby Murcer	

Season	HR	RBI	BA	SA	Bases	Highlights
1972 NL	40 Johnny Bench	125 Johnny Bench	.333 Billy Williams	.606 Billy Williams	410 Billy Williams	Nate Colbert of the San Diego Padres hits 5 home runs and knocks in 13 runs in a doubleheader.
1972 AL	37 Dick Allen	113 Dick Allen	.318 Rod Carew	.603 Dick Allen	404 Dick Allen	Roberto Clemente gets his 3,000th hit on September 30. AL MVP Dick Allen becomes only the fourth man to hit a home run into the center-field bleachers at Comiskey Park.
1973 NL	44 Willie Stargell	119 Willie Stargell	.338 Pete Rose	.646 Willie Stargell	455 Darrell Evans	On July 21, Hank Aaron joins the 700-homer club. A month later, Willie Mays hits his final home run as a Met, 660. On April 6, Ron Blomberg steps in as the game's first designated hitter, a rule first proposed 45 years before.
1973 AL	32 Reggie Jackson	117 Reggie Jackson	.350 Rod Carew	.531 Reggie Jackson	377 Sal Bando	
1974 NL	36 Mike Schmidt	129 Johnny Bench	.353 Ralph Garr	.546 Mike Schmidt	416 Mike Schmidt	On April 8, Hank Aaron breaks Babe Ruth's career home run record. On October 2, Aaron homers in his last NL at-bat. Al Kaline doubles for hit 3,000 on September 24.
1974 AL	32 Dick Allen	118 Jeff Burroughs	.364 Rod Carew	.563 Dick Allen	370 Jeff Burroughs	
1975 NL	38 Mike Schmidt	120 Greg Luzinski	.354 Bill Madlock	.541 Dave Parker	411 Greg Luzinski	On May 4, Astros first baseman Bob Watson scores baseball's 1,000,000th run. On April 8, Frank Robinson becomes the game's first black manager and responds with a home run in his first at-bat. Rennie Stennett goes 7 for 7, collecting two hits in an inning twice, as the Pirates bomb the Cubs 22–0.
1975 AL	36 George Scott/Reggie Jackson	109 George Scott	.359 Rod Carew	.566 Fred Lynn	422 John Mayberry	
1976 NL	38 Mike Schmidt	121 George Foster	.339 Bill Madlock	.576 Joe Morgan	406 Mike Schmidt	Bill Madlock goes 4 for 4 on the final day of the season to steal the batting title from Ken Griffey Sr., who had been sitting idle to protect his lead.
1976 AL	32 Graig Nettles	109 Lee May	.333 George Brett	.502 Reggie Jackson	347 George Brett/Rod Carew	George Brett slips past teammate Hal McRae in a controversial race in the AL. Hank Aaron hits his last home run, 755, on July 20. George Brett gets at least 3 hits in 6 consecutive games, a record.
1977 NL	52 George Foster	149 George Foster	.338 Dave Parker	.631 George Foster	449 George Foster	Japanese slugger Sadaharu Oh hits his 756th career home run. George Foster is the first man in 12 years to hit 50 home runs.
1977 AL	39 Jim Rice	119 Larry Hisle	.388 Rod Carew	.593 Jim Rice	435 Jim Rice	Rookie Ted Cox of the Red Sox gets 6 hits in his first 6 at-bats.
1978 NL	40 George Foster	120 George Foster	.334 Dave Parker	.585 Dave Parker	400 George Foster	Pete Rose joins the 3,000-hit club on May 5; later in the summer he hits in 44 consecutive games.
1978 AL	46 Jim Rice	139 Jim Rice	.333 Rod Carew	.600 Jim Rice	464 Jim Rice	Davey Johnson and Mike Ivie each hit their second pinch-hit grand slam of the season in June, the first two to ever do it twice in the same year. Willie McCovey hits his 500th home run on June 30.

Season	HR	RBI	BA	SA	Bases	Highlights
1979 NL	48 Dave Kingman	118 Dave Winfield	.344 Keith Hernandez	.613 Dave Kingman	425 Mike Schmidt	Twelve years after meeting in the World Series, Lou Brock and Carl Yastrzemski get their 3,000th hits within 30 days of one another. Bob Watson becomes the first man to hit for the cycle in both leagues.
1979 AL	45 Gorman Thomas	139 Don Baylor	.333 Fred Lynn	.637 Fred Lynn	426 Jim Rice	
1980 NL	48 Mike Schmidt	121 Mike Schmidt	.324 Bill Buckner	.624 Mike Schmidt	431 Mike Schmidt	After making a serious run at .400, George Brett finishes the year at .390, the highest batting average in the majors since Ted Williams hit .406 in 1941.
1980 AL	41 Ben Oglivie/ Reggie Jackson	122 Cecil Cooper	.390 George Brett	.664 George Brett	390 Reggie Jackson	
1981 NL	31 Mike Schmidt	91 Mike Schmidt	.341 Bill Madlock	.644 Mike Schmidt	301 Mike Schmidt	Pete Rose has to sit through a two-month players strike before he can break Stan Musial's NL hit record with 3,631; on the eve of the strike, Nolan Ryan stymies Rose in his bid to break the mark. The strike shortens what might have been the greatest season of Mike Schmidt's career.
1981 AL	22 Eddie Murray/ Bobby Grich/ Dwight Evans/ Tony Armas	78 Eddie Murray	.336 Carney Lansford	.543 Bobby Grich	300 Dwight Evans	
1982 NL	37 Dave Kingman	109 Al Oliver/ Dale Murphy	.331 Al Oliver	.547 Mike Schmidt	396 Dale Murphy	Harvey's Wallbangers, the Milwaukee Brewers, produce the league's top two run scorers, top two in total bases, three of the top five in RBI, two of the top five in batting average, and the leader in doubles, homers, and slugging average. To top it off, Robin Yount, Cecil Cooper, and Paul Molitor place 1-2-3 in hits, all topping 200 for the season.
1982 AL	39 Gorman Thomas/ Reggie Jackson	133 Hal McRae	.332 Willie Wilson	.578 Robin Yount	437 Dwight Evans	
1983 NL	40 Mike Schmidt	121 Dale Murphy	.323 Bill Madlock	.540 Dale Murphy	408 Dale Murphy/ Mike Schmidt	On July 24, George Brett's game-breaking home run against the Yankees is waved off due to excessive pine tar on his bat. The Royals' protest is upheld, and KC wins the game a month later. Bill Madlock wins his fourth batting title.
1983 AL	39 Jim Rice	126 Jim Rice/ Cecil Cooper	.361 Wade Boggs	.563 George Brett	401 Cal Ripken	
1984 NL	36 Mike Schmidt/ Dale Murphy	106 Mike Schmidt/ Gary Carter	.351 Tony Gwynn	.547 Dale Murphy	411 Dale Murphy	Pete Rose joins Ty Cobb in the 4,000-hit club and Reggie Jackson enters the 500-homer club. Don Mattingly goes 4 for 5 on the season's final day to hold off teammate Dave Winfield for the batting title. Mattingly is the first Yankee since Mickey Mantle to take the crown.
1984 AL	43 Tony Armas	123 Tony Armas	.343 Don Mattingly	.541 Harold Baines	431 Dwight Evans	

Season	HR	RBI	BA	SA	Bases	Highlights
1985 NL	37 Dale Murphy	125 Dave Parker	.353 Willie McGee	.577 Pedro Guerrero	422 Dale Murphy	On August 4, the same day that Tom Seaver is winning his 300th game, Rod Carew reaches the 3,000-hit plateau. On September 11, Pete Rose passes Ty Cobb on the all-time hit list.
1985 AL	40 Darrell Evans	145 Don Mattingly	.368 Wage Boggs	.585 George Brett	426 Don Mattingly	
1986 NL	37 Mike Schmidt	119 Mike Schmidt	.334 Tim Raines	.547 Mike Schmidt	391 Mike Schmidt	Don Mattingly sets Yankees records for hits (238) and doubles (53) in a season. An apparent lock for the Hall of Fame, back problems will begin to slowly erode Mattingly's abilities in 1987.
1986 AL	40 Jesse Barfield	121 Joe Carter	.357 Wade Boggs	.573 Don Mattingly	441 Don Mattingly	
1987 NL	49 Andre Dawson	137 Andre Dawson	.370 Tony Gwynn	.597 Jack Clark	443 Dale Murphy	Mike Schmidt's 500th home run proves to be a game winner against the Pirates on April 18. Mark McGwire obliterates the rookie home run record with 49. Padres catcher Benito Santiago establishes a rookie record by hitting in 34 consecutive games.
1987 AL	49 Mark McGwire	134 George Bell	.363 Wade Boggs	.618 Mark McGwire	429 Wade Boggs	
1988 NL	39 Darryl Strawberry	109 Will Clark	.313 Tony Gwynn	.545 Darryl Strawberry	392 Will Clark	On June 11, pitcher Rick Rhoden starts for the Yankees at DH. Wade Boggs becomes the first man to hit .360 in consecutive seasons since Al Simmons hit .381 and .390 in 1930–31.
1988 AL	42 Jose Canseco	124 Jose Canseco	.366 Wade Boggs	.569 Jose Canseco	425 Jose Canseco	
1989 NL	47 Kevin Mitchell	125 Kevin Mitchell	.336 Tony Gwynn	.635 Kevin Mitchell	432 Kevin Mitchell	Commissioner Bart Giamatti bans Pete Rose from baseball for gambling, then dies of a heart attack eight days later. Kirby Puckett and Tony Gwynn both win batting titles on the last day of the season.
1989 AL	36 Fred McGriff	119 Ruben Sierra	.339 Kirby Puckett	.543 Ruben Sierra	408 Fred McGriff	
1990 NL	40 Ryne Sandberg	122 Matt Williams	.335 Willie McGee	.565 Barry Bonds	394 Ryne Sandberg	The Reds intentionally walk Andre Dawson five times in one game. Ken Griffey Sr. and Ken Griffey Jr. become the first father-son combination in the same lineup on August 31 against the Royals. They go on to hit back-to-back home runs against the Angels. Cecil Fielder becomes the first 50-homer man in the AL since Roger Maris.
1990 AL	51 Cecil Fielder	132 Cecil Fielder	.329 George Brett	.592 Cecil Fielder	429 Cecil Fielder	
1991 NL	38 Howard Johnson	117 Howard Johnson	.319 Terry Pendleton	.536 Will Clark	380 Howard Johnson	Frank Thomas produces more bases than any AL hitter outside of Fenway Park since Harmon Killebrew, foreshadowing the beginning of a long stretch of hitting exploits. Base totals will climb to levels not seen since the 1940s and 1950s.
1991 AL	44 Cecil Fielder/Jose Canseco	133 Cecil Fielder	.341 Julio Franco	.593 Danny Tartabull	447 Frank Thomas	

Season	HR	RBI	BA	SA	Bases	Highlights
1992 NL	35 Fred McGriff	109 Darren Daulton	.330 Gary Sheffield	.624 Barry Bonds	422 Barry Bonds	Robin Yount and George Brett each collect their 3,000th hits in September. Dave Winfield knocks in 100 runs at age 40.
1992 AL	43 Juan Gonzalez	124 Cecil Fielder	.343 Edgar Martinez	.585 Mark McGwire	429 Frank Thomas	
1993 NL	46 Barry Bonds	123 Barry Bonds	.370 Andres Galarraga	.677 Barry Bonds	491 Barry Bonds	On September 7, Mark Whiten homers 4 times and knocks in 12 runs, tying both major league records. Dave Winfield gets his 3,000th hit nine days later. Barry Bonds records the highest slugging average since Mickey Mantle in 1961.
1993 AL	46 Juan Gonzalez	129 Albert Belle	.363 John Olerud	.632 Juan Gonzalez	455 Ken Griffey Jr.	
1994 NL	43 Matt Williams	116 Jeff Bagwell	.394 Tony Gwynn	.750 Jeff Bagwell	365 Jeff Bagwell	A players strike cuts short brilliant and potentially legendary seasons by Matt Williams, Ken Griffey, Jeff Bagwell, Frank Thomas, Albert Belle, and Tony Gwynn.
1994 AL	40 Ken Griffey Jr.	112 Kirby Puckett	.359 Paul O'Neill	.729 Frank Thomas	400 Frank Thomas	
1995 NL	40 Dante Bichette	128 Dante Bichette	.368 Tony Gwynn	.620 Dante Bichette	412 Barry Bonds	Eddie Murray gets his 3,000th hit on June 30. Ken Caminiti hits home runs from both sides of the plate 3 times in 4 games. The White Sox and Tigers hit 12 home runs in a 14–12 pitchers' duel on May 28. Albert Belle becomes the only man to top 50 homers and 50 doubles in the same season.
1995 AL	50 Albert Belle	126 Mo Vaughn/ Albert Belle	.356 Edgar Martinez	.690 Albert Belle	450 Albert Belle	
1996 NL	47 Andres Galarraga	150 Andres Galarraga	.353 Tony Gwynn	.639 Ellis Burks	469 Barry Bonds	Eddie Murray hits his 500th home run on September 6, joining Willie Mays and Hank Aaron as the only players with both 500 home runs and 3,000 hits. Ten days later, Paul Molitor triples for his 3,000th hit.
1996 AL	52 Mark McGwire	148 Albert Belle	.358 Alex Rodriguez	.730 Mark McGwire	474 Albert Belle	The Orioles establish a team record with 257 home runs, one of three teams to break the previous mark held by the 1961 Yankees.
1997 NL	49 Larry Walker	140 Andres Galarraga	.372 Tony Gwynn	.720 Larry Walker	487 Larry Walker	Larry Walker's 487 bases is the most since Mickey Mantle in 1956. With 58 spread over two leagues, Mark McGwire becomes the only man other than Babe Ruth to hit 50 home runs in consecutive seasons.
1997 AL	56 Ken Griffey Jr.	147 Ken Griffey Jr.	.347 Frank Thomas	.646 Ken Griffey	469 Ken Griffey Jr.	
1998 NL	70 Mark McGwire	158 Sammy Sosa	.363 Larry Walker	.752 Mark McGwire	545 Mark McGwire	Mark McGwire and Sammy Sosa both break the single-season home run mark held by Roger Maris, connecting for 70 and 66, respectively. McGwire collects more bases than any man since Jimmie Foxx in 1932, setting a new National League record in the process. Sammy Sosa knocks in more runs than any player in 49 years, and more than any National Leaguer since Hack Wilson in 1930. Greg Vaughn of the Padres produces the most over-looked 50-homer season in history.
1998 AL	56 Ken Griffey Jr.	157 Juan Gonzalez	.339 Bernie Williams	.655 Albert Belle	480 Albert Belle	

Season	HR	RBI	BA	SA	Bases	Highlights
1999 NL	65 Mark McGwire	146 Mark McGwire	.379 Larry Walker	.710 Larry Walker	490 Mark McGwire	Mark McGwire breaks his own record with 135 home runs in two seasons. He becomes the first man to reach 400 home runs and 500 home runs in consecutive seasons. Tony Gwynn and Wade Boggs, who both repeated as batting champions in 1987 and 1988, go into the 3,000-hit club in the same season. Boggs, the ultimate slap hitter, becomes the only man to go into the club with a home run.
1999 AL	48 Ken Griffey Jr.	165 Manny Ramirez	.357 Nomar Garciaparra	.665 Manny Ramirez	453 Rafael Palmeiro	

Bibliography

Banks, Kerry. *The Babe Ruth Era.*

Bouton, Jim. *Ball Four.*

Carter, Craig (ed.). *The Sporting News Complete Baseball Record Book.*

Cohen, Richard, and David S. Neft. *The World Series.*

———. *The Sports Encyclopedia: Baseball.*

Crisfield, D. W. *The Louisville Slugger® Book of Great Hitters.*

Einstein, Charles (ed.). *The Fireside Book of Baseball,* vols. I–III.

Halberstam, David. *October 1964.*

Herskowitz, Mickey, and the Mantle family. *A Hero All His Life.*

James, Bill. *Guide to Baseball Managers.*

———. *Historical Baseball Abstract.*

———. *The Politics of Glory.*

LaMar, Steve. *The Book of Baseball Lists.*

Lowry, Philip J. *Green Cathedrals.*

Monteleone, John, and Mark Gola. *The Louisville Slugger® Ultimate Book of Hitting.*

McConnell, Bob, and David Vincent (eds.). *The Home Run Encyclopedia.*

McCullough, Bob. *My Greatest Day in Baseball: 1946-1997.*

Mead, William B. *Two Spectacular Seasons.*

Myers, Doug. *Essential Cubs.*

———. *Scouting Report: 1997.*

Nathan, David. *Baseball Quotations.*

Nemec, David. *The Great Encyclopedia of 19th Century Major League Baseball.*

Obojski, Robert. *Bush League.*

Okrent, Daniel, and Steve Wulf. *Baseball Anecdotes.*

Pepe, Phil. *Talkin' Baseball: An Oral History of Baseball in the 1970s.*

Reichler, Joseph. *Baseball's Great Moments.*

Ritter, Lawrence. *The Glory of their Times.*

Rose, Pete, and Roger Kahn. *Pete Rose: My Story.*

Scheinin, James. *Field of Screams.*

Schell, Michael. *Baseball's All-Time Best Hitters.*

Seidel, Michael. *Streak.*

Skipper, John C. *Inside Pitch: Classic Baseball Moments.*

Smith, Robert. *Baseball in the Afternoon.*

Thorn, John, and Pete Palmer (eds.). *Total Baseball.*

Index

About the Authors

While Doug Myers may be the worst hitter ever produced by Montgomery High School in Skillman, New Jersey, he probably came closer than any to fulfilling his potential. This is his fifth book, his fourth on baseball, and third for Contemporary (*Essential Cubs* and *The Louisville Slugger® Complete Book of Pitching*). He lives in Bear, Delaware, with his wife, Cindy, and is currently working on a series of children's books that will soon be going into beta test on newborn twins.

Brian Dodd is a light-hitting middle infielder from Toronto, Canada, who stays in the lineup because of his soft hands and ability to turn two. An investment banker in his spare time, Brian focuses his energies on the twin gifts of reading and writing. He currently resides in Ridgewood, New Jersey, with his first and only wife, Dana, and their little darlings, Lucy and Quincy.